SOCIETY FOR NEW TESTAMENT STUDIES
MONOGRAPH SERIES

GENERAL EDITOR
MATTHEW BLACK, D.D., F.B.A.

9

THE TENDENCIES OF THE
SYNOPTIC TRADITION

THE TENDENCIES OF
THE SYNOPTIC
TRADITION

E. P. SANDERS

Wipf & Stock
PUBLISHERS
Eugene, Oregon

Wipf and Stock Publishers
199 West 8th Avenue, Suite 3
Eugene, Oregon 97401

The Tendencies of the Synoptic Tradition
By Sanders, E.P.
Copyright©1969 Cambridge University Press
ISBN: 1-57910-512-2
Publication date 10/16/2000
Previously published by Cambridge University Press, 1969

To my Mother
and
In memory of my Father

CONTENTS

CONTENTS

CONTENTS

PREFACE

Criteria for distinguishing the relatively early form from the relatively late form of parallel traditions have interested me ever since Professor W. R. Farmer introduced me to the mysteries of the Synoptic problem. I did not doubt that there were firm criteria for this task until I had begun the present study. My initial intention was only to confirm them and to apply them systematically to the Synoptics themselves, which had not been done before. I soon was led to question the sureness of the criteria which are in general use, however, and felt obliged to organize the study in such a way as to test the criteria themselves. I have still attempted to apply them to the Synoptics, sometimes with interesting results.

This study was initially prepared during the years 1964–6 as a doctoral dissertation at Union Theological Seminary. It appears here with only minor alterations. In revising the manuscript for the press, I have done what I could to insure that the many lists in the book are accurate. I shall be glad to learn of mistakes and omissions which remain. I was also able to take some account of literature which has appeared since the work was initially completed. But it should be noted that no attempt has been made at bibliographical completeness on each of the many issues which are discussed. I have intended primarily to investigate the first-hand sources rather than to discuss a full range of viewpoints on each topic. It would have been instructive and entertaining to write a history of the use of the criteria which are discussed here, but that would have made the work far too long.

I am especially grateful to Professor W. D. Davies, who supervised the work, for his generosity in sharing his wisdom and critical acumen with me during the period of research and writing. His sympathetic interest has encouraged me throughout, and his probing questions have repeatedly led to the strengthening of the work. Professor Louis Martyn has given counsel and support which have measurably improved the work. I am indebted to them both, as well as to the other members of the doctoral committee, Professors John Knox and

Samuel Terrien, who offered helpful suggestions at several points. It perhaps goes without saying that mentioning those who have so kindly helped me is not intended to remove responsibility for the shortcomings of the work from my own shoulders.

My thanks for sharing in the typing and proofreading of a difficult manuscript go to Mrs Lyman Lauver, Mrs Bruce Gillies, Mrs George Boyd, and my wife, who added these tasks to her other responsibilities. Her support and help have been indispensable throughout the course of the work.

McMaster University, Hamilton, Ontario   E.P.S.
January 1969

ABBREVIATIONS

Act. Pil.	Acts of Pilate.
B.F.C.T.	Beiträge zur Förderung christlicher Theologie.
ctr.	contrast.
Epiph.	Epiphanius.
E.T.	English translation.
Exp. Times	*The Expository Times.*
F.R.L.A.N.T.	Forschungen zur Religion und Literatur des Alten und Neuen Testamentes.
Gosp. Ebion.	Gospel of the Ebionites.
Gosp. Heb.	Gospel of the Hebrews.
H.-S.	Hennecke-Schneemelcher, *New Testament Apocrypha*, vol. I.
H.T.R.	*Harvard Theological Review.*
Haer.	*Heresies, Against Heresies.*
J.B.L.	*Journal of Biblical Literature.*
J.B.R.	*Journal of Bible and Religion.*
J.T.S.	*Journal of Theological Studies.*
Jos. of Arim.	The Narrative of Joseph of Arimathea.
Lat.	Latin.
Legg	S. C. E. Legg, *Nouum Testamentum Graece.*
Liddell and Scott	H. G. Liddell and R. Scott, *Greek-English Lexicon.*
N.T.S.	*New Testament Studies.*
Nat. Mary	The Gospel of the Nativity of Mary.
Nestle	E. Nestle and K. Aland, *Novum Testamentum Graece.*
Nov. Test.	*Novum Testamentum.*
Oxy.	Oxyrhynchus.
p., pap.	papyrus.
Protev. Jms.	The Protevangelium of James.
Pscud.	Pseudo-.
R.H.Ph.R.	*Revue d'Histoire et de Philosophie Religieuses.*
R.H.R.	*Revue de l'Histoire des Religions.*
de Santos	Aurelio de Santos Otero, *Los Evangelios Aprocrifos.*
Th. Lit. Zeit.	*Theologische Literaturzeitung.*
T.U.	Texte und Untersuchungen.

T.W.B.N.T.	*Theologisches Wörterbuch zum neuen Testament.*
U.B.S. text	*The Greek New Testament*, ed. by K. Aland, M. Black, B. M. Metzger, and A. Wikgren. Published by the United Bible Societies, 1966.
Vig. Chr.	*Vigiliae Christianae.*
V.T.	*Vetus Testamentum.*
Westcott and Hort	B. F. Westcott and F. J. A. Hort, *The New Testament in the Original Greek.*
Z.N.T.W.	*Zeitschrift für die neutestamentliche Wissenschaft.*

EDITORIAL NOTE

In preparing the passages printed in appendix v, I have always consulted, and frequently relied heavily upon, the English translations available in Hennecke-Schneemelcher, *New Testament Apocrypha*, vol. 1 (E. T. edited by R. McL. Wilson), and in various volumes of the series, *Writings of the Anti-Nicene Fathers* (originally titled *The Ante-Nicene Christian Library*).

Otherwise, the translations, including those of passages from the New Testament, are my own. They are, for the most part, as literal as possible, even to the point of producing poor English. The aim was to enable the reader readily to grasp wherein one version of a tradition is different from another.

CHAPTER I

THE PROBLEM

THE NEED FOR CRITERIA

The early Christian tradition about 'all that Jesus began to do and teach', like the Jewish tradition alongside which it grew, was a living and developing tradition. This has been accepted by scholars of all persuasions. Thus Bonnard, who wishes to emphasize the kerygmatic unity of the early tradition, observes that one would expect to see such a theological tradition passed down in a tightly controlled form. But actually we do not find it so. 'Theologically coherent at its base, the Christian tradition reveals, until about the year 95, a prodigious liberty, a creativity both marvelous and disquieting for the historian.'[1] The German form critics, as is well known, especially emphasize the creative role of the early Christian communities in shaping and developing the tradition. But even Riesenfeld, who has helped lead a reaction against that view, and who argues for a fixed and controlled tradition both in Judaism and Christianity, grants that 'variations in the material took place in the process of tradition' in both spheres.[2] In a similar way Gerhardsson points out that not all of the Christian tradition was passed down with the same precision. Thus the sayings of Jesus show fewer changes than do the narrative material and the redactional framework, but even they are sometimes reworked.[3] Whether one wishes to emphasize or minimize the degree of creativity on the part of the early communities, and thus the degree of change which took place in the tradition, problems are posed

---

[1] Pierre Bonnard, 'La Tradition dans le nouveau Testament', *R.H.Ph.R.* XL (1960), 21–2. Cf. also the statement by André Lacocque, 'La Tradition dans le Bas-Judaïsme', *R.H.Ph.R.* XI (1960), 6: 'ce sera l'œuvre unique de la Tradition d'empêcher la sclérose, de faire que l'Écriture ne soit pas statique, mais dynamique.'

[2] Harald Riesenfeld, *The Gospel tradition and its beginnings* (London, 1957), pp. 18, 22.

[3] Birger Gerhardsson, *Tradition and transmission in early Christianity* (Lund, 1964), pp. 44–5. See also *Memory and manuscript* (Uppsala, 1961), pp. 334 f. and the comments by W. D. Davies, *The Setting of the Sermon on the Mount* (Cambridge, 1964), appendix xv, pp. 464 ff.

for the historian, as Bonnard has indicated. There are really two basic problems: how much material was created in the communities, and what development the material—whatever its origin—underwent during the course of its transmission. These two problems are closely related, and one's attitude toward the one will bear some relation to one's attitude toward the other. Nevertheless, they are separable. It is the purpose of this study to inquire into the latter problem: what was the tendency of the tradition; how much did it develop, and in what ways? A proper elucidation of this problem will elucidate the other also, and some light will be shed on the question of the role of the Christian communities in creating new material.

The concern of this study, then, is to analyze early tradition about Jesus in order to see what tendencies, if any, its development reveals. The chief result of such a study might be expected to be the development of criteria for judging the relative antiquity of parallel traditions. The question is, when two forms of one pericope exist, how one distinguishes the relatively earlier from the relatively later. Lacking apparent references to historical events (such as occur in Mt. 24. 15//Mk. 13. 14//Lk. 21. 20), how can the relative age of different forms of the same story be fixed?

The answer has always been that one may distinguish relatively early from relatively late forms of a certain story on the basis of knowledge of how the tradition as a whole developed. The later tradition will show certain characteristic changes when compared with the earlier tradition. It is our purpose to examine these characteristic changes in order to determine if they really be characteristic, and if so, how characteristic they are. We are thus concerned to examine the validity of 'internal criteria', that is, criteria for assessing relative age which are based on knowledge of the internal development of the early Christian tradition.

In order that the point and significance of this problem may properly be grasped, we may now briefly indicate four areas in which such criteria are not only useful but necessary. Indeed, these are four areas in which such criteria—whether rightly or wrongly—have already been used.

First of all, there is the existence of extra-canonical material which is more or less parallel with canonical material. Wherever such material exists, the possibility may be, and has been, raised whether the non-canonical material may not preserve a form of tradition older than that found in the canonical Gospels. This could conceivably be the case if the extra-canonical material appears to go back to a tradition independent of the canonical Gospels. The most recent and most striking instance of this possibility is the material in the Coptic Gospel of Thomas which is parallel to the canonical Synoptic material. The problem posed by the Gospel of Thomas will be discussed more fully below (pp. 40–3); here we need only point out that its existence requires criteria for determining the relative age of the material it has in common with our Synoptics. Thus, for example, Montefiore has argued that in some instances 'Thomas provides a text which may be more original than that of the Synoptic Gospels'.[1] He naturally employs criteria for making this assertion: the more detailed and vivid is earlier,[2] the secondary is sometimes more compressed,[3] the simplest is to be preferred,[4] and the like.

Even before the discovery of the Gospel of Thomas, however, the existence of material parallel to, but independent of and possibly more original than the Synoptics had been postulated. This theory has been put forward especially with respect to the Didache,[5] but Köster would extend it to include a considerable part of the Synoptic tradition found in the Apostolic Fathers.[6]

In the second place, there exists the possibility that our Synoptics themselves made use of parallel but independent traditions. There are at least three different theories to consider here.

[1] Hugh Montefiore and H. E. W. Turner, *Thomas and the Evangelists* (London, 1962), p. 52.
[2] *Ibid.* pp. 50 f.   [3] *Ibid.* pp. 51 f.   [4] *Ibid.* pp. 61–3.
[5] See, for example, Richard Glover, 'The Didache's quotations and the Synoptic Gospels', *N.T.S.* v (1958), 12–29. Glover thinks that the Didache did not use Matthew and Luke, but a collection of sayings comprising both 'Q' and 'M' material. The Didache sometimes preserves a more authentic form of a saying than do our canonical Gospels.
[6] Helmut Köster, *Synoptische Überlieferung bei den apostolischen Vätern* (Berlin, 1957). Köster's view will be discussed more fully below. As an example pertinent to the present point, however, we may mention in dealing with I Clem. 13. 2 and 46. 8, Köster concludes that the author of I Clement had access, even if indirectly, to the *Vorstufe* of the Synoptics. He thinks that at 46. 8, especially, Clement had a tradition related to Q rather than to our Synoptics themselves. See pp. 12–19.

3   1-2

(1) Several scholars have suggested that translation variants may be found within our Synoptics.[1] The point is that certain variations in wording, between, let us say, Matthew and Mark, can be explained as different translations of a common Aramaic word. Thus νηστεύειν (Mk. 2. 19 a), νηστεῦσαι (Lk. 5. 34), and πενθεῖν (Mt. 9. 15 a) may be seen as 'variant renderings of the ambiguous Aramaic *'ith 'anne'*.[2] Dalman criticized a similar view when it was put forward by Resch,[3] but the persistence of it cannot be ignored. We cannot deal with the ramifications of such a possibility here, but can only note that if a later Gospel could have had a translation of an Aramaic word other than that used in its main Gospel source, then presumably it must have had access to a tradition at least partially independent of the main Gospel source. The possibility of the existence of such independent traditions requires the search for criteria for determining relative antiquity.

(2) It has long been thought that there are places in which

---

[1] The principal works to be mentioned here are C. C. Torrey, *Our translated Gospels* (New York, 1936), and Matthew Black, *An Aramaic approach to the Gospels and Acts*[3] (Oxford, 1967). Joachim Jeremias, *The parables of Jesus*, 2nd English ed., E.T. by S. H. Hooke (New York, 1963), has also noted what appear to be translation variants. This view has been supported by J. W. Doeve, 'Le Rôle de la tradition orale dans la composition des Évangiles synoptiques', *La Formation des Évangiles* (Bruges, 1957), pp. 72 f.; by Köster, *op. cit.* p. 40; and by W. G. Kümmel, *Einleitung in das neue Testament*[13] (Heidelberg, 1964), p. 26.

[2] Jeremias, *op. cit.* (1st Eng. ed.), p. 42 n. 82. More examples of possible translation variants are given in Appendix 1 below.

[3] Gustaf Dalman, *Die Worte Jesu* (Darmstadt, 1965), p. 35. See the English translation, *The words of Jesus*, E.T. by D. M. Kay (Edinburgh, 1902), pp. 43 f. Dalman writes as follows: 'The fact that Greek synonyms *may* often be traced back to one Hebrew word, though sometimes several Hebrew synonyms also may be discovered, in no way proves that a Hebrew word really lies behind the Greek synonyms. One might almost as well name an Aramaic or an Arabic word, and then in the same way proceed to argue an Aramaic or Arabic original... Only in the case of striking deviations among the variants could a testimony in favour of a Semitic original be inferred with *some* degree of certitude, provided there was found a Semitic term which perchance so solved the problem of the divergent readings, that the one appears, with good reason, to be a misunderstanding easily possible, the other the correct interpretation of the Semitic expression. Even then, however, it would remain questionable whether the divergent readings had not arisen through other causes, so that it is only by accident that a Semitic term appears to account for the deviation. This must indeed be always the most plausible supposition...' Although Resch wished to use 'translation variants' to prove a Hebrew rather than an Aramaic origin of the Gospels, Dalman's strictures of his position would apply also to any argument depending on variant translations from Aramaic.

4

the sources of our Synoptic Gospels overlap.[1] Thus at the Beelzebub controversy, Mark and Q are said to overlap. Sometimes Q and M are thought to have overlapped.[2] All such instances raise the problem of which of the overlapping traditions is earlier.

(3) The view of W. L. Knox[3] and L. Cerfaux[4] raises the possibility of overlapping traditions from another angle. These scholars have put forth the view that there existed small literary units anterior to our Gospels. It follows that one of the later Gospels could have followed such a unit where it paralleled his main Gospel source, and thus have preserved the small unit better than did the earlier Gospel. Cerfaux, in fact, declines to assert the absolute priority of one Gospel to another, and stresses their independence.[5]

Any theory which envisages the possibility of parallel but independent traditions' being available to the canonical evangelists must use criteria to distinguish the earlier from the later.

The Synoptic problem itself, though closely related to the possibility of independent but parallel traditions, deserves separate mention as an area of study which requires the criteria which we plan to investigate.

(1) The hypothesis that Matthew and Luke used Q independently requires such criteria in order to distinguish the more original form of a Q saying.[6]

(2) All more or less complicated solutions to the Synoptic problem must rely, in part at least, on such criteria.[7] The view, for example, which envisages a highly developed oral tradition

[1] See B. H. Streeter, *The Four Gospels* (London, 1961), pp. 186–91. Besides the Beelzebub controversy (Mk. 3. 23–30 parr.), Streeter lists Mt. 10. 1–16 parr., Mk. 1. 1–8 parr., Mk. 1. 9–13, and Mt. 13. 31–3 parr.
[2] *Ibid.* pp. 281–5.
[3] W. L. Knox, *The sources of the Synoptic Gospels*, ed. Henry Chadwick (2 vols.; Cambridge, 1953 and 1957).
[4] L. Cerfaux, 'Les Unités littéraires antérieures aux trois premiers évangiles', *La Formation des Évangiles*, pp. 24–33.
[5] *Ibid.* pp. 24 and 33.
[6] See, for example, Streeter, *op. cit.* p. 183.
[7] More or less complicated solutions to the Synoptic problem are not in short supply. See, for example, the six solutions which Heuschen lists of the many which have been offered to account for the agreements of Matthew and Luke against Mark (J. Heuschen, 'La Formation des Évangiles', *La Formation des Évangiles*, pp. 16 f.). He concludes that a simple theory of Matthew's dependence on Mark is not adequate to account for the evidence (p. 17).

5

opens the possibility that Luke or Matthew could, at a certain passage, have employed the oral tradition rather than Mark.[1] All forms of the Ur-Markus theory must reckon with the possibility that Matthew and Luke could have preserved the Ur-Gospel better than did Mark. The Ur-Gospel theory has had a long life, and may not be said to be dead even yet. Bultmann, for example, while not making much use of it, has never given it up. He remains open to the possibility that 'Matthew and Luke possessed Mark and the *Logia* in different recensions, and [thus] it is quite probable that the form of the Gospel of Mark used by them was earlier than the one with which we are familiar'.[2] Many other scholars have appealed to such a theory to account for what they consider to be secondary features in Mark *vis-à-vis* Matthew and/or Luke.[3] All such appeals, needless to say, rest on an assurance that what is relatively early can be distinguished from what is relatively late.

(3) Most scholars who have dealt extensively with the Synoptic Gospels, whether explicitly accepting an Ur-Gospel theory or not, have found some passages in which either Matthew or Luke or both seem to have an earlier form than

[1] See Doeve, *op. cit.*

[2] Rudolf Bultmann, 'The New Approach to the Synoptic Problem', *Journal of Religion*, VI (1926), 338. Cf. also *Die Erforschung der synoptischen Evangelien*[4] (Berlin, 1961), p. 9 (English translation by F. C. Grant, 'The study of the Synoptic Gospels', in *Form Criticism* [New York, 1962], pp. 13 f.); *Die Geschichte der synoptischen Tradition*[5] (Göttingen, 1961), pp. 7, 18 and often (English translation by John Marsh, *The History of the Synoptic Tradition* [New York, 1963], pp. 6, 20).

[3] We may give here only a few examples. See J. H. Scholten, *Das älteste Evangelium* (Elberfeld, 1869), p. 168; Bernhard Weiss, *Das Marcusevangelium und seine synoptischen Parallelen* (Berlin, 1872), p. vii and often (e.g., when contrasting Mk. 5. 11 with the Matthean parallel, he notes that it is 'augenfällig' that 'Marcus hier eine erleichternde und darum secondäre Darstellung hat', p. 177); F. Spitta, *Die synoptische Grundschrift in ihrer Überlieferung durch das Lukasevangelium* (Leipzig, 1912), pp. 463 f. The view of P. Wernle (*Die synoptische Frage* [Tübingen, 1899]), who attributes instances in which Mark has a secondary form when compared with Matthew and Luke to textual revision of the text of Mark, is not really different from an Ur-Markus hypothesis. See p. 58. Sir John Hawkins was of a similar view. While wishing to reject the Ur-Markus hypothesis, he found about ten instances in which a later editor changed the Mark used by Matthew and Luke. See *Horae Synopticae*[2] (Oxford, 1909), p. 152. A similar view is that of T. F. Glasson, 'Did Matthew and Luke use a "Western" text of Mark?' *Exp. Times*, LV (1943/4), 180–4 and *ibid.* LXXVII (1966), 120 f. Hadorn (*Die Entstehung des Markus-Evangeliums* [Gütersloh, 1898]) also noted that the secondary matter in our Mark requires either an Ur-Markus hypothesis or the acceptance of Matthew's priority. He chose the latter course, however. See pp. 12, 159.

that in our Mark. To take a recent example, Köster thinks that Mt. 24. 30 b retains the original form of Mark, while the present Mk. 13. 26 is later.[1] A more extensive list may be found in Appendix II.

(4) More fundamentally, however, the basic solution to the Synoptic problem which has formed the foundation for work on the Synoptics for over half a century has now been challenged, principally by B. C. Butler[2] and W. R. Farmer.[3] Both Butler and Farmer have challenged, rightly to my view, the opinion that the two-document hypothesis can be established by appeal to such general considerations as the order of pericopes.[4] Surely one response to this challenge is that the priority of Mark is to be proved by a comparison of it in individual passages with Matthew and Luke.[5] Such a comparison, of course, requires criteria of relative antiquity and presupposes knowledge of the tendency of the tradition. Further, Farmer wishes to employ the criteria which have been in common use to show that they actually support Matthew's priority.[6]

This study is written with one eye on the problem we have just mentioned. In my view, the study of the Synoptic problem is at a stage at which the comparison of individual passages in the Gospels, with the appropriate criteria in hand, is necessary. It is for this reason, as we shall presently see, that the criteria are not derived from a comparison of the Synoptics with one another (as was done by Bultmann, for example), but are derived from an investigation of the post-canonical Synoptic tradition. Whatever criteria are derived may then be applied to the Synoptic Gospels themselves. This method should shed light on the Synoptic problem.

The ultimate need for criteria for testing relative antiquity, however, comes from the problem of the origins and development of Christian thought. As the form critics clearly perceived, the tradition developed not only after it first came to light in our earliest Gospel, but was developing already before it was

---

[1] Köster, op. cit. p. 188.
[2] B. C. Butler, The originality of St Matthew (Cambridge, 1951).
[3] W. R. Farmer, The Synoptic problem (New York, 1964).
[4] G. M. Styler, 'The priority of Mark', excursus IV in C. F. D. Moule, The birth of the New Testament (New York, 1962), p. 225, grants that 'formal relationships do not by themselves compel one solution to the synoptic problem'.
[5] See the remarks by Styler, ibid. pp. 227–30.   [6] Farmer, op. cit. pp. 227–8.

written and incorporated as we now have it. It is to be assumed that knowledge of the tendency of the tradition after it comes into view can be used to cast light on how it had already been developing.[1] Thus if proper criteria can be established, they can be used not only to test which of two or more parallel traditions available to us is the earlier, but also to indicate what the tradition most probably was like and what developments it most probably underwent before it reached the form in which we now have it. Here the question of oral tradition need not be decided.[2] We investigate written tradition because that is all that is available to us. Many scholars now think that there would have been little difference between written and oral tradition during the first century, however, so that the tendencies of the one are presumably the tendencies of the other.[3] We must operate on this presumption, although it cannot be tested. Even if it should be the case that oral tradition was not so rigid as some seem to think, that does not of itself mean that oral tradition was a great deal different from written tradition, since written tradition itself was by no means inflexible, as we shall see.[4]

THE PRESENT SITUATION AND THE TASK

It is obvious, then, that criteria for determining the relative age of two or more parallel passages, based on knowledge of the tendency of the tradition, are needed. But are they not already

[1] Cf. F. C. Grant, 'Where form criticism and textual criticism overlap', *J.B.L.* LIX (1940), 14.

[2] This formulation stands in the closest agreement with that of Bultmann. After describing how laws of the development of tradition may be ascertained, he notes that 'if we are able to detect any such laws, we may assume that they were operative on the traditional material even before it was given its form in Mark and Q, and in this way we can infer back to an earlier stage of tradition than appears in our sources. Moreover it is at this point a matter of indifference whether the tradition were oral or written, because on account of the unliterary character of the material one of the chief differences between oral and written traditions is lacking'. *Die Geschichte*, p. 7 (E.T. p. 6).

[3] This is implicit, for example, in Gerhardsson's stress on the accuracy of oral transmission. See *Memory and manuscript*, pp. 130 ff. So also F. C. Grant, *art. cit.* pp. 11–21.

[4] It would be possible to enumerate other areas in which internal criteria for determining relative antiquity are used. See, for example, Brown's use of them in comparing John with the Synoptics in *The Gospel according to John* (i–xii) (New York, 1966), pp. 237–44.

8

available to us? Are not the tendencies of the tradition already so well known that firm criteria can be derived from them, and have these criteria not already been used in a meaningful way to illumine the problems which we have just outlined? It is certainly true that virtually every scholar who has dealt with the Synoptic tradition has employed criteria of the type which we have in view. It is, it appears, a common assumption today that these criteria have been derived, or at least confirmed, by studying bodies of material comparable to the Synoptics and that they represent universal laws of the development of material of the Synoptic type.[1]

This generalization has been primarily reached through discussion with others who are interested in the New Testament. We may cite some statements in support of it, however. G. Bornkamm writes as follows: '[Form criticism] has shown that from the character of the Gospel tradition we can recognize reasonably clearly the laws and forms of the pre-literary oral tradition...We find numerous parallels to these forms and laws of tradition, particularly in the rabbis' method of teaching, in the apocalyptic tradition, but also in popular oral tradition in general.' See *Jesus of Nazareth* (E.T. by Irene and Fraser McLuskey with J. M. Robinson) (New York, 1960), p. 218. If by the phrase 'laws of tradition' Bornkamm means laws governing the development of tradition, he clearly thinks that such laws have been found in popular material outside the canon. It is this assumption, as we shall show below, which is incorrect.

A second example of this assumption is found in W. G. Kümmel, *Einleitung in das neue Testament*[13], pp. 21 f. He writes: '[Form criticism] transferred to the material of the Synoptic tradition observations which had been made by literary-historical research in other areas, above all in the Old Testament literature (H. Gunkel, H. Gressmann). Popular tradition follows, in the reproduction and formation of its materials, fixed laws, which differ according to literary category (fairy tale, saga, historical narrative, hymn, saying with this or that aim, and the like).' Here it is supposed that each literary category has laws both of formation *and transmission* ('reproduction', *Wiedergabe*). The context of Kümmel's discussion shows that his view of form criticism is that its *investigations of other literature* had revealed laws of construction *and transmission* which apply also to the Synoptics. We shall show below that this view of what form criticism did is incorrect. See also the discussion of Klijn's view on p. 31 below.

[1] The word 'laws' in this work refers to generalizations based on behaviour which is observed to be more or less uniform; that is, it refers to the characteristic developments of the tradition. See further Bultmann's definition, p. 17 below, and the discussion on pp. 272 f. below.

It is further commonly assumed that these criteria have been applied systematically to the Synoptic Gospels, and that the differences among the Synoptic Gospels conform to these universal tendencies in such a way as to support the common solution to the Synoptic problem.

We may here briefly mention as an example a matter which will be discussed more fully in chapter IV. Kümmel (*op. cit.* pp. 29 f.) states that Mark's Greek is more popular and Semitic than that of Matthew and Luke. He considers this decisive proof for the priority of Mark. Such a statement assumes two things: (1) Research has shown that popular and Semitic Greek is improved in the course of the tradition, but that 'better' Greek is not made more popular and Semitic. (2) A review has been made of vulgarisms and Semitisms in the Synoptics, and the results point decisively toward Mark's priority; that is, there is not a significant number of instances in which Matthew or Luke has the more vulgar or Semitic text. Neither assumption is well founded, as we shall show below.

The assurance with which these or similar assumptions are held is easily seen in the work of many scholars today. We may take one example of this assurance. In discussing II Clem. 5. 2–4//Mt. 10. 16//Lk. 10. 3, Köster comments that 'der sekundäre Charakter dieser Stelle [in Clement] zeigt sich schliesslich auch noch darin, dass Petrus als Frager ausdrücklich genannt wird'.[1] He refers, as proof of the canon, to one passage, Mt. 15. 15//Mk. 7. 17, and cites Bultmann, *Geschichte der synoptischen Tradition*, pp. 71 f. (E.T. pp. 67 f.). Actually, however, the criterion is by no means so clear. It is not difficult to find a passage in which Mark, rather than Matthew, explicitly names Peter (see Mt. 21. 20//Mk. 11. 21). In this instance, indeed, Bultmann recognized that the tendency of the tradition was by no means uniform, or rather that in some instances the general tendency was reversed.[2] It is questionable how much assurance should be laid on such a canon.

Despite the assurance with which certain criteria are sometimes used today, we must observe that, in point of fact, neither of the two assumptions upon which such assurance is based is justified. That is, it is not the case that the criteria have been established by exhaustive, or even by fairly comprehensive work on the relevant literature, nor is it the case that these criteria

[1] Köster, *op. cit.* p. 98.
[2] See the passage referred to by Köster.

have been systematically employed in the study of the Synoptic Gospels.

That this is the true situation may readily be seen by studying the work of the scholars who have used literary criteria in the past. This may be done here in only a very brief and highly selective way. It is necessary to show, to some extent, the limitations of the work of previous scholars in order to make the point of this present study fully comprehensible. I hope it will be clear, however, that in criticizing the work of others, I wish only to supplement tasks which have already been begun and to refine methods which have already been initiated.

In discussing the individual criteria in the chapters which follow, we shall give examples of their use by early scholars. The basic thrust of our present study, however, must relate to the form-critical school,[1] since it is there that these criteria have been used most self-consciously. In form criticism they were tied, for the first time, to a total view of the Synoptics. Since the criteria which we investigate have been derived from knowledge of the tendencies of the tradition, and since the tendencies of the tradition could be properly comprehended only if the nature of the tradition were rightly grasped, there should be a direct relation between the criteria established and the nature of the material. It is primarily in the work of the form critics, especially Rudolf Bultmann, that an attempt has been made to relate the tendency of the tradition to the nature of the material which was being handed down. Thus it is necessary to deal, although briefly, with the nature of the Synoptic material, as seen by the form critics.

The old view that the Gospels are biographies[2] was vigorously

[1] For a useful survey of the twentieth-century work which led up to form criticism, see B. S. Easton, *The Gospel before the Gospels* (New York, 1928). His analysis of the principal works of the form critics is on pp. 31–53. E. Fascher's work, *Die formgeschichtliche Methode* (Giessen, 1924), is also useful for a general review of form criticism. Fascher, however, gives almost all his attention to discussion of forms and almost none to the tendency of the tradition. Recently J. Rohde has summarized and analyzed the work of the form critics. (See the summary of his Berlin dissertation in *Th. Lit. Zeit.* xc (1965), 226–8). Apparently he does not deal with the laws of transmission either, however.

[2] See, for example, C. W. Votaw, 'The Gospels and contemporary biographies', *American Journal of Theology*, xix (1915), 45–73 and 217–49. Votaw distinguished between historical and popular biographies and compared the Gospels with the latter. The relation of the Gospels to contemporary biographies should not be entirely overlooked, as it tends to be, and Votaw's articles are still of use in any discussion of the Gospel *Gattung*.

attacked by form critics, especially by K. L. Schmidt.[1] In his concentration upon separating the individual pericopes from their narrative framework, he sought parallels to the Synoptics among other literature similarly composed of individual pieces woven together. Although he granted that perhaps the closest parallels to the individual pericopes in the Synoptics are to be found in Rabbinic literature,[2] Rabbinic literature offers no parallel to the Synoptics as a whole. Perhaps the best parallels can be found in later *Kleinliteratur*, such as certain of the monastic collections of the deeds of community leaders.[3]

A note is struck here which is of the highest importance for the form critics' view of the Synoptic material. That material is unliterary and anonymous. Dibelius especially emphasized the sociological and anti-individualistic view which form criticism took of the Christian tradition. He contrasted folk tradition with a more elevated style of narration and 'Kollektivkunst' with 'individuelle Kunstleistung'. He stressed that the Gospel material was passed down by anonymous transmitters.[4] Bultmann also placed emphasis on the role of the Christian communities in creating, shaping, and transmitting the Gospel material.[5]

Now if the Gospel traditions are folk tradition, it should follow that the laws of the transmission of folk traditions also apply to the transmission of the Gospel tradition. The form

[1] K. L. Schmidt, 'Die Stellung der Evangelien in der allgemeinen Literaturgeschichte', ΕΥΧΑΡΙΣΤΗΡΙΟΝ (Göttingen, 1923), 2. Teil, pp. 50–134. For more recent studies of the question concerning what type of literature the Gospels are, see also J. M. Robinson's article, 'ΛΟΓΟΙ ΣΟΦΩΝ. Zur Gattung der Spruchquelle Q', *Zeit und Geschichte*, Dankesgabe an Rudolf ¡Bultmann, ed. E. Dinkler (Tübingen, 1964), pp. 77–96; and K. Grobel, *The Interpreter's Dictionary of the Bible*, *s.v.* Gospels. We may additionally note that Bowman thinks that 'the Gospel Form as a whole' is derived from the Passover Haggadah. See *The Gospel of Mark* (Leiden, 1965), pp. xiii, xiv. Bowman here supports the view of David Daube, though without referring to it. See Daube, *The New Testament and Rabbinic Judaism* (London, 1956), pp. 168, 188 f.

[2] Schmidt, 'Die Stellung der Evangelien', p. 125.

[3] *Ibid.* pp. 102 ff.; 129. Schmidt refers to the *Historia Monachorum* of Rufinus, the *Historia Lausiaca* of Palladius, and the *Apophthegmata Patrum*, which gives an especially good example of how oral traditions were compiled. There are no bodies of tradition precisely parallel to the Gospel tradition, however.

[4] M. Dibelius, 'Zur Formgeschichte der Evangelien', *Theologische Rundschau*, n.F. 1 (1929), 185–216. See especially pp. 188 f., 202.

[5] See, for example, his discussion of the church's role in creating and shaping apophthegms in *Die Geschichte*, pp. 49–56 (E.T. pp. 48–54) and 64–73 (E.T. pp. 61–9).

critics seem to take account of this necessity by speaking of the laws of each form.[1] One would gather from such a phrase that the forms which they have in mind are those common to the Gospels and similar folk traditions, and that the laws of transmission for each form can be learned by observing the behavior of the forms in the various traditions in which they occur. Actually, as we shall see, this is not quite the method pursued by the form critics, although it would be a reasonable and logical one. We may now take each of the major form critics in turn to see how he arrived at the laws of the development of the tradition.

Analysis of the form-critical method of establishing the tendencies of tradition

According to Dibelius, the critic must ask about the motive for spreading the tradition and for the laws under which it spread, and apparently the two are interconnected. The motive was to further the mission of the church; the sermon was the means to this end.[2] Thus the law which governs the tradition is conformity to the sermon form. 'We may suppose that the manner in which the deeds of Jesus were narrated was determined by the requirements of the sermon.'[3] The result was a paradigmatic style. Besides the 'sermon-law', there was another law at work: the catechetical. Catechesis imposed its own laws upon the isolated sayings of Jesus.[4] Dibelius distinguishes the two kinds of tradition, each of which had its own laws, by comparing the sayings of Jesus with Jewish halacha and the narrative about Jesus with the haggada.[5] As an example of the kind of law which Dibelius had in mind, we may cite his description of the paradigms, which were used in sermons. The paradigms are characterized by external rounding off, brevity and simplicity (which are not necessarily characteristic of any folk tradition, but which are necessary to the purpose of the preacher),[6] a

[1] The phrase 'the laws which work in each form' is to be found in R. Reitzenstein, *Hellenistische Wundererzählungen*, p. 99 (cited by H. J. Cadbury, *The making of Luke-Acts* [London, 1958], p. 142). See also the phrase 'the laws of style of a specified literary form', R. Bultmann, *Die Erforschung*, pp. 19-20 (E.T. p. 29).
[2] M. Dibelius, *Die Formgeschichte des Evangeliums*[4] (Tübingen, 1961), p. 12.
[3] *Ibid.* p. 25.   [4] *Ibid.*
[5] *Ibid.* p. 26. The comparison is not a very happy one.   [6] *Ibid.* p. 51.

13

'realistic unwordly' coloring, frequently a concluding word of Jesus, and a thought useful for preaching.[1] It must be carefully noted that, although preaching provides the law under which the tradition spread, Dibelius does not mean that this law was a law of development. On the contrary, the 'laws' of the paradigmatic form are simply its characteristics, and its characteristics in its purest state. The paradigm form, for Dibelius, has no laws of development, but only characteristics. Any development must be away from the purity of the form. Thus an understanding of the characteristics of the paradigm does provide criteria for determining relative authenticity, but the criteria are negative. The closer to the pure form, the earlier the paradigm is; the farther away, the later.[2]

The Christian material did develop, and Dibelius accounts for its development. Although the paradigm form itself did not develop, paradigms were changed into other things—first of all, into less pure paradigm forms. This change, however, was not germane to the paradigm, but was simply the process of making the material literary. When the Gospel material began to be written, it became not just 'material', but also reading matter for Christians. 'Der Prozess der Literarisierung nahm seinen Anfang.'[3] For example, in the narrative of the sons of Zebedee (Mk. 10. 35–45), verses 38–40 show signs of developing into a legend, since they are interested in secondary characters. This interest is absent from the pure paradigm, and is therefore a secondary development.[4]

⌈So we see that, for Dibelius, the laws of the development of the Christian tradition are not derived from observing the development of other folk tradition, but by analyzing the needs and activities of the Christian communities.⌋ These needs required a certain form with certain characteristics. Any difference from the pure form must be a later development. In what ways, if at all, the forms of the Christian tradition would have developed cannot be discovered from a comparison of any literature other than the Christian, since no other literature would represent the same type of communities with the same type of needs.[5]

---

[1] Ibid. pp. 42–55.   [2] Ibid. p. 58.   [3] Ibid. p. 39.   [4] Ibid. pp. 57 f.
[5] Dibelius notes, for example, that the propaganda purpose of the paradigms distinguishes them from folk tales (ibid. p. 289).

In his summary statements about the methods of form criticism,[1] Rudolf Bultmann mentions two fundamental ways of working toward decisions about relative antiquity in the Synoptic material. In the first place, Bultmann agrees with Dibelius that the closer one comes to a pure representative of a certain form the earlier the tradition.

> If...we can succeed in identifying a particular literary type and its laws of style, we can then frequently distinguish an original tradition from secondary additions. We thus obtain a test for determining the age of a literary utterance by noting whether it appears in the original pure form belonging to this type of literature or whether it shows marks of further stylistic development.[2]

Bultmann's forms correspond more closely to forms known outside the Christian tradition than do Dibelius's. His criteria of what constitutes the characteristics of the pure form are more likely to be derived from a study of examples of that form in Hellenistic and Rabbinic literature than from an analysis of how it must have been used in the Christian communities.[3] Thus, in discussing the *Streitgespräche*, he shows that Rabbinic examples of this type agree essentially in form with Synoptic examples and argues that this formal agreement 'provides us with the criterion for eliminating the additions that destroy the force of the argument...'.[4]

We see, then, that the characteristics of a certain form, which are established or confirmed by a study of comparative material, serve as a criterion for determining relative age. Departures

---

[1] See the introductory chapter to *Die Geschichte, Die Erforschung*, and 'The new approach'.

[2] Bultmann, 'The new approach', p. 344.

[3] This is partially a result of difference of method. Dibelius began with the early Church and worked out to the Christian tradition. He presented a section on analogies in Greek and Rabbinic literature only after having discussed the Christian materials (see *Die Formgeschichte*). As a consequence, his forms were determined more by his understanding of the needs of the early Church than by a comparison with Greek or Rabbinic parallels. Bultmann, on the other hand, took the Synoptic material itself as his starting point and analyzed it by comparing it with other literature. He then drew conclusions about the early Church on the basis of his analysis of the material. Both Dibelius and Bultmann had to work in a circle to a certain extent, and so their methods are not so much opposed as it might at first seem; nevertheless, a real difference in methodology and result is discernible. See Bultmann, *Die Geschichte*, pp. 5 f. (E.T. p. 5) and also the discussion by Gerhardsson in *Memory and manuscript*, pp. 9 f.

[4] *Die Geschichte*, p. 46 (E.T. p. 45).

15

from the pure form are relatively younger than the elements of a passage which belong properly to the form.

It is obvious that such considerations do not lead to the formulation of general laws governing the transmission of tradition, since the criteria would, in theory at least, vary from form to form. Thus Bultmann notes that indications of circumstance and place are foreign to *miracle stories*;[1] when such indications are found in miracle stories, they are usually later additions, since they are deviations from the pure form. Yet it must be noted that distinctions according to what form is being considered are somewhat misleading. Bultmann himself points out that several of the characteristics of miracle stories are also characteristics of apophthegmata.[2] It should nevertheless be borne in mind that Bultmann frequently made such judgements only with reference to particular forms. They do not necessarily apply to the transmission of material in general.

We may describe the use of the characteristics of each form as a negative method for determining relative age, since it usually functions by eliminating intrusive elements. In addition, and more important for our present purpose, Bultmann utilized positive, universally applicable laws of the development of tradition.[3] But before turning directly to these, it is necessary to clarify his terminology. The fundamental distinction is between the *characteristics* and the *development* of tradition. When speaking of the characteristics, Bultmann also uses such terms as the *form* of the tradition,[4] the laws of *style*,[5] and the formal characteristics[6] of a certain literary type. When speaking of the development of tradition, he employs such terms as the laws which govern *transmission*,[7] the *history* of the tradition,[8] and the *tendency* of the tradition.[9] The distinction between characteristics and development was quite clear to Bultmann, although it seems frequently not to have been grasped. Thus he writes of the desirability of recognizing 'not only the appropriate

[1] *Ibid.* p. 257 (E.T. pp. 241 f.).   [2] *Ibid.*
[3] For the view that the 'general laws which govern the transmission of material' do not vary from form to form, see 'The new approach', pp. 344 f.
[4] *Die Geschichte*, p. 7 (E.T. p. 6).
[5] *Die Erforschung*, p. 19 (E.T. p. 29).
[6] *Die Geschichte*, p. 258 (E.T. p. 243).
[7] 'The new approach', p. 345. See also *Die Erforschung*, p. 20 (E.T. p. 30).
[8] *Die Geschichte*, pp. 7 f. (E.T. pp. 6 f.).
[9] *Ibid.* p. 37 (E.T. p. 37); p. 55 (E.T. p. 53).

16

laws of style of a specified literary form but also the laws by which the further development of material takes place, *i.e.*, a certain orderliness in change by which a body of tradition is always controlled in its growth'.[1] The discovery of the laws of style, or characteristics, depends heavily upon the investigation of comparative literature. But how are the general laws of the development of tradition derived? The summary statements on the methodology of form criticism make it abundantly clear that Bultmann derived his understanding of how the material as a whole tended to change from a study which has nothing to do either with the characteristics of certain forms or with the folk character of the Synoptic tradition. Bultmann accepted and utilized the literary criteria which had been used by scholars before him. These literary criteria he derived by studying how the Synoptic material itself was actually changed in the course of transmission. In the first place, he noted that despite the uncertainties caused by the question of an Ur-Markus and the difficulties of textual criticism, 'we may still discern a certain regularity in the way Matthew and Luke use Mark'. It is more difficult, but sometimes possible, 'by comparing Matthew and Luke to recognize what laws governed the development of material from Q to Matthew and Luke'. Secondly, the way in which the Apocryphal Gospels developed and changed the Synoptic material may be studied with an eye to deriving criteria. Thirdly, and 'quite fundamentally', he mentions the history of the text as a source for such criteria.[2] That is, the positive, general laws of transmission are derived from a study of the Christian tradition itself.

Yet Bultmann, in his discussions of laws of transmission, does refer to the usefulness of comparative literature. 'The ability to make the necessary distinctions [between older and later elements] can be developed by studying the general laws which govern popular transmission of stories and traditions in

---

[1] *Die Erforschung*, pp. 19 f. (E.T. p. 29). For the distinction, see also 'The new approach', pp. 343 ff.

[2] *Die Geschichte*, p. 7 (E.T. p. 6). See also *Die Erforschung*, p. 20 (E.T. pp. 29 f.); 'The new approach', p. 345 ('the study of the laws which govern literary transmission can be approached by observing the manner in which the Marcan material was altered by Matthew and Luke', etc.); M. Goguel, *R.H.R.* xciv (1926), 138.

17

other instances, for example, in the case of folk-tales, anecdotes, and folk-songs.'[1] Similarly, he mentions that light can be thrown on the laws of development (once they are arrived at by a study of the Christian literature) by a study of Buddhist Fairy stories.[2] It is doubtless references such as these which have led to the view that form criticism derived laws of transmission from other literature and applied them to the Synoptics.[3]

According to Bultmann's own statements of his methodology, the laws of transmission are fundamentally derived from the study of the Christian tradition. The role of comparative literature here is a very subordinate one. Indeed, it seems to be mentioned as a possible avenue of investigation rather than one which Bultmann actually employed. At any rate, it does not figure significantly in his published work. He scarcely ever compares the development (as opposed to the characteristics) of the Christian tradition with the development of non-Christian tradition. The difficulty of doing so is obvious: where are there bodies of folk-literature which can be studied at successive stages of their transmission? Even where variant forms of the same tradition exist (*e.g.* in Rabbinic literature), it is often difficult to show that one is a lineal descendent of another.

Bultmann, then, in his summary statements about the methods of form criticism, lays stress on comparative material for analyzing the form of the Christian tradition, while emphasizing that the laws of transmission are best studied in the Christian materials themselves. He always notes, however, that study of comparative material does have a subordinate role to play in studying the laws of transmission. As one works through

---

[1] 'The new approach', p. 345. See also *Die Erforschung*, p. 20 (E.T. p. 30).

[2] *Die Geschichte*, p. 8 (E.T. p. 7).

[3] See pp. 9 f. above and also I. F. MacKinnon, '"Formgeschichte" and the Synoptic Problem: Present Position', *Canadian Journal of Religious Thought*, IX (1932), 191.

[4] Bultmann had read widely in the comparative literatures and had doubtless formed opinions about the tendencies operative in their transmission, but he does not use them scientifically in this regard as he does in establishing the characteristics of certain forms. For the most part, students of folk-literature do not emphasize the kinds of laws of transmission about which Bultmann spoke and which concern us here. See, for example, H. M. and N. K. Chadwick, *The growth of literature*, 3 vols. (Cambridge, 1932, 1936, 1940).

18

the *History of the Synoptic Tradition*, it becomes clear that he observed these priorities. When he makes observations about the laws of transmission, the history of the tradition, or the tendency of the tradition, he usually does so on the basis of a discussion of changes which occur in the Synoptics themselves and in the later Christian literature.[1] Similarly, when he makes observations about the laws of style, the characteristics of the tradition, or the form of the tradition, he frequently adduces Rabbinic and Hellenistic parallels.[2] Occasionally he illustrates a law of transmission from non-Christian material. But these instances only serve to reinforce my point that the laws of transmission have not been established outside of the Christian material itself. For instance, in discussing the tendency to make supplementary expansions, Bultmann cites Abodah Zarah IV. 7 and its parallel in the Mekilta, Par. Jethro, Par. 6. He writes that 'the argument in the first passage as to why God does not destroy the heathen deities is subordinated in the second to a comprehensive discussion about God's relationship to idolatry, and in addition is enlarged by an added quotation of scripture'.[3] Bultmann's use of this example requires several comments. (1) It *is* only an example. Bultmann does not undertake to show, nor does he refer to anyone else as having shown, that expansion is a general characteristic of Rabbinic passages. For all we know, there may be many more cases of abbreviation than of expansion. Thus it is clear that the law of expansion has not been proved in Rabbinic literature and then applied to the Synoptic material. It seems more likely that the reverse process has taken place. (2) Bultmann does not find it necessary to show that the passage from the Mekilta is a lineal descendent of the passage from the Mishnah. For all we are told, the two passages could have altered a common ancestor in different ways and actually provide examples of diverse tendencies. (3) Bultmann funda-

---

[1] See, for example, *Die Geschichte*, p. 37 (E.T. p. 37) on the tendency to specify the disciples as companions of Jesus; pp. 54 f. (E.T. pp. 52 f.) on the tendency to standardize Jesus' opponents; pp. 71 f. (E.T. pp. 67 f.) on the tendency to develop apophthegmata by the addition of more precise details; pp. 93 ff. (E.T. pp. 89 ff.) on the tendency to expand sayings; pp. 256 ff. (E.T. pp. 241 ff.) on the tendency to add details and novelistic coloring to miracle stories.

[2] See, for example, *ibid.* pp. 42 ff. (E.T. pp. 41 ff.) on the style of the *Streitgespräche* (especially p. 46, E.T. p. 45); pp. 68 f. (E.T. p. 65) on certain stylistic characteristics of apophthegmata.   [3] *Ibid.* p. 63 (E.T. p. 60).

2-2

mentally recognizes that the tendency of expansion has not been proved from the Rabbinic literature, although the use he makes of that literature in this instance, when added to his summary references to the 'general laws which govern popular transmission of stories and traditions...',[1] somewhat obscures this. All he really claims to show by a few references to Rabbinic literature on the point of expansion is 'that Rabbinic stories did occasionally undergo supplementary expansion'.[2] He is showing that what he claims did take place in the Christian literature is not unnatural, since it at least occasionally took place elsewhere. There is no question of deriving a law from elsewhere and applying it to the Christian literature, however. Such use of comparative literature does not even serve to confirm a tendency of the Synoptic tradition, since it is not shown that the general tendency existed in the literature being compared.

We shall subsequently have occasion to note the relationship between Bultmann's two methods of judging relative antiquity (purity of form and general laws of transmission) and to offer a brief criticism of the first method. For the present, it will suffice to say that this study primarily relates to the second method employed by Bultmann—the investigation of the general tendencies of change in the Synoptic material.

The British form critic, Vincent Taylor, also used literary laws based on the same evidence which Bultmann employed. Thus he writes that 'the modifications which the later Synoptists make in their sources furnish grounds for inferring the kind of changes for which we must make allowance in Mark and Q'.[3] Taylor is not unqualifiedly certain of the ability of studies comparing the Gospels to produce sure laws, however, even though such studies are bolstered by appeal to the later use of the Synoptic tradition: '"Laws of the tradition" can be suspected [to exist], even if they cannot be laid down as hard and fast rules, and further evidence of changes is supplied by the textual tradition and the Apocryphal Gospels.'[4] Taylor also mentions knowledge about the earliest period, derived from the epistles of Paul, Acts, and James, and com-

---

[1] 'The new approach', p. 345.
[2] *Die Geschichte*, p. 63 (E.T. p. 59), emphasis removed.
[3] Vincent Taylor, *The formation of the Gospel tradition* (London, 1957), p. 26.
[4] *Ibid.*

parison with parallel matter as ways of determining the original forms of the Gospel material.[1]

On the question of whether the earliest tradition is that nearest to the pure form, however, Taylor differs from Dibelius and Bultmann. The tradition in its origin was more or less formless—rough, detailed, and unfit for transmission. The older it got, however, the more closely it was conformed to the typical types of tradition known in Judaism and Hellenism. It was rounded, smoothed, shortened, and conventionalized.[2] This difference between Taylor and the German form critics is of considerable significance, especially for the question of whether details tend to be added, and it will be discussed below. We may here only point out that Taylor supports his view by appeal to some experiments he had carried out, apparently with his students, which indicated the shortening of oral stories in the course of transmission.[3] It is significant that Taylor, like Dibelius and Bultmann, never investigated the tendency of material more or less parallel to that in the Synoptics and more or less contemporaneous with it. Like Dibelius and Bultmann, he viewed such material as primarily useful for determining the typical characteristics of certain forms of tradition, but not the typical tendency of those forms.

Evaluation of the form-critical method of establishing the tendencies of the tradition

It has been necessary to emphasize this last point because of what apparently is a fairly common assumption concerning the laws of the tradition, namely, that they have been derived by

[1] *Ibid.*   [2] *Ibid.* pp. 122–6.

[3] *Ibid.* pp. 202–9. Taylor refers to these experiments in his discussion of miracle stories (p. 124), but the example he cites is not a miracle story. He apparently intends the conclusions drawn from his experiments to apply to narrative material in general. We may also note that the circumstances of his experiments could hardly have duplicated the process of the kind of oral transmission depicted by Gerhardsson. Taylor's experiments seem to show how personal reminiscence would be told at second hand rather than how oral tradition would have been transmitted. In addition, the case is somewhat prejudiced, since the initial form of the example he chose is so replete with details and circumstance that it could hardly have been accurately repeated. Taylor presupposes that the original tradition was very detailed, and that determines his choice of the example (see p. 203). Had he presupposed the opposite, the result could well have been the reverse.

studying the course of development of traditions which, though non-Christian, parallel the Christian materials in type and age, and that these laws thus derived may be considered the more or less universal tendency of tradition. This assumption, wherever it is held, is unjustified. Although the form critics compared the Christian tradition with other traditions, they did so in order to understand the formal characteristics of the tradition, not the types of changes it underwent. Even McGinley, who investigates some Rabbinic and Hellenistic healing stories and compares them to those in the Synoptics,[1] does not compare different forms of the same story at different levels of transmission in order to discover the laws of transmission characteristic of healing stories. To my knowledge, this has never been done. Until it is done I do not see how we can speak of the tendencies of each form, in contrast to the characteristics of each form, on which the form critics did so much excellent work.[2]

That the form critics, in establishing the characteristics of each form, actually were correct in comparing the Gospel literature to folk traditions has been questioned.[3] It will be readily seen, however, that this question is of small significance for our present study, since in any case the tendencies of change and development in the Gospel tradition were not derived from a study of the tendencies of change and development in folk tradition. It is true that the characteristics of each form, which were derived from an analysis of folk literature, were used as negative criteria for determining relative age (because the tradition was presumed to develop away from the pure form). But even this view was not proved by appeal to evidence. That is, the form critics did not show, outside of the Synoptic Gospels, that there was a body of tradition which had at first existed in pure forms, but whose purity of form had been corrupted by the passage of time. Indeed, as we have seen,

[1] L. J. McGinley, *Form-criticism of the Synoptic healing narratives* (Woodstock, Maryland, 1944), pp. 96–154.
[2] I hope, in the near future, to make a small effort in this direction by comparing different versions of the same stories in the Rabbinic materials. Some possibility for such a study also exists in Greek popular traditions. A few of the healings of Asclepius, for example, appear in more than one version.
[3] See, for example, McGinley, *op. cit.* p. 153. 'The synoptic narratives so differ from the analogies adduced, that their very form indicates a different origin and development' (italics removed). See also p. 5.

22

Vincent Taylor differs on this point completely from Dibelius and Bultmann. In both cases the argument is *a priori* and does not rest on an examination of particulars. Nor may it be thought that the process of degeneration of form may be observed clearly in the Synoptic Gospels themselves. For example, in the story of the healing of the paralytic (Mt. 9. 1–8//Mk. 2. 1–12//Lk. 5. 17–26) Matthew's version is closer to the pure form described by Dibelius than is Mark's.[1] The question of what purity of form indicates about relative age is concerned almost altogether with the matter of the addition or omission of details, and will be discussed later under the section on details. As we shall see, the view of Dibelius and Bultmann is somewhat inconsistent.

How, then, will the other method pursued by Bultmann and Taylor of developing criteria be evaluated? First of all, it will be recalled, they developed criteria by showing how Matthew and Luke had changed Mark and Q. It will be obvious that for the present study this method is not feasible, since we wish to use the criteria, among other things, to test the more important solutions to the Synoptic problem. But even apart from this, it must be pointed out that the method was not an altogether happy one. In the first place, we may note that Dibelius was of the view that, although the dependence of Luke on Mark could be established on the basis of the order of events, this was not so of the dependence of Matthew on Mark. That could only be established by 'the dependence in detail of the Greek text of Matthew upon that of Mark'.[2] To prove 'dependence in detail', of course, requires certain criteria for determining the relatively early and the relatively late. But if these criteria were only derived, as in the case of Bultmann, from a study of the differences in detail between Matthew and Mark, it is clear that the argument is completely circular. On the one hand, criteria may be established by comparing Matthew with Mark; then on the other, Matthew may be shown to be secondary to Mark by these same criteria. Secondly, one could point out that the laws allegedly derived from a comparison of our Gospels

---

[1] Dibelius (*Die Formgeschichte*, pp. 46–51) characterizes paradigms as being brief and simple. Matthew's version is both briefer and simpler (lacking in the details of Mk. 2. 1–2, 4) than Mark's. See also McGinley's comments on p. 24 below.

[2] M. Dibelius, *A fresh approach to the New Testament and early Christian literature* (London, 1937), p. 55.

23

are not really consistent with the differences between our Gospels. Thus McGinley points to a fundamental contradiction:

It is a well-known fact that picturesque details—a sign of modification of the original form according to form-critical standards—are often more abundant in the Marcan version of a story than in the parallels in Luke and Matthew. Indeed, for an entire category of the Gospel narratives, Dibelius feels obliged to ascribe the more 'primitive' style of Matthew to a modification of a modification found in Mark![1] In general, then, the deduction of the laws that governed the development of forms in the tradition prior to its fixation in the Gospels, by a comparison of Q or Mark with Matthew and Luke, may be said to be quite difficult, if not impossible.[2]

McGinley's point may be reinforced by referring to the recent work of Held on Matthew's use of miracle stories.[3] Held observes that many miracle stories which, in their Markan form, Dibelius classified as Tales (*Novellen*), are, in their Matthaean form, closer to Paradigms.[4] He does not note that, according to Dibelius, Tales are generally later than Paradigms and, indeed, developed from them.[5] Thus, in Dibelius's terms, many of Matthew's miracle stories are formally earlier than Mark's. Thus we see that the attempt to derive laws of transmission from seeing how Matthew and Luke used Mark and Q raises the most serious difficulties; it even comes into direct conflict with using purity of form as a test of relative antiquity.

It is in line with this to observe that the form critics did not derive laws of transmission from the Synoptics systematically. That is, as far as we can judge from published works, all of the instances of change on one point or other were not noticed, but only examples taken. This led to a certain over-simplification of the 'laws'. To choose an example already used, we may take the matter of names. Bultmann is of the view that names tend to be added, and in one place lists three points at which either Matthew or Luke has a name not in Mark. He fails to list, however, all those instances in which Mark has a name not in Matthew or Luke.[7] It is to this incomplete citation of evidence

[1] His reference is to Dibelius, *Formgeschichte*, p. 74.
[2] McGinley, *op. cit.* pp. 14 f.
[3] In Bornkamm, Barth, and Held, *Tradition and interpretation in Matthew* (London, 1963), pp. 165–299.
[4] *Ibid.* pp. 212, 242 f.   [5] *Die Formgeschichte*, pp. 96 f. (E.T. pp. 99 f.).
[6] *Die Erforschung*, p. 23 (E.T. p. 33).
[7] These instances are listed in the appropriate category in chapter III. Cf. also Farmer, *op. cit.* p. 134 n.

24

that we referred in saying that the supposition that the laws have been systematically used in the study of the Synoptics, wherever it may exist, is unjustified. The laws were derived from a partial examination of the evidence, and partially used in the study of the Synoptics. Whether one wishes to derive the laws from the Synoptics and apply them elsewhere or derive them elsewhere and apply them to the Synoptics, the same criticism holds: the Synoptic evidence has not been completely and systematically presented.

This last criticism applies also to the attempt to derive laws from examining how the Synoptic material was changed in the Apocryphal Gospels and in the later manuscripts. On the assumption that there was some continuity of how the material was changed, such study should prove fertile. It is, in fact, the very study undertaken here. Our criticism of Bultmann and Taylor, who mentioned this study as a way for learning the tendencies of the tradition, is only that they did not do it thoroughly. Taylor scarcely ever refers to the Apocryphal litera-ture, and Bultmann does so only to give examples of laws which he already believed to have been operative. To use once more the example of names, Bultmann mentions four instances in which an Apocryphal Gospel has added a name to the Synoptic tradition.[1] One would receive the impression that this was a consistent tendency. But what of instances in the Apocryphal Gospels in which names drop out?[2] The criticism need not be elaborated or belabored. One cannot establish tendencies by citing only examples. What is needed is a thorough investiga-tion of all the evidence, considering how many instances there are which point in each direction. Listing only some instances, all of which point in one direction, is neat, but useless and even misleading. It is a complete[3] investigation of the post-canonical Synoptic tradition which is the goal of this study.

Now the principal points which have been made about the ways in which the form critics developed and used laws of transmission can be summarized.

[1] *Die Erforschung*, pp. 22 f. (E.T. p. 33).
[2] These instances are listed in the appropriate category in chapter III.
[3] 'Complete' is used in the sense that all the evidence on each side which is found in a given body of literature is presented. Section three below will describe the literature which is used.

25

1. The form critics did not derive laws of transmission from a study of folk literature, as many think.

2. They derived them by two methods: (*a*) by assuming that purity of form (or, in the case of Taylor, impurity of form) indicates relative antiquity, and (*b*) by determining how Matthew and Luke used Mark and Q, and how the later literature used the canonical Gospels.

3. The first method is based on *a priori* considerations.

4. In so far as it depends on the use of Mark and Q by Matthew and Luke, the second is circular and therefore questionable.

5. The two are sometimes in direct conflict, although the form critics did not observe this.[1]

6. In any case, the form critics did not derive the laws from or apply the laws to the Gospels systematically, nor did they carry out a systematic investigation of changes in the post-canonical literature.

It is the purpose of this study to meet this last defect. Before describing the method and materials of the present study, however, we must look briefly at the related work of Birger Gerhardsson.

The relation of this study to 'Memory and manuscript'

Gerhardsson, in his book *Memory and manuscript* (1961) and its sequel *Tradition and transmission in early Christianity* (1964), has set out upon the ambitious program of offering an alternative to form criticism, at least as it was conceived by Dibelius and Bultmann. In order to understand the nature of the Christian tradition and how it was transmitted, Gerhardsson studies first of all the more or less contemporary Jewish literature and then Hellenistic pedagogics.[2] This study leads him to stress the accuracy of oral tradition in passing down material unchanged, or virtually so.[3] But as Gerhardsson is at pains to point out, he does not investigate the tradition as such, but 'the technical process by which [it] was transmitted'.[4] In stressing the tech-

---

[1] In addition to p. 24 above, see also p. 146 n. 3 below.
[2] See *Tradition and transmission*, p. 47 n. 115.
[3] See *Memory and manuscript*, pp. 130–6. Note also the statement that if Jesus taught, 'he must have required his disciples to memorize', p. 328.
[4] *Tradition and transmission*, p. 12 n. 20.

nique of oral transmission, he naturally lays great emphasis on what the Rabbis said about how they taught and learned. This has the effect of minimizing the actual differences which occur between two different forms of any one Rabbinic story, so that Gerhardsson's work, thus far at least, leads one to expect little change in material transmitted orally. Thus far the problem of how the material was altered has scarcely arisen in Gerhardsson's work.

It may be helpful to define this study over against Gerhardsson's. He dealt with the methods of teaching and learning which were operative primarily in Rabbinic Judaism, but also in Hellenism.[1] By his very method he was led to stress the rigidity of the tradition.[2] We study the changes which actually took place in the post-canonical Synoptic tradition. We naturally shall stress the changing character of the tradition. This study, in other words, is an individual study of a particular aspect of the early Christian tradition. We cannot derive from it a total view of that tradition, but it should serve as a contribution to a total view. In the conclusion some indications may be given of what the significance of our study for the larger problem is. Any attempt to shape a comprehensive view of the nature of the early Christian tradition will have to consider both the facts of change, some of which we shall here present, and the factors making for continuity and stability stressed by Gerhardsson. The one may serve as corrective to the other.

Put in another way, where Gerhardsson studied the Rabbinic material, we study the Christian in its own right. Without denying the value of comparative studies, we may point to the following factors which give the early Christian tradition a certain claim on uniqueness over against both the Rabbinic material and folk traditions. (1) Belief in the living Lord presumably fostered more creativity than one finds in the Rabbinic

---

[1] The view of B. S. Easton may be compared to Gerhardsson's: 'If, then, we are to form a just picture of the earliest Christianity, we must think of it as busily engaged in teaching its converts the sayings of the Second Moses.' The material of the early Christian tradition was 'the material used by the catechists in preparing converts to face the approaching Messianic judgment'. See 'The first Evangelic tradition', *J.B.L.* L (1931), 151, 154.

[2] This is not to say that Gerhardsson denies that the tradition changed. In *Memory and manuscript*, p. 98, he discusses changes which were made in the Rabbinic materials by redactors in the colleges. The general emphasis of his work, however, is on the precision with which tradition was transmitted.

27

material.[1] In a section on the 'distinctiveness of the Christ-tradition', Gerhardsson notes the charismatic element in the Christian tradition but warns that we should not emphasize this element at the expense of recognizing the 'rational mechanisms' of the early Church's teaching.[2] (2) The oral period was of very short duration when compared to that of the Old Testament, the Rabbinic tradition, and epic material; and thus the Christian tradition probably did not undergo the same changes as did the materials which remained longer in the oral state.[3] (3) The Christian material was transmitted in more than one language.[4] The multi-lingual character of the early Christian tradition provided a source of variation. It should not be expected that material which passed from one language and culture to another would have been so free of change as material which stayed in the same language and was maintained by members of a relatively small and static group. (4) The Christian tradition was doubtless transmitted by people who were not trained in passing on oral tradition in the way described by Gerhardsson.[5] One of the real accomplishments of Gerhardsson's work is to show how difficult accurate transmission of oral tradition is and the discipline and training required to effect it. The rapid spread of Christianity, especially into the West, seems to preclude the possibility that the various widely spread churches could have relied on trained transmitters. They must, therefore, have learned and retained the Christian tradition in a way other than that which obtained in the Rabbinic academies. The problem of method of transmission is discussed more fully in Appendix III. (5) Despite certain similarities with folk literature, the Christian tradition is not really of that genre, at least in the way that fairy tales are.[6]

For these reasons, we seem justified in saying that the Christian tradition was, in certain respects, unique. It follows that, helpful though studies comparing it with other literature are, there is a need to study the course of its development in its own

---

[1] The influence of prophecy and 'charismatic authority' on the early Christian tradition is emphasized by Amos Wilder, 'Form-history and the oldest tradition', *Neotestamentica et Patristica*, Freundesgabe Oscar Cullmann, ed. W. C. van Unnik (Leiden, 1962), p. 5.
[2] *Tradition and transmission*, pp. 46 f.   [3] Cf. *ibid.* p. 46.
[4] Cf. *ibid.* p. 45.   [5] *Memory and manuscript*, pp. 93–122.
[6] See the discussion by McGinley, *op. cit.* p. 153.

28

right. We do this by tracing the changes which occurred in the Synoptic material when it was employed by later writers. What material is to be used will be the point of discussion in the next section. Here we may conclude by noting that the work intends to be a contribution to form criticism. The purpose of the work is complementary to the purpose of form criticism as described by its inaugurator:

Die Formgeschichte stellt sich...die...Aufgabe, Entstehung und Geschichte dieser Einzelstücke zu rekonstruieren, somit die Geschichte des vorliterarischen Ueberlieferung aufzuhellen, und — im Falle der Synoptiker — eine Art 'Paläontologie der Evangelien' (K. L. Schmidt nach Overbeck in RGG² II 638) zu schaffen.[1]

THE MATERIAL

We must now define what literature will be used in our study of how the post-canonical Synoptic material changed. The principal groups of material, which we shall discuss one by one, are the texts of the New Testament, the Synoptic material in the early Fathers, and the Apocryphal literature. No one of these three groups bears the same relation to our Synoptic Gospels that one Gospel bears to another. There are difficulties which hamper our use of each group, as we shall see. Nevertheless, these groups present the only possibility of seeing how the Synoptic material fared after it had been employed in the Synoptic Gospels themselves. By studying all three groups it should be possible to draw general conclusions as to the tendencies of the Synoptic material which will have some validity when applied to the differences among our canonical Gospels and to the pre-canonical tradition.

The textual tradition

It was Fascher's view that

tradition criticism and text criticism stand before the same methodological problems, insofar as they, in the quest for the original form or original text, seek to reach behind the transmitted forms by means of the 'laws' of oral tradition or of the *Sitz im Leben*...[2]

[1] 'Zur Formgeschichte', pp. 187 f.
[2] Erich Fascher, *Textgeschichte als hermeneutisches Problem* (Halle, 1953), p. 3. Fascher's book is a consideration of the theological significance of textual variants, especially their significance for the hermeneutical problem.

29

Doubtless many proponents of the eclectic school of textual criticism would agree, inasmuch as they seek the earliest form of the text by the use of internal criteria which are based principally on knowledge of the author's style and of the general tendencies of scribes.[1] Bultmann also apparently regarded the tendency of the later scribes to be the same, by and large, as the tendency of earlier transmitters of the material, since he listed the manuscript tradition as one source for determining the laws of development.[2] De Jonge came to a similar conclusion on the basis of a study of the manuscripts of the Testaments of the Twelve Patriarchs. After noting that a newly discovered Aramaic fragment of the Testament of Levi is parallel to the Greek MS *e*, he observed that 'the case of MS *e* shows, that "Traditionsgeschichte" and textual history cannot [*scil.* should not] be separated too strictly'.[3]

This view has been criticized, however, principally by Klijn.[4] Klijn notes that both Fascher and Karnetzki[5] wish to apply to the written text the laws which form criticism showed to have been operative in the development of the oral tradition. Klijn does not doubt either that these laws have been established by the form critics independently of the study of the written text or that *at some stage* the written text changed in accordance with those laws. He doubts, however, that these laws were still operative in the period from which our manuscripts come. He would thus argue that the laws of form criticism should not be applied to the study of the written texts of the fourth century and later.[6] It would follow from this that a study of the written texts would not, in Klijn's view, reveal the laws of development of the early tradition. A complication arises, however, since, according to Klijn, influences *other* than those which shaped the

---

[1] See the recent discussion by Bruce M. Metzger, *The text of the New Testament* (New York, 1964), pp. 175–9. For a statement of the eclectic method, see G. D. Kilpatrick, 'Western text and original text in the Gospels and Acts', *J.T.S.* XLIV (1943), 24–36.

[2] See p. 17 above. F. C. Grant, 'Where form criticism and textual criticism overlap', pp. 14 f., was of the view that the earliest period of textual transmission would not have been much different from the preceding period of oral transmission, although the change would eventually prove revolutionary.

[3] M. De Jonge, *Testamenta XII Patriarcharum* (Leiden, 1964), p. xi.

[4] A. J. Klijn, 'A survey of the researches into the Western Text of the Gospels and Acts (1949–1959)', part II, *Nov. Test.* III (1959), 161 ff.

[5] 'Textgeschichte als Überlieferungsgeschichte', *Z.N.T.W.* XLVII (1956), 170–80.

[6] Klijn, *op. cit.* p. 162.

development of the early tradition might have had *similar effects* on the later textual tradition. That is, the causes may have changed while the results remained the same. Thus Klijn writes that

the influences of translations (compare d on D), pedantic copyists (grammatical alterations), apocryphal writings (addition of names and geographical alterations) and dogmatics very often caused the same deviations as those due to the laws of form criticism in the very beginning.[1]

Klijn's criticism of Fascher's view, however, does not prevent us from using the manuscript tradition in our investigation. It will be noted that Klijn is of the view that form criticism had independently established laws of change in the earliest tradition. These laws of change, in his view, were caused by other motivations than those he ascribes to the manuscript copyists. We have already seen, however, that the form critics actually did not establish laws of change independently of that very written tradition (the manuscript and the apocryphal) to which Klijn refers. Nor can it be done. Thus one cannot appeal to form criticism as having established, for the early transmitters, other motivations than those mentioned by Klijn. As a matter of fact, it seems likely that all but one of the motivations for change which Klijn mentions as governing the manuscript tradition would have been operative earlier. The one exception would be grammatical alterations. But even this motivation may well have been present in the work of the later Gospel writers. Multi-lingualism, dogmatic concern, and novelistic (apocryphal) interest may very well antedate the scribes to whom Klijn refers.

There are, nevertheless, problems in using the manuscript tradition. The first is the problem of circularity. Since in some cases the original readings or the best manuscripts have been determined, partly at least, on the basis of internal criteria, it follows that any analysis of how those original readings were changed will simply reflect the criteria by which they were chosen in the first place. This problem is largely mitigated, however, by considering that the Koine (sometimes called Byzantine or Syrian) text-type has been shown to be later than the Alexandrian and 'Western' text-types apart from internal

[1] *Ibid.*

criteria. In the first place, the witness of the Fathers supports this judgement.[1] Further, there is sufficient evidence in the Koine text-type of conflation of other text-types to prove its secondary character.[2]

Even when this text-type is shown to be secondary, however, it still does not bear the relationship to the other text-types which one Gospel bears to another. To take an example, the scribes, on the whole, regarded the text as holy and official. Under such circumstances we need look for relatively little creativity.[3] On small points, however, such as the tendency toward or away from explicitness, this text-type may be of some use.

A special problem is raised in respect to the so-called Western text, and especially in respect to its major representative, codex D. It has been argued, principally by Wensinck[4] and

[1] Thus Hort writes that 'before the middle of the third century, at the very earliest, we have no historical signs of the existence of readings, conflate or other, that are marked as distinctively Syrian by the want of attestation from groups of documents which have preserved the other ancient forms of text. This is a fact of great significance, ascertained as it is exclusively by external evidence...'. See Westcott and Hort, *The New Testament*, vol. II (New York, 1882), pp. 114–15. The want of early Patristic support for the distinctively Koine (or Syrian) text-type was also confirmed, against Hort's critics, by F. G. Kenyon, *Handbook to the textual criticism of the New Testament* (London, 1901), pp. 274–7.

[2] See Westcott and Hort, *op. cit.* pp. 93–107. This position has been challenged by G. D. Kilpatrick in 'The Greek New Testament text of today and the *Textus Receptus*', *The New Testament in historical and contemporary perspective* (Essays in Memory of G. H. C. Macgregor, ed. by H. Anderson and William Barclay, Oxford, 1965, pp. 189–206). Kilpatrick argues that not all instances of apparent conflation in the Koine text are really conflation, that other text-types also have conflate readings, and that in any case the readings of the Koine text, like those of the Western, should be considered on their own merits rather than rejected out of hand because they occur in a certain text-type. Kilpatrick's general point is well taken, but his eclecticism is so consistent that he seems never to consider that an 'inferior' reading could have been substituted for a 'superior' reading in the history of the text. This problem will be discussed more fully in chapter IV. For the present, it seems wisest to accept the best modern critical texts as presenting the right readings and to consider deviations from them as later changes. This policy doubtless will lead to some errors, but I think that the number of really questionable readings in the lists which follow will prove to be negligible.

[3] The concern for accurate transmission on the part of the scribes was not equally strong at all periods and places, however. On the looseness of transmission and lack of editorial control in the late Byzantine manuscripts, see E. C. Colwell, 'The complex character of the Late Byzantine text of the Gospels', *J.B.L.* LIV (1935), 211–21. Colwell believes that there was a similar lack of control in the earliest period, until about A.D. 300.

[4] A. J. Wensinck, 'The Semitisms of Codex Bezae and their relation to the non-Western text of the Gospel of Saint Luke', *The Bulletin of the Bezan Club*, XII (1937). Cited by M. Black, *An Aramaic approach*, p. 5.

32

whish
has now
been proven false

Black,[1] that D is shown, by the presence of Aramaisms, to preserve, at many places, an original reading over against the Alexandrian text. This view has been criticized, rightly to my view, by Yoder and Klijn. Yoder comes to two conclusions on this point:

(1) When one takes into account not only the instances of Semitic phenomena in codex Bezae, but also the Bezan variants which abandon Semitisms found in other MSS, the net increase of Semitisms is sometimes inconsequential, while in other respects this MS actually reveals fewer Semitisms than found in the B Aleph text; and (2) oft-times the data are concentrated in limited areas of the text, thus detracting from the supposed homogeneity of the Bezan text.[2]

On the basis of a review of all the variants in D, Yoder is of the opinion that

their grammatical cast is almost totally consonant with vernacular Greek of the early Christian centuries, while exhibiting also some striking resemblances to the LXX.[3]

Klijn, referring to Wensinck's work on D, noted that he only compared it with B Aleph.

The result of this limited number of witnesses was that he overlooked the possibility of many so-called aramaisms being not more than latinisms caused by the influence of d on D. In this case Black's study shows a great advantage. Apart from D, the latin and syriac versions are constantly referred to…The question, however, is whether we are dealing with aramaisms or syriasms. As long as the relation between D—old syr—old lat —diat has not been solved it is rather hazardous to base too many conclusions on semitisms in D.[4]

A final difficulty with the view of Black may now be pointed out. One might receive the impression that in the passages in which he finds a Semitism in D, the only difference between D and the generally accepted text of ℵ B is that D has an Aramaism not found in the latter. This is frequently not the case, however.

[1] Black, An Aramaic approach, pp. 25–31 and passim (3rd ed. pp. 28–34).
[2] J. D. Yoder, 'Semitisms in Codex Bezae', J.B.L. LXXVIII (1959), 317. As an example of the second point, we may cite Yoder's evidence concerning parataxis, the frequency of which in the Gospels is frequently regarded as being due to Semitic influence. He points out that Bezae shows a tendency toward parataxis in Acts, but the reverse tendency in Luke and Mark. See pp. 318 f.
[3] Ibid. p. 321.
[4] Klijn, 'A survey of the researches into the Western Text of the Gospels and Acts', p. 161.

To take one notable example, Black has noticed parataxis in the D text of Mark 14:4. It does not occur in the usually read text. The two readings, however, are simply not the same. D has οἱ δὲ μαθηταὶ αὐτοῦ διεπονοῦντο καὶ ἔλεγο.[1] The Nestle text reads ἦσαν δέ τινες ἀγανακτοῦντες πρὸς ἑαυτούς. While it is true that the D text has two finite verbs linked with καί and that the ℵ B text does not, it can hardly be thought that the ℵ B text is a result of correcting the more Semitic text of D. Thus it does not follow that the more Semitic D text is earlier. Which is the earlier reading must be judged by canons other than that of Semitism, for the Semitism here is only incidental to the variant, not the cause of it.

There is another way in which this passage shows the care which must be exercised in using an apparent Semitism to establish the earlier reading. There is a possible Semitism in the ℵ B text of 14:4: πρὸς ἑαυτούς may be regarded as translating an ethical dative. Dr Black, as a matter of fact, when listing uses of parataxis chooses the text of D,[2] but when listing the uses of the ethical dative chooses the text of ℵ B.[3] We really cannot have our cake and eat it too. There is no reason to suppose that any reading ever had both the ethical dative and the parataxis. So we have no alternative but to conclude that a reading containing one of these 'Semitisms' was created somewhere in the transmission of the text. Nothing could show more sharply that an apparent Semitism in D is not *ipso facto* proof of an earlier reading. This last point supports the conclusions of Yoder and Klijn, and it seems best to follow them in not evaluating D's readings more highly than is usually done.[4] The evaluation of D which is accepted here is supported by a recent article by K. Aland, in which he points out that new papyri, especially 𝔓⁷⁵, show that the conjunction of D with the Old Latin cannot be regarded so highly as it has been.[5] /

In sum, we have no new evaluation to offer of either the

---

[1] The text is that of F. H. Scrivener, *Bezae Codex Cantabrigiensis* (Cambridge, 1864).
[2] Black, *An Aramaic approach*², p. 50 (3rd ed. p. 68).
[3] *Ibid.* p. 77 (3rd ed. p. 103).
[4] It may additionally be noted that H. J. Vogels, *Die Harmonistic im Evangelientext des Codex Cantabrigiensis* (Leipzig, 1910), shows harmonistic readings in D. Harmonisation sometimes caused the scribe to omit, against what otherwise seems to be a tendency to add. See, for example, Mt. 5. 11 and Lk. 6. 22.
[5] K. Aland, 'Neue Neutestamentliche Papyri II', *N.T.S.* xii (1966), 193–210.

Koine or 'Western' text. We follow here the most prevalent
modern views of textual criticism as they are represented in the
texts edited by Westcott and Hort and by Nestle. Thus we take
an agreement between the major modern texts to represent an
original reading. Really questionable readings (as where Nestle
disagrees with Westcott and Hort) are not used in this study.[1]

We may also use the information derived from observing
how individual manuscripts or small groups of manuscripts
differ within each text-type. Any instance in which one or more
manuscripts differs from what is obviously the correct reading
we take as giving the type of evidence for which we seek. The
procedure will be to use the only full textual apparatus available, that of Legg on Matthew and Mark, and to catalogue all
of the changes from what must have been the original reading
which bear on the categories under discussion. (These categories will be explained later.) Experiments with using smaller
critical apparatuses have proved that an inaccurate picture is
derived from them. Further, we shall actually list only the
changes in the first half of Matthew (chapters 1. 17 through 15)
and in the second half of Mark (chapters 9 through 16). Only
half of the total evidence collected, in other words, is to be
presented. This limitation is observed for purely physical
reasons. I am satisfied that the cutting of the evidence in half
in this way offers no distortion of the total view. The important
thing is to record all the changes within a certain body of literature which bear on a certain point one way or the other, and
not to select only the changes which go in one direction.

The early Fathers

In dealing with the question of intentional alteration of readings, Titus notes that the quotations from the New Testament
in the Apostolic Fathers are 'too loose and uncertain' to permit

---

[1] The new edition of the Greek New Testament sponsored by the United Bible
Societies and edited by Aland, Black, Metzger, and Wikgren (Stuttgart, 1966)
had not been published when this study was being prepared. I have subsequently
tried to take it into account, however, and have noted in the lists which follow
instances in which the new edition (cited as the U.B.S. text) differs from Nestle
and Westcott and Hort.

[2] Legg's standard of accuracy seems to be sufficient for the present purpose. His
work in any case is the only one which is sufficiently complete.

discussion of the motivation of changes in reading, while Origen is too text-conscious and critical. The intervening Fathers quote the New Testament sufficiently literally, but also with enough 'spontaneous creativity' to be useful.[1] The same considerations apply to our study. As we shall see immediately below, the Apostolic Fathers are hardly usable here. We exclude the third-century Fathers for the reason adduced by Titus: their view of the New Testament prevented them from altering it spontaneously. That is, the tradition was no longer developing, so laws of development can no longer be seen. These later Fathers belong in the area of text criticism, and their witness is listed there. We have also, however, had to eliminate from consideration the Synoptic material in Irenaeus and Clement of Alexandria. This elimination was dictated purely by physical considerations: the size of the material was too large to allow its inclusion in this study. It may be that a subsequent study can meet this defect. We may discuss briefly the principal Fathers whose work we use.

The Apostolic Fathers, for the most part, as Titus noted, quote the New Testament with such freedom that it is difficult to use them in showing how the New Testament material was changed. In addition, there is the question of whether, in passages parallel to the Synoptic Gospels, these early writers were actually using our canonical Gospels. Thus, for example, Glover[2] and Audet[3] think that the Didache depended on a source or sources other than our Synoptics.[4] Both seem to think the source or sources to have been used independently by the Didache and by Matthew and Luke. This problem was early studied as a whole by a committee of the Oxford Society of Historical Theology[5] and more recently by Helmut Köster.[6] In neither study are many passages found in which it can be

[1] E. L. Titus, *The motivation of changes made in the New Testament text by Justin Martyr and Clement of Alexandria* (Chicago, 1945), p. 4.
[2] Richard Glover, 'The Didache's quotations and the Synoptic Gospels', *N.T.S.* v (1958), 12–29.
[3] Jean-Paul Audet, *La Didachè: Instructions des Apôtres* (Paris, 1958), esp. pp. 166–86.
[4] B. C. Butler, 'The literary relations of Didache, Ch. xvi', *J.T.S.* xi (1960), 265–83, differs with Glover and Audet. Butler thinks that Did. 16 depends on Luke (or possibly proto-Luke) and on a source which he names M (g). He notes that this source is not distinguishable from Matthew.
[5] *The New Testament in the Apostolic Fathers* (Oxford, 1905).
[6] *Synoptische Überlieferung bei den apostolischen Vätern.*

36

thought with some assurance that the Father in question drew directly on one or more of our canonical Gospels.

Köster's view is that there existed a free oral tradition which, until about the year 150, could be drawn upon. This oral tradition paralleled the Synoptics, and was, in part at least, the very *Vorstufe* of the Synoptics themselves.[1] Thus most of the Apostolic Fathers actually stand on the same level as the Synoptic Gospels with regard to the early Christian tradition. Both the early Fathers and the canonical Gospels drew from the same resources.[2] The only clear exceptions are II Clement[3] and Did. 1. 3–2. 1,[4] which Köster regards as having used our Synoptic Gospels, or at least as having used sources which were themselves dependent upon our Gospels.

It is clear that such a view prohibits our use of any among the Apostolic Fathers but II Clement and Did. 1. 3–2. 1. If the others did not use our Synoptics directly, we naturally cannot show how they changed the Synoptic material, since in that case we do not have their sources. I am by no means persuaded of the accuracy of Köster's view as a whole.[5] But it cannot be denied that there is a distinct possibility that, for example, I Clement drew upon non-canonical sources, even if one does not think of a 'free tradition'[6] being maintained in the oral state until the year 150. Since quotations of the Synoptic material, except in the two places named, tend for the most part to differ so widely from our Synoptics, however, we think it best to limit the material used from this group to II Clement and Did. 1. 3–2. 1.

The only other principal group of Fathers before Irenaeus is the group known as the Apologists. The members of this group are Aristides, Justin, Tatian, Athenagoras, Theophilus of Antioch, and Hermias.[7] Of these, Aristides, Hermias, and Tatian do not quote directly from the New Testament, although Tatian does refer to the hidden treasure of Mt. 13. 44 in chapter 30 of his *Address to the Greeks*. Athenagoras and Theophilus do not quote extensively from the Synoptics, so that the principal source here is Justin.

[1] *Ibid.* p. 3. [2] *Ibid.* p. 258. [3] *Ibid.* pp. 62–111, esp. 110 f.
[4] *Ibid.* pp. 217–39, esp. 229. [5] See p. 296 n. 1 below.
[6] The phrase is Köster's, *passim*.
[7] The date at which Hermias wrote is very uncertain. The others fall in the second half of the second century.

There has been some debate about Justin's use of the Synoptics. Several scholars have thought Justin to have had access to a non-canonical source in part paralleling the canonical Gospels. Bousset noted points at which he thought Justin had an earlier and more original form of a saying than that in the Synoptics. He concluded that Justin had access to the 'Sammlung von Herrenreden, die unserm Matth. und Luk. vorlegen hat'.[1] Scholars as a whole have not accepted this view, and, indeed, I think it to be untenable.[2] It can be shown that when Justin quoted the same Synoptic passage in two different places, he frequently quoted it once in Matthew's form and once in Mark's or Luke's.[3] Such instances make it almost incredible that he was using in these passages sources behind our Synoptics. But if it can be shown that at these passages he used our Synoptics, the assumption is that he also used them elsewhere, unless very strong evidence to the contrary is forthcoming. Since I know of no such evidence, I take it that Justin used our Synoptics rather than their sources.

More recently Köster has revived the suggestion that Justin used a Gospel harmony.[4] This argument has been developed

[1] Wilhelm Bousset, *Die Evangeliencitate Justins des Märtyers* (Göttingen, 1891), p. 114. Glover, *op. cit.* p. 29, also thinks Justin may have had access to Q. Glover unfortunately seems to wish to have F. C. Burkitt's support for his view. He states (p. 29) that 'F. C. Burkitt observed that nine-tenths of the examples of Christ's ethical teaching given by Justin in his *First Apology* were drawn from Q'. (The reference is to F. C. Burkitt, *The Earliest Sources for the Life of Jesus*, p. 44, *apud* T. W. Manson, *The Teaching of Jesus*, p. 28.) This statement is doubly misleading. In the first place, Burkitt referred only to the ethical teachings cited in Apol. 1. 15 f., not to those used in the whole Apology. In the second place, Burkitt did not say that the examples were 'drawn from Q', but that they 'came out of passages derived from Q' (Burkitt, *ad loc. cit.*), that is, from places in Matthew and Luke which depend on Q. Burkitt was simply pointing out the ethical richness of the Q material. Actually, he did not doubt that Justin knew and used our canonical Gospels. See *The Gospel history and its transmission* (Edinburgh, 1911), p. 257.

[2] The question of whether or not the 'memoirs' mentioned by Justin were our Gospels was much debated in the nineteenth century. See the balanced summary of the discussion in G. T. Purves, *The testimony of Justin Martyr to early Christianity* (New York, 1889), pp. 170–5. His discussion of the problem itself occupies pp. 175–213. A. J. Bellinzoni, Jr., *The sayings of Jesus in the writings of Justin Martyr* (Leiden, 1967), has now shown decisively that Justin did not use Q or any other sayings source older than our Gospels. See pp. 21 n., 25 n., 28 n., 139, and often.

[3] See Justin, Apol. 1. 16. 7 and Dial. 101. 2; Dial. 51. 2 and 76. 7.

[4] Köster, *op. cit.* pp. 86–91. For the earlier discussion, see Purves, *op. cit.* pp. 206–11.

38

further by Bellinzoni.[1] Although Bellinzoni's work, while generally persuasive, does not convince me at all points, it is not necessary to enter into a detailed discussion of it here. It must suffice to say that Bellinzoni has shown, at the very least, that Justin frequently cites Synoptic passages in harmonized readings which are also known from later writers. It thus appears that Justin made some use of harmonies and collections of harmonized sayings material which continued in circulation. I think that such passages as those referred to in n. 3, p. 38 above show that Justin did not always use harmonies. In any case, however, the harmonies which Justin used, as Bellinzoni shows, were harmonies of our Gospels, so that we may still use Justin's quotations as providing evidence of how the Synoptic material was changed.[2]

In order to investigate the way in which Justin reflects changes in the Synoptic material, we must assume that we now have access to a text of the Synoptics which is earlier than Justin. While present critical texts of the New Testament do not rest on manuscripts which can be dated before Justin's time, this constitutes very little difficulty. Justin did not quote very accurately from the New Testament, and his citations of it show how one not concerned with literal transmission would alter the material. Thus the possibility of his having preserved an authentic reading very rarely arises. Where Justin does quote more or less literally, he can sometimes be seen to agree with the Old Syriac and Old Latin.[3] We have already indicated that present critical texts rest upon text-types which are superior to the Western text, despite some attempts to re-evaluate the latter.[4]

Daniel Ruiz Bueno has conveniently assembled the Greek texts of the second-century apologists, together with a Spanish translation, in one volume.[5] It is this volume which I have used in comparing the Synoptic material in the Apologists with the Synoptic Gospels themselves. Ruiz Bueno has not, however, made fresh editions of the text. For the Apologies of Justin, he

[1] *Op. cit.* See also his review of W. A. Shotwell, *The biblical exegesis of Justin Martyr* (London, 1965) in the *J.B.L.* LXXXV (1966), 124 f.
[2] See Bellinzoni, p. 139
[3] See F. G. Kenyon, *Handbook to the textual criticism of the New Testament*, p. 210.
[4] See pp. 32–5 above.
[5] *Padres apologistas Griegos* (Biblioteca de Autores Cristianos) (Madrid, 1954).

prints the text of G. Rauschen;[1] for the Dialogue, that of
Georges Archambault.[2] For the Embassy of Athenagoras, he
uses the text of J. Geffcken;[3] for the Apology of Theophilus
(Three Books to Autolycus), that of G. Bardy.[4]

The procedure has been to note every instance in which a
quotation from the Synoptics in one of the Fathers differs from
our Synoptic Gospels, and, if it relates to one of our categories,
to list it in the proper place.

The Apocryphal Gospels

There are few problems which stand in the way of our use of the
Apocryphal Gospels. We need not even decide the dating of
each of the individual Gospels within close limits, since it is not
doubted that they actually made use of our Synoptics, nor can
it be said that they, being late, regarded the Synoptic Gospels
as holy and unchangeable. They may have been late, but their
attitude toward the Gospel material did not compel them
toward inflexibility in the use of it. This is readily seen by
examining the number and type of alterations of the Synoptic
material which appear in the Apocryphal Gospels. Many of
these will be listed in the chapters which follow.

The principal problem here is whether or not we shall make
use of the recently found Gospel of Thomas. The question is
whether this document did make use of our Synoptic Gospels
or whether its author possessed independent sources. The leading scholar who has most extensively argued that Thomas
depends upon a source independent of, and perhaps earlier
than our Synoptics is G. Quispel. Quispel thinks that some of
the sayings of Jesus in Thomas come from 'a Jewish-Christian
Gospel originally written in Aramaic'.[5] He shows that there

---

[1] *S. Iustini Apologiae duae* (Bonnae, 1911).
[2] *Justin, Dialogue avec Tryphon* (Textes et Documents) (Paris, 1909).
[3] *Zwei griechische Apologeten* (Leipzig, 1907).
[4] *Théophile d'Antioche* (Sources Chrétiennes) (Paris, 1948).
[5] G. Quispel, 'The Gospel of Thomas and the New Testament', *Vig. Chr.* XI
(1957), 189–207, esp. 189. Quispel also presents his general view in 'Some
remarks on the Gospel of Thomas', *N.T.S.* v (1958), 276–90. See also, by the
same author, 'L'Évangile selon Thomas et les Clémentines', *Vig. Chr.* XII (1958),
181–96; 'L'Évangile selon Thomas et le Diatessaron', *Vig. Chr.* XIII (1959),
87–117; 'L'Évangile selon Thomas et le "Texte Occidental" du Nouveau
Testament', *Vig. Chr.* XIV (1960), 204–15.

are parallels and agreements between sayings in Thomas and the quotations in the Pseudo-Clementine writings (which he thinks came from a Jewish-Christian source), the Diatessaron, and the Western text. He thinks the latter agreements may be due to common influence from the Gospel according to the Hebrews.[1] He concludes that Thomas at certain points maintains an Aramaic tradition independent of the Synoptics.[2] This view is basically supported by Montefiore[3] and Guillaumont.[4] Jeremias[5] and Hunzinger[6] are among other scholars who find an independent and perhaps quite early tradition embodied in Thomas.

Gärtner, however, argues against Quispel that 'when we find that many of the readings of the *Gospel of Thomas* are so close to the Diatessaron, the *Pseudo-Clementines* and the "Western Text", it seems quite clear that we are here dealing with a common textual tradition, which might easily be condemned as "heretical"'.[7] Schrage makes the same point, noting further that this relationship of Thomas to the Western text, which he regards as the normal text of the second century, actually confirms the dependence of Thomas upon the Synoptics.[8] As to

---

[1] 'The Gospel of Thomas and the New Testament', p. 203.
[2] *Ibid.* p. 207. Since some of the sayings in the Gospel of Thomas show similarities with Luke where he differs from Mark, and since Thomas used none of our Synoptics, Quispel concludes that Luke had access to the same special source used by Thomas. See 'Some Remarks', pp. 280-1.
[3] Hugh Montefiore, 'A comparison of the parables of the Gospel according to Thomas and of the Synoptic Gospels' in H. Montefiore and H. E. W. Turner, *Thomas and the Evangelists*, pp. 40-78.
[4] Antoine Guillaumont, 'Sémitismes dans les Logia de Jésus retrouvés à Nag-Hamâdi', *Journal Asiatique*, 246 (1958), 113-23. Guillaumont notes certain similarities between some of the sayings in Thomas which have Synoptic parallels and the Syriac version of the same sayings. He thinks this may indicate a Syrian origin for the sayings in Thomas (p. 117). But he also thinks that the agreement of the Coptic with the Syriac may indicate the *original* syntax of a saying, as in Logion 16 = Lk. 12. 51-3. He proposes a reconstruction of the passage in Luke on the basis of the Coptic and Syriac (p. 119). Guillaumont also thinks that Logion 107 and Mt. 18. 12-13//Lk. 15. 3-6 are independent translations of the same Aramaic (p. 120).
[5] Joachim Jeremias, *The parables of Jesus* (second Eng. ed.), p. 24.
[6] Claus-Hunno Hunzinger, 'Aussersynoptisches Traditionsgut im Thomas-Evangelium', *Th. Lit. Zeit.* LXXXV (1960), 843-6.
[7] Bertil Gärtner, *The theology of the Gospel according to Thomas* (New York, 1961), p. 63. Turner ('The Gospel of Thomas: its History, Transmission and Sources', in Montefiore and Turner, *op. cit.* p. 26) takes the same view.
[8] Wolfgang Schrage, *Das Verhältnis des Thomas-Evangeliums zur synoptischen Tradition und zu den koptischen Evangelienübersetzung* (Berlin, 1964), p. 18.

41

the Semitisms, Klijn warns that they may be 'syriasms' as well as 'aramaisms', since the sayings in Thomas 'went through a syriac speaking environment'.[1] Schrage has further noted that some of the 'Aramaisms' found by Quispel and others actually seem to have come from the Coptic version of the New Testament.[2] Gärtner further argues that many of the sayings in Thomas depend upon our Synoptics because they are conflated (he says 'compounded') from two or more sayings, usually from Matthew and Luke. Thomas thus falls into the common pattern of harmonization.[3]

Perhaps the primary question, however, is methodological. Schrage argues that if, in any of the instances in which Thomas has material parallel to material in the Synoptics, it can be definitely shown that Thomas has used our Synoptics, the presumption is that he did so in instances in which definite proof one way or the other is lacking.[4] Montefiore also grants that it is unlikely that Thomas used both our Synoptic Gospels and 'sources independent of the Synoptic Gospels but containing some similar material'.[5] His procedure differs from Schrage's, however. Montefiore first looks for traditions parallel to but apparently independent of the Synoptics,[6] and then raises the possibility that Thomas 'derived none of his material from the Synoptic Gospels'.[7] Schrage begins with traditions in which dependence upon the Synoptics is surest, Montefiore with traditions in which dependence upon the Synoptics is least sure. In my view, Schrage's method is the better one, and it seems more likely that Thomas used our Synoptics than that he used some other traditions.[8]

It must be granted, however, that the matter is not yet finally settled. The material requires yet more investigation, even though Schrage's work now probably sets the pattern for future

[1] Klijn, 'A survey of the researches into the Western Text of the Gospels and Acts', pp. 167 f.
[2] Schrage, *op. cit.* pp. 13 f.   [3] Gärtner, *op. cit.* pp. 65, 68.
[4] Schrage, *op. cit.* pp. 10 f.
[5] Montefiore, *op. cit.* p. 41.
[6] *Ibid.* p. 42. Although the main body of Montefiore's article deals only with parables, the discussion of whether Thomas knew our Gospels includes other sayings material.
[7] *Ibid.* p. 46.
[8] For further literature and other names on each side of the debate, see Schrage, *op. cit.* p. 3 nn. 8 and 12.

work in this area.[1] This uncertainty, however, together with another factor, renders the Gospel of Thomas unusable for our purposes. The other factor, which is really the decisive one, is that, even if Thomas did use our Synoptics, he did so in a curious way, a way apparently, in many respects, unlike that of most other later authors. For one thing, the material in Thomas frequently is so loosely related to our Synoptics that it is almost impossible to enumerate and categorize what changes have taken place. Then again, the changes are governed by Thomas's own theology more frequently than is usually the case. When so many changes are governed by a distinctive theology, it is very difficult to isolate any general tendency of the tradition. It may be that more work on Thomas will make it useful for our purpose, but for the present it seems better to attempt to establish criteria elsewhere, where the changes in the tradition and their motivations are somewhat clearer.

A second problem which arises with respect to our use of the Apocryphal materials is that, thanks to recent discoveries, some of these materials are now available to us in documents which are earlier than or as early as the manuscripts upon which our present New Testament text is based. The principal documents in this category are the Bodmer papyrus of the Protev. Jms., the Egerton papyrus, the Fayum fragment, and the Oxyrhynchus papyri.[2] These documents cannot accurately be said to change a text which is later than they. But it must be remembered that many of the readings which are found in the manuscripts upon which our New Testament text is based (primarily B ℵ) are earlier than the manuscripts themselves. On this assumption, it would still be possible to speak of how a document from the early third century 'changed' a reading that actually is not known to us until it appears in a manuscript of the late third or fourth century. For the sake of accuracy, however, we shall not speak of how these early documents changed the New Testament text, but of how they differ from it. Thus, instead of

---

[1] Schrage, p. 9, accepting Köster's view of the duration of oral tradition, reckons with the possibility that Thomas, besides drawing directly on our Synoptics, may have been influenced by the oral tradition. He also does not exclude the possibility that in a few instances Thomas may have had access to a tradition independent of the Synoptics; see p. 8. In any case, the author, following the custom of the time, would have quoted the Gospel tradition in a loose way.

[2] For publication data, see Aurelio de Santos Otero, *Los Evangelios Apocrifos*[2] (Madrid, 1963), pp. 76 ff.

43

saying that an early papyrus omits a phrase from Matthew, we shall say that it lacks it.[1]

For noting the differences between the Synoptic material in the Apocryphal Gospels and the Synoptics themselves, I have used the recent edition of the Apocryphal Gospels by Aurelio de Santos Otero.[2] This useful book gives the Greek or Latin text of the Apocryphal Gospels which have a Greek or Latin original, together with a Spanish translation. Gospels which were originally written in some language other than Greek or Latin are given in Spanish translation. The text printed is usually that of Tischendorf.[3] As with the Fathers who are used, it has been my intention to list every change which bears on our categories which took place in the Synoptic material used by apocryphal writers. Any omissions, and I hope they are few, are purely the result of oversight.

In conclusion, it should be emphasized that not one of the three traditions which we study here is related to our canonical Gospels in the same way that they are related to one another. Further, the three traditions do not relate to the canonical Gospels in the same way. The textual tradition will not reveal the tendencies of transmitters who had a free hand in altering the material as they chose, but the tendencies of copyists who intended (for the most part) to transmit the material unchanged. The changes which nevertheless occurred in the textual tradition will be revealing for showing the natural inclinations of copyists, but will be limited in scope. The material derived from the writings of the early Fathers will show what changes occurred when a saying or narrative was freely and loosely quoted. Although this material is of relatively small size, it is quite important, since the Fathers' method of quotation may be the closest we can come to the method followed in the earliest period. The Apocryphal Gospels show how the Synoptic tradition was changed when it was reproduced with an eye toward popular consumption. We learn here how the material was changed when there was no necessity to observe the order, meaning, or wording of the original.

---

[1] This problem hardly arises with regard to the papyrus manuscripts of the New Testament, since most of them were published and collated after Legg had prepared the critical apparatus which is used in this study. They were not used by Legg and consequently do not appear here.

[2] de Santos, *op. cit.*   [3] *Evangelia Apocrypha*[2] (Lipsiae, 1876).

The question will be whether, from a study of sources so diverse, general tendencies will come into view. If they do, we may with some justification suppose that these same tendencies existed elsewhere. The tendencies which produced changes in the material in the post-canonical period may well have produced changes in periods to which we have no direct access. A study of this material, then, should be of importance to the study of the pre-canonical Synoptic tradition. Despite the differences in genre, the study of the post-canonical material should also aid in the assessment of the differences among our canonical Gospels. The tendencies of the later period may also have obtained in the earlier.

Now it only remains to say a brief word about the categories to be investigated. They are basically three: length, detail, and Semitism. Each of them has several subdivisions. In addition, two miscellaneous items will be considered in a fourth chapter. The question in each case is the same: was the tendency of the tradition toward greater length or toward abbreviation, toward detail or simplicity, toward Semitism or better Greek? In each chapter we shall present the evidence from the manuscript tradition, the Fathers, and the Apocryphal literature which bears on each point, draw whatever conclusions seem appropriate, and then present the differences among the canonical Gospels themselves on each point. Thus, for example, we shall see in how many instances the manuscript tradition, the Fathers, and the Apocryphal tradition change a good Greek reading to a more Semitic reading, how many times they change a Semitic reading to a better Greek reading, and finally how many times Matthew has a Semitic reading not in Mark, Mark one not in Matthew, and so forth.

It should be noted that in no case does this study investigate a criterion which has not already been used by some scholar or other. It was originally intended to seek to discover new criteria as well as to test old ones. An investigation of the material, however, revealed no changes of any significance which had not already been dealt with by some scholar. Once or twice it appeared that a new criterion had been discovered, but further research always revealed a prior user.

45

CHAPTER II

INCREASING LENGTH AS A POSSIBLE TENDENCY OF THE TRADITION

INTRODUCTION

We turn first to the question of whether the tradition tended to become longer or shorter. It is very difficult to separate the question of length from that of detail, and there is bound to be some overlapping. Nevertheless, there is some point in considering the two separately.

Scholars are by no means all of one mind on the question of length, or perhaps it would be more accurate to say that most scholars do not think the tradition moved in only one direction. In textual criticism the rule that the shorter reading is better has been long established, but it has by no means gone unchallenged. The most forceful challenge came from A. C. Clark, who maintained that just the opposite was the case.

Nowhere is the falsity of the maxim *brevior lectio potior* more evident than in the New Testament. The process has been one of contraction, not of expansion. The primitive text is the longest, not the shortest. It is to be found not in Bℵ, or in the majority of Greek MSS., but in the 'Western' family, i.e. in the ancient versions and the Codex Bezae (D).[1]

Clark, who came to the study of the New Testament from Latin classics, argued that the easiest thing in the world is to omit.[2] He was able, indeed, to provide abundant examples showing that substantial portions of text were sometimes omitted by scribes.[3] The principal cause of omission was homoeoteleuton or homoeoarcton. Thus the omissions would be the length of one line or a multiple of that length. Clark's studies convinced him that the Gospels were transmitted through 'a series of MSS written in extremely narrow columns'. He thought the line length was 10–11 letters.[4] He then considered instances in which one manuscript or group of manuscripts

[1] A. C. Clark, *The primitive text of the Gospels and Acts* (Oxford, 1914), p. vi.
[2] A. C. Clark, *The Acts of the Apostles* (Oxford, 1933), pp. xlv ff.
[3] A. C. Clark, *The descent of manuscripts* (Oxford, 1918), pp. 1–31.
[4] *Primitive text*, p. 21.

46

does not have a passage found in others. He showed that frequently the number of letters in the passage in question is a multiple of some number between 9 and 12 (allowing some variation from the standard length of 10–11 letters), and concluded that the shorter readings are the result of the omission of entire lines.[1]

Clark's method of dealing with the text of Acts was somewhat different. Here he thought that the ancestor of all our present manuscripts of Acts was written in 'sense-lines of varying length', as D is throughout.[2] He eventually came to regard the shorter text of Acts as the result of deliberate excisions.[3]

To the first method Kenyon[4] points out several objections. (1) Examination of early Greek papyri shows that the line length supposed by Clark is too short: there are usually from sixteen to thirty letters to a line.[5] (2) The line length upon which Clark based his work is so short that a disputed reading of virtually any length over eight letters could be explained as an omission of one or more lines. The line length of 9–12 letters allows all passages except those whose length is 13–17, 25, or 26 letters to be claimed as a multiple of the basic unit.[6] (3) Many of the readings which Clark claims to have been omitted by scribal error are sense-units. Kenyon comments that 'where the omissions correspond with recognizable units of sense, other possibilities come into play, with higher degrees of probability'.[7] Clark's theory that the text of the New Testament was steadily shortened by omissions caused by homoeoteleuton does not withstand these criticisms. Such omissions did occur, but not with sufficient frequency to justify Clark's thesis. His thesis also does not account for the actual relationships among the manuscripts now available. As Kenyon showed, the shorter text (usually ℵ B) cannot be explained as having descended from the longer text (usually D) by a process of accidental omission.

The second theory advanced by Clark, that in Acts the ancestor of all our manuscripts was written in sense-lines, some of which were consciously excised, is also not persuasive. Kenyon points out that it is unlikely that such an arrangement of the text was adopted only in Acts. In the second place, Jerome

[1] *Ibid.* pp. 57–66.　　[2] *Ibid.* p. vii.　　[3] *Acts*, p. xxxi.
[4] F. G. Kenyon, *The Western text in the Gospels and Acts* (London, 1939).
[5] *Ibid.* p. 20.　　[6] *Ibid.* p. 21.　　[7] *Ibid.* p. 23.

mentions that the orations of Demosthenes and Cicero were written in such a way and 'announces his intention of applying this method to Isaiah'. 'His very words', Kenyon observes, 'are a proof that he had never known it applied to texts of the Bible.' In the third place, such a method of writing is unlikely to have been followed at an early date because of the wastage of space which is involved.[1] These considerations do not of themselves show that D, which Clark championed, is always later than ℵ B or that the longer reading is never right.[2] They do show that Clark's argument that the longer reading is better cannot be maintained.[3]

Even though it is thought that Clark's position as a whole is wrong, no scholar would wish to argue that omissions did not occur. Thus, for example, in discussing the 'Western' text, Hatch points out that both omissions and additions took place. He observes, however, that the omissions 'are fewer than the additions, and the passages omitted are shorter than those which have been added'.[4] On the assumption that D is later, it shows a greater tendency to add than to omit, although both tendencies are present to some extent.

The problem of length arises in an interesting way in the discussion of the text and later paraphrases of the Protoevangelium of James. De Strycker, who has recently discussed this problem, points out that the later paraphrases frequently expand the material. 'Often, the words of the characters are elaborated into veritable discourses. New episodes are inserted in the course of the narrative.' Thus the Armenian Infancy Gospel, after narrating the offerings made by Joachim when he learned of the pregnancy of his wife (Protev. Jms. 4. 3 ff.), adds that a

---

[1] *Ibid.* p. 24.

[2] Thus Aland ('Neue Neutestamentliche Papyri II', 196 f.) has recently accepted, on the strength of $\mathfrak{P}^{75}$, six longer readings in Lk. 24 where Westcott and Hort had preferred D's shorter text ('Western non-interpolations'). In a seventh case (Lk. 24. 32), $\mathfrak{P}^{75}$ supports the longer text of D against c e syr^{c,s}. Westcott and Hort had accepted the shorter text. K. W. Clark, *J.B.L.* LXXXV (1966), 1–16, also observes, against the 'Western non-interpolation' theory, that the longer text is sometimes right.

[3] Kilpatrick ('The Greek New Testament text of today and the *Textus Receptus*', p. 196) thinks that length in itself is not a reliable criterion for evaluating variant readings. Sometimes the longer is earlier and sometimes the shorter; if the best reading cannot be distinguished on some other ground, it is doubtful if the criterion of length will decide the issue.

[4] W. H. P. Hatch, *The 'Western' Text of the Gospels* (Evanston, 1937), p. 24.

lamb was also offered in the name of the child which was to be born. Further, from the lamb, when slaughtered, there flowed not blood, but milk, as a sign of the purity of the coming child (Mary). A second example of expansion is found in the Syriac paraphrase of the Protev. Jms. According to this paraphrase, Mary was entrusted at the age of twelve to the care of an old priest named Zadok and his wife Sam'ī, whereas in the Protev. Jms. (chapter 9) she goes directly from the temple to the house of Joseph. De Strycker concludes that 'one sees how the material never ceased growing'.[1]

Nevertheless, de Strycker does not conclude that the tendency toward growth was a one-way street. There are three sections in which the newly discovered Bodmer Papyrus of the Protev. Jms. is considerably shorter than the regular text as printed by Tischendorf.[2] De Strycker argues that the Bodmer Papyrus is secondary to the longer text. The following points are important in his argument. (1) The shorter text is difficult to understand without reference to the longer text. The shorter text is sometimes absurd and inconsistent. At other points, it is obscure.[3] In one place, for example, the subject of a verb cannot be identified.[4] (2) The style of the shorter text does not correspond to that of the Protev. Jms. as a whole.[5] (3) The shorter text has several phrases in common with the longer text which fit better in the longer text.[6] These phrases in the shorter

[1] Émile de Strycker, *La Forme la plus ancienne du Protévangile de Jacques* (Bruxelles, 1961), pp. 378 f.
[2] The sections are 18. 2–19. 1; 20. 1–4; 21. 2–3. De Strycker prints both the longer and shorter texts for easy comparison (*op. cit., ad loc.*). Both texts may also be compared in English translation in Hennecke-Schneemelcher, *New Testament Apocrypha*, vol. 1 (Philadelphia, 1963), pp. 383–6. The problem of the date of the Protev. Jms. is referred to in Appendix IV.
[3] The speech of Joseph to the midwife in the short text at 19. 1 is vague and obscure. It reads as follows: 'And he found one who was just coming down from the hill country, and he took her with him, and said to the midwife: "Mary is betrothed to me; but she conceived of the Holy Spirit after she had been brought up in the temple of the Lord."' See de Strycker, *op. cit.* pp. 383 f.
[4] In 20. 1 the short text reads: 'And she entered and made her ready, and Salome examined her condition.' But who 'entered and made her ready'? See *ibid.* p. 385.
[5] In 20. 1 the short text reads: 'And Salome cried out that she had tempted the living God.' De Strycker (p. 385) points out that the Protev. Jms. never uses indirect discourse.
[6] In 20. 4 the short text reads: 'And she did so, and Salome was healed.' Since 'she' was none other than Salome, the insertion of the name with 'healed' is strange. The phrase 'Salome was healed' is also in the long text, where it is not awkward. See *ibid.* p. 387.

text 'are regularly obscure and harsh, and the connections among themselves and with the context are not satisfactory; in the long text, on the other hand, they are completely appropriate and sensible'.[1]

Thus de Strycker warns against thinking that the shorter text is necessarily the earlier. In support of this point, he refers to the three forms in which the Letters of Ignatius appear. Of the three, the one of middle length is universally regarded as genuine. It has been both abridged and expanded. 'There are also', he reminds us, 'revisers who prune and abridge.'[2] J. B. Lightfoot has discussed the method of the abbreviator of Ignatius, whose work appears in a Syriac recension which was published by W. Cureton in 1845. Lightfoot suggests that he was filling a few leaves of parchment which would otherwise have gone to waste and simply copied what he had space for. He omitted larger portions, but from these he would still include a terse maxim here and there which struck his eye.[3]

It would be possible to discuss other instances of abbreviation, such as occur in II Clement[4] and the Ebionite Gospel,[5] as well as a multitude of instances of expansion, but surely the point thus far is clear: both abbreviation and expansion took place. Thus we may already conclude that it is an oversimplification to speak of a uniform tendency as Quispel does in discussing a saying which is in both the Gospel of Thomas and the Gospel of the Hebrews. He concludes that Thomas used Hebrews, rather than vice versa, since the form of the saying in Thomas is longer. 'It is a law of text-criticism, form-criticism and source-criticism that short forms tend to become longer.'[6]

We may now present the evidence which we have collected on the subject, in order to see if any patterns emerge. The

---

[1] *Ibid.* pp. 383–91. The quotation is from p. 391.   [2] *Ibid.* p. 379.
[3] J. B. Lightfoot, *The Apostolic Fathers*, vol. I, pt. ii, pp. 320–7, esp. 325.
[4] On abbreviation in II Clement, see Köster, *op. cit.* p. 73. An example of abbreviation is II Clem. 9. 11: 'For the Lord said, "My brothers are these who do the will of my Father."' The saying is eleven words in Greek. Mt. 12. 50 reads: 'For whoever does the will of my Father in the heavens, he is my brother and sister and mother.' The saying is twenty words in Greek. Cf. also II Clem. 4. 2 (13 words) and Mt. 7. 21 (25 words).
[5] The Ebionite Gospel omits, for theological reasons, Matthew's genealogy. See Epiph., *Haer.* 30. 14. 3, cited by Vielhauer in Hennecke-Schneemelcher, *op. cit.* p. 125.
[6] '"The Gospel of Thomas" and the "Gospel of the Hebrews"', *N.T.S.* XII (1966), 379.

categories are, I think, self-explanatory. It must be especially noted that no attempt has been made to catalogue all of the new material in the Apocryphal Gospels, or to catalogue all of the canonical material excluded from them. We only note instances in which a passage which is being used is expanded or abbreviated. The creation of new speeches is noted only when they fall in the midst of material taken from the canonical Gospels in such a way as to expand the material. A special problem arises with regard to the Apocryphal Gospels of which only fragments survive. The presumption should be that new speeches so preserved originally fitted into a canonical context, and so these speeches are listed in the appropriate place. Translations of the more significant fragments are found in Appendix v.

METHOD OF CITATION

The following notes explain the manner in which evidence is cited in the lists.

A. The manuscripts.

1. For the uncials, the regular symbols are employed. Greek and Hebrew symbols are transliterated into English, however, by using the first two letters of the English name of the Hebrew or Greek letter. Thus Al indicates Codex Sinaiticus (א), De indicates Δ, Ph indicates Φ, and so on.

2. The symbol Ko (for Koine) is used to indicate the uncials E F G H K M S U V Y Om when they concur in a certain reading. It corresponds to Legg's $. The uncials represented thus are about the same as those represented by the symbol 𝕶 in the Nestle apparatus. Ko does not include minuscules, however, as does Nestle's 𝕶.

3. Minuscules are not cited individually, but are counted. 4Gr means that a reading is supported by 4 Greek minuscules.

4. Family 1 and Family 13 are cited as Fam 1 and Fam 13. Together they are cited as Famm 1 & 13. When one or more members of a family differs from the others, the number of dissenting manuscripts is placed after a minus sign in parentheses. Thus Fam 1 (− 2) means that two members of Family 1 differ from the others.

5. A plus sign indicates that, according to Legg, some minuscules not named support a certain reading. Thus 7 + Gr

means that Legg lists seven Greek minuscules in support of the reading and indicates that others also support it.

6. Greek lectionaries are cited as Greek minuscules.

7. Manuscripts of versions, like Greek minuscules, are not individually cited. Each version is distinguished, but the various manuscripts of each version are only numbered. Thus 4It indicates that four of the Old Latin manuscripts support a certain reading. 2Sy indicates that a reading is supported by two of the Syriac text-types (Peshitta, Sinaitic, Curetonian, etc.). 2Cop means that a reading is supported by both the Coptic Sahidic and the Coptic Bohairic. If no number is put before the abbreviation of a version, all the manuscripts and types of that version support the reading.

8. The Fathers who are cited in Legg's apparatus are indicated by the usual abbreviations.

B. The Fathers and the Apocryphal Gospels are cited by abbreviations which should be self-explanatory. Citations from papyrus fragments are by number of the papyrus and the line.

C. Other symbols.

1. The plus sign (+) indicates that the cited sources add the words which follow it to the original text. We may take an illustration: Mt. 8. 32 C³ E K L S U V X Pi 5 + Gr 1Cop Aeth 'herd + of swine'. This means that the correct text of Mt. 8. 32 has only 'herd', but that the manuscripts and versions listed add the genitive phrase 'of swine'. If the addition precedes the words to which it is added, it is set in parentheses and preceded by a plus sign, thus: 'he commanded (+ his disciples) to go.' Such an arrangement indicates that the cited sources have added 'his disciples'.

2. The minus sign (−) is used in the same way as the plus sign. What is omitted is regularly set in parentheses, however, for the sake of clarity.

3. Underlining is used to indicate that a pronoun is explicit in Greek. Thus '*you* see' means that *humeis* is written in the Greek, while 'you see' means that it is not.

D. The Gospels.

For the sake of convenience, all the lists which compare the Gospels with each other are composed as if the shorter text were always earlier. Thus instances in which Matthew is longer than Mark are listed as Matthean 'additions' to Mark, while instances in which Mark is longer than Matthew are listed as Marcan 'additions' to Matthew. I do not actually suppose that by choosing the shortest reading from among our Gospels we should arrive at the original text of the Gospel narrative, but the lists are composed as if that were the case. We may take the following example: Mt. 19. 23 & Mk. 10. 23; ctr. Lk. 18. 24 'said + to his disciples'. This means that Matthew and Mark read 'said to his disciples', but that Luke has only 'said'. The phrase 'to his disciples' is listed as an 'addition' to Luke by Matthew and Mark, although it may really be an omission by Luke. This procedure should not be confusing, and it enables us quickly to grasp how often each Gospel is longer than each of the others.

Plus signs, minus signs, parentheses, and underlining are used in the lists comparing the Gospels as they are in the other lists, and with the same meanings.

THE EVIDENCE FROM THE POST-CANONICAL TRADITION[1]

1a   Addition of all or part of an Old Testament quotation

THE TEXTUAL TRADITION

Matthew

3. 3   To the quotation from Is. 40. 3, 5It add Is. 40. 4 and part of vs. 5.

4. 6   1Vg 2Sy Aeth Eph 'concerning you + that they should guard you' 2Vg + 'that they should guard you in all (your) ways' (from Ps. 90. 11).

13. 14   D 9It add 'go and say to this people' (from Is. 6. 9).

15. 8   C N W X Ga (De) Pi Si Ph 0106 Ko Most Minusc. 2It 1Sy 'this people + draws near with their mouth' (from Is. 29. 13).

Mark

10. 7   All uncs but Al B Ps; Most Minusc. It Vg 2Sy 2Cop Geo Bas add 'and shall cleave to his wife' (Gen. 2. 24).

15. 28   L P Y^mg Ga De Th Pi Si 0112 Ko Famm 1 & 13 9 1 Gr It(2) Vg 3Sy 1Cop Geo Aeth Arm add this entire quotation: 'And the scripture was fulfilled which says, "He was reckoned with the lawless"' (Is. 53. 12).

---

[1] Since the lists of changes in the post-canonical tradition are considered to comprise a kind of critical apparatus, Greek words are left unaccented.

1b Omission of all or part of an Old Testament quotation

Matthew

3. 3   1Sy omits 'voice crying in the wilderness' (Sy^s).
3. 3   1It 1Sy omit 'make straight his paths' (Sy^s).
13. 14 1It omits 'you see and'.
13. 14 1It omits all of the quotation in vs. 14.
13. 14 1It omits second half of the quotation in vs. 14.
13. 15 1It omits 'they see' through 'they turn and'.
13. 15 2It omit 'they see' through 'they understand and'.
13. 15 1It omits 'and I heal them'.
13. 15 1Sy omits 'and they turn and I heal them'.
15. 8   Om omits 'and honors me with the lips'.

Protev. Jms. 21. 2, cf. Mt. 2. 5, 6. Has 'For thus it is written', as in Mt. 2. 5, but omits the actual quotation in Mt. 2. 6.

Pseud. Matt. Lat. 15. 1. After Lk. 2. 22, omits 2. 23, a quotation from the O.T.

Nat. Mary 10. 2. Omits Mt. 1. 22–3, a statement of the fulfillment of prophecy and a quotation.

2a Additions to speeches

Matthew

5. 28   2Gr 'I say to you+do not desire'.
5. 44   D L W De Th Pi Si Ko Fam 13 7+Gr 4It Vg 3Sy 1Cop Aeth Arm Tat add 'Bless the ones cursing you; do good to those who hate you' (Lk. 6. 27, 28)/2Gr Clem Lucif add only the first half/7It 1Vg Cass add only the second half.
5. 44   D L W De Th Pi Si Ko Fam 13 6+Gr 5It 1Vg 3Sy Arm Clem 'Pray for those who (+insult you) and persecute you' (Lk. 6. 28).
7. 1   L Vg add 'condemn not and you will not be condemned' (Lk. 6. 37).
7. 21   At end, C² W Th Ph 4Gr 10It Vg 1Sy Aug Cyp Hil+'this one will enter into the kingdom of the heavens'.
8. 7   Al* adds 'follow me'.
8. 21   At end, 2Sy add 'and I will come'.
9. 3   At end, 3It 1Vg add 'who is able to forgive sins but one, God?'
9. 22   1Gr 1It add 'go in peace'.
9. 28   2Sy 'Yea, Lord,+we believe'.

10. 12   Al* D L W Th Pi Fam 1 14+Gr It Vg Arm Geo 'salute it, +say-
ing, "Peace to this house"'.

15. 27   At end, 4Sy Tat add 'and live'.

Mark

9. 47   1Gr 'remove it+and cast (it) from you'.

9. 49   A D N X Ga Th Pi Si Ph Ps Ko Fam 13 7+Gr 4It Vg 2Sy 1Cop
Aeth add 'and every sacrifice will be salted with salt', and the like.

10. 20   At end, K M N W Y Th Pi Si Fam 13 14Gr 2It 1Sy 1Geo Arm add
'what yet do I lack?'/1Geo adds 'what must I do?'

10. 21   K M N W Y Th Pi Si Fam 13 25+Gr 1Sy 2Cop 1Geo Aeth Clem
add 'if you want to be perfect'.

10. 21   At end, A G N W X Y Ga Pi Si Ph Ko Famm 1 & 13 7Gr 2It 2Sy
1Cop 1Geo Aeth Arm Iren add 'taking up (your) cross'.

10. 28   At end, Al 2Gr 2It add 'what then shall we have' (Mt. 19. 27).

11. 10   At end, Fam 1 1Gr add 'peace on earth and glory in the highest'/
3Gr add 'peace in heaven and glory' before 'hosanna'.

11. 26   This verse is added by A C D N X Y Ga Th Pi Si Ph Ko (− 1) Famm
1 & 13 5+Gr It (−4) Vg (− 1) 2Sy Aeth Cyp Aug.

11. 31   D Th Ph Fam 13 4Gr 7It 'saying+what shall we say'.

13. 2   At end, D W It (− 3) Cyp add 'and after three days another shall be
raised without hands'.

13. 11   A Th X Y Ga De Pi Ph Ko Fam 13 (− 1) 11+Gr 2It 2Sy Arm 'do
not be anxious+nor practise'.

14. 19   At end, A D X Y Ga Th Pi Si Ph 0116 Ko Famm 1 & 13 10+Gr
It (− 1) 1Sy Geo Arm Or add 'and another, "Is it I?"'

14. 22   E F H M² S V X Y Ga Si Om 0116 Fam 13 6+Gr 1It 1Cop 'take
+and eat'.

14. 22   At end, 1It adds 'for it is broken for many for the remission of sins'.

14. 65   N U W X De Th Si 067 Fam 13 15+Gr 1Sy 1Cop Geo Aeth Arm
'prophesy+Christ, who is the one striking you' and the like (Mt.
26. 68).

16. 7   Fam 1 4Gr 1Geo 'say that+he is raised from the dead, and'.

Cf. also Mark 11. 3   Text: τι ποιειτε τουτο/D Th Fam 13 5Gr 6It Arm:
τι λυετε τον πωλον/Fam 1 3Gr 1Sy Geo: τι. Here one makes more
explicit, another shortens.

THE APOCRYPHAL AND PATRISTIC TRADITIONS

Gosp. Heb. Jerome, Contra Pelag. III. 2 (see Appendix v. 3); cf. Mt. 18. 21 f.
A new saying on the ubiquity of sin even in the prophets is added. (This
is found also in the Jewish Gospel to Mt. 18. 22. See de Santos, p. 46.)

Gosp. Heb. Ps. Orig. Lat. (see Appendix v. 4); cf. Mt. 19. 16 ff. A new saying on the difficulty of fulfilling the law is added.

Egerton Pap. 2 Frag. 1, lines 22–41. Cf. Mt. 8. 1–4 parr. After the vocative in Mt. 8. 2, this speech appears: 'Wandering with lepers and eating with them in the inn, I also became a leper.' (The text is somewhat uncertain.)

Act. Pil. 4. 3; cf. Jn. 18. 31. 'Take him (+and bring him into your synagogue) and judge him according to your law.'

Just. Dial. 51. 2; cf. Mt. 16. 21 parr. Justin adds 'and again to appear in Jerusalem and then again to eat and drink with his disciples'.

Just. Apol. 1. 16. 12; cf. Mt. 13. 43. Justin adds 'but the unrighteous shall fall into the eternal fire'.

Just. Dial. 115. 6; cf. Mt. 7. 2. 'For with what judgment you judge, (+it is right for you) to be judged.'

2b Omissions from speeches

THE TEXTUAL TRADITION

Matthew

3. 12 1Gr omits 'and he will clear his threshing-floor' (perhaps by homoeoteleuton).

10. 12 1It omits 'salute it'. Cf. category 2 a.

Mark

9. 35 Fam 1 (−1) 3Gr omit 'last of all and'.

9. 37 1Gr* omits 'receives me; and whoever receives me'.

9. 37 1It omits 'in my name receives me; and whoever receives me'.

9. 37 1Gr 1It 1Geo omit 'not me but'. Very clear abbreviation.

9. 38 6Gr omit 'and we rebuked him, because he does not follow you'.

9. 50 1Gr omits 'have salt in yourselves and be at peace with one another'.

10. 27 De Ps Fam 1 (−1) 14Gr 1It Arm omit 'for all things are possible with God'.

10. 30 Al 1Gr 2It omit 'houses and brothers and sisters and mothers and children and fields'. Al 1Gr 1It also omit 'with persecution'.

11. 9 1Gr omits 'hosanna! Blessed is the one coming in the name of the Lord'.

11. 10 1Gr omits 'Blessed is the coming kingdom'. (Perhaps to avoid repetition.)

11. 30 15Gr omit 'answer me'.

12. 14 D 1Gr It (−2) 2Vg omit 'shall we give or not give'/E 1Geo omit 'or not'/1Gr omits 'give or not'.

13. 15 2Gr 2It Aug omit 'nor let him go in'. Clear abbreviation./1Gr omits 'nor let him go in to take anything from his home'.

14. 13 Or omits 'follow him'.

14. 22 De* 2It 1Cop omit 'take'.

14. 44 1It omits 'and lead away safely'.

56

14. 64 1It omits 'you have heard the blasphemy. How does it appear to you?'
14. 68 1It 1Sy omit 'neither do I know'.
16. 6 Al* omits 'you seek the Nazarene'.
16. 6 2It omit 'he is not here'.

THE APOCRYPHAL AND PATRISTIC TRADITIONS

Act. Pil. 3. 2, cf. Jn. 18. 37. (− 'I might witness to the truth.')
Just. Apol. i. 15. 13; cf. Mt. 5. 45. Just. has only 'he causes his sun to shine upon sinners and righteous and evil' (omits 'rain').
Just. Apol. i. 16. 11; cf. Mt. 7. 23. Omits 'I do not know you'.
Just. Apol. i. 16. 12; cf. Mt. 13. 43. Omits 'in the kingdom of their father' (but this omission helps to achieve better balance; see the addition cited in 2a above).
Just. Apol. i. 16. 5. Omits Mt. 5. 34b–36, which give examples of how not to swear. Justin was only interested in the principle. He quotes 5. 34a and 37.
Theoph. iii. 14. Omits Mt. 5. 45.
II Clem. 6. 1; cf. Lk. 16. 13 par. Omits 'for either he hates the one', etc.

3a Addition of speeches

THE TEXTUAL TRADITION

Matthew

9. 25 1It Vg 'he took her hand + and said, "Girl, arise"'.

Mark

After Mk. 11. 26, Mt. 7. 7–8 is added by M 20Gr.

THE APOCRYPHAL AND PATRISTIC TRADITIONS

Gosp. of the Heb. Clem. Alex. ii. 9, v. 14 (see Appendix v. 1). New sayings which appear to be based on Mt. 11. 28.
Gosp. Heb. Origen In Io. 2. 6 (see Appendix v. 5). New saying based on Mt. 4. 1, 8.
Gosp. Heb. Jerome, Comm. 1 in Mt. 12. 13 (see Appendix v. 2). A new speech is given to the man with the withered hand.
Gosp. Heb. Jerome Comm. iv in Is. 11. 2 (de Santos, p. 41; H.-S. pp. 163 f.). Cf. Mt. 3. 16. The Holy Spirit makes an extended speech to Jesus when the latter comes out of the water.
Gosp. Heb. Jerome, Contra Pelag. iii. 2 (see Appendix v. 6). A new speech is made out of bits and pieces of synoptic texts.

57

Gosp. Ebion. Epiph. Haer. 30. 16. 4 f. (de Santos, p. 53; H.-S. p. 158). A new saying is created, apparently based on Mt. 5. 17 f. and Jn. 3. 36 f. 'I am come to do away with sacrifice, and if you cease not from sacrificing, the wrath of God will not cease from you.'

Pap. Oxy. 1. 30–5 (see Appendix v. 12). A new saying (based on Lk. 4. 23) is created.

Epitome Clementina 1 c. 96 (de Santos, p. 115). A new saying is created on the analogy of Mt. 18. 7: '"It is necessary for the good things to come, and blessed", he said, "(is he) through whom they come".'

Protev. Jms. 11. 2. After Lk. 1. 30, the following speech is added: 'When she heard this, she doubted in herself and said: "Shall I conceive of (*apo*) the Lord, the living God, and bear as every woman bears?"'

Protev. Jms. 12. 2; cf. Lk. 1. 39–45. New sayings are added. See Appendix v. 17.

Pseud. Matt. 15. 2; cf. Lk. 2. 28. Simeon is given a new speech, based on the promise of Lk. 2. 26: 'God hath visited his people, and the Lord hath fulfilled his promise.'

Pseud. Mt. 15. 2, end (de Santos, p. 213). MS B adds a speech of the infant Jesus to Simeon.

Act. Pil. 3. 1. For Jn. 18. 32 (which is a reference back to a prophecy of Jesus) Pil. has a new saying: 'Pilate said: "Has God said to you not to kill, but (allowed) me?"'

Joseph of Arim. 3. 2, 3. A long speech is made by each robber, based on Lk. 23. 39 ff.

Joseph of Arim. 3. 4. Jesus makes a long speech after the 'in Paradise' of Lk. 23. 43.

Just. Apol. 1. 16. 10. 'For whoever hears me and does what I say, hears the one who sent me.' Formed on analogy with Lk. 10. 16. The same saying is found in Apol. 1. 63. 5, but there 'and does what I say' is omitted.

Just. Dial. 35. 3. ἔσονται σχίσματα καὶ αἱρέσεις. (I Cor. 11. 19: δεῖ γὰρ καὶ αἱρέσεις ἐν ὑμῖν εἶναι...)

3b Omission of speeches

THE TEXTUAL TRADITION

Mark

9. 35 D 2It omit the saying.

14. 72 D 1Gr 1It omit 'before the cock crows twice you will deny me thrice'.

THE APOCRYPHAL TRADITION

Jos. Arim. 2. 4 omits Mt. 26. 50//Lk. 22. 48 (not in Mark). It is Jesus' reply to Judas.

4a Addition of dialogue

THE TEXTUAL TRADITION

Matthew

9. 21   1 It adds Mk. 5. 29–33, with some changes.

Mark

10. 19   1 It 'you know the commandments. + He said, "Which". And Jesus said to him' (Mt. 19. 18).

THE APOCRYPHAL TRADITION

Gosp. Heb. Jerome, Contra Pelag. III. 2 (see Appendix v. 6). Cf. Mt. 18. 21 f. The conversation is expanded: Jesus initiates it; Peter replies; Jesus answers.

Gosp. Ebion. Epiph., 30. 13. 7 f. (see Appendix v. 8). There is an extended conversation incorporating Mt. 3. 17 and 3. 14 f.

Protev. Jms. 21. 2. After Mt. 2. 5, a new conversation between Herod and the Magi is added.

Pseud. Thom. 19. 4. After Lk. 2. 49, a new conversation is added: 'And the scribes and Pharisees said: "Are you the mother of this child?" And she said: "I am." And they said to her: "Blessed are you among women, for God has blessed the fruit of your womb (cf. Lk. 1. 42). For such glory and such virtue and wisdom we have neither seen nor heard of."'

Act. Pil. 3. 2; cf. Jn. 18. 37. After 'what is truth?', the conversation continues: 'Jesus says to him: "Truth is from heaven." Pilate says: "Is there not truth upon earth?" Jesus says to Pilate: "You see how those who speak the truth are judged by (*apo*) those who have authority upon earth."'

Act. Pil. 4. 1. After Mt. 26. 61, this conversation is added: 'Pilate says: "What temple?" The Jews say: "The one which Solomon built in forty-six years, this one says (he will) destroy and build it in (*dia*) three days."'

Act. Pil. 16. 2. Inserts in the middle of Lk. 2. 34 the following: '"I give you good tidings concerning this child." And Mary said: "Good, my Lord?" And Simeon said to her: "Good."'

II Clem. 5. 2–4. After the equivalent of Lk. 10. 3, adds: 'Peter answering says to him: "If then the wolves tear the lambs?" Jesus said to Peter: "Let the lambs not fear the wolves after their death."' Then quotes the equivalent of Lk. 12. 4 f. par.

4b   Omission or curtailment of dialogue

THE APOCRYPHAL AND PATRISTIC TRADITIONS

Joseph. Arim. 2. 4. Omits Mt. 26. 50//Lk. 22. 48 (as does Mk.). The verse contains Jesus' reply to Judas.

Gosp. Heb. Ps. Orig. Lat. (see Appendix v. 4). The conversation between Jesus and the rich man is curtailed.

Just. Apol. I. 16. 7; cf. Mk. 10. 17 parr. Justin omits the young man's question to Jesus and Jesus' rhetorical question. Similarly Dial. 101. 2. Justin's interest in the passage was restricted to 'good teacher' and Jesus' principal saying.

5a   The creation of new scenes and events

THE TEXTUAL TRADITION

Matthew

3. 15   At end. 2It add 'and when he was baptized, a great light flashed forth from the water, so that all who had come together were afraid', and the like./Eph adds 'and when he was baptized a great light flashed forth from the water'.

THE APOCRYPHAL AND PATRISTIC TRADITIONS

Gosp. Heb. Jerome, de Viris Ill. 2 (de Santos, p. 38; H.-S. p. 165). A new post-resurrection appearance to James is created.

Gosp. Ebion. Epiph. Haer. 30. 13. 7 f. The following is added to Lk. 3. 22: 'And immediately a great light shone round about the place.'

Oxy. Pap. 840 (see Appendix v. 11). This is a new story, taking its starting-point from Mk. 11. 27.

Pap. 11710 (de Santos, p. 84). This passage shows how new material could be created for familiar characters. The two statements of Nathanael are taken from Jn. 1. 49, 29. 'Nathanael confessed and said: "Rabbi (ῥαμβιού) Lord, you are the Son of God." The Rabbi (ὁ ῥαμβίς) answered him and said: "Nathanael, go in the Sun." Nathanael answered him and said: "Rabbi Lord, you are the lamb of God, which takes away the sins of the world." The Rabbi answered him and said...'

Fragm. P. Ryl. III. 463. New material is created for Andrew, Peter and Mary.[1]

Pseud. Matt. 17. 1; cf. Mt. 2. 16. After saying that Herod was angry, Pseud. Matt. adds: 'And he sent through all the roads, wishing to seize them and put them to death.'

---

[1] This is a fragment of the Gospel of Mary, which is more fully available in Coptic (P. Berol. 8502). The connection of the new material with Synoptic material is very slight.

Gosp. Pet. 4–5. 'And Pilate sent to Herod and begged his body. And Herod said: "Brother Pilate, even if no one had begged him, we should bury him, since the Sabbath is drawing on" (cf. Lk. 23. 54). For it stands written in the law: "The sun shall not set on one that has been put to death."' (Cf. Jn. 19. 31.)

Arabic Inf. Gosp. 7; cf. Mt. 2. 11. After the Magi present their gifts, adds: 'Then the Lady Mary took one of the swaddling bands, and, on account of the smallness of her means, gave it to them; and they received it with the greatest marks of honour.'

Arabic Inf. Gosp. 53. After Lk. 2. 50, adds: 'Then those teachers asked Mary whether He were her son; and when she signified that he was, they said: "Blessed art thou, O Mary, who hast brought forth such a son."'

Pseud. Matt. Lat. 16. 2; cf. Mt. 2. 11. After 'gave gifts', adds 'and to the child himself they offered each of them a piece of gold'.

Just. Dial. 88. 3. 'When Jesus went down into the water, and a fire was kindled in the Jordan.'

Addendum: Creation of new material

In all the Apocryphal Gospels, most of the material does not appear in the canonical Gospels, so the very existence of the former is proof of the tendency to create new material. Some examples of new material being created for familiar characters are these:

1. The role of Nicodemus is considerably expanded in the Act. Pil. His role on behalf of Jesus occupies chapter 5 and portions of chapters 12 and 15.

2. Joseph of Arimathea plays an enlarged role from chapter 12 of Act. Pil. on. But note that in the Act. Pil. the disciples play almost no role at all.

6a   Addition of actions

THE TEXTUAL TRADITION

Matthew

3. 10   reads: 'every tree therefore that does not bear good fruit is cut down and thrown into the fire.' 1Gr reads '...and thrown into the fire and burned'. This is abbreviated as follows:

3. 10   1Gr adds 'and burned'.

4. 24   2Sy add 'he placed his hand upon each one of them'.

8. 32   3Gr add 'he turned to them'.

9. 11   M 10 + Gr 1It 1Vg 1Geo 1Sy 'your teacher eats + and drinks'.

9. 28   Ph 2It add 'pleading'.

12. 1   1It 1Sy Eph Tat add 'rubbing them with their hands', and the like.

15. 23   2Sy 'he cries out + and comes'.

Mark

9. 27   Vg adds 'and he gave him back to his father' (Lk. 9. 42)/1Sy has
         this in place of 'and he rose'.
9. 28   W Th ($\mathfrak{P}^{45}$) Fam 13 (− 1) 4Gr 'his disciples + came up (to him)'.
11. 8   A D N X Y Ga Th Pi Si Ph Ko Most Minusc. It Vg 2Sy 1Cop Geo
         add 'they spread (them) in the way'.
12. 3   1Gr adds 'and they killed'.
12. 4   A C N X Ga Th Pi Si Ph Ko Fam 13 5 + Gr 2Sy Aeth '(+ having
         stoned) they beheaded'.
14. 68   A C D N X Y Ga De Th Pi Si 067 Ko Famm 1 & 13 8 + Gr It (− 1)
         Vg 2Sy 1Geo Aeth Arm Eus add 'and the cock crew'.
15. 23   G Fam 1 '(+ having tasted) he did not take'.
15. 25   At end, 1Cop adds 'and they kept watch on him'.
15. 39   A C N X Y Ga De Pi Si Ko Most Minusc. It Vg 2Sy Aeth Aug
         '(+ crying out) he gave up the ghost'; similarly D W Th 1Gr 1Sy
         Geo Arm Or. 0112 1It add 'crying out', but omit 'he gave up the
         ghost'.

Cf. also Mt. 11. 3. For 'he said', 1It has 'he sent word to Jesus saying'.

THE APOCRYPHAL TRADITION

Protev. Jms. 11. 1–2 (see Appendix v. 14). Several actions added.
Protev. Jms. 12. 2 (see Appendix v. 17). Actions added.
Pseud. Mt. Lat. 15. 2; cf. Lk. 2. 28. After narrating that Simeon took Jesus
   up into his arms (Pseud. Matt. has 'cloak'), Pseud. Matt. adds 'and
   kissed his feet'.
Pseud. Thom. 19. 1; cf. Lk. 2. 43. For Lk.'s 'when the days were completed',
   Thom. has 'and after the passover + they returned to their house'.

6b Omission of actions

THE TEXTUAL TRADITION

Matthew

9. 22   1Sy omits 'and seeing'.
12. 1   1Gr omits 'and they ate'.

Mark

9. 15   1Gr omits 'were greatly amazed, and running'.
9. 27   W P45 1Gr 2It 2Sy omit 'and he rose'.
10. 50   Ga omits 'leaping to his feet'.
11. 8   W 1It 1Sy omit 'and others branches, having cut (them) from the
         fields'.
11. 13   D 3Gr 6It omit 'coming up to it'.
14. 1   2Gr omit 'they might kill'.

14. 54   1Gr (122*) omits 'and warming himself'.
14. 67   1Gr (517) omits 'warming himself'.
14. 67   1Sy omits 'looking at him'.
15. 14   1Gr omits 'but they cried out the more, "Crucify him"'.
15. 24   1Gr omits 'casting lots for them'.
15. 29   1Gr omits 'wagging their heads'.
15. 36   D omits 'gave him to drink, saying'.
15. 36   1It (d) omits 'placing (it) on a reed'.
15. 41   C D De 7Gr 1It omit 'and ministered to him'.
15. 44   2Gr 1It omit 'and calling the centurion he asked him if he was already dead'.
15. 46   1Geo omits 'taking him down wrapped him in the linen shroud'. (Probably by homoeoteleuton.)
15. 46   De omits 'he wrapped him in the linen shroud and laid him'. (Probably by homoeoteleuton.)
Cf. also Mk. 15. 21. M* 1Gr omit 'that he should pick up his cross'.

THE APOCRYPHAL TRADITION

Egerton Pap. 2. Fragm. 1. Lines 22-41 (de Santos, p. 98); cf. Mt. 8. 1-4 parr. Lacks 'stretching forth his hand he touched him'.
Act. Pil. 10. 1; cf. Lk. 23. 34. Omits 'cast lots'.

Addendum: Other instances of expansion

THE APOCRYPHAL AND PATRISTIC TRADITIONS

Pseud. Matt. Lat. 16. 1; cf. Mt. 2. 2. '(+they made strict inquiry of the Jews), saying.'
Arundel Lat. Inf. Gosp. 90. The story of the Magi is considerably expanded.
Pseud. Thom. 19. 2; cf. Lk. 2. 47. Has 'How he, being a child, was shutting the mouths of the elders and teachers of the people, explaining the main points of the law and the parables of the prophets' for Lk.'s 'at his understanding and his answers'.
Act. Pil. 1. 1; cf. Lk. 11. 15. '(+he is a sorcerer), and by Beelzeboul', etc.
Arabic Inf. Gosp. 50; cf. Lk. 2. 41-5. The story is expanded by insertion of the questions asked of Jesus (in 50, 51, 52). See also abbreviation, below.
Act. Pil. 11. 2. This verse is inserted between Lk. 23. 48 and 49. The author has been following Lk. very carefully. See Appendix v. 16.
Just. Dial. 76. 5. Mt. 15. 41. Has 'which the father prepared' for Mt.'s 'prepared'.

Addendum: Other instances of abbreviation

THE TEXTUAL TRADITION

Matthew

4. 18   1Gr omits 'two brothers, Simon the one called'; thus reads: 'he saw Peter'.

10. 2   For 'James the (son) of Zebedee and John his brother', Sy⁹ has 'James and John, the sons of Zebedee'.

14. 24   Text: 'was many stadia distant from the land' (six words); Al C D L P W X Ga De Pi Si 084 0106 Ko Most Minusc. It Vg 1Sy Eus: 'was in the midst of the sea' (four words).

Mark

9. 13   X 'and they did (– to him whatever they wanted), just as it is written'.

11. 17   1Gr (– 'not written that'); 1Gr (– 'written that').

11. 29   For this verse, 1Gr has only 'I shall ask you one thing and answer me'.

12. 8   For this verse (10 words), 2Gr have Lk. 20. 15*a* (7 words).

12. 21   1It omits this verse and adds 'likewise they took' to vs. 22. 2Gr 1It (– 'and the second took her and died not leaving seed').

12. 39   For this verse, 1It has 'and first place in the session'.

12. 41   D omits 'casts copper money into the treasury. And many rich men'. The resultant text is 'the crowd cast much'.

14. 58   For 'we heard him saying', Al has 'he said'.

14. 72   For 'the word as Jesus said to him', Fam 1 has 'the word of Jesus, saying'; 1Gr has 'the word of Jesus'.

THE APOCRYPHAL AND PATRISTIC TRADITIONS

Gosp. Heb. Ps. Orig. Lat. (see Appendix v. 4); cf. Mt. 19. 16 ff. Omits Jesus' question ('why ask me', etc.) and the following sentences. Has only the command 'fulfill the law and the prophets'. The commandments are not enumerated: The young man replies 'that I have done'.

Gosp. Heb. same. Omits Mt. 19. 23*b*–24*a* and 25 ff. See Appendix v. 4.

Gosp. Ebion. Epiph. 30. 13. 6 (see Appendix v. 9). Conflates and summarizes.

Trad. Matt. Clem. Alex. Strom. IV. 6 (see Appendix v. 10); cf. Lk. 19. 1 ff. Much abbreviated.

Fayum Fragm. (see Appendix v. 27); cf. Mt. 26. 31–4 parr. Fayum abbreviates and conflates Mt. and Mk.

Protev. Jms. 11. 1–2; cf. Lk. 1. 28–30. Omits Lk. 1. 29.

Protev. Jms. 12. 2 (see Appendix v. 17); cf. Lk. 1. 39–45. Jms. has 86 words to Lk.'s 113, despite some additions.

Pseud. Matt. Lat. 15. 2; cf. Lk. 2. 25. Omits 'expecting the consolation' to end of verse.

Pseud. Matt. Lat. 15. 2. Omits Lk. 2. 27. (The information that Simeon was in the temple had already been given.)

Pseud. Matt. Lat. 15. 2. Omits Lk. 2. 33–5.

Pseud. Matt. 15. 3; cf. Lk. 2. 38. Has 'And coming up she adored the child, saying: "In him is the redemption of the world"' for Lk.'s 'And coming up at that very hour, she gave thanks to God, and spoke of him to all who were looking for the redemption of Jerusalem'.

Pseud. Matt. Lat. 17. 2; cf. Mt. 2. 13–14. Has 35 words for Mt.'s 51 (in the Vulgate). The verses are also put in another place.

Pseud. Matt. 25. 1. For Mt. 2. 19–20, has only 'After no long time the angel said to Joseph: "Return to the land of Judah, for they are dead who sought the child's life."'

Pseud. Thom. 19. 1; cf. Lk. 2. 43. Omits 'did not know'.

Act. Pil. 9. 1. Skips from 'whom do you want (that) I release to you' (Mt. 27. 17) to the words after 'whom do you want (that) I release to you among the two' (Mt. 27. 21).

Act. Pil. 13. 1; cf. Mt. 28. 3. Has 'and he shone like snow and like lightning' for Mt.'s 'his appearance was as lightning, and his raiment white as snow'.

Jos. Arim. 2. 1–3. 1. The story of the trials is severely summarized.

Arabic Inf. Gosp. 6–7. Summarizes Lk. 2. 21–39 and Mt. 2. 1–12.

Arabic Inf. Gosp. 7. So abbreviates Mt. 2. 1–12 as not even to mention Herod. Thus the sentence in Arabic Inf. Gosp. 9 'when Herod saw that the Magi had left him, and not come back to him...' (cf. Mt. 2. 16) is incomprehensible.

Arabic Inf. Gosp. 50. Abbreviates Lk. 2. 41–5. The story is also expanded; see above.

Just. Apol. 1. 15. 4; cf. Mt. 19. 12. Has 27 words for Mt.'s 37.

Just. Apol. 1. 15. 10; cf. Lk. 6. 34. Has 'This also the tax-collectors do' for Lk.'s 'Even sinners lend to sinners, to receive back the equivalent'.

Just. Apol. 1. 15. 14. For Mt. 6. 25b–26//Lk. 12. 23–4, Justin has only 'are you not better than the birds and the beasts? And God feeds them'.

Athen. 12. 3; cf. Mt. 5. 46 par. Mt. has two 'if' clauses, two 'what reward' (and the like) clauses, and two conclusions. Lk. has three of each. Athen. has two 'if' clauses (one from both Mt. and Lk., one adapted from Lk.), one 'what reward' clause, and no conclusions. His version is: ἐὰν γὰρ ἀγαπᾶτε τοὺς ἀγαπῶντας καὶ δανείζητε τοῖς δανείζουσιν ὑμῖν, τίνα μισθὸν ἕξετε;

II Clem. 4. 2; cf. Mt. 7. 21. Clem. has 'will be saved' for 'will enter into the kingdom of heaven' and 'righteousness' for 'the will of my Father who is in heaven'.

Addendum: instances in which the shorter of two possible readings is chosen

Just. Apol. I. 15. 9. Has 'also the evil ones do this'. Lk. 6. 32: 'also the sinners love the ones who love them'; Mt. 5. 46: 'do not the tax-collectors do the same?'

Just. Apol. I. 15. 16; cf. Mt. 6. 33//Lk. 12. 31. Justin chooses Lk.'s shorter form, omitting 'first' and 'and its righteousness', although he agrees with Mt. against Lk. in reading 'all'.

Just. Apol. I. 19. 6; cf. Lk. 18. 27 parr. In the saying 'the things impossible with men', etc., Just. agrees with Lk.'s shorter form, but he omits Lk.'s *estin* in agreement with Mt. and Mk.

Just. Dial. 51. 2; cf. Mt. 16. 21 parr. Omits 'to go up to Jerusalem' (as do Mk. and Lk.) and 'and be rejected' (as does Mt.).

Just. Dial. 76. 7; cf. Mt. 16. 21 parr. Omits 'to go up to Jerusalem' (as do Mk. and Lk.).

Just. Dial. 81. 4; cf. Mt. 22. 30 parr. 'angels (–in heaven)' (as also Lk.).

Just. Dial. 93. 2; cf. Mk. 12. 30 parr. Justin has Luke's short form for the second commandment, 'and your neighbor as yourself'.

Athen. 33. 2; cf. Mt. 19. 9//Mk. 10. 11f. Athen. has Mt.'s shorter form.

Athen. 33. 2; cf. Mt. 19. 9//Mk. 10. 11f. Omits Mt.'s 'except for adultery', as does Mk.

Mt. 5. 29 has 'pluck it out and cast it from you'; Mk. 9. 47 has 'cast it out'; Just. Apol. I. 15. 2 has 'cut it out', thus choosing Mk.'s shorter form. Justin's word 'cut out' occurs in Mt. 5. 30.

On the basis of these lists, we may make the following observations:

1. Some slight tendency may be observed toward omitting all or part of a quotation from the Old Testament. This is especially the case when the later writer is using Matthew, who may have been thought to use the O.T. too much. When Mark is being used, however, the reverse tendency seems to exist, so far as the scant evidence allows any judgement to be made.

2. The MSS show a slight tendency to add to speeches rather than to shorten them, while the other evidence, though very scant, is fairly evenly balanced. No real tendency can be observed here.

3. There is a clear tendency in the Apocryphal Gospels to create new speeches. The manuscripts have no scope to follow such a tendency. The scribes of the period from which our manuscripts come very rarely altered the text to the extent of

adding an entire speech. Since the quotations from the Fathers do not preserve the narrative character of the Gospels, but are only isolated citations, they also have no possibility of giving characters new speeches.

4. [The Apocryphal Gospels also show a clear tendency to create new dialogues.] This includes the tendency to make what was previously a speech into dialogue by the insertion of a new speech. See, for example, the first and last items in the list of dialogues from the Apocryphal Gospels.

5. There is also a tendency on the part of the Apocryphal Gospels to create new scenes and events. In the case of the fragments, as we have already noted, we cannot tell how the new material was related to the old. We must also note here that the Apocryphal Gospels leave out a great deal of the Synoptic material, even of that portion on which they draw. These excisions are very difficult to catalogue, but what is said in the addendum to category 5 a about the role of the disciples in the Acts of Pilate should be noted.

6. The evidence for the addition and omission of actions is fairly evenly balanced. No tendency can be observed here.

So we see that numbers 3, 4, and 5 in the list above represent the clearest tendencies of the tradition in this group. Of these, number 4 is the strongest. Not one of the tendencies is universal. Numbers 3 and 5 are especially subject to *redaktionsgeschichtlich* considerations. That is, an author may well have tended to add new speeches and new scenes, but he would omit scenes and speeches which did not interest him. Here the evidence of Justin is important, especially for the tendency to omit some sayings. Thus, as we saw,[1] in citing Mt. 5. 34–7 he gives the principle ('do not swear at all') but not the particulars ('neither by heaven', and so forth). Here we should refer to the work of Burton, who saw very clearly the relation between length and the interest of the author. In discussing principles of literary criticism, he lists six points which indicate secondary character. Four of these bear on the problem of length: (1) 'insertion by one writer of material not in the other, and clearly interrupting the course of thought or symmetry of plan in the other'; (2) 'clear omission from one document of matter which was in the other, the omission of which destroys the connection';

---

[1] In category 2 b.

(3) 'insertion of matter the motive for which can be clearly seen in the light of the author's general aim, while no motive can be discovered for its omission by the author if he had had it in his source'; (4) 'vice versa, omission of matter traceable to the motive natural to the writer when the insertion could not thus be accounted for'.[1]

The consideration that a writer expands what interests him and abbreviates what does not also affects number 4 in our list, but not so forcefully as it affects numbers 3 and 5. This is especially true of the tendency to expand already existing dialogues or to make a dialogue out of a conversation. This tendency may be more closely related to a love of novelistic color than to special interest in the material. Sometimes the expanded conversation conveys no additional information, but is expanded only by the insertion of 'prodding' questions, such as Mary's question and Simeon's answer in Act. Pil. 16. 2.

It must be granted, however, that none of the differences in this category is very strong for establishing the tendency of the tradition. We are likely to learn more about the policy and interests of a certain editor than about a tendency common to most transmitters.[2]

For this reason, the relations of the Gospels to each other in the matter of length will be of considerable interest, even if length cannot confirm or deny the priority of one to another. We should expect that the earliest Gospel will be the one which has the fewest speeches, the shortest dialogues, and the fewest 'scenes' in parallel material, unless the evangelists can be shown to have had editorial policies which would cause the matter to go another way. In other words, Mark will be expected to be the shortest in these respects unless Matthew and Luke can be shown to have been interested in abbreviation, or at least disinterested in those matters which are in Mark but not in their Gospels.

---

[1] Ernest DeWitt Burton, *Principles of Literary Criticism and the Synoptic Problem* (Chicago, 1904), p. 198. Cited by Farmer, *op. cit.* p. 229.

[2] For example, Bellinzoni, *op. cit.* p. 81, notes Justin's tendency to be concise.

THE EVIDENCE FROM THE SYNOPTIC GOSPELS

The true relation of Matthew and Mark in the matter of length has been the subject of some debate. Herder argued that Mark, being the shorter, was more original. 'Is this not the more natural view? Is not the shorter, the unadorned, probably the earlier, to which then on other occasions explanations, fullness, roundness are added?'[1] Most scholars, however, recognizing that in a majority of the individual pericopes Matthew and Luke are shorter than Mark, have had to attribute to them abbreviating tendencies. Thus Bultmann noted that Matthew 'abbreviates Mark's stories by omitting small novelistic features'.[2] It is usually said that Matthew did this in order to gain room for the addition of more essential material.[3] The question then becomes, whether the differences between Mark and Matthew can actually be explained on this hypothesis. Weiss, for example, doubted it in some cases. He could not think that Matthew, in order to save space, or from a deficient interest in details, excised the verse about stretcher-bearers carrying the ill man onto the roof (Mk. 2. 4).[4] It is this question which we must bear in mind as we examine the following lists.

1′ Old Testament quotations in one Gospel but not in another

Matthew

Mt. 4. 4 has 'man shall not live by bread alone, but by every word that proceeds from the mouth of God'. Lk. 4. 4 has 'man shall not live by bread alone'. This is abbreviated as follows:

4. 4; ctr. Lk. 4. 4 + 'but by every word', etc.

8. 17; ctr. Mk. 1. 34 and Lk. 4. 41. Mt. adds here the formula quotation 'he took our sickness', etc.

10. 36; ctr. Lk. 12. 53 + 'a man's enemies', etc. See Mic. 7. 6.

12. 17–21; ctr. Mk. 3. 12. Mt. adds 'Behold my servant', etc.

---

[1] Cited from Kümmel, *Das neue Testament* (Freiburg/München, 1958), pp. 97–8.
[2] *Die Geschichte*, p. 378 (E.T. p. 353). It is thus difficult to see how Quispel can claim that the tendency of short forms to become longer is a law of form and source criticism. See *N.T.S.* XII (1966), 378.
[3] For example, see B. H. Streeter, *The Four Gospels*, p. 158.
[4] J. Weiss, *Das älteste Evangelium*, p. 3; cf. p. 155. See also Wilhelm Bussmann, *Synoptische Studien*, I (Halle, 1925), p. 75.

13. 14; ctr. Mk. 4. 12 and Lk. 8. 10. Mt. adds 'You hear and do not understand', etc.

13. 35; ctr. Mk. 4. 34. Mt. adds the formula quotation 'I open my mouth in parables', etc.

16. 27; ctr. Mk. 8. 38 and Lk. 9. 26. Mt. adds 'He will repay to each', etc.

19. 5; ctr. Mk. 10. 7 + 'and be joined to his wife'.

19. 19; ctr. Mk. 10. 19 and Lk. 18. 20 + 'and love thy neighbor as thyself'.

21. 4, 5; ctr. Mk. 11. 3 and Lk. 19. 31. Mt. adds the formula quotation 'Say to the daughters of Zion', etc.

21. 33 and Mk. 12. 1; ctr. Lk. 20. 9 + 'and he set a hedge around it', etc.

21. 42 and Mk. 12. 11; ctr. Lk. 20. 17 + 'this is from the Lord, and is it marvelous in our eyes?'

24. 31; ctr. Mk. 13. 27 + 'with a great trumpet'. See Is. 27. 13.

26. 31; ctr. Mk. 14. 27 'the sheep + of the shepherd'.

26. 64 and Mk. 14. 62; ctr. Lk. 22. 69. Mt. and Mk. add 'and coming upon (or, with) the clouds of heaven'.

27. 43; ctr. Mk. 15. 32 + 'he trusted in God', etc. See also category 2' below.

Mark

1. 2; ctr. Mt. 3. 3 and Lk. 3. 4 + 'behold! I send my messenger', etc. Cf. Mt. 11. 10; Lk. 7. 27.

6. 34; ctr. Mt. 14. 14. Mk. adds 'because they were as sheep without a shepherd'.

8. 18; ctr. Mt. 16. 9. Mk. adds 'having eyes you do not see', etc.

9. 48; ctr. Mt. 18. 9. Mk. adds 'where their worm does not die', etc. (See Bussmann, I, p. 87.)

11. 17; ctr. Mt. 21. 13 and Lk. 19. 46. Mk. adds 'for all the nations (or, Gentiles)'.

12. 29; ctr. Mt. 22. 37 and Lk. 10. 27. Mk. adds 'Hear, Israel, the Lord your God is one Lord'.

12. 30; ctr. Mt. 22. 37 and Lk. 10. 27 + 'and with all your strength'.

Luke

3. 5–6; ctr. Mt. 3. 3 and Mk. 1. 3 + every valley', etc.

Summary

Matthew is longer than Mark 11 times.	Mt:Mk::11:7
Matthew is longer than Luke 10 times.	Mt:Lk::10:1
Mark is longer than Matthew 7 times.	Mk:Lk::7:1
Mark is longer than Luke 7 times.	
Luke is longer than Matthew 1 time.	
Luke is longer than Mark 1 time.	

2′ Speeches longer in one Gospel than in another

Matthew

4. 10; ctr. Lk. 4. 8 + 'Depart, Satan'.

5. 41; ctr. Lk. 6. 29 + 'and if anyone forces you to go with him one mile, go with him two'.

8. 26 and Mk. 4. 40; ctr. Lk. 8. 24 f. + 'Why are you afraid?'

9. 13; ctr. Mk. 2. 17 and Lk. 5. 31 + 'Go and learn what this means: "I want mercy and not sacrifice."'

9. 17 (+ 'and both are kept safe' [also conclusion]) and Lk. 5. 39 (+ 'and no one after drinking old wants new; for he says, "The old is good".'); ctr. Mk. 2. 22.

11. 23 f.; ctr. Lk. 10. 15 + 'Because if the mighty works which have happened among you had happened in Sodom', etc. (Also conclusion.)

12. 5–7; ctr. Mk. 2. 26 and Lk. 6. 4 + 'Or have you not read that on the sabbath the priests in the temple profane the sabbath', etc.

12. 11; ctr. Mk. 3. 3 and Lk. 6. 8 + 'who is the man among you who has one sheep', etc.

12. 45; ctr. Lk. 11. 26 + 'Thus it will be also for this evil generation.' (Also conclusion.)

13. 12; ctr. Mk. 4. 11 and Lk. 8. 10 + 'whoever has, it will be given to him', etc.

13. 56; ctr. Mk. 6. 3 + 'From whence therefore are all these things?' (This is repetitious; see also Mk. 6. 2 and Mt. 13. 54.)

14. 16; ctr. Mk. 6. 37 and Lk. 9. 13 + 'They need not go away'.

16. 11 ('How is it that you do not perceive that I did not speak about bread? Beware of the leaven of the Pharisees and Sadducees.'); ctr. Mk. 8. 21 ('Do you not yet understand?'). Mt.'s is also explanatory.

16. 23; ctr. Mk. 8. 33 + 'You are a scandal to me'.

17. 12; ctr. Mk. 9. 13 + 'And they did not know him'.

17. 12*b*; ctr. Mk. 9. 13 + 'So also the Son of man will suffer at their hands'.

17. 23 and Mk. 9. 31; ctr. Lk. 9. 44 + 'and they shall kill him and on the third day he shall be raised', and the like.

18. 7 (cf. Lk. 17. 1); ctr. Mk. 9. 42 + 'Woe to the world on account of *skandala*', etc.

18. 8; ctr. Mk. 9. 43 + 'and cast it from you'.

18. 9; ctr. Mk. 9. 47. Same.

19. 27; ctr. Mk. 10. 28 and Lk. 18. 28 + 'What then will be to us?' Note semitism.

19. 28; ctr. Mk. 10. 29 and Lk. 18. 29 + 'You who have followed me, in the new age', etc.

21. 3 and Mk. 11. 3; ctr. Lk. 19. 31 + 'And immediately he will send him (them)'.

21. 21; ctr. Mk. 11. 22 +'Not only the thing of the fig tree will you do'.

21. 43; ctr. Mk. 12. 11 and Lk. 20. 17 +'The kingdom of God will be taken away from you', etc.

22. 17; ctr. Mk. 12. 14 and Lk. 20. 22 +'Tell us, therefore, what do you think?'

22. 18 and Mk. 12. 15; ctr. Lk. 20. 23 +'Why do you tempt me?'

24. 30; ctr. Mk. 13. 26 and Lk. 21. 27 +'Will appear the sign of the Son of man in heaven, and then all of the tribes of the earth will mourn'.

24. 36 and Mk. 13. 32; ctr. Lk. 21. 33 +'No one knows that day and hour', etc. (Luke 'saves' Jesus.)

26. 40 and Mk. 14. 37; ctr. Lk. 22. 46 +'Are you not able to watch with me one hour?' See also Mk. 14. 37, same category and conflation.

26. 63; ctr. Mk. 14. 61 and Lk. 22. 67 +'I adjure you by the living God'.

26. 65; ctr. Mk. 14. 63 and Lk. 22. 71 +'He blasphemed'.

26. 68 and Lk. 22. 64; ctr. Mk. 14. 65 +'Who is it who strikes you?'

27. 40; ctr. Mk. 15. 30 +'If you are the Son of God'. See also Lk. 23. 37: 'If you are the King of the Jews'.

27. 43; ctr. Mk. 15. 32 +'He trusted in God; let him deliver him now, if he wants him (also category 1' above); for he said, "I am the Son of God"'.

28. 7; ctr. Mk. 16. 7 'Say+he is raised from the dead'.

Mark

1. 15; ctr. Mt. 4. 17 +'The time is fulfilled' and 'Believe in the Gospel'.

2. 7 and Lk. 5. 21; ctr. Mt. 9. 3 +'Who is able to forgive sins but God?' (Explains 'he blasphemes'.)

2. 9; ctr. Mt. 9. 5 and Lk. 5. 23 +'and take up your bed'.

2. 19; ctr. Mt. 9. 15 and Lk. 5. 34 +'For whatever time they have the bridegroom with them, they cannot fast'. (Answers the preceding rhetorical question.)

2. 27; ctr. Mt. 12. 7 and Lk. 6. 5 +'The sabbath was made for man, and not man for the sabbath'.

4. 3; ctr. Mt. 13. 3 and Lk. 8. 5 +'Hear'.

4. 7; ctr. Mt. 13. 7 and Lk. 8. 7 +'And it did not bear fruit'. (Also conclusion.)

4. 8; ctr. Mt. 13. 8 and Lk. 8. 8 +'growing up and increasing'.

5. 34 and Lk. 8. 48; ctr. Mt. 9. 22 +'Go in peace'. Mk. also adds 'and be healed from your disease'.

7. 8; ctr. Mt. 15. 9 +'Leaving the commandment of God, you hold fast the tradition of men'.

7. 13; ctr. Mt. 15. 6 +'And many such things you do'.

7. 18–19a; ctr. Mt. 15. 17 'Whatever enters a man (or, the mouth) (+cannot defile him, since it enters not his heart but) his stomach'.

7. 27; ctr. Mt. 15. 26 + 'Let the children first be fed'. (The effect is to weaken Jesus' rejection of Gentiles.)

9. 12; ctr. Mt. 17. 11 + 'And how is it written of the Son of man, that he should suffer many things and be treated with contempt?'

9. 13; ctr. Mt. 17. 12 + 'as it is written of him'.

9. 39; ctr. Lk. 9. 50 + 'For there is no one who does a mighty work in my name and can then soon speak evil of me'. (Explanatory.)

9. 41; ctr. Lk. 9. 50 + 'For whoever gives you a cup of water to drink', etc.

9. 45; ctr. Mt. 18. 8. Mk. has a separate saying for the foot, whereas Mt. handles foot and hand together.

10. 24; ctr. Mt. 19. 24 and Lk. 18. 24 + 'Children, how difficult it is to enter into the kingdom of God'.

10. 30; ctr. Mt. 19. 29 and Lk. 18. 30 + 'houses and brothers and sisters and mothers and children and lands, with persecutions'.

10. 38; ctr. Mt. 20. 22 + 'or to be baptized with the baptism', etc.

10. 39; ctr. Mt. 20. 23 + 'and you will be baptized', etc.

11. 23; ctr. Mt. 21. 21 + 'but believes that what he has said will happen'.

11. 30; ctr. Mt. 21. 25 and Lk. 20. 4 + 'Answer me'.

12. 23; ctr. Mt. 22. 28 and Lk. 20. 33 + 'when they rise'. (Redundant.)

13. 23; ctr. Mt. 24. 25 + 'But you beware'.

14. 6; ctr. Mt. 26. 10 + 'Leave her alone'. (Gives the point of the following speech.)

14. 7; ctr. Mt. 26. 11 + 'And when you want you are able to do good for them'.

14. 13*b* and Lk. 22. 10*b*; ctr. Mt. 26. 18 + 'A man carrying a jar of water will meet you. Follow him.' (Also detail.)

14. 15 and Lk. 22. 12; ctr. Mt. 26. 18 + 'And he will show you a large upper room furnished and prepared. There prepare for us.'

14. 37 (+ 'Simon, do you sleep?') and Lk. 22. 46 ('Why do you sleep?'); ctr. Mt. 26. 40. But see Mt. 26. 40, same category. Also see conflation, Mark.

Luke

4. 6; ctr. Mt. 4. 9 + 'because it is given to me and to whomever I wish to give it'. (Explanatory of the preceding statement.)

7. 7; ctr. Mt. 8. 8 + 'wherefore I did not presume to come to you'. (Explanatory of the preceding statement.)

8. 12; ctr. Mt. 13. 19 and Mk. 4. 15 + 'in order that he may not, believing, be saved'. (Gives purpose.)

8. 50; ctr. Mk. 5. 36 + 'and she shall be saved'.

9. 13; ctr. Mt. 14. 17 (cf. Mk. 6. 37*b*) + 'unless we are to go and buy food for all these people'.

9. 44; ctr. Mt. 17. 22 and Mk. 9. 31 + 'Place these words in your ears'.

9. 48; ctr. Mk. 9. 37 + 'For he who is least among you, this one is great'.

12. 52; ctr. Mt. 10. 34 + 'For there will be from now on five divided in one house, three against two and two against three'.
20. 2; ctr. Mt. 21. 23 and Mk. 11. 28 + 'Tell us'.
20. 18; ctr. Mt. 21. 43 and Mk. 12. 11 + 'everyone who falls upon that stone', etc.
21. 8; ctr. Mt. 24. 5 and Mk. 13. 6 + 'The time is near'.

Summary

Mt. longer than Mk. 26 times.	Mt:Mk::26:29
Mt. longer than Lk. 22 times.	Mt:Lk::22:14
Mk. longer than Mt. 29 times	Mk:Lk::18:9
Mk. longer than Lk. 18 times.	
Lk. longer than Mt. 14 times.	
Lk. longer than Mk. 9 times.	

3′ Speeches present in one Gospel but not in another

Matthew

12. 23; ctr. Lk. 11. 14 + 'Is this the Son of David?' The verbatim agreement in this passage is slight, however.
12. 38; ctr. Lk. 11. 29 + 'We wish to see a sign from you'. Cf. Lk. 11. 16. (In Lk., Jesus initiates the discourse.)
12. 48 and Mk. 3. 33; ctr. Lk. 8. 20 + 'Who is my mother and who are my brothers?'
14. 18; ctr. Mk. 6. 38 and Lk. 9. 14 + 'Bring them here to me'.
14. 33; ctr. Mk. 6. 52 + 'Truly you are the Son of God'.
16. 17–19; ctr. Mk. 8. 29 and Lk. 9. 20 + 'Blessed are you, Simon Barjonah', etc.
16. 22; ctr. Mk. 8. 32 + 'God forbid, Lord! This shall never happen to you'.
*18. 21; ctr. Lk. 17. 4 Peter aks 'How many times shall my brother sin against me', etc.
*19. 18; ctr. Mk. 10. 18 and Lk. 18. 19 + 'He says, "Which?"'
*22. 42; ctr. Mk. 12. 35 and Lk. 20. 41 + 'They say to him, "The son of David"'.
26. 42; ctr. Mk. 14. 39. Mt. repeats Jesus' prayer a second time, while Mk. has 'saying the same thing'. (Contrast Mk. 11. 4//Mt. 21. 6.)
26. 50; ctr. Mk. 14. 45 + 'Jesus said to him, "Friend, ἐφ' ὃ πάρει"'. (See also Lk. 22. 48.)
26. 52 ff. (+ 'return your sword to its place', etc.) and Lk. 22. 51 (+ 'No more of this'); ctr. Mk. 14. 47.
26. 72; ctr. Mk. 14. 70 + 'I do not know the man'. (See also Lk. 22. 58.)

* An asterisk indicates that the new speech creates a dialogue or expands one.

THE EVIDENCE FROM THE SYNOPTIC GOSPELS

Mark

1. 37; ctr. Lk. 4. 42 + 'Everyone is searching for you'.
2. 12 (+ 'We never saw anything like this') and Lk. 5. 26 (+ 'We have seen a paradox today'); ctr. Mt. 9. 8.
3. 3 and Lk. 6. 8; ctr. Mt. 12. 10 + 'He says... "Rise up (Lk. + "and stand") in the midst"'.
3. 11 (cf. Lk. 4. 41); ctr. Mt. 12. 16 The demons cry out 'You are the Son of God'.
5. 41 and Lk. 8. 54; ctr. Mt. 9. 25. Mk. and Lk. add a command to the girl to rise.
6. 15 f. and Lk. 9. 8–9; ctr. Mt. 14. 2. Mk. and Lk. have estimates of who Jesus is in addition to that in Mt., as well as Herod's speech, 'John, whom I beheaded', etc.
6. 22; ctr. Mt. 14. 6 + 'Ask me whatever you want', etc.
6. 31; ctr. Mt. 14. 13 and Lk. 9. 10 + 'Come away by yourselves to a lonely place, and rest a while'.
*9. 16; ctr. Mt. 17. 14 and Lk. 9. 37 + 'What are you discussing with them?'
9. 25; ctr. Mt. 17. 18 and Lk. 9. 42 + 'You deaf and dumb spirit, I command you', etc.
9. 26; ctr. Mt. 17. 18 and Lk. 9. 42 + 'He is dead'.
16. 3; ctr. Mt. 28. 4 and Lk. 24. 1 + 'And they were saying to one another, "Who will roll away for us the stone from the door of the tomb?"'

Luke

4. 41; ctr. Mk. 1. 34 The demons cry out 'You are the Son of God'. Cf. Mk. 3. 11 above.
*10. 26; ctr. Mt. 22. 36 and Mk. 12. 29 + 'He said to him, "How is it written in the law? How do you read?"' There is no verbatim agreement between Mark and Luke, however, and only moderate agreement between Matthew and Luke.
*12. 41; ctr. Mt. 24. 44 Peter asks, 'Lord, are you telling this parable for us or for all?'
*20. 16; ctr. Mt. 21. 41 and Mk. 12. 9 + 'Hearing, they said, "God forbid!"'
20. 39 (+ 'Teacher, you say well') and cf. Mk. 12. 28 (+ 'seeing that he answered them well'); ctr. Mt. 22. 33 f.
*22. 8; ctr. Mt. 26. 17 and Mk. 14. 12 Jesus says, 'Go prepare for us the Passover, in order that we may eat'.

Cf. also reports of speech

Mark

1. 30 and Lk. 4. 38; ctr. Mt. 8. 14 +Statement that the disciples told Jesus about Peter's mother-in-law's illness. (Perhaps explanatory.)
1. 34 and Lk. 4. 41; ctr. Mt. 8. 16 +'And he did not permit the demons to speak', etc.
3. 9; ctr. Mt. 12. 15 and Lk. 6. 17 +'And he told his disciples to have a boat ready for him', etc.
4. 34; ctr. Mt. 13. 34 +'But privately to his own disciples he explained everything'. See also Mk. 4. 10; 7. 17; 9. 28; 9. 33; 10. 10.
5. 43 and Lk. 8. 56; ctr. Mt. 9. 25. Jesus commands that his cure of Jairus' daughter not be told.
14. 5; ctr. Mt. 26. 9 +'And they reproached her'.

Luke

11. 16; ctr. Mt. 12. 24 and Mk. 3. 22 +'But others, tempting, sought a sign from heaven from him'.
18. 36; ctr. Mt. 20. 30 and Mk. 10. 47 +'He asked what this should be'.

Summary
(Parentheses include reports of speech)

Mt. longer than Mk. 10 times.   Mt:Mk::10:11(17)
Mt. longer than Lk. 8 times.   Mt:Lk::8:9(14)
Mk. longer than Mt. 11 times (17 times).   Mk:Lk::7(8):5(7)
Mk. longer than Lk. 7 times (8 times).
Lk. longer than Mt. 9 times (14 times).
Lk. longer than Mk. 5 times (7 times).

4′ Dialogues in one Gospel but not in another

Matthew

3. 14 f.; ctr. Mk. 1. 9 and Lk. 3. 21. Mt. adds a dialogue between Jesus and John concerning why John should baptize Jesus.
15. 12–14; ctr. Mk. 7. 15. Mt. adds an exchange between the disciples and Jesus about the Pharisees being offended.
15. 23 f.; ctr. Mk. 7. 25. The disciples say 'send her away', etc. Jesus replies, 'I was only sent to the lost sheep of the house of Israel'.
16. 22–3 and Mk. 8. 32–3; ctr. Lk. 9. 22. Mt. adds the conversation between Peter and Jesus in which Jesus rebukes Peter for dissuading him from accepting his death. (Luke may 'save' Peter here.) Mark, however, does not give Peter's actual speech.
17. 19 f. and Mk. 9. 28 f.; ctr. Lk. 9. 43. Mt. and Mk. have the disciples ask 'Why were we not able to cast it out?' Mt. has Jesus reply, 'Because

76

of your little faith', etc. Mk. has him reply, 'This kind cannot be driven out except by prayer'.

19. 10–12; ctr. Mk. 10. 12. The disciples say it is better not to marry, and Jesus replies.

21. 41; ctr. Mk. 12. 9 and Lk. 20. 16. By adding 'they say to him', Mt. changes the speaker and makes a speech into dialogue.

26. 25; ctr. Mk. 14. 21. + 'Answering, Judas, who betrayed him, said, "It is not I, Rabbi?" He says to him, "you said"'. (See also Lk. 22. 23.)

27. 21; ctr. Mk. 15. 12. Pilate asks, 'Which of the two do you want me to release for you?' The people answer, 'Barabbas'.

Mark

5. 9 and Lk. 8. 30; ctr. Mt. 8. 29. + 'Jesus asked him, "What is your name?" And he says to him, "Legion"', etc.

5. 18 ff. and Lk. 8. 37 ff.; ctr. Mt. 8. 34. Mk. and Lk. add a conversation between the former demoniac of Gerasa and Jesus.

5. 30 ff. and Lk. 8. 45 f.; ctr. Mt. 9. 21. + 'And Jesus...said, "Who touched me?" And the disciples said, "You see the crowd"', etc. Lk. also adds another response by Jesus: 'Jesus said, "Someone touched me"', etc.

5. 35 ff. and Lk. 8. 49 ff.; ctr. Mt. 9. 22. The head of the synagogue is told that his daughter is dead (cf. Mt. 9. 18). Jesus replies, 'Do not fear, only believe'.

6. 24; ctr. Mt. 14. 8. + 'She said to her mother, "What shall I ask?" And she said, "The head of John the baptizer"'.

6. 37*b*–38*a*; ctr. Mt. 14. 17 and Lk. 9. 13. + They said, 'shall we go and buy', etc. (Cf. Lk. 9. 13, end.) He said, 'How many loaves have you', etc.

8. 19 f.; ctr. Mt. 16. 9 f. Jesus' speech is made into a dialogue in Mark by the insertion, at the proper places, of the disciples' answers: 'twelve' and 'seven'.

9. 21–4; ctr. Mt. 17. 17 and Lk. 9. 42. Mk. adds the extensive dialogue between Jesus and the father of the epileptic child.

10. 2–5; ctr. Mt. 19. 3, 7–8. Mk. inserts this question by Jesus: 'What did Moses command you?', thereby increasing the changes of speakers.

12. 32–4; ctr. Mt. 22. 40 and Lk. 10. 28. Mk. adds a conversation between the scribe and Jesus.

Luke

9. 59; ctr. Mt. 8. 21 f. Without adding any words, Lk. adds one exchange. Mt. has: another said, Jesus said. Lk. has: Jesus said, another said, Jesus said. (Note, Jesus here initiates.)

22. 70; ctr. Mt. 26. 64 and Mk. 14. 62 + 'They all said, "Are you then the Son of God?" And he said to them, "You say that I am"'. (Cf. Mt. 26. 64: 'you say'.)

Summary

Mt. longer than Mk. 7 times (9 times).
Mt. longer than Lk. 4 times (7 times).
Mk. longer than Mt. 10 times (11 times).
Mk. longer than Lk. 5 times (6 times).
Lk. longer than Mt. 6 times (10 times).
Lk. longer than Mk. 1 time (4 times).

Parentheses show figures resulting from taking into account additions of speeches (category 3) which either make a dialogue of a speech or which extend dialogue.

$$Mt:Mk::7(9):10(11)$$
$$Mt:Lk::4(7):6(10)$$
$$Mk:Lk::5(6):1(4)$$

5′ Scenes and events in one Gospel but not in another

Matthew

14. 28–31; ctr. Mk. 6. 50. The story of Peter's walking on the water.
17. 6–7; ctr. Mk. 9. 7 and Lk. 9. 35. 'When the disciples heard this, they fell on their faces, and were filled with fear. But Jesus came and touched them, saying, "Rise, and have no fear".'
21. 14–16; ctr. Mk. 11. 11 and Lk. 19. 45 f. The healing of the blind and lame in the temple, and Jesus' conversation with the chief priests and the scribes.
27. 19; ctr. Mk. 15. 10. 'But while he was sitting on the judgment seat, his wife sent to him, saying, "Let there be nothing between you and that righteous man, for I have suffered much today in a dream on account of him".'
27. 24–5; ctr. Mk. 15. 14 and Lk. 23. 23. The story of Pilate's washing of his hands and the response of the crowd. [The motif of Pilate's innocence also appears in Lk. 23. 20 ('desiring to release Jesus'); 23. 22 ('I have found in him no crime deserving death', etc.); 23. 25 ('to their will'); and Mk. 15. 15 ('wishing to satisfy the crowd').]
27. 51b–53; ctr. Mk. 15. 38 and Lk. 23. 46. 'And the earth shook, and the rocks were split; the tombs also were opened, and many bodies of the saints who had fallen asleep were raised, and coming out of the tombs after his resurrection they went into the holy city and appeared to many.'
28. 2–4; ctr. Mk. 16. 2 and Lk. 24. 1. The angel rolls away the door. But see also Mk. 16. 3, category 3′ above.

Mark

2. 4 and similarly Lk. 5. 18b–19; ctr. Mt. 9. 2. 'And not being able to bring him up to him on account of the crowd, they removed the roof above

78

him; and when they had made an opening, they let down the pallet on which the paralytic lay.'

5. 15 f. and similarly Lk. 8. 35 f.; ctr. Mt. 8. 34. 'And they come to Jesus and behold the demoniac sitting there, clothed and in his right mind ...; and they were afraid. And those who had seen it told how it happened to the demoniac, and about the swine.'

9. 14*b*-16; ctr. Mt. 17. 14 and Lk. 9. 37. '...and scribes arguing with them. And immediately all the crowd, when they saw him, were greatly amazed, and ran up to him and greeted him. And he asked them, "What are you discussing with them?"' See also additional speech.

9. 20-4; ctr. Mt. 17. 17 and Lk. 9. 42. Mk. puts here the story of the convulsing of the epileptic and the conversation between Jesus and the father of the boy. Lk. 9. 42 states that 'the demon tore and convulsed him'.

9. 35; ctr. Mt. 18. 1 and Lk. 9. 47. 'And he sat down and called the twelve, and he said to them, "If any would be first, he must be last of all and servant of all".' (Cf. Mt. 20. 26 f. parr.)

10. 49*b*-50; ctr. Mt. 20. 32 and Lk. 18. 40. 'And they call the blind man saying to him, "Be of good cheer, rise, he calls you". Then casting off his garment he rose to his feet and went to Jesus.'

11. 4-5 and similarly Lk. 19. 32-4; ctr. Mt. 21. 6. 'And they went away, and found a colt tied at the door out in the open street; and they untied it. And those who stood there said to them, "What are you doing, untying the colt?"' (Mt. has 'and did'.)

14. 51-2; ctr. Mt. 26. 56 and Lk. 22. 53. This is the story of the youth who fled naked.

15. 8; ctr. Mt. 27. 16. 'And the crowd came up and began to ask [Pilate] to do thus for them.'

15. 44-5; ctr. Mt. 27. 58 and Lk. 23. 52. 'But Pilate wondered if he were already dead, and calling the centurion, he asked him if he had been dead long. And when he learned from the centurion, he granted the body to Joseph.' Cf. also result, Mt. 27. 58*b*.

Luke

7. 4-6*a*; ctr. Mt. 8. 7. '[The elders of the Jews] coming to Jesus besought him earnestly, saying, "He is worthy to have you do this for him, for he loves our nation, and he built us our synagogue". And Jesus went with them. When he was not far from the house, the centurion sent friends to him, saying to him...'

7. 20-1; ctr. Mt. 11. 3. 'And when the men had come to him, they said, "John the Baptist has sent us to you, saying, 'Are you he who is to come, or shall we look for another?'" In that hour he cured many of diseases and plagues and evil spirits, and on many that were blind he bestowed sight.'

79

9. 31–33 a; ctr. Mt. 17. 3 and Mk. 9. 4. '... who appeared in glory and spoke of his departure, which he was to accomplish at Jerusalem. Now Peter and those who were with him were heavy with sleep but kept awake, and they saw his glory and the two men who stood with him. And as the men were parting from him...'

22. 43–4; ctr. Mt. 26. 39 and Mk. 14. 36. The story of the appearance of the angel while Jesus was praying in the garden. These verses may, however, not be original. See the MSS.

Summary

Mt. longer than Mk. 7 times.	Mt:Mk::7:10
Mt. longer than Lk. 5 times.	Mt:Lk::5:7
Mk. longer than Mt. 10 times.	Mk:Lk::6:2
Mk. longer than Lk. 6 times.	
Lk. longer than Mt. 7 times.	
Lk. longer than Mk. 2 times.	

6′ Actions in one Gospel but not in another

Matthew

8. 15 (+'she rose up') and Lk. 4. 39 (+'immediately rising up'); ctr. Mk. 1. 31.

9. 1; ctr. Mk. 2. 1 +'embarking in a boat, he crossed over'. But see Mk. 2. 2, circumstance.

9. 25 (+'going in') and Mk. 5. 40 (+'he takes the father of the child and the mother and those with him and enters where the child was'); ctr. Lk. 8. 53.

12. 1 (+'and to eat') and Lk. 6. 1 (+'and they ate, rubbing [the grain] with their hands'); ctr. Mk. 2. 23.

12. 49 (+'and stretching forth his hand toward his disciples') and Mk. 3. 34 (+'looking about on those who sat about him'); ctr. Lk. 8. 21.

14. 12; ctr. Mk. 6. 29 +'and going they announced to Jesus'.

19. 15 ('and placing his hands on them he went away') and Mk. 10. 16 ('and embracing them he blessed them, putting his hands on them'); ctr. Lk. 18. 17.

19. 26 and Mk. 10. 27; ctr. Lk. 18. 26 +'looking at them'.

21. 8 and Mk. 11. 8. The cutting and spreading of branches; ctr. Lk. 19. 36.

22. 19 and Mk. 12. 16; ctr. Lk. 20. 24 +'and they brought (to him a denarius)'.

22. 22; ctr. Mk. 12. 17 and Lk. 20. 26 +'and leaving him he went away'. Cf. Mk. 12. 12, same category.

26. 30 and Mk. 14. 26; ctr. Lk. 22. 39 +'having sung a hymn'.

26. 44; ctr. Mk. 14. 40 +'and leaving them again, going away he prayed for a third time, saying the same thing again'.

26. 57 (+'then they seized') and Lk. 22. 54 (+'then arresting'); ctr. Mk. 14. 53.

26. 65 and Mk. 14. 63; ctr. Lk. 22. 71. +the high priest rends his garment.

26. 71 and Mk. 14. 68; ctr. Lk. 22. 58 +'and he went out into the porch (gateway)'.

27. 26 and Mk. 15. 15; ctr. Lk. 23. 25. The scourging of Jesus.

27. 29; ctr. Mk. 15. 17 +'and they put a reed in his right hand'.

27. 36 (+'and sitting down they kept watch over him there') and Lk. 23. 35 (+'and the people stood watching'); ctr. Mk. 15. 25.

Mark

1. 7; ctr. Mt. 3. 11 and Lk. 3. 16 'I am not able (+bending down) to loose'.

1. 35; ctr. Lk. 4. 42 +'There he prayed'.

1. 43; ctr. Mt. 8. 3 and Lk. 5. 13 +'And having sternly charged him, he immediately sent him away'.

3. 5 and Lk. 6. 10; ctr. Mt. 12. 12 +'And he looked around at them'.

4. 36; ctr. Mt. 8. 18 and Lk. 8. 22 +'And leaving the crowd, they took him as he was'.

5. 6; ctr. Lk. 8. 28 'seeing, +they ran'.

5. 42; ctr. Mt. 9. 25 and Lk. 8. 55 'She rose+and walked'.

6. 5; ctr. Mt. 13. 58 +'Except he laid his hands on a few sick people and healed them'. (This has the same effect as Mt.'s phrase 'many mighty acts'.)

6. 12 f. and Lk. 9. 6; ctr. Mt. 10. 14 The disciples went out, preached, cast out demons, anointed, and healed.

6. 53; ctr. Mt. 14. 34 +'They anchored'.

7. 30; ctr. Mt. 15. 28 +'She went away into her house and found the child lying in bed'.

9. 27; ctr. Mt. 17. 18 and Lk. 9. 42 +'seizing his hand he raised him' etc.

9. 36; ctr. Mt. 18. 3 and Lk. 9. 48 +'taking him in his arms'.

10. 17; ctr. Mt. 19. 16 and Lk. 18. 18 'a certain one+running and kneeling'.

10. 21; ctr. Mt. 19. 21 and Lk. 18. 22 'Jesus+looked at him'.

10. 23; ctr. Mt. 19. 23 and Lk. 18. 24 'Jesus+looked around'.

11. 11; ctr. Mt. 21. 17 +'looking around at everything'.

12. 12; ctr. Mt. 21. 46 and Lk. 20. 19 +'and leaving him they went away'. Cf. Mt. 22. 22, same category.

14. 3; ctr. Mt. 26. 7 +'She broke the jar'.

14. 65; ctr. Mt. 26. 68 +'And the guards received him with blows'. See also Lk. 22. 65: 'And many other things, blaspheming, they said against him.'

14. 67; ctr. Mt. 26. 69 +'She looked at him'. See also Lk. 22. 56: 'looking steadily at him'.

Luke

4. 40; ctr. Mt. 8. 16 and Mk. 1. 33 '(+Laying his hands on each of them), he healed'.
6. 8; ctr. Mk. 3. 3 +'And rising he stood'.
7. 9; ctr. Mt. 8. 10 '(+Turning) he said'.
8. 5; ctr. Mt. 13. 4 and Mk. 4. 4 +'It was trampled'.
20. 17; ctr. Mt. 21. 42 and Mk. 12. 10 +'looking at them'.
22. 51; ctr. Mt. 26. 52 and Mk. 14. 47 +'And touching his ear he healed him'.
22. 61; ctr. Mt. 26. 74 and Mk. 14. 72 +'And turning, the Lord looked at Peter'.
23. 48; ctr. Mt. 27. 54 and Mk. 15. 39 The multitudes returned home beating their breasts.

Summary

Mt. longer than Mk. 9 times.   Mt:Mk::9:19
Mt. longer than Lk. 11 times.   Mt:Lk::11:9
Mk. longer than Mt. 19 times.   Mk:Lk::22:11
Mk. longer than Lk. 22 times.
Lk. longer than Mt. 9 times.
Lk. longer than Mk. 11 times.

Miscellaneous differences of length
Matthew

9. 20 and Lk. 8. 44; ctr. Mk. 5. 27 '(+the hem of) his garment'.
10. 15; ctr. Lk. 10. 12 '(+the land of) Sodom'.
18. 6; ctr. Mk. 9. 42 and Lk. 17. 2 'in (+the depth of) the sea'.

Mark

6. 21 ('But an opportunity came when Herod on his birthday gave a banquet for his courtiers and officers and the leading men of Galilee'); ctr. Mt. 14. 6 ('But when Herod's birthday came').

Luke

6. 17; ctr. Mk. 3. 8 '(+the seacoast of) Tyre and Sidon'.
7. 31; ctr. Mt. 11. 16 '(+the men of) this generation'.

Our evidence did not lead us to think that any clear tendency was to be observed in the first two items taken, the length of quotations from the Old Testament and the length of speeches. The relation of Matthew and Mark in these respects is in agreement with this, in that neither one is consistently longer than the other in regard to the second item, additions to speeches, while Matthew's greater length in respect to quotations from the Old Testament is doubtless an expression of his own preference, rather than a sign of lateness. Luke is considerably shorter than Matthew and Mark in both categories.

In the third category, the addition of new speeches, the situation is basically the same. Matthew and Mark are close together. Luke is shorter than Mark. Here the relation of Matthew and Luke is approximately even, however. But if we take into account reports of speeches, Mark and Luke are both considerably longer than Matthew.

In the fourth category there once again is no clear difference between Matthew and Mark. Luke is somewhat longer than Matthew but shorter than Mark. The relationships are not greatly altered by considering instances in which a new speech makes a dialogue of a speech or extends dialogue. Since this category appeared to be the strongest one for establishing the tendency of the tradition, the result of applying it to the Synoptics is somewhat confusing. Luke appears to be later than Matthew but earlier than Mark, while the relation of Matthew and Mark is unclear.

Mark is clearly longer than Matthew and Luke in the 'new scene' category, however, while Luke is also longer than Matthew. Unless *redaktionsgeschichtlich* considerations determine otherwise, Matthew here appears to be earlier than Mark and Luke, and Luke earlier than Mark.

In the category of physical actions, Mark once again emerges considerably longer than Matthew and Luke. Luke and Matthew are fairly evenly balanced.

It is clear that far-reaching conclusions on the basis of the relative length of the Gospels in the categories which we have just discussed would be uncalled for. The Synoptic tradition in the post-canonical period did not consistently become either longer or shorter. There was some tendency for later writers to add speeches, to expand dialogues, and to introduce new scenes into material that was being used. But enough tendency toward abbreviation existed[1] to prevent us from laying much emphasis on the tendency to expand in these three ways. Even

---

[1] See especially the addendum on 'other instances of abbreviation' after category 6b above.

if we allow some value to these three categories for testing relative antiquity, they shed little light on the Synoptic problem. It may only be said that they do not support the two-document hypothesis, since none of them supports Mark's priority. The category of the addition of speeches favors Luke's priority to Matthew and Mark, but does not distinguish between Matthew and Mark. The category of the expansion of dialogues supports the priority of Matthew and Mark to Luke, but again does not distinguish between Matthew and Mark. The 'new scene' category supports the order Matthew, Luke, Mark. It is doubtful, however, that these categories should be given much weight in assessing the Synoptic relationships.

It is interesting to observe that the only relation which remains consistent throughout each category is that of Mark and Luke: Luke is always shorter than Mark in the lists above. The relation of Matthew and Luke is on the whole fairly evenly balanced, although in the more significant fourth and fifth categories, and perhaps in the third (if reports of speeches are counted), Luke is longer than Matthew. Mark tends on the whole to be longer than Matthew, although the figures are usually close together. The differences in the important categories are not sufficient to make any judgements one way or another.

 These lists are revealing for the question of *Redaktionsgeschichte*, however. They seem in the first place to contradict the notion that Matthew abbreviated Mark. This is an important issue, and it deserves some further discussion.

Streeter observed that Augustine's view of Mark as an abbreviator of Matthew could not be maintained, since Matthew is usually shorter than Mark where the two Gospels are parallel.[1] He continues,

Now there is nothing antecedently improbable in the idea that for certain purposes an abbreviated version of the Gospel might be desired; but only a lunatic would leave out Matthew's account of the Infancy, the Sermon on the Mount, and practically all the parables, in order to get room for purely verbal expansion of what was retained. On the other hand, if we suppose Mark to be the older document, the verbal compression and omission of minor detail seen in the parallels in Matthew has an obvious purpose, in that it gives more room for the introduction of a mass of highly important teaching material not found in Mark.[2]

[1] *Op. cit.* pp. 157 f. [2] *Ibid.* p. 158.

This view of the matter has been taken by many other scholars.[1] Nevertheless, it cannot be maintained. We may list two principal arguments against it. (1) Streeter argues that, if Mark used Matthew, he would have to be thought of as omitting Matthew's teaching material *for the sake of* purely verbal expansion. But this is a serious misapprehension of the situation. Mark's 'purely verbal expansions' are in no way equivalent in bulk to Matthew's teaching material. He could have expanded the narrative verbally and still have included most of Matthew's teaching material (if he had wanted it) without producing a Gospel longer than Matthew or Luke. Thus Streeter's attempt to ridicule the notion that Mark eliminated teaching material *in order* to expand the narrative material is misdirected.

(2) In the same way, it is not reasonable, as Streeter claimed it to be, to think that Matthew's elimination of Mark's narrative details (on the assumption that Matthew used Mark) would have given him room to introduce the teaching material which is in Matthew but not in Mark. (*a*) Mark's details, again, are not comparable in bulk to Matthew's teaching material. (*b*) As Bussmann pointed out repeatedly, although Matthew does not have many of the narrative elements which are in Mark, he does have approximately the same amount and type of material elsewhere.[2] Thus one would have to suppose that Matthew condensed Mark's material in some passages, not to add new teaching material, but to expand Mark's material in other passages or to add new narrative material. This is not persuasive.

This last point, taken from Bussmann, is confirmed in two ways. In the first place, the lists presented above do not show any great overall differences in length between Matthew and Mark in parallel passages. Matthew is not consistently shorter than Mark, or at least not much shorter. In the second place, we may give some statistical evidence.

In the triple tradition there are about 83 pericopes. In these, Mark has a total of approximately 8,598 words, Matthew a total of approximately 8,325 words. That is a difference of 273 words. Of these 83 pericopes, Mark is longer than Matthew in 44, while Matthew is longer than Mark in 37. There are two ties. This slight difference certainly does not indicate consistent

---

[1] E.g. Hawkins, *Horae Synopticae*[2], pp. 125 ff., 158 ff.
[2] *Op. cit.* pp. 85–7. Cf. pp. 150f. below.

abbreviating by Matthew. We might also note that of the 273 words by which Mark is longer than Matthew in the triple tradition, 190, a little over two-thirds, are to be found in the story of the Gerasene Demoniac (Mk. 5. 1–20 parr.). So in the other 82 pericopes, Matthew managed to save only a total of 83 words, barely an average of one word per pericope. The generalization that Matthew abbreviates Mark simply does not account for this evidence.

These results are unchanged when we consider the material common to Matthew and Mark alone. Of 16 pericopes, Mark is longer in 8 and Matthew longer in 7, with one tie. Mark has a total of 1,858 words, Matthew a total of 1,659 words, a difference of 199 words. Of these 199, 111 occur in one pericope (Mk. 6. 17–29//Mt. 14. 3–12). While here there is more average difference, the fact that Matthew is longer than Mark almost half the time prevents the generalization that he abbreviates.

In the total of the triple and double traditions, counting 99 pericopes, Mark is 472 words longer than Matthew. But if we take just three of these pericopes (Mk. 5. 1–20//Mt. 8. 28–34; Mk. 5. 21–43//Mt. 9. 18–26; Mk. 6. 17–29//Mt. 14. 3–12), we see that in these three pericopes alone Mark is a total of 537 words longer than Matthew. This means that in the total of the other 96 pericopes, Matthew is actually 65 words longer than Mark. This consideration should lay to rest the generalization that Matthew abbreviates Mark, or at least that he abbreviates Mark for the sake of saving space for teaching material.

A special problem is raised with regard to the three pericopes just mentioned, however. Why is Matthew so much shorter than Mark in these three places? Even here the actual differences do not support the hypothesis of abbreviation. In the story of the Gerasene demoniac, for example, Mark has two themes ordinarily dear to Matthew—the worship of Jesus (Mk. 5. 6)[1] and the testimony of the healed man (Mk. 5. 18–20),[2] neither of which is in the Matthean parallel. It does not seem that Matthew would have omitted these themes here in order to save space. We may summarize this discussion by

---

[1] Matthew uses προσκυνέω 13 times, Mark 2 times, and Luke 2 times. It occurs 59 times in the New Testament.

[2] See, for example, Mt. 9. 26. He has, against Mark and Luke, 'and this report) (φήμη) went out into all that land'.

observing that the hypothesis of abbreviation does not account for the actual relationship between Matthew and Mark, either in terms of the material as a whole or of individual differences.[1]

In the case of Luke the matter is somewhat different. Without giving comparable statistics, we may note that Luke is shorter than Mark much more consistently than is Matthew, as indeed we saw in our lists above. Since his relation to Matthew is not the same, however, it is somewhat difficult to argue that Luke was a consistent abbreviator. Nevertheless, the hypothesis of abbreviation is more likely in the case of Luke than of Matthew.

As we saw above, whatever evidence there is in the category of length for the solution of the Synoptic problem weighs against the two-document hypothesis, and especially against Mark's priority, unless it can be offset by the *redaktionsgeschichtlich* consideration that Matthew and Luke were abbreviators. In the case of Matthew, I think the title of abbreviator is unjustified, although it may be applied to Luke with more justice. Thus this category does not indicate Mark's priority to Matthew, and his priority to Luke is supported only to the extent to which Luke is thought to have been an abbreviator. Further discussion of this question must now be postponed until the evidence concerning detail is presented, which is closely related to the evidence concerning length.

[1] Held, *op. cit.* pp. 165 ff., sees Matthew's 'abbreviation' of some of Mark's miracle stories to be for the purpose of interpretation rather than saving space. Matthew's expansion of other miracle stories serves the same purpose. This adds powerful support to our arguments against seeing Matthew as an abbreviator.

CHAPTER III

INCREASING DETAIL AS A POSSIBLE
TENDENCY OF THE TRADITION

INTRODUCTION

The general category of 'detail' covers a large number of lesser categories, but they may all be discussed together. The view of the German form critics with regard to details, in Bultmann's words, was that as

narratives pass from mouth to mouth, or when one writer takes them over from another, their fundamental character remains the same, but the details are subject to the control of fancy and are usually made more explicit and definite.[1]

Dibelius was of the same view. In discussing short stories about Jesus, he points out that they were intended only to bear witness to Jesus. Thus everything was as compressed as possible. Dibelius contrasts this situation with the 'secular, artistic medium', which would amplify such matters as when and where the event took place and employ portraiture for secondary figures. He concludes that

the less that [secular, artistic] medium was used, the more is it likely that the narrative arose in that earliest period when the Christian church was still cut off from the influences of a secular manner of narration.[2]

These scholars saw the naming of characters and the full description of them to be examples of how the material grew more detailed.

As soon as the apophthegm is affected by an interest in history or developed story telling we meet with more precise statements. This is shown in the first place by a specific description of the questioner.[3]

In Bultmann's view the general tendency was to substitute particular characters (such as Peter) for general names (dis-

---

[1] Bultmann, *Die Erforschung*, p. 22 (E.T. p. 32). The addition of details was held by Bultmann to be a general tendency of all oral tradition. See 'The new approach', pp. 345 f., where all of his examples are from the Synoptic tradition, however.   [2] Dibelius, *A fresh approach*, pp. 38–9.
[3] Bultmann, *Die Geschichte*, p. 71 (E.T. p. 67).

ciples).[1] He meets here a difficulty, however, caused by the fact that it is sometimes Mark who has the proper name rather than Matthew and Luke.

Without prejudice to what has been said on p. 310[2] about the secondary tendency to individualize by the giving of names, I think it probable that those sections of the tradition which use the names of individual disciples come from an earlier time when the idea of the Twelve as Jesus' constant companions had not yet been formed or successfully carried through.[3]

Thus those awkward places at which Mark has a proper name while another Gospel has the general term 'disciples' are explained as due to a later interest in the Twelve as a group.[4] Bultmann's explanation is not overly convincing, however, since in the passages he names Matthew does not use the word 'twelve', and, indeed, does not use it so often as Mark anyway.[5] This explanation also makes it impossible to tell when the mention of the disciples is early because it refers to a large and unspecific group and when it is late because it refers to the Twelve. But Bultmann has at least taken into account the conflicting evidence on this point, which cannot be said for those who think the mention of a particular name is always later than the use of a general term.[6]

Bultmann thinks the naming of disciples to be original in Mk. 5. 37; 9. 38; 10. 35; and probably 13. 3. In 1. 29 and 9. 2 only Peter was originally named. The other names were added 'under the influence of 1. 16–20'. In 1. 29 the other names were not in the original edition of Mark, however, but have been added by a copyist.[7]

Streeter saw the matter of names in another way.

It is a law of the evolution of tradition that names to which no incident of dramatic interest is attached tend, either to gather incidents round themselves, or else to drop out.[8]

---

[1] *Ibid.* pp. 71 f. (E.T. pp. 67 f.).   [2] P. 338 in the German edition.

[3] *Die Geschichte*, p. 370 (E.T. p. 345).

[4] Bultmann indicates that Matthew has a special interest in the Twelve in *Die Geschichte*, p. 71 (E.T. p. 67).

[5] The word 'twelve' occurs the following number of times in the Synoptics: 13 in Mt.; 15 in Mk.; 12 in Lk.

[6] So apparently J. Weiss, *Earliest Christianity* (New York, 1959), II, 686; and Köster, *op. cit.* pp. 98, 103.

[7] *Die Geschichte*, p. 370 (E.T. p. 345). W. L. Knox, *The sources of the Synoptic Gospels*, I, 103, differs with Bultmann with regard to Mk. 13. 3. Knox thinks the names there to be typical of apocryphal tradition.

[8] Streeter, *The Four Gospels*, p. 349.

He does not tell us where he discovered this 'law of the evolution of tradition', but it is an interesting one and should be kept in mind in studying the lists on names.

Not only names, but also times and places are details singled out by Bultmann as usually secondary. In the introductions to narratives, notices of time 'are always the work of an editor'.[1] Virtually the same thing is true of mentions of place.

> Since precise indications of place are obviously unsuited to the apophthegmatic style, we cannot avoid the question whether they are all secondary additions.[2]

After giving some examples, however, he qualifies his judgement on mentions of place.

> Elsewhere we cannot with confidence distinguish the place locations as editorial; and even if it is not in keeping with the style, it is still not impossible for the early tradition itself to have passed on this or the other apophthegm complete with localization.[3]

Other scholars have taken just the opposite view to that of Dibelius and Bultmann. C. H. Weisse was of the opinion that, while perhaps not every single detail in Mark went back to the eye-witness account of Peter, most did. He thought it could be shown that an author who wrote in the circumstances in which Mark wrote (namely, on the basis of Peter's account) would give an account fuller of details than would his successors. As the first author of the Gospel story, he would not only have details from the mouth of Peter, but would also tend to include details to give the narrative 'Gestalt und Farbe, und dadurch Haltung und Bestehen'.[4]

Jülicher took a similar view. In discussing Mk. 2. 1–12 parr., for example, he stated that 'that Mark's account is here the earliest may be assumed from the very vividness of his description...'. He especially refers to the mention of the paralytic's

---

[1] *Die Geschichte*, p. 363 (E.T. p. 338).   [2] *Ibid.* p. 68 (E.T. p. 64).
[3] *Ibid.* p. 68 (E.T. p. 65). Cf. also the statement on p. 363 (E.T. p. 338): 'Generally speaking the geographical scene is a matter of indifference to the story and would hardly have been bound up with it originally. On the other hand perhaps not all geographical statements are editorial conjectures; some may well have been found in the ancient tradition and transferred from it to other stories.' Here he expands his judgement about geographical statements from apophthegmata to the tradition as a whole.
[4] C. H. Weisse, *Die evangelische Geschichte* (Leipzig, 1838), I, 65–6.

having been borne by four. Mark has 'the freshest and most living picture'.[1] Most scholars who have argued that details indicate an earlier tradition have done so on the grounds that details are to be expected in an eye-witness record. These scholars think that Mark reflects an eye-witness report and thus reason that his details are early. We have already seen that this was the view of Weisse. We may also mention as representatives of such a view Sir John Hawkins[2] and V. H. Stanton.[3] Since the rise of form criticism, however, this view has been represented most thoroughly by Vincent Taylor.

Taylor discusses details in a chapter in his commentary on Mark on 'The Historical Value of the Gospel'. He says that

if the vivid details in Mark are original, they are of the greatest importance in assessing its historical value. In themselves lifelike touches are not a sure criterion, since they may be due to the exercise of a vivid imagination, but they present data on which a judgment may be based, especially if their character and distribution are considered.[4]

Their character is such as comports with their having come from an eye-witness, and the distribution is such as to deny them to Mark himself. This second point is especially forceful. The argument runs thus: if the details do not come from Peter, they come from Mark (there being, in much of the material, no intermediary); Mark can be shown not to have been interested in adding details, since some of the material in his Gospel is lacking in them, even though they are common enough in his Gospel generally; therefore, what details there are in Mark come from the eye-witness source. Thus Taylor can argue that,

---

[1] Adolf Jülicher, *An introduction to the New Testament,* translated by Janet Penrose Ward (London, 1904), p. 350.

[2] See, for example, *Horae Synopticae*[2], p. 126, on 'context supplements' and p. 127 and n. 2 on Mk. 3. 9.

[3] *The Gospels as historical documents* (Cambridge, 1909), II, 325–6. Stanton, in explaining how Matthew could have been led to omit so many interesting details from Mark, argues in part as follows: 'We ought not to assume that whatever seems significant to us must have seemed so in another age. The vivid touches in Mark's narratives are prized by us as indications that his informant was an eye-witness. They had not the same importance for our first evangelist because the authenticity of the record was either not in question, or in so far as it was, would not have been defended on this ground.' See also p. 145.

[4] *The Gospel according to St Mark* (London, 1959), p. 135. Cf. *The Formation,* pp. 41–3.

if it be doubted that Mark's details provide historical recollec-
tions, 'it is necessary to account for the relative want of vivid
details in the narratives already classified as "'Markan Constructions"'.[1] He refers to such passages as Mk. 3. 13–19a;
3. 19b–21; 4. 10–12, etc.[2]

Taylor also argues from the inconsequence of the details to
their authenticity.

> What point, for example, is there in mentioning 'the hired servants' (1. 20),
> the fact that the paralytic was 'borne of four' (2. 3) [there follows a long
> list], unless these things were known and remembered?[3]

Despite all the arguments on behalf of details, however, it is
clear that Taylor, as the first quotation from his work indicated,
does not really think that details are self-authenticating as
indications of an early tradition. Only the details in Mark may
be regarded as indicating an early source. Thus he notes that
the 'one' of Mk. 10. 17//Mt. 19. 16 becomes a 'young man' in
Mt. 19. 22 and a 'ruler' in Lk. 18. 18. Again, in the Gospel
according to the Hebrews, the 'one' is 'two men', and the
detail is added that one of them scratches his head in puzzle-
ment. None of these details is early.[4] Taylor clearly states that
some details are early and some late, and states the criteria for
distinguishing them.

> Length and detail alone will not indicate a primitive story, otherwise we
> might so describe the account of the Raising of Lazarus (Jn. 11. 1–46). Only
> where details are not due to literary activity and are not subservient to
> doctrinal interests, can we be sure that we have to do with primitive stories.[5]

Similarly, Taylor distinguishes between what happened in the
'genuine historical tradition' of the Gospels and in the apocryphal literature. The loss of peripheral matters and concentration on the central figure, he says, 'is exactly what ought
to be the history of a genuine historical tradition; it is the reverse
of that which is found in the apocryphal literature'.[6]

There is a world of problems here. In the first place, such a
statement indicates that the tendency of the apocryphal tradition differed from that of the earlier Gospel tradition. Yet
Taylor had himself stated that light could be shed on the

---

[1] Taylor, *The Gospel according to St Mark*, p. 140.   [2] *Ibid.* pp. 82–5.
[3] *Ibid.* pp. 139–40.   [4] *Formation*, p. 66.
[5] *Ibid.* p. 126.   [6] *Ibid.* p. 166.

history of the early Gospel tradition by investigating the apocryphal literature.[1] In the second place, there is the supposition that the details which are due to 'literary activity' can be distinguished from those which are not. What Taylor means by 'literary activity', which he also calls 'literary art',[2] has primarily to do with good literary style. Thus in discussing the description of the demoniac in Mk. 5. 2–5, he comments that 'the roughness of this description relieves the story of the charge of literary embellishment; while the amount of detail forbids us to suppose that we have here a mere product of the community'.[3] Presumably if the details were due to 'literary activity', they would have been added with more grace! This leaves out of account the fact that the very detailed Apocryphal Gospels were frequently written quite roughly, without any discernible 'literary art'. There can be little doubt that Taylor actually would not like to be in the position of attributing primitiveness to poorly written details or lateness to well written ones.[4]

We may repeat that, for Taylor, details in Mark are early, but those which occur elsewhere are not. The real point of departure for him, as for Weisse, Stanton, and Hawkins, is that Mark rests, partially at least, on Peter's eye-witness account. It is Taylor's view that there is a positive correlation between the more detailed sections in Mark's Gospel and the sections which depend on Peter's testimony.[5] The view that Mark's Gospel rests partially upon Peter's account is derived from the testimony of the early Fathers, especially Papias and Irenaeus.[6]

We should refer at this point to the work of Cadbury, who has a balanced view of how the tradition developed with regard to details. Cadbury notes that uninteresting things tend to be

[1] See above, p. 20. [2] *Formation*, p. 126. [3] *Ibid.* pp. 122 f.
[4] The idea that any details which may have been added to the tradition must have been the result of artful literary embellishment, an idea which removes the suspicion of lateness from Mark's details, did not originate with Taylor. Thus F. H. Woods, 'The origin and mutual relation of the Synoptic Gospels', *Studia Biblica et Ecclesiastica* (Oxford, 1890), II, 95, writes as follows: 'It is in itself far more probable that the graphic details of St Mark, many of them of no importance from a religious or doctrinal point of view, should have fallen out in the more elaborate works of later evangelistic compilers, than that they should have been added by a later writer by way of embellishment, specially by one like St. Mark, who gives us little or no evidence of literary skill.'
[5] *The Gospel according to St Mark*, p. 82.
[6] *Ibid.* p. 26.

forgotten. Further, what is remembered is even told with a view to its interest. 'Unessential details tend to be omitted promptly, so much so that they cause remark when, as occasionally in Mark's gospel, they are retained.' He continues,

the place, the person, the time, in so far as they are not bound up with the point of the incident, tend to disappear...The settings of Jesus' sayings were early lost if the saying was memorable and complete in itself.[1]

This is true of miracle stories as well as sayings:

The circumstances are briefly told—the event and the effect. After repeated re-telling even the names of the persons and places disappear.[2]

As to Mark's details, Cadbury seems to agree with Taylor:

The stories [in Mark] are told with an objectivity and with a vividness of detail which suggest primitiveness quite as much as they suggest an editor's naïveté.

He adds that 'the present compiler does not betray any subjectiveness of his own'.[3]

Actually, however, Cadbury does not quite share Taylor's view. He thinks that the details and Aramaisms in Mark only show it to be relatively earlier than Matthew and Luke. The Markan material actually has behind it a rather complicated history. The material as a whole is of a 'secondary character', despite a few primitive remains. Thus he points out that

the literary structure of the book and the apparent history of its materials suggest that processes of gestation and development have been at work. This is compatible with the retention of primitive elements, but not compatible with a theory of the primitiveness of the whole.[4]

On pp. 87–8 of *The making of Luke-Acts*, Cadbury describes the position taken by Taylor and others and shows that he disagrees with it. Nevertheless, his view as to the relative primitiveness of details in Mark is the same as Taylor's.

Like Taylor also, Cadbury does not think that details are always early.

We should recall that meeting the current toward elimination of names is the counter current of late development, which localized legend and gave to simplified matter the verisimilitude of proper names...[5]

---

[1] H. J. Cadbury, *The making of Luke-Acts*, pp. 34–5. [2] *Ibid.* p. 51.
[3] *Ibid.* p. 79. [4] *Ibid.* p. 89; cf. also pp. 83–4.
[5] *Ibid.* p. 59. He gives examples from the Apocryphal Gospels. See also 'Between Jesus and the Gospels', *Harvard Theological Review* (1923), p. 89.

It is clear that Cadbury actually thinks of a kind of circle. The Gospel materials 'have passed from their original connection to their present connection through an intermediate stage of reduction to single units'.[1] The earliest tradition, then, was detailed, but the details were lost quite rapidly as the material was passed down in isolated pericopes. Details were once more added at a late stage when novelistic interest led to the filling out of the material. On this view details themselves do not prove primitiveness, but are the indications of it in documents already thought to be early.

W. S. Taylor, depending primarily on F. C. Bartlett's *Remembering*, came to a similar conclusion. He argued that the tendency of remembered material is to conform progressively to the conventional. It becomes shorter and less detailed. Single novel details are sometimes retained, however, as are details which are repeated. After a period of simplification a period of elaboration may begin, but still in the direction of conventional forms. General statements tend to be made concrete.[2]

The view of one other scholar with regard to details should now be briefly mentioned. Bussmann was of the opinion that details tended to be added. Luke, the least detailed Gospel, represents the earliest form of the narrative tradition, while Mark, the most detailed, represents the latest form.[3] Bussmann's theory was that a source document G (*Geschichtsquelle*) lay behind the Synoptic triple tradition, but had been used by our evangelists in different recensions. Luke used the earliest form and Matthew the second, while Mark itself is actually the third recension of the source G.[4] The principal criterion for establishing this sequence is the matter of details. Bussmann's view will be discussed again below.

Most of the discussion about details has centered around names of people and places and colorful items of information. We include in this category, however, also other matters of explicitness. Frequently explicitness involves a proper name, but not always. It may be that in one document the subject or object of a verb is understood, while in another it is supplied,

[1] *Ibid.* p. 50.
[2] W. S. Taylor, 'Memory and the Gospel Tradition', *Theology Today*, xv (1958), 472–94.
[3] Wilhelm Bussmann, *Synoptische Studien*, i, 85 ff. [4] *Ibid.* pp. 67, 111.

95

perhaps by the addition of a pronoun rather than a proper name. Schmid noted this, and thought that one of the ways Matthew and Luke improved Mark was by adding a subject or object or by making it more definite. His evidence, however, (twelve instances in which Matthew and Luke are more explicit, two in which Mark is) is so selective as to be misleading.[1] Stanton also regarded it as a sign of editorial work whenever Matthew or Luke has a subject where Mark is indefinite.[2] Further, Cadbury noted that Josephus added subjects when I Maccabees had a subject understood. Josephus also changed indefinite verbs ('they did so and so') by supplying a named person as subject.[3] The following lists pay a great deal of attention to this kind of evidence, which includes not only additions of new subjects but also making words more concrete, as by the substitution of a noun for a pronoun and the like. The subdivisions into which the material is divided should be self-explanatory.

THE EVIDENCE FROM THE POST-CANONICAL TRADITION

1a The addition of the subject

THE TEXTUAL TRADITION

Matthew

2. 14 reads as follows: 'And having risen up, he took the child and his mother...' 2It Prisc read: 'And having risen up, Joseph took the child and his mother...' This is abbreviated as follows:

2. 14 2It Prisc 'Joseph took'.

3. 6 C² 1Gr Hil 'All were baptized'.

3. 6 2Sy '*each one* confessing'.

3. 7 1Gr 1It 1Vg 'John seeing'.

3. 14 All but Al* B 1Sy 1Cop Eus 'John prevented'.

* 4. 4 D 1Gr 6It 2Sy Aeth

* 4. 12 C** L P W Ga De Th Si Ko Famm 1 & 13 7 + Gr 7It 4Sy 2Cop Aeth Arm Geo

* 4. 18 E De Om L 3 + Gr 5It Vg 1Sy

* 4. 19 C² 1Gr 4It 5Vg 2Sy Aeth

---

[1] Josef Schmid, *Matthäus und Lukas* (Freiburg, 1930), pp. 75 ff.
[2] Stanton, *op. cit.* II, 51.
[3] Cadbury, *The making of Luke-Acts*, pp. 174 f.
* An asterisk indicates that 'Jesus' is the subject added.

* 4. 21   1Sy
* 4. 23   Al C* D 10+Gr It (− 1) Vg 4Sy 1Cop Aeth Arm also C³ W Ga
           De Pi Si Ko 6+Gr Geo
* 5. 1   5It Vg 1Sy Geo
  5. 12   U 3It 2Sy 'their fathers persecuted'.
* 8. 3   All uncs but Al B C* Z; 5+Gr 10It Vg 5Sy 1Geo Hil
* 8. 7   All but Al B 2Gr 1It 1Sy 1Cop
  8. 18   6It 2Vg Hil 'he commanded (+his disciples) to go'.
  8. 25   C* C² E K L M S U V Ga De Pi Om W X Th Si Ph Famm 1 & 13
           13+Gr 4It 4Sy Aeth Geo Got Vg 'the disciples come'.
* 8. 26   6It 2Sy Arm
* 8. 32   C 7It 1Sy
* 9. 1   C* C³ F Th² 047 Fam 13 (− 1) 21Gr Vg
  9. 4   All uncs but Al B C D Fam 13 10+Gr 'you meditate'.
* 9. 12   All uncs and minusc but Al B D 047 4Gr also 12It Vg 1Cop Arm
           Got 3Sy Aeth
* 9. 28   1Geo
* 9. 29   1It
* 9. 36   G 2Gr 2It 2Vg 3Sy also C M N Si Fam 13 (− 1) 7Gr
*10. 1   C³ L Th² Fam 13 (− 1) 6Gr 1It 1Sy
*11. 20   C K L N W Y Th Pi Si Fam 13 18+Gr 2It 2Vg Sy 1Cop Aeth Geo
  12. 2   8It Vg 'not lawful (+for them) to do'.
*12. 3   Th 10Gr 3It
  12. 3   L Y Th Si^mg Ph Fam 13 (− 1) 3+Gr 8It 2Sy 'he hungered'.
*12. 9   C E G N Si 1Gr 3It 1Sy Arm Geo
*12. 11   Geo
*12. 13   1Geo
  12. 13   11Gr 'his hand was restored'.
*12. 25   All uncs but Al B D Most minusc 11It Vg 1Sy Aeth Arm Geo
*12. 39   1Gr
*12. 48   Geo
*13. 11   Geo
  13. 17   3Gr 3It 1Vg Eph Eus 4Sy 'you see'.
13. 31   L
*13. 33   1Sy
*13. 36   All uncs but Al B D Most minusc 3It 2Sy
*13. 37   7It
*13. 52   C N U Si 5Gr 1Sy 1It 1Vg
*13. 54   1Sy
  14. 6   Geo 'her dance pleased'.
  14. 11   4Gr 2Vg 1Sy 1Cop also 1It 4Vg also 7It 'the girl brought'.
*14. 14   All uncs but Al B D Th Most minusc 4It 1Sy Geo Or

        * An asterisk indicates that 'Jesus' is the subject added.

7   97   S S T

*14. 18   8It 1Sy 1Geo

*14. 22   C³ L X Ga Th² Pi Ko Fam 13 6+Gr 7It

*14. 25   C³ E F G K L M U X Y Th Pi Ph Fam 13 6+Gr 6It 3Sy 1Cop Aeth Arm Geo

*14. 29   E 1Gr 1Sy

*15. 3   1It 1Geo 1Sy

*15. 10   1Sy

15. 10   2It '*you* hear'.

*15. 13   5It

*15. 16   All uncs but Al B D O Z Most minusc 2It 1Sy Geo

*15. 23   5It Aeth

*15. 24   1It

*15. 26   1Sy

*15. 29   1Gr

*15. 36   7It Vg

Mark

* 9. 2   W𝔓⁴⁵ Fam 13 1Gr

9. 8   2Sy 'his disciples looking around'.

* 9. 9   2Gr Aeth

* 9. 12   2It

* 9. 16   1Geo

* 9. 19   Fam 13 3Gr 2It 3Sy 1Geo also W Th 𝔓⁴⁵ 2Gr

* 9. 21   Ph Fam 1 5Gr 4It 3Sy Aeth also N Th Si

9. 26   2It Arm 'the child became as dead'.

9. 26   1It 'the child is dead'.

* 9. 28   1It 2Sy

* 9. 29   G 2It 3Vg

* 9. 33   Om 4Gr

* 9. 35   1It 1Sy

*10. 1   1It

10. 5   D Ps 11Gr 6It 1Sy 1Cop 1Geo 'Moses wrote'.

*10. 11   1Gr 1It

10. 24   A C D N X Y Ga Th Pi Si Ph Ko All minusc It (−2) Vg 3Sy 1Cop Geo Arm Clem 'it is difficult (+for those who trust in riches) to enter'/W 1It '(+for a rich man) to enter'.

10. 27   C² D N W Th Si Fam 13 8Gr 1It 2Sy Arm 1Cop 1Geo Aeth '*this is impossible*'.

*10. 32   F H Ga 6Gr 1Sy

*10. 36   Si Ph 1Gr

10. 48   1Gr '*he* cried out'.

*11. 1   3Gr

* An asterisk indicates that 'Jesus' is the subject added.

*11. 1 1Sy

*11. 11 1Gr 2It 1Sy Aeth Arm also A N X Y Ga Pi Si Ph Ko Fam 13
6+Gr 1It 1Sy

*11. 14 X Y Ga Pi² Ko (−2) 4+Gr also W 0188 1Cop

*11. 15 Geo

*11. 15 A N X Y Ga Th Pi Si Ph Ko Fam 13 (−1) 6+Gr 2It 2Sy

11. 20 1It 'the disciples passing by'/1It 'those who were with him passing
by'.

11. 23 A N X Y Ga Th Pi Si Ph Ps Ko Fam 13 10+Gr 7It 2Sy Arm
'(+whatever he says) will be'.

11. 29 A K Y Pi also E F H S U V X also Al D N W X Ga Th Si Ph Ko
𝔓⁴⁵ Famm 1 & 13 14+Gr It (−1) Vg 3Sy Geo '*I* ask'.

11. 29 Alᶜ '*I* will tell'.

*12. 1 2It

12. 13 2Gr 'the chief priests and the scribes sent'.

12. 14 D 1Gr 3It 'the Pharisees ask' for 'they say'.

*12. 15 D G Th Famm 1 & 13 5Gr It Aeth Arm

*12. 16 1Geo

12. 27 A D X Ga Th Pi Si Ph Ko (−1) Fam 13 8+Gr 5It Vg 2Sy 1Geo
Arm also G Fam 1 4Gr 3It 1Sy 2Geo Aeth '*you* are led astray'.

*12. 41 A D W X Ga Th Pi Si Ph Ko Famm 1 & 13 10+Gr It Vg 4Sy
1Cop Aeth Arm Geo Or (3 diff. readings)

*12. 43 5Gr 1It 2Sy 1Geo

13. 7 8Gr 3It Vg (2 diff. subjs.) 'it is necessary (+for all things, for these
things) to happen'.

14. 8 A C D X Y Ga De Pi Si Ph Ko 0116 8+Gr It Vg '*this one* did'.

14. 12 1Sy 'The Jews sacrificed'.

*14. 16 2Gr

*14. 20 1Gr

*14. 22 Al A C L P X Y Ga De Th Pi Si Ph Ps 0116 Ko Most minusc
5It Vg 2Sy 1Cop 1Geo Aeth Arm

14. 31 A C G M N S U W Th Si Ph Om Famm 1 & 13 13+Gr 2Sy Geo
Aeth Arm 'Peter said'.

14. 44 1Gr '*I* shall kiss'.

14. 50 N W Th Si Fam 13 10Gr 2It Vg 'the disciples leaving'.

14. 51 A C² N P X Y Ga Pi Si Ph 0116 Ko 6+Gr 1It 1Sy Aeth Arm also
W Th Famm 1 & 13 9Gr Geo 1Sy 'the youths seized him'.

*14. 61 Al A 12Gr 1Sy 1Geo Aeth

14. 64 G N W Si Fam 1 11Gr 1It Geo Arm '*all* heard'.

14. 70 M 1It '*you* are of them'.

*15. 2 N Si 2Gr Geo Aeth

15. 6 W Fam 13 1Gr 1It 1Cop 'the governor released'.

* An asterisk indicates that 'Jesus' is the subject added.

15. 10   2Sy 'Pilate knew'.
15. 26   D 2Gr 3It 1Sy 1Geo '*this is* the king'.
15. 36   1Gr 'the rest [said]' for 'saying'. Cf. Mt. 27. 49.
*15. 44   1It
15. 46   D Th Si 4Gr It (−1) Vg 1Sy Aug 'Joseph bought'.
16. 2   1Gr 'women come'.
16. 6   D 1It 'the angel says'.
9. 10   1Gr 'the disciples seized'.
9. 50   W Fam 13 (−1) 3Gr 1Cop Arm '*you* have'.
11. 4   1It 'those two went away'.
12. 27   Th Fam 13 4Gr 'God is (+God) of the living'.
12. 32   E F H W 092 1+Gr also D G Th Fam 13 7Gr It (−2) Vg 2Sy
         2Cop 1Geo Arm Euseb Hil 'God is one'.
13. 18   Al^c A X Y Ga De Pi Si Ph Ps Ko Fam 1 8+Gr 2It Vg 2Sy 2Cop
         2Geo Aeth also L Th 8Gr 5It 1Geo Arm 'your flight may not be'.
         Cf. Matthew.
14. 41   D W Th Ph Fam 13 7Gr 7It

The Jewish Gospel to Mt. 15. 5 (de Santos, p. 47) adds the pronoun 'you'
    as subj.
Protev. Jms. 21. 3; cf. Mt. 2. 11. 'and (+the Magi) saw'.
Pseud. Matt. Lat. 15. 1; cf. Lk. 2. 22 '(+Joseph) took'. But Lk. has a plural
    verb.
Pseud. Matt. Lat. 16. 2; cf. Mt. 2. 10. '(+the Magi), seeing the star'.
Pseud. Thom. 19. 3; cf. Lk. 2. 49. '(+Jesus) said'.
Gosp. Pet. 10; cf. Mk. 14. 61. '(+*he*) held his peace'.
Act. Pil. 3. 1; cf. Jn. 18. 30. '(+The Jews) answered'.
Act. Pil. 10. 1; cf. Lk. 23. 34. '(+the soldiers) divided'.
Act. Pil. 10. 2; cf. Lk. 23. 43. '(+Jesus) said'.
Act. Pil. 13. 1; cf. Mt. 28. 6. '(+the Lord) lay'. So also A C D L W Ga De
    Pi Si Ko Most minusc It (−1) Vg 3Sy. Ph has 'Jesus lay'. 5Gr have
    'The body of the Lord lay'.
Jos. Arim. 2. 4; cf. Mt. 26. 48 par. 'whomever (+I) kiss'.
Just. Apol. 1. 15. 11; cf. Mt. 6. 19. Adds 'you'.
II Clem. 5. 4; cf. Mt. 10. 28. '(+*you*) do not fear'.

    * An asterisk indicates that 'Jesus' is the subject added.

1b The omission of the subject

THE TEXTUAL TRADITION

Matthew

1. 24   reads: 'Joseph, having risen up...did as the angel of the Lord commanded him. 2Gr 1Vg read: 'Having risen up..., he did...' This is abbreviated as follows:

1. 24   '(−Joseph) having risen'.

* 3. 16   3Gr 1It Vg 2Sy Eus

* 4. 1   2Gr 1Geo

* 4. 17   1Gr

6. 9   2Gr '(−you) pray'.

8. 8   Fam 1 1Gr 1It 1Cop '(−my child) will be healed'.

8. 9   1Gr '(−I) am'.

* 8. 13   2Gr

* 8. 14   7Gr 1Cop

* 8. 22   Al 1Gr 4It 1Sy

8. 32   1Geo

* 9. 15   M 1Gr

9. 18   1Gr '(−he) speaking'.

* 9. 19   1Vg

* 9. 22   Al* D 1Gr 6It 1Sy

* 9. 23   1Gr

9. 25   1Sy '(−the girl) arose'.

* 9. 28   8Gr 1Sy

* 9. 35   2Gr 2Vg

10. 2   D 3It 1Sy 'and (−coming up, Pharisees) asked'.

10. 16   1Gr '(−I) send'.

10. 32   1Sy Epiph '(−I) shall confess'.

10. 33   2Vg Epiph '(−I) shall deny'.

*11. 7   2Cop

11. 10   Z 1Gr 3It Vg 2Sy 1Cop Geo '(−I) send'.

*11. 25   1Gr

*12. 15   1Gr

12. 24   1Gr '(−this one) does not cast out'.

12. 27   1Gr '(−I) cast out'.

12. 28   M 047 10Gr 4It 1Sy '(−I) cast out'.

*13. 34   1It

*13. 57   Al 1Gr

14. 2   1It 2Sy '(−he) is raised'.

14. 11   2Cop '(−his head) was brought'.

*14. 13   0106 1Gr

* An asterisk indicates that 'Jesus' is the subject omitted.

14. 16 Al D 6Gr 2It 3Sy 2Cop Aeth
14. 20 1It '(–all) ate'.
14. 26 Al* Th 10Gr 10It Vg Cop Eus Aug '(–the disciples) seeing'.
14. 27 Al D 084 5Gr 3It 1Sy 2Cop Eus
14. 28 1Sy (subj. of inf.) 'command (–me) to come'.
14. 31 E 1Vg
*15. 21 4Gr 1Cop
*15. 28 D Ga 1Gr 1It 1Vg 2Sy 1Cop
*15. 29 D (?) 1Gr 3It
*15. 34 7Gr 1Cop
15. 37 1Gr 1It '(–all) ate'.

Mark

9. 15 1Sy '(–all the crowd) seeing'.
9. 21 De 1It 2Vg '(–this) has been'.
* 9. 23 1Gr
9. 25 Al* '(–I) command'.
* 9. 39 D W Famm 1 & 13 (–1) 2Gr
10. 4 Th 1Gr 4It '(–Moses) permitted'.
*10. 5 3Gr
*10. 18 De
*10. 21 A K Y De Pi 9Gr
10. 28 W '(–Lo! we) have left'.
*10. 29 Ga
*10. 38 De Th 4Gr 1It 1Sy 1Cop
*10. 39 6Gr
*10. 42 1Sy 1Geo W 1Gr
10. 48 2Gr 3It 2Vg '(–many) rebuked'.
*10. 51 Th 1Gr
*10. 52 W 1Sy 1Cop 1Geo
11. 3 1Gr 4It Vg Aeth 'what is (–this) you do'?
*11. 6 1Gr
11. 11 B 2Gr '(–the hour) being already late'.
11. 12 1Gr 'while (–they) were going out'.
11. 14 De 1Gr 'may (–any one) eat'.
*11. 22 1Gr
*11. 29 9Gr
*11. 33 1Sy
*12. 17 W Th 4Gr 2It 1Cop 1Geo
12. 19 1Gr 'if (–a brother) should die'.
*12. 24 1It
12. 26 1Gr '(–God) spoke to him (–saying)'.

* An asterisk indicates that 'Jesus' is the subject omitted.

*12. 29 W 1Gr

*12. 35 W 1Gr

12. 35 W '(— the Christ) is the Son of David'.

*13. 2 W Th 2Gr 3It 2Vg

13. 3 1Gr 'while (— he) was sitting'.

*13. 5 3Gr 2It

13. 12 1Gr '(— brother) will hand over'.

13. 13 W Si 1Vg '(— this one) will be saved'. See also omission of casus pendens.

13. 19 1It 'which (— God) made'.

13. 20 W 4Gr 1Geo '(— the Lord) shortened'.

13. 29 1Gr (— υμεις) οταν ιδητε.

*14. 18 4Gr 3It 1Cop

14. 21 D 1Gr 1It '(— the Son of man) is handed over'.

14. 21 2Sy 1Cop Iren 'if (— that man) had not been born'.

14. 22 W 'while (— they) were eating'.

14. 23 1Sy '(— all) drank'.

*14. 27 1Gr 3It

*14. 30 X

*14. 30 Al C D De Ph 2 + Gr It(− 2) 1Geo

14. 41 1Gr '(— the Son of man) is handed over'.

*14. 48 1Gr

14. 50 N 12Gr '(— all) fled'.

*14. 62 4Gr

14. 64 1Gr '(— all) condemned'.

14. 65 1Vg '(— certain ones) began'.

14. 65 D 2It '(— the guards) received'.

14. 68 D 1Gr It Vg '(— you) say'.

15. 10 B 4Gr 1Sy 1Cop '(— the chief priests) handed him over'.

15. 11 1Gr '(— the chief priests) stirred up'. (Omitted by lectionary 17.)

*15. 34 D Th 1Gr 1It 1Sy 1Cop

15. 35 De '(— and certain of the ones standing by, hearing) said'.

THE APOCRYPHAL AND PATRISTIC TRADITIONS

Pseud. Thom. 19. 3; cf. Lk. 2. 48. '(— your father and I) seek'.

Just. Apol. 1. 15. 12; cf. Mt. 16. 26. Omits 'man'.

Just. Dial. 76. 4; cf. Mt. 8. 11. '(— many) shall come'. Also Dial. 120. 6 and 140. 4.

II Clem. 3. 2; cf. Mt. 10. 32. '(— I) shall confess'.

* An asterisk indicates that 'Jesus' is the subject omitted.

2a   The addition of the direct object

THE TEXTUAL TRADITION

Matthew

2. 3   reads: 'When Herod heard, he was astounded.' Geo reads: 'When Herod heard this, he was astounded.' This change is indicated as follows:

2. 3   Geo
2. 9   Geo
4. 23   Al*
5. 17   3It 1Sy 2Cop
5. 17   2Sy 2Cop
6. 9   4It
6. 14   L 5Gr 6It Vg 1Cop Aeth Aug Faust
6. 18   1Gr
8. 4   Ga 3Gr (makes double negative)
8. 10   C N Si 14+Gr It Vg All vss
8. 10   N Si 1Gr Geo
8. 25   All uncs but Al B C Most minusc All vss
9. 8   1Gr
9. 27   All but B D 1Gr 2It
10. 31   M W Fam 13(−1) 7Gr 1It 4Vg 1Cop
11. 1   1Gr 3It 7Vg (Four different objects are added by various of the MSS.)
11. 14   2Cop Aeth
12. 2   C D L De Th Fam 13 10Gr 8It 3Sy
12. 13   6It 4Sy Aeth 1Geo 2Cop (diff. obj.)
12. 30   Al 2Gr 1Cop Aeth
12. 34   D* 1It
12. 44   D 1It (noun) 3It Vg 1Cop Geo (pron.)
13. 3   6Gr 3It Vg 1Sy Eph
13. 44   2It 4Sy (makes Sem.)
13. 48   P S De Ph Om 7Gr 2Sy
14. 3   All uncs but Al* B Most minusc It(−1) Vg 3Sy 2Cop
14. 3   3It 2Vg 3Sy 2Cop 1Gr
14. 11   M 5Gr 2Cop
14. 19   2Sy
14. 30   W (inf. obj. of vb.)

Mark

9. 26   Al* A C³ N X Y Ga Th Pi Si Ph Ko Most minusc It(−4) Vg 3Sy 2Cop Aeth Arm
10. 4   N 1Sy 1Cop

10. 5   1It
10. 16   1Gr
10. 32   Fam 13 1Gr 1It
10. 34   A* C N W X Y Ga Pi Si Ph Ps Ko Fam 13 7+Gr Vg
11. 17   1Gr 1It
12. 8   1It 1Sy 1Cop
12. 38   F 3Gr 3It (cf. add. dat.)
12. 41   W
12. 43   1Gr 2It
13. 14   D 3It
13. 19   2Gr
14. 1   3Gr
14. 1   3It 2Sy 1Gr
14. 15   Or
14. 20   A 1Gr 4It Vg 1Sy 2Cop also 2It
14. 68   M Y 6Gr
14. 68   1Gr
15. 1   W Fam 13(−1) 9Gr 2Sy 2Cop Aeth
15. 8   D 2It
15. 29   2Cop Eus
15. 32   C³ D E F G H M* P V² Ga Th Pi² Si Famm 1 & 13 21+Gr It 4Vg
         1Sy 1Cop Geo Aeth Arm Eus
15. 35   1Gr

THE APOCRYPHAL TRADITION

Pseud. Matt. Lat. 16. 1; cf. Mt. 2. 8. 'when you have found + him.'
Nat. Mary 10. 2; cf. Mt. 1. 24. 'he took (+ the virgin) [as] his wife.'
Pseud. Thom. 19. 2; cf. Lk. 2. 45. 'not finding + him.'
Act. Pil. 4. 1; cf. Mt. 26. 61. 'to build + it.' So also all MSS of Mt. but B Th
         8Gr Arm Geo Or.
Act. Pil. 10. 1; cf. Lk. 23. 35. 'beholding + him.'
Act. Pil. 10. 1; cf. Lk. 23. 35. 'mocked + him.'
Act. Pil. 13. 3; cf. Mt. 28. 14. 'we shall persuade + him.'[1] So also all MSS
         of Mt. but Al B Th 1Gr 1It.
Jos. Arim. 1. 4; cf. Mt. 26. 61. Jos. has 'to raise *it*' for Mt.'s 'to build'.
II Clem. 5. 4; cf. Lk. 12. 5. 'after killing + you.'

2b   The omission of the direct object

Matthew			
1. 19	1Gr	2. 16	Z
2. 8	2Geo	2. 22	1Sy
		3. 11	Or

[1] The U.B.S. text accepts the αὐτὸν in Mt. 28. 14.

5. 15	4Gr	13. 30	D It(−2) Vg
5. 28	De Pi^suppl mg	13. 39	2It
5. 41	L De 1It	13. 51	1Sy
5. 42	1It	14. 5	Si
5. 44	3Gr	14. 12	1Geo
7. 29	1Vg Arm	14. 19	1Gr 1It 1Sy
8. 3	1Gr	14. 22	D 1Gr 6It Arm
8. 31	2Gr	14. 30	2Gr
9. 9	1Gr	14. 35	1Gr
9. 24	2Gr	14. 36	B* 2Gr 1It Or
10. 17	C* 1Gr	15. 23	Z Arm
13. 3	L V 2Gr 1It 1Vg	cf. 6. 33	4Gr Just. 'the kingdom (−
13. 30	D 1Gr 4It		and his righteousness).'

Mark

9. 12	1Gr	12. 8	Geo 1Gr 1It Arm
9. 15	Fam 1(−1) 1Gr 2Geo	12. 8	Al L W X De Ko(−1)
9. 15	1Gr		Famm 1 & 13 7+Gr 4It
9. 18	De 1Gr Arm		Vg
9. 18	Al D W 1It	12. 14	2Gr
9. 18	1Gr 1It	12. 19	1Gr
9. 20	1It	12. 28	1It
9. 22	K 1Gr 2Geo Arm	12. 34	Al D L W De Th Fam 1
9. 27	W 1Gr 1Geo		8+Gr It(−1) Vg 2Sy Geo
9. 27	3Gr		Aeth Arm Hil
9. 36	W Th Fam 1 2Gr Arm	12. 37	2Gr
9. 39	D 1Gr 4It	13. 11	1Gr
9. 39	1Geo	14. 1	7Gr 2It
9. 50	M Ga Fam 1 6Gr It	14. 3	2It
10. 34	De	14. 30	L Th 1Gr
10. 34	N 1Gr	14. 31	2Gr
10. 42	2Gr also Fam 1(−1) 2Gr	14. 44	3Gr 1It 1Sy
	also W 1Gr	14. 62	1Gr
10. 49	1Gr	14. 65	2Gr
11. 2	2Gr	14. 67	1Gr
11. 18	A K Pi 7 Gr 2It	15. 2	1Gr
11. 22	1Gr 3It 1Cop (obj. gen.:	15. 4	B* 2Gr
	makes 'faith' abs.)	15. 12	B
12. 1	1It	15. 13	1Gr
12. 3	1Gr	15. 15	1Gr
12. 5	X	15. 24	3Gr
		15. 32	2It

Pseud. Thom. 19. 2; cf. Lk. 2. 46. 'both hearing (–them) and asking them.' The first 'them' in Lk. is in the genitive.

Act. Pil. 13. 3; cf. Mt. 28. 15. 'taking (–money).'

Act. Pil. 14. 1; cf. Mk. 16. 15. 'preach (–the Gospel).'

Cf. also Pseud. Thom. 19. 2; cf. Lk. 2. 44. 'among (en) their kinsfolk (–and acquaintances).'

Justin Apol. I. 15. 1; cf. Mt. 5. 28. εμοιχευσε (–αυτην). So also De Pi. This may improve the grammar.

Just. Apol. I. 15. 10; cf. Lk. 6. 30//Mt. 5. 42. 'asks (–you).'

Just. Apol. I. 15. 11; cf. Mt. 6. 19. '(–treasures).' Same 15. 11, 12; cf. Mt. 6. 20.

Athen. 12. 3; cf. Mt. 5. 46 par. 'the ones loving (–you).'

Athen. 32. 1; cf. Mt. 5. 28. μεμοιχευκεν for Mt.'s εμοιχευσεν αυτην. See Just. Apol. I. 15. 1 above.

Just. Dial. 133. 6; cf. Lk. 6. 27. 'the ones hating (–you).'

Just. Dial. 133. 6; cf. Lk. 6. 28. 'the ones cursing (–you).'

Athen. 11. 1; cf. Lk. 6. 28. 'the ones cursing (–you).'

3a The addition of indirect objects and equivalent πρός phrases

THE TEXTUAL TRADITION

Matthew

1. 21 reads: 'She will bear a son...' 2Sy read: 'She will bear to you a son...' This is indicated as follows:

1. 21 2Sy

2. 6 C K Ga 11Gr Or

2. 8 D 2Gr 1It 3Sy Aeth

3. 16 Al^b C D^suppl L P W Ga De Si Ko All minusc It Vg 2Sy 1Cop Aeth Arm Hip Aug

3. 17 D 5It 2Sy

4. 4 4Gr 1It 3Vg 3Sy

5. 22 L Th Famm 1 & 13(–1) 3+Gr 2Sy 1Cop Arm Geo Tat

5. 27 L M De Th 5+Gr 8It 3Sy 1Geo Eus Iren

6. 14 1Gr

6. 15 Al D 6Gr It Vg 4Sy 2Cop Arm Geo Aug

7. 15 7It Vg 2Sy

8. 8 U 2It 1Cop

8. 8 4It 4Vg 2Sy

8. 10 2Gr

8. 19 3It 2Cop Aeth

8. 25 C* Vg

9. 2   D De** 2Gr 1It 1Vg Or Iren Aug also L X Th Pi Ph Fam 13 5 + Gr It Vg Sy 2Cop Arm Geo Iren
9. 4   D N Th Si Fam 13 6Gr 3It 1Vg 3Sy 2Cop Arm Geo
9. 5   3Gr Tert
9. 5   8Gr 8It Sy 2Cop Aeth Arm Geo
9. 12 All uncs but Al B C* D X Most minusc 4It 3Sy 1Cop Aeth Arm Geo Got
9. 14 1Gr 1Geo
9. 18 C³ F G L U Fam 13(−1) 4 + Gr Geo
9. 23 C L W Y Ga De Th Pi Ph Ko 5 + Gr 3It 3Sy Geo Got
9. 28 Al* 9It Vg 2Sy Arm
9. 29 1Sy 1Geo
10. 5 2Sy
10. 9 1Sy Arm
11. 1 1Gr
11. 2 2It Hil
11. 17 All uncs but Al B D Z 8 + Gr 5It 4Vg 4Sy Aeth Arm 1Geo Aug
11. 18 Th Fam 13 11Gr 3Sy
12. 13 4It 1Vg Hil
12. 30 1Sy
12. 31 All uncs but Al B Fam 13 8 + Gr 8It Sy 1Geo 1Cop Aeth
12. 38 2Sy Arm
13. 10 C 1It
13. 11 All uncs but Al C Z Most minusc It Vg Sy 1Cop Arm Geo[1]
13. 12 1Gr 1It 2Sy 1Cop Arm
13. 29 D N O Th Si 1Gr 5It 3Vg 2Sy 2Cop Geo
13. 36 3Sy
13. 37 All uncs but Al B D Most minusc 5It Vg Sy Arm Geo
14. 9 Th Fam 13 14Gr 2Sy 1Cop Aeth Arm also 1It
14. 18 P 4Gr 2It Vg 3Sy 2Cop Geo
14. 24 Th Ph 5Vg 6It 1Sy (dat. obj. after adj.)
15. 12 F 2It 2Sy 2Cop
15. 16 O Si 9Gr 4Sy Geo 1It 2Cop Aeth (2 diff. adds.)
15. 22 L W X Ga De Pi Ph o119 Ko Most minusc 6It Vg 1Sy Aug
15. 23 1Sy
15. 26 3Gr Geo also 2It 3Sy
15. 32 Al C K Pi 19Gr 3Sy 2Cop Aeth 1Geo
15. 34 D 2Gr 1Vg 3Sy 1Geo

Mark

9. 33 A N W X Y Ga Th Pi Si Ph Ko Famm 1 & 13 9 + Gr 1It 4Sy 1Cop 2Geo Aeth Arm

[1] 'To them' is bracketed in the U.B.S. text.

108

9. 39   1Gr 2It 2Sy also 1Cop

10. 2   2Gr

10. 4   2It

10. 14   1Cop 1Geo

10. 27   2Gr

10. 27   2Sy 1Cop Aeth Ga Th 2Gr

10. 29   Al 1Gr/1Gr/1Geo/1It

10. 40   7It Vg Aeth

11. 2   4Gr

11. 3   2Gr 2Sy

11. 6   D M W Th Ph Famm 1 & 13(−1) 12+Gr It Vg 2Sy 2Cop Geo
Aeth

11. 26   D 10+Gr 6It Vg 2Sy

11. 31   1Sy Aeth

11. 31   D M W Th Famm 1 & 13 5Gr It(−3) Vg 2Sy 1Cop Geo Aeth Arm

12. 1   C² N W Th Si Ps 4Gr 3Sy 2Cop Aeth Arm Or/1It

12. 1   1Gr

12. 3   D 3It

12. 6   2Gr 1Sy Aeth 'beloved + to him'.

12. 16   1Gr 2It Vg 2Cop 2Sy Aeth

12. 17   All uncs but B D (sup. by 𝔓⁴⁵) All minusc It(−2) Vg 3Sy 2Cop
Geo Aeth Arm Aug

12. 28   5Gr/2Cop 1Geo

12. 28   De

12. 29   W Th Fam 13(−1) 6Gr 2It Arm/D 5It/1It 1Sy/1Gr/1Geo/A C X
Ga Pi Si Ph Ko 5+Gr 3It Vg 1Sy Aug

12. 38   3Gr 1Sy/A X Ga Pi Si Ph Ko(−1) Fam 1(−1) Fam 13(−1) 5+Gr
3It Vg 1Sy 1Cop Geo(−1) Aeth (Cf. add. dir. obj.)/D Th 1Gr 3It

13. 21   1Sy

14. 3   Fam 13 1Gr

14. 6   D W Th 2Gr It(−3) 2Vg 2Sy 2Cop 1Geo Aeth Arm

14. 11   De 3Gr 1Cop Aeth

14. 12   D De Th Ps 9Gr It(−2) Vg 1Cop 1Geo Aeth Or

14. 16   4Gr

14. 16   1Gr

14. 18   9Gr 1It 2Vg 1Sy 2Cop 1Geo Arm Aeth

14. 22   W De Th 2Gr 2It 2Sy 1Cop Aeth

14. 37   1Gr 3It

14. 45   E G H S V Y Ph Om 0116 10+Gr 1Sy also N Si 3Gr

14. 52   1Cop

14. 53   A D (N) P X Y Ga Pi Si Ph Ps Ko 6+Gr 3Sy 1Cop 1Geo Arm/C

14. 60   1Sy 1Cop Aeth

14. 61   1Sy 2Geo

14. 62 D G W Th Famm 1 & 13 7Gr It(−1) Vg 3Sy 2Cop 2Geo Aeth
Arm Or
14. 65 D Th 2Gr 3It 1Sy Geo Arm
14. 65 Ps 4Gr 4It/1Gr 1It Vg/1Gr/N U X De Th Si 067 13+Gr 1Sy 1Cop
Geo Aeth Arm/1Sy
14. 66 D Th 6It Eus
14. 67 D 3It 2Sy 2Cop
14. 68 1Geo
15. 15 F 2Gr 1It 2Vg 3Sy Geo
15. 31 Th 1Gr 1Cop

THE APOCRYPHAL TRADITION

Egerton Pap. 2, Fragm. 1, line 33 (de Santos, p. 98). Mt. 8. 2. 'coming up+
to him.'
Pseud. Matt. Lat. 16. 1. Mt. 2. 7. 'called the Magi+to himself' (*ad se*).
Pseud. Matt. Lat. 17. 2. Mt. 2. 13. 'said+to him.'
Act. Pil. 3. 2. Jn. 18. 34. 'Jesus answered+to Pilate.' (dative)
Act. Pil. 3. 2. Jn. 18. 35. 'Pilate answered+to Jesus.' (*pros*)
Act. Pil. 3. 2. Jn. 18. 37. 'answered+to him.'

3b The omission of indirect objects and equivalent πρός phrases

THE TEXTUAL TRADITION

Matthew

2. 5	Al^cor 1Gr 1It Vg Geo	12. 2	1Gr 1Vg
3. 15	1It 1Sy 1Cop	12. 18	1Gr
4. 6	1Sy	12. 38	N W X Y G De Pi Ph
4. 9	Arm		Ko(−1) Fam 1 6Gr 1It
4. 10	1Gr 2Geo		1Sy Arm
5. 30	2Vg	12. 47	Al^a
5. 40	Or	12. 48	W Z 1It
6. 18	1Gr	13. 13	L 1It Cyr
7. 9	1Gr	13. 14	2It 1Sy
8. 19	1Cop	13. 27	2Cop
8. 20	1Sy	13. 28	3Gr 1Geo
8. 21	2Gr	13. 28	1Gr
9. 14	X 2Gr 1Sy 2Geo Got	13. 36	2Gr 1Sy
9. 18	Fam 1 10Gr 2Cop	14. 4	Al* 2Gr 1Vg 1Cop
9. 30	2Gr	14. 15	1Gr Geo
11. 4	2Gr	14. 16	4Gr 5It 1Cop Arm
11. 25	1It 2Sy	14. 18	Arm
11. 28	3Gr 1It	14. 27	4Gr
		14. 28	De 10Gr 6It Vg

14. 28	3Gr		10. 52	4It
14. 35	1Gr		11. 2	Fam 1(−1) 1Gr 1Sy 1Geo
15. 1	2Gr		11. 5	1It 1Sy 1Cop
15. 3	D 3It 1Geo		11. 6	D 1Gr 6It 1Vg
15. 12	1Vg Arm		11. 17	1It
15. 15	3Gr 1It 1Cop		11. 21	1It 1Cop
15. 28	Th 1Gr 3It 1Sy		11. 22	1Cop
15. 33	1It		11. 23	1Sy 1Geo Aeth
			11. 25	3Gr 4It

Mark

			11. 28	1Geo
9. 4	1It		11. 31	1Sy
9. 9	1Gr 1It		11. 33	1Geo
9. 17	A N X Y Ga Pi Si Ph Ko Many minusc 3It Vg 1Sy		11. 33	1It
			12. 1	1Gr 2It 1Sy 1Geo
9. 19	C* Fam 13 7Gr 1It 1Geo		12. 2	W
9. 20	D It(−1)		12. 4	Fam 1(−1) 2Gr 1Cop Arm
9. 21	1Gr 2Vg 1Sy		12. 6	D It 1Vg 2Geo
9. 23	2Cop		12. 13	D 7It 1Cop
9. 25	Th 𝔓⁴⁵ 4Gr 2It 1Vg Geo		12. 16	1Gr
9. 31	B 1It		12. 16	W Famm 1 & 13(−1) 9Gr 4It 1Sy Geo
9. 38	4Gr 2It		
9. 42	U W 2Gr		12. 26	3Gr 1Sy
10. 3	1It		12. 28	4Gr
10. 5	D 2Gr 1It		12. 43	1Gr
10. 5	D Fam 13 6Gr 5It Geo Arm		13. 1	1Gr
			13. 4	2Gr
10. 14	Geo		13. 5	3+Gr
10. 18	7Gr Clem		14. 4	D Th 1It/3It 1Geo 1Sy
10. 20	K Y Pi 5Gr 6It Vg 1Geo		14. 6	V* 2Gr 1It Arm
10. 21	1Gr Clem		14. 15	Or
10. 26	1Gr Clem		14. 19	K Pi 1Gr 4It Vg
10. 27	2Gr 1It		14. 21	1It
10. 28	2It 1Sy		14. 24	B
10. 32	1Gr		14. 29	Th 3Vg
10. 35	A N W X Y Ga Pi Si Ph Ps Ko Famm 1 & 13 5+Gr It(−2) Vg 1Sy 2Geo Aug		14. 30	W
			14. 34	1Gr
			14. 40	5Gr 1Cop
			14. 45	2Gr
10. 36	2Gr 5It		14. 48	1Gr
10. 37	3It Vg 1Geo		14. 54	1It
10. 39	D W Th Fam 1(−1) 9Gr It (−3)		14. 61	6Gr 3It 1Sy 2Geo Arm
			14. 65	W o67 Famm 1(−1) & 13 1Gr 2Sy Arm
10. 52	1Sy Pers		
			14. 67	D 3It

14. 70	D 1It	15. 14	Al* Ps
15. 2	W 3Gr 4It Aug	15. 41	Ps 1It
15. 6	1It	15. 41	N Si

THE APOCRYPHAL AND PATRISTIC TRADITIONS

Act. Pil. 3. 1; cf. Jn. 18. 31. 'said (− to them).'

Act. Pil. 3. 2; cf. Jn. 18. 37. 'said (− to him).'

Just. Apol. 1. 16. 2; cf. Mt. 5. 22. 'angry (− at his brother).'

4a   The addition of non-adjectival prepositional phrases

THE TEXTUAL TRADITION

Matthew

2. 2   reads: 'We have come to worship him.' Vg reads: 'We have come with presents to worship him.' This is indicated as follows:

2. 2	2Vg
2. 13	B
2. 14	2It
2. 17	D 2It
3. 16	D 1Gr 7It 3Vg 1Sy Hil
4. 3	Eph
4. 10	C² D E L M U Z Ga Om 14+ Gr 4It 3Sy 2Cop Aeth Arm 1Geo/4It Vg Eph
4. 11	2Sy Eph
5. 12	2It 2Sy
5. 42	2Cop Arm 1It 1Sy
6. 4	L W X De Th Pi Si Ph Ko Fam 13 6+ Gr 9It 4Sy Aeth Arm Geo
6. 6	L W X De Th Pi Si Ph Ko Fam 13 9+ Gr 7It 2Sy Aeth Arm Geo
6. 18	E De 10+ Gr 6It Aeth Arm
8. 14	Ph 1Gr
9. 13	C E G K L M S U V^{mg} X Y Ga^{mg} Th Om Fam 13 5+ Gr 3It 3Vg 3Sy 2Cop Aeth Epiph Eus Just Bas Aug Hil
9. 15	D 7It 4Vg 1Sy Bas
9. 35	Al* C³ E F G K L M U X Y Ga Th Pi Fam 13 3+ Gr 2It Vg 1Sy Aeth Arm Geo
10. 1	L 6Gr 2It
10. 7	N Si 2Gr
10. 21	1Sy
12. 4	6Gr
12. 11	1It
12. 23	1It 1Sy
12. 27	1Sy
13. 6	1Sy

14. 7   It(−2) Vg 2Sy 1Cop Aeth
14. 20   1Sy
14. 24   1Gr
15. 22   D 1It
15. 30   1Gr
Cf. also Mt. 8. 29 'They cried out+with a loud voice' (φωνη μεγαλη) 1Gr
         1Sy
Mt. 9. 16 'No one sews on... + with a needle' (ραπτει) 2Gr

Mark

9. 1   D 1Gr 5It
9. 24   A² C³ D N X Y Ga Th Pi Si Ph Ko Most minusc It Vg 3Sy
9. 26   D (De) 1Gr 9It Vg 2Sy 1Cop 1Geo
9. 30   2Sy Aeth
9. 35   1Gr 1It 1Cop Bas
9. 42   A B C² L N W X Ga Th Pi Si Ph Ps Ko All minusc 5It Vg 3Sy
         2Cop Geo Aeth Arm
9. 45   1It 1Sy 2Cop also 1Sy 1Cop Arm
9. 45   A D N X Ga Th Pi Si Ph Ko(−1) Fam 13 5+Gr 3It Aeth
10. 22   W
10. 40   Al* Ph Fam 1 4Gr/Th 4Gr also 1It 1Sy
11. 10   A N X Y Ga Pi Si Ph Ko(−1) 4+Gr 1It 1Sy Aeth Catt
11. 13   W Fam 13 2Gr 2Sy 2Cop 2Geo
12. 1   2Cop 1Sy
12. 20   Al^a*mg Th Fam 13 7Gr 2It 4Vg 1Cop 1Geo Arm also D 7It
13. 2   3It Cyp ('in the temple' for 'here')
13. 10   D 3It Vg
13. 20   D 2Gr 6It Arm
13. 27   4Gr
13. 28   D Th 6Gr 1It Arm
14. 5   1Sy
14. 7   1It
14. 24   W Fam 13 6Gr 2It 1Vg 1Cop
14. 25   1Vg 1Sy 2Cop
14. 27   G 2Gr 6It 2Vg 1Sy 1Cop/A C² E F K M N U W Y Th Pi* Si Ph
         Famm 1 & 13 6+Gr 2It 5Vg 2Sy 1Cop Geo Aeth Arm/5Gr 1It
         Vg(rells) 1Cop
14. 29   E G U Fam 1 5Gr 2It Vg 1Geo Aeth
14. 34   G 0112 Fam 1 4Gr 3It 1Cop 1Sy
14. 35   D G Th Si Famm 1 & 13 10Gr It(−3) 1Vg 1Sy Arm
14. 37   F 6Gr 2It 1Vg 1Cop 1Geo
14. 40   2Gr ('heavy+with sleep': dat. only) 2It 2Vg (Same, but with
         prep.)
14. 52   1Sy

14. 52   A D N P W X Y Ga De Th Pi Si Ph Ko Famm 1 & 13 8+Gr
         It(−2) Vg 2Sy Geo Arm Aug
14. 61   W Th Ph Fam 13 3Gr 1Sy 2Geo Arm Or
14. 64   2Gr Cf. category 7a below.
15. 1   D 1Gr Or 5It
15. 7   2It
15. 19   2Sy 1Cop ('in his face' for 'him')
15. 24   1Sy
16. 8   1It

THE APOCRYPHAL AND PATRISTIC TRADITIONS

Gosp. Ebion. Epiph. Haer. 30. 13. 6 (de Santos, p. 51); cf. Mk. 1. 4. Add
'in the Jordan River' (from Mk. 1. 5). Cf. 4b below.

Protev. Jms. 11. 2; cf. Lk. 1. 31. 'shall conceive + of (ek) his word.'

Protev. Jms. 11. 3; cf. Lk. 1. 38. 'behold the handmaid of the Lord + before
him.'

Protev. Jms. 11. 3; cf. Lk. 1. 35. 'that which is born + of (ek) you.'

Protev. Jms. 14. 1; cf. Mt. 1. 19. 'put her away secretly + from me.'

Protev. Jms. 12. 3; cf. Lk. 1. 24. 'she hid herself + from the sons of Israel.'
Cf. 18b.

Pseud. Matt. Lat. 15. 3; cf. Lk. 2. 36. 'there was + in the temple.'

Pseud. Matt. Lat. 16. 2; cf. Mt. 2. 12. 'warned + by an angel.'

Pseud. Matt. Lat. 17. 2; cf. Mt. 2. 17. Add 'by the way of the desert'.

Ps. Thom. 19. 1; cf. Lk. 2. 41. 'to the feast of passover + with their fellow-
travelers.'

Act. Pil. 3. 2; cf. Jn. 18. 33. 'called Jesus + kat' idian.'

Act. Pil. 10. 1; cf. Lk. 23. 36. 'vinegar + with gall' (from Mt. 27. 34).

Act. Pil. 13. 1; cf. Mt. 28. 2. 'The stone + from the mouth of the cave.'

Carta del domingo (de Santos, p. 675); cf. Mk. 13. 31 parr. 'shall not pass
away + eis ton aiōna.'

Just. Apol. 1. 15. 1; cf. Mt. 5. 28. 'heart + before God' (παρα τω θεω).

Just. Apol. 1. 33. 5; cf. Lk. 1. 32. 'you shall conceive + from (ek) the Holy
Spirit.'

Just. Dial. 103. 6; cf. Mt. 4. 10. 'depart + behind me' (from Mt. 16. 23
parr.).

4b The omission of non-adjectival prepositional phrases

THE TEXTUAL TRADITION

Matthew

1. 22	2Gr		2. 15	2Vg Arm
2. 1	1Gr		3. 9	1Sy Aeth Or Aph
2. 4	D Ga 1It 2Sy		3. 11	1It
			3. 11	1Gr

3. 11	1It 1Vg 1Cop Cyp Hil	10. 11	Th Fam 1 4Gr
4. 1	1Gr	10. 17	3It
4. 5	2Gr	10. 28	1Gr
4. 18	2Geo	10. 30	1It '(−now in this time).'
4. 23	3Gr	10. 31	K*
5. 12	1Vg	10. 46	Th 1Gr D 7It (εκειθεν
5. 28	Clem		for απο Ιερειχω)
5. 42	D 1Gr 2It Clem	10. 46	1Gr
8. 5	1It 1Sy	10. 52	2Geo
8. 10	3Gr	11. 1	1Gr
8. 28	W	11. 1	D 1Gr 6It Vg Or
8. 28	2Gr 1Sy	11. 9	1It
9. 10	1Gr	11. 11	1Gr
9. 18	1Sy	11. 13	0188 2It 2Sy
11. 7	1Gr (also prop. name)	11. 14	1It
11. 29	Al* 2Gr	11. 15	1Gr 1It
12. 1	1It	12. 2	Ps 1Gr 1Sy
12. 5	1Sy ('in the temple'	12. 32	1Gr 1It
	prhps. adj.)	13. 1	1It
13. 21	1Gr 1Sy	13. 3	2Gr 1It 1Cop 1Geo
13. 34	2Gr	13. 16	1Gr 2It 2Vg
13. 48	2Sy	14. 1	D 3It
13. 57	L 7Gr 2It 1Vg	14. 9	1Gr
14. 8	D 1It	14. 33	1Sy 1Cop
14. 10	1It	14. 35	2It 1Geo
14. 13	Ga 1Gr 2Sy	14. 51	W Fam 1 2It 1Sy 1Cop
14. 23	2Gr	14. 54	1Gr 1It
14. 24	3Gr	14. 54	2Gr
14. 25	1Sy 1Geo	14. 56	1Gr
14. 26	4Gr 1It 1Cop	14. 72	Al L 1Gr 1It 1Vg
15. 33	1Gr	15. 24	3It
Cf. 12. 5	1Sy Tat (−τοις σαββασιν).	15. 31	1Gr 1Cop
Cf. 12. 10	1Sy *ibid.*	15. 39	2Gr
		15. 45	1It 1Sy
Mark		16. 3	1Sy
9. 2	4Gr 1It 2Sy 1Cop Aeth	16. 5	1It
9. 7	2It	Cf. 12. 2	1Gr (−τω καιρω).
9. 28	Ps 𝔓⁴⁵	Cf. 14. 30	S (−ταυτη τη νυκτι).
9. 34	A D De 5It 1Sy	Cf. 15. 34	1It (−τη ενατη ωρα).
10. 10	K W 7Gr		

THE APOCRYPHAL AND PATRISTIC TRADITIONS

Gosp. Ebion. Epiph. Haer 30. 13. 6; cf. Mk. 1. 4. Omits 'in the desert and preaching' and 'for forgiveness of sins'. Cf. 4a above.

Gosp. Ebion. Epiph. Haer. 30. 13. 7 f.; cf. Mt. 3. 15. 'fitting (–for us).'
Protev. Jms. 21. 1; cf. Mt. 2. 1. 'Magi (–from the East).'
Protev. Jms. 21. 2; cf. Mt. 2. 5. Omits 'through the prophet'.
Protev. Jms. 22. 1; cf. Mt. 2. 16. Omits 'in Bethlehem and in all its regions'.
Pseud. Matt. Lat. 17. 1; cf. Mt. 2. 16. Omits 'and in all its regions'.
Pseud. Matt. Lat. 15. 1; cf. Lk. 2. 24. Omits 'according to what is said in the law of the Lord'.
Ps. Thom. 19. 5; cf. Lk. 2. 51. Omits 'in her heart'.
Ps. Thom. 19. 5; cf. Lk. 2. 52. Omits 'with God and man'.
Act. Pil. 2. 1; cf. Mt. 27. 19. Omits 'in a dream'. (A Matthaean phrase.)
Act. Pil. 3. 2; cf. Jn. 18. 37. Omits second 'unto this'.
Act. Pil. 3. 2; cf. Jn. 18. 37. Omits 'into the world'.
Just. Apol. 1. 15. 10; cf. Mt. 5. 42. Omits 'from you'.
Just. Apol. 1. 16. 2; cf. Mt. 5. 41. Omits 'with him'.
Just. Apol. 1. 16. 11; cf. Mt. 7. 22. Omits 'in that day'.
Cf. also Just. Apol. 1. 15. 14; cf. Mt. 6. 25. Omits 'in your soul', τη ψυχη.
Cf. also Just. Apol. 1. 15. 14; cf. Mt. 6. 25. Omits 'for your body', τω σωματι.
Cf. also Pseud. Matt. Lat. 15. 3; cf. Lk. 2. 38. Omits αυτη τη ωρα.

5a The addition of adjectives and adjectival phrases

THE TEXTUAL TRADITION

Matthew

1. 25   reads: 'And he did not know her until she bore a son.' Many manuscripts read: 'And he did not know her until she bore her first-born son.' This is indicated as follows:

1. 25   C D* N W Ga De Pi Si Ko Most minusc Epiph 4It Vg 2Sy Arm Aug Tat also D^{cor} L 2It Aeth Arm '(+first-born) son'.
2. 6   1Gr 'the (+new) Israel'.
4. 16   1Sy Aug '(+great) light'.
6. 15   M 9Gr 2It 4Vg Aeth Arm Aug 'your (+heavenly) Father'.
7. 12   8It Vg 'all (+good)'.
8. 16   De 9It Vg 1Cop Hil '(+unclean) spirits'.
8. 19   047 '(+good) teacher'.
8. 29   1Gr '(+the living) God'.
9. 16   L* 2It 1Cop 'from the (+old) garment'.
9. 28   Al* D 2Gr 4It 4Vg 1Sy 'the (+two) blind men'.
10. 20   Aph '(+Holy) Spirit'.
10. 29   12Gr 5It 3Vg 2Cop Aeth Or 'Father+who is in heaven'.
11. 2   C³ L X Ga Pi Ph Ko Famm 1 & 13(–1) 7+Gr 4It Vg 1Sy 1Cop Aeth Or 1Geo (δυο for δια).
12. 13   5Gr 'the man+who had the withered hand'.
12. 43   2It 'arid (+and desert) place'.

116

13. 32   1 Sy 1Cop Aeth 1Geo '(+great) tree'.

13. 33   1Sy '(+wise) woman'.

13. 42   2Gr 2Vg 1Cop 1Geo '(+burning) furnace' and the like.

13. 47   2Sy '(+large) net'.

13. 50   2Gr 1It 1Cop as 13. 42.

14. 2   D Ph 4It Vg 'John the Baptist+whom I beheaded'.

14. 30   All uncs but Al B 073 Most minusc It Vg Sy Aeth Arm Geo
        '(+strong) wind'.

15. 32   1Gr '(+twelve) disciples'.

15. 34   1It ('two' for 'few').

15. 36   Al* 6Gr 2It 1Geo '(+two) fish'.

Mark

9. 7   0131 'beloved son+whom I have chosen'/Al^a De ' +in whom I
       am well pleased' (from Mt. 17. 5).

9. 17   3Gr 'dumb (+and deaf) spirit'. Cf. 5 b below.

9. 19   W 𝔓^45 Fam 13 6Gr 'faithless (+and perverted) generation'.

9. 20   1Gr 2It 1Cop '(+unclean) spirit'.

9. 25   1Gr 1It '(+unclean) spirit'.

9. 31   3Gr '(+sinful) men'.

9. 47   1Gr '(+right) eye'.

10. 12   1Gr 'her (+own) husband'.

10. 20   4Vg '(+good) teacher'.

12. 28   1Gr 'first (+and great) commandment'.

13. 14   A X Y Ga De Th Pi Si Ph Ko Famm 1 & 13 6+Gr 4It 2Vg 2Sy
        Aeth also 1It 1Gr 'abomination. . . +which was spoken by Daniel
        the Prophet', etc.

13. 22   1Gr '(+great) signs'.

14. 13   1Gr 'city+which is opposite you'.

14. 24   A P X Y Ga De Pi Si Ph 0116 Ko Famm 1 & 13 7+Gr It(−1)
        Vg 3Sy 1Geo Aeth Arm 'the (+new) covenant'.

15. 46   Al 1Geo '(+great) stone'.

THE APOCRYPHAL AND PATRISTIC TRADITIONS

Pap. Oxy. 1. 7, lines 36–41 (de Santos, pp. 90 f.); cf. Mt. 5. 14. Has 'city
   built. . .and established' for Mt.'s 'city placed'. Addition of adjectival
   participle.

Pseud. Matt. Lat. 16. 2; cf. Mt. 2. 11. '(+great) gifts.'

Act. Pil. 4. 1; cf. Mt. 27. 24. 'the blood of this+righteous man.' 'Righteous'
   also added by many MSS.

Act. Pil. 9. 4; cf. Mt. 27. 24. 'this (+righteous) one.'

Act. Pil. 11. 3; cf. Lk. 23. 53. 'a (+clean) linen cloth.'

Ps. Thomas 19. 2; cf. Lk. 2. 44. 'a journey of (+one) day.'

Gosp. Ebion. Epiph. Haer. 30. 13. 4 f.; cf. Mt. 3. 4b 'wild honey + of which the taste was of manna, as a cake (dipped) in oil'.

Nat. Mary 10. 2; cf. Mt. 1. 20. 'For that which is born (+ and which now vexes thy soul, is the work not of man, but) of the Holy Spirit.'

Act. Pil. 13. 1; cf. Mt. 28. 5. 'the women + who waited at the tomb.'

Act. Pil. 16. 2; cf. Lk. 2. 25. Simeon is called 'the great teacher'.

Jos. Arim. 2. 3; cf. Mt. 26. 15. Has 'hand over the one who takes away the law and plunders the prophets' for Mt.'s 'hand him over'.

Just. Apol. 1. 16. 7; cf. Mk. 10. 18 parr. 'God, + who made all things.'

Just. Apol. 1. 15. 13; cf. Lk. 6. 36. '(+ good and) merciful' two times. Dial. 96. 3 has '(+ good and) merciful' once.

5b The omission of adjectives and adjectival phrases

THE TEXTUAL TRADITION

Matthew

3. 4   2Sy '(−leather) girdle'.
3. 10   Iren '(−good) fruit'.
4. 21   1Sy 'James (−the [son] of Zebedee)'.
5. 12   1Sy 'Prophets (−who were before you)'.
5. 39   D 2It 2Sy Aph Eph Adam '(−right) cheek'.
6. 14   1Sy '(−heavenly) Father'.
8. 24   1Gr '(−great) storm'.
8. 26   1Gr '(−great) calm'.
10. 1   1Gr '(−twelve) disciples'.
11. 1   7Gr '(−twelve) disciples'.
12. 36 X 3Gr '(−idle) word'.
12. 45 2Gr '(−seven) other spirits.'/1Sy 'seven (−other) spirits'.
13. 45 1Sy '(−beautiful) pearls'.
13. 46 D Th 3Gr 8It 1Sy 2Cop '(−one) costly pearl'.
15. 13 Hil 'my (−heavenly) Father'.
15. 36 5Gr '(−seven) loaves'.

Mark

9. 17   1Sy '(−dumb) spirit'.
9. 25   W 𝔓⁴⁵ Fam 1 1Sy Geo '(−unclean) spirit'.
10. 38 1Sy '(−which I am baptized)'.
10. 39 1It (−same).
11. 10 De Fam 1(−1) 5Gr 1It '(−coming) kingdom'.
11. 25 1It 'Father (−in the heavens)'.
12. 42 D Th 1Gr It(−2) Arm '(−poor) widow'.
13. 19 D Th 2Gr 7It Arm '(−which God created)'.
13. 20 1It '(−whom he chose)'.

14. 15 7Gr '(−large) upper room'.
14. 15 A M* De 7+Gr 5It Vg 1Geo Arm '(−prepared)'.
14. 71 Al 1It '(−whom you say)'.
15. 12 A D W Th Fam 1 7Gr It Vg 1Sy 1Cop Geo Arm '(−whom you call)'.
15. 24 D 2Gr 3It 1Sy '(−who would take what)'.
Cf. also the following in Mark:
11. 28 W Th 2Gr 5It 1Sy Geo Arm 'who gave you this authority (−that you do these things)'?
14. 30 Al C* D W 2Gr It(−4) 3Vg Aeth Arm '(−twice)'.
14. 30 1Geo '(−thrice)'.
14. 72 Al C* W De Si 2Gr 5It Geo Aeth '(−twice)'.

Egerton Pap. 2, Fragm. 1, line 9; cf. Jn. 5. 39 '(−eternal) life'.
Gosp. Ebion. Epiph. Haer. 30. 14; cf. Mt. 12. 50 'my father (−in the heavens)'.
Act. Pil. 11. 3; cf. Lk. 23. 50 f. Omits 'a man good and just—he had not consented to their purpose and deed'.
Protev. Jms. 24. 4; cf. Lk. 2. 25. Omits Lk.'s description of Simeon.
Just. Apol. 1. 16. 2; cf. Mt. 5. 41. '(−one) mile'.
II Clem. 3. 2; cf. Mt. 10. 32 'my Father (−in the heavens)'.
II Clem. 9. 11; cf. Mt. 12. 50 'my Father (−who is in the heavens)'.

6a The addition of a noun in the genitive

Matthew

2. 1 1It 'King+of Judah'/1Cop +'of the Jews'.
3. 7 1Gr 'the baptism+of John'.
4. 16 1Gr 'region+of darkness'.
4. 23 1Gr 'kingdom+of God'.
5. 29 2Gr Adam 'Gehenna+of fire'.
6. 2 1Gr 'streets+of the city'.
6. 32 1Gr 2Sy
6. 33 All uncs but Al B Most minusc 9It Vg Sy Geo Aug 'Kingdom+of God'/1Gr Clem Just +'of the heavens'/+'his', see add. pron. (No add.: Al 4It 3Vg Tert)
7. 26 1It 'sand+of the sea'.
8. 28 Vg 'the other side+of the sea'.
8. 32 C³ E K L S U V X Pi 5+Gr 1Cop Aeth 'herd+of swine'.
9. 1 2It 'city+of Judea'.
9. 10 1Cop 'house+of Simon'.

9. 18   1Sy 'rabbi of their synagogue' for 'ruler'.

9. 23   1Sy 'ruler + of the synagogue'.

9. 35   1Gr 'kingdom + of God'.

12. 35   L 13Gr 3It Vg Aeth Arm 3Sy Aug 'treasury + of (his) heart'.

12. 35   L 8Gr 2Vg 2Sy Arm Aug Same.

12. 47   Al^a 1Gr 'a certain one + of his disciples'.

13. 4   E* K M Th Pi Si Ph Fam 13 9 + Gr 2It 2Vg 2Sy 2Cop Aeth Arm Geo Or 'the birds + of heaven'.

13. 22   Vg 'word + of God'.

13. 35   All uncs but Al^b B Most minusc 8It Vg 1Sy 2Cop Hil/6It 1Sy 2Geo 'foundation + of the world'.[1]

13. 47   2Gr 11It Vg 1Cop Aeth 'every kind + of fish'.

13. 49   1Gr 'angels + of God'.

14. 12   1Geo 'body + of John'.

14. 15   1Sy 'crowds + of men'.

15. 11   1Cop Aph 'out of the mouth + of man'.

Mark

9. 29   1It/1It 'this kind + of demon(s)'.

9. 45   F/3It Vg 1Sy 'Gehenna + of (inextinguishable) fire'.

9. 47   A C N X Y Ga Th Pi Si Ph Ko(−1) Fam 13 6 + Gr 5It Vg 2Sy 1Cop Aeth 'Gehenna + of fire'.

10. 37   1Cop 'in the glory + of your kingdom'. Cf. W Fam 13 1Gr 'in the kingdom of your glory'.

11. 15   2Sy 'the temple + of God'.

11. 27   D 1Gr 'elders + of the people'.

12. 2   1Sy 1Cop 1Geo 'at the time + of fruit'.

12. 9   1Geo 'tenants + of the vineyard'.

12. 25   5Gr 1It/1Gr/Fam 13(−2) 4Gr 'angels + of God'.

12. 29   E F G H S V Y Ga Fam 13 7 + Gr 1Sy/A C K M U Pi Si Ph 10 + Gr 2It Vg 1Sy/2It/1Gr/X 2Gr 1Sy Arm/D W Th 2Gr 3It/Fam 1(−1)/ 2Gr 'first + of all the commandments', etc.

13. 1   D 8It Vg 'buildings + of the temple'.

13. 19   1Gr 'creation + of the world'.

14. 4   W Fam 13 1Gr 1Sy 'some + of the disciples'.

14. 27   E F K M Y Pi* 10 + Gr 3It 2Vg 1Geo 'sheep + of the shepherd'.

14. 49   N W Th Ph Fam 13 7Gr 1Sy Geo Arm 'the writings + of the prophets'.

14. 58   1Gr 'the temple + of the body'./2It + 'of God'.

14. 62   1Gr Vg 1Cop 'the power + of God'.

14. 64   W Th 1Sy (cf. category 7a below). 'blasphemy + of his mouth'.

15. 1   1Gr 'elders and scribes + of the people'.

---

[1] The phrase 'of the world' is placed in brackets in the U.B.S. text.

15. 16   2Gr Th M 6+Gr 'palace+of Caiaphas'.
15. 29   1Gr 1Vg 'temple+of God'.
15. 45   3Vg 1Cop 'body+of Jesus'.

THE APOCRYPHAL AND PATRISTIC TRADITIONS

Egerton Pap. 2, Fragm. 1, line 29 (de Santos, p. 98); cf. Jn. 7. 30. 'his hour+ of betrayal'.
Protev. Jms. 22. 2; cf. Lk. 2. 7. 'in a manger+of oxen'.
Pseud. Matt. Lat. 15. 3; cf. Lk. 2. 37. 'the temple+of the Lord'.
Act. Pil. 9. 1; cf. Mt. 27. 15 par. 'the feast+of the unleavened bread'.
Just. Dial. 35. 3; cf. Mt. 24. 11. 'lead astray many+of the faithful'.
II Clem. 5. 4; cf. Mt. 10. 28 and Lk. 12. 5 'Gehenna+of fire'.

6b   The omission of a noun in the genitive

THE TEXTUAL TRADITION

Matthew

1. 20   1Gr 'angel (−of the Lord)'.
3. 16   1Vg 'spirit (−of God)'.
4. 4   1It 'the mouth (−of God)'.
5. 20   1Sy 'kingdom (−of the heavens)'.
13. 11   6It 1Sy Eus (same as 5. 20).
13. 19   1Gr 'the word (−of the kingdom)'.
15. 31   X 1Gr 'the God (−of Israel)'.

Mark

9. 35   1Gr Vg 'servant (−of all)'.
10. 23   1Gr 'kingdom (−of God)'.
13. 14   1Gr 'abomination (−of desolation)'.
13. 19   W 2Gr Geo 'beginning (−of creation)'.
14. 4   D Fam 1 2Gr 2It 1Sy 1Geo 'destruction (−of ointment)'.
14. 24   1It 'my blood (−of the covenant)'.
14. 47   D 1It 'a certain one (−of the bystanders)'.
15. 36   1Gr 'sponge (−of vinegar)'.
16. 3   1It 'door (−of the tomb)'.

THE APOCRYPHAL TRADITION

Arundel Latin Infancy Gospel 90; cf. Mt. 2. 5. 'Bethlehem (−of Judah)'.
Act. Pil. 4. 1; cf. Mt. 26. 61. Has 'this temple' for 'temple of God'.
Act. Pil. 11. 3; cf. Lk. 23. 51. 'a city (−of the Jews)'.
Act. Pil. 13. 1; cf. Mt. 28. 2. 'an angel (−of the Lord)'.

7a The addition of a personal pronoun in the genitive

THE TEXTUAL TRADITION

Matthew

1. 23   reads: 'God with us.' 3Sy Tat read: 'our God with us.' This is abbreviated as follows:

1. 23   3Sy Tat 'our God'.

1. 24   4Sy Aeth 'his sleep'.

1. 25   1Cop C D* N W Ga De Pi Si Ko Most minusc Epiph 4It Vg 2Sy Arm Aug Tat 'her son'.

3. 7   All uncs but Al* B Most minusc It Vg 4Sy 1Cop Aeth Arm Aug 'his baptism'. Cf. category 6a above.[1]

3. 11   1Gr 'his sandals'. Cf. Semitic wording.

3. 12   B E L U W 7Gr 4It Vg Sy Aeth Arm 1Geo Iren 'his storehouse'. But cf. omission of pronoun below.[2]

4. 20   K W Pi 9+Gr 6It 1Vg 4Sy 2Cop Aeth 1Geo 'their nets'.

4. 22   Al* Aeth 'their boat'./2It Vg 1Sy 1Cop 'their nets'.

5. 3   2Sy 'their spirit'.

5. 25   5Gr Geo 'your adversary'.

5. 40   Al Si 13Gr 4Sy 2Cop Aeth Arm Geo 'your garment'.

6. 22   B 1Gr It Vg Aeth Aug Or Hil 'your eye'.

6. 33   B 2Gr 2Cop Aeth Aph 'his kingdom'. Cf. also category 6a above. But B reads, τὴν δικαιοσύνην καὶ τὴν βασιλείαν αὐτοῦ.

8. 3   Al 1Gr 2Sy 2Cop 'his hand'.

8. 4   N Si 5Gr Geo 'your gift'.

8. 6   1It 2Vg 2Cop Aeth 'my house'.

8. 13   All uncs but Al B Most minusc 4Sy 1Cop Aeth Arm Geo Got 'his servant'.[2]

8. 16   1Sy Aeth 'their demons' for 'the spirits'.

8. 20   1Cop 'their nests'.

8. 20   6It Vg 4Sy 2Cop Cyp Aug Faust 'his head'.

8. 21   All uncs but Al B Most minusc 6It Vg Sy 1Cop Aeth Arm Geo Got 'his disciples'.[2]

9. 6   1 Geo 'their sins'.

9. 10   1Cop 1It 'his house'. Cf. category 6a above.

10. 21   3Sy 1Cop 'his brother'.

10. 21   3Sy 1Cop 'his child'.

10. 21   1Geo 'their parents'.

10. 24   Al F M W Fam 13(−1) 9+Gr 2Sy 2Cop Aeth Arm Geo 'his teacher'.

10. 25   De* 'his slave'.

[1] 'His' is accepted by the U.B.S. text.
[2] 'His' is bracketed in the U.B.S. text.

10. 27   2Sy 'your ear(s)'.

10. 27   Fam 1 1Gr 1Cop 'your roofs'.

10. 28   1Geo 'your bodies'.

10. 28,   1Cop 'your soul and your body'.

10. 37   2Sy 1Geo 'his father'.

10. 37   2Sy 1Geo 'his mother'.

10. 37   2Sy Aeth 1Geo 'his son'.

11. 16   All uncs but Al B D Z Most minusc Sy 1Cop Aeth Arm Geo 'their playmates'.

11. 20   1Gr 'their cities'.

11. 25   1Sy 1Cop 'my father'.

11. 29   4Sy 2Cop Aeth 'my heart'.

12. 1   Geo 'their grain fields'.

12. 20   X 12Gr 'his judgment'.

12. 34   Vg 'his mouth'.

12. 35   Vg 1Cop 'his treasury'.

12. 35   1Cop 'his treasury'.

12. 46   (De*) 9Gr It(−3) Vg Other vss Or 'his mother'.

12. 50   2Cop Aeth 'my sister'.

12. 50   1Vg 3Sy 2Cop Aeth 'my mother'.

13. 10   C X 11Gr 6It 3Vg 4Sy 2Cop Aeth 1Geo Eus 'his disciples'.

13. 15   Al C Ph 6Gr 7It 3Sy 2Cop Aeth Arm 'their ears'/1Gr 'his ears'.

13. 15   1Gr 3Sy 2Cop Aeth 'their eyes'.

13. 15   Al[b] 1Gr 3Sy 2Cop Aeth 'their ears'.

13. 20   W X De 2Gr 2It 1Sy Vg 'my word'.

13. 22   W 'my word'. Cf. category 6a above.

13. 23   W 2Gr 1It 1Sy (same).

13. 27   2Sy 'our Lord'.

13. 30   1Gr 1It 4Vg 'my reapers'.

13. 36   7Gr Arm Or 'his house'.

13. 38   Aeth 'his field'.

13. 48   1Cop 'their vessels'.

14. 6   D 'his daughter'.

14. 6   Aeth Geo 'in (+their) midst'.

14. 12   Al* D L Si 18Gr 7It 3Sy 1Geo 1Cop 'his body'.

14. 13   1It

*14. 15   All uncs but Al B Z Most minusc It(−a) Vg Sy 2Cop Aeth Geo Or

*14. 19   Th 047 Fam 13 8Gr 5It Vg 3Sy 1Cop Aeth Geo

*14. 22   B E F K P X Th Pi Si Fam 13 8+Gr 9It Vg 3Sy 2Cop Aeth

*14. 26   Si 1Sy

14. 31   1Vg 3Sy 2Cop

* An asterisk indicates that 'his' is added to 'disciples'.

15. 2   2Sy 'our elders'.

15. 2   All uncs but Al B De; Fam 13 7 + Gr 9It Vg 4Sy 2Cop Aeth Aug
'their hands'.[1]

15. 4   C** K L M N U W Y Th Pi Si Ph Fam 13 12 + Gr 7It 3Sy 2Cop
1Geo Or 'your father'.

15. 4   N W 8Gr 7It 3Sy 2Cop 1Geo 'your mother'.

15. 4   3Sy 2Cop Epiph 'his father and his mother'.

15. 5   1It 2Sy 2Cop Arm 1Geo 'his father'.

15. 5   Ga 1It 1Vg 1Sy 2Cop 'his mother'.

15. 5   1It 2Sy 'my gift'.

15. 8   1Geo

*15. 12   All uncs but Al B D Th Fam 1 5 + Gr It(−2) Vg Other vss

*15. 33   All uncs but Al B Most minusc 4It 4Sy Aeth Geo

*15. 36   All uncs but Al B D Th 4 + Gr 9It Vg 3Sy 1Cop Aeth

*15. 36   Ga 1It 2Sy 2Cop Aeth

Mark

* 9. 14   Th Fam 13(−1) 2Gr 5It Vg 1Sy 1Cop 1Geo Aeth

  9. 18   A C³ N X Y Ga Th Pi Si Ph 067 Ko 8 + Gr 2It 4Sy 2Cop Aeth
Arm

  9. 35   1Sy 'his twelve'.

  9. 41   Al* C³ W X Y Ga Pi² Ko(−3) 9 + Gr/D De Th H M Fam 13(−1)
6 + Gr It Vg 2Sy 2Cop Aeth Or

  9. 44   2Gr

  9. 46   2Gr

  9. 48   Ps 4Gr 1It 3Sy 2Cop 1Geo Aeth

  10. 2   2It 1Vg 2Sy 2Cop 1Geo

  10. 7   Al (D) M Ps 5Gr 5It 2Sy 2Cop 1Geo (Legg in error cites B here.)
'his mother'.

*10. 10   A D N W X Y Ga Pi Si Ph Ko Famm 1 & 13 6 + Gr It Vg 3Sy
2Cop Geo Aeth

*10. 13   D Th 2Gr 4It 2Sy Aeth

  10. 19   Al* C F N W Th Si 10 + Gr It(−5) 3Vg 2Sy 2Cop Geo Aeth

*10. 24   D De Th Fam 1 3Gr It(−2) 1Sy 1Geo

  10. 29   1Gr 2Sy

  10. 32   3Gr 'his twelve disciples' for 'the twelve'/2Sy 'his twelve'.

  10. 40   Ps 6 + Gr 1It 3Sy 1Cop 1Geo Aeth

  10. 43   1Gr

  12. 2   2Sy

  12. 6   A N X Ga Pi Si Ph Ko 8 + Gr also W Fam 1(−1) 2Gr 'his beloved'.
Cf. category 3a above.

---

[1] 'Their' is accepted by the U.B.S. text.

* An asterisk indicates that 'his' is added to 'disciples'.

12. 9   1Gr 1It

12. 19   A D X Ga Pi Si Ph Ko Fam 13 8+Gr It Vg 2Sy 2Cop 2Geo Aeth Arm

12. 33   Al L 2Gr 1Sy 'your heart'./1Sy 'his heart'.

12. 33   1Gr 'your strength'.

12. 33   1Sy 'his strength'.

12. 33   Al* De W 1Gr 2Cop 'your strength'/1Gr 2Sy 'his strength'.

13. 12   2Sy Aeth 'his brother'.

13. 12   2Sy 'his child'.

13. 12   1Sy 2Cop 'his parents'.

13. 15   2Gr

13. 27   Al A C X Y Ga De Th Pi Si Ph Ps 0116 Ko All minusc 4It Vg(−1) 3Sy 2Cop Geo Aeth Arm Or 'his angels'.

13. 28   2Sy

14. 8   1Gr

14. 9   2Sy

*14. 16   A C D P W X Y Ga Th Pi Si Ph 0116 Ko Fam 13(−1) 6+Gr It Vg 3Sy 1Cop

14. 17   Aeth 'his twelve disciples' for 'the twelve'/2Sy 'his twelve'.

14. 36   W Fam 13 1Gr 2Sy Aeth

14. 37   1It

14. 54   Fam 13 1Gr

14. 55   1Sy

14. 56   4Gr 2It 1Vg 2Sy 2Cop Geo

14. 60   1Gr

14. 64   D G N Si o67 Famm 1 & 13 2Gr 2It 4Vg 1Sy 1Geo Aeth 'his blasphemy'/2Gr 'his blasphemy out of his mouth'. Cf. categories 6a and 4a above.

15. 7   1Gr

15. 20   1Sy

15. 27   1It 2Sy 2Cop 1Geo Aeth

15. 45   D 2It 2Sy 1Geo

16. 6   D W Th 1Gr 5It 1Sy

Cf. also Mt. 8. 34 'they asked+of him' (αυτου) 2Gr 4It Vg Sy (with prep.) 2Cop 1Geo

13. 17   'to hear+from me' 8Gr (μου) Eph (*a me*)

Pseud. Thom. 19. 2; cf. Lk. 2. 44 '(+their) relatives'.

Act. Pil. 9. 4; cf. Mt. 27. 24. '(+his) hands'.

Act. Pil. 11. 1; cf. Lk. 23. 48. '(+their own) breasts'.

Act. Pil. 16. 2; cf. Lk. 2. 28. '(+his) arms'. So also Ko D Th Many minusc

Just. Dial. 49. 3; cf. Mt. 3. 12 par. '(+his) winnowing fan.'

* An asterisk indicates that 'his' is added to 'disciples'.

7b The omission of a personal pronoun in the genitive

THE TEXTUAL TRADITION

Matthew

1. 21   Epiph Hil Cyp '(–their) sins'.
2. 2   2Geo '(–his) star'.
3. 4   7It Vg '(–his) garment'.
3. 4   1Vg '(–his) food'.
3. 12   E L U 12+Gr 7It Vg Sy Arm 2Geo Just Iren Clem '(–his) wheat'.
4. 22   4It Vg Iren
4. 23   1Gr '(–their) synagogues'.
4. 24   De
5. 20   1Gr
5. 29   2Gr
5. 32   1Geo Clem
6. 3   Aug Hil
6. 6   Si 3Vg 1Sy '(–your) closet'.
6. 6   1Gr 1It 2Sy '(–your) door'.
6. 14   D '(–their) trespasses'.
6. 14   3Gr '(–your) father'.
6. 15   1It '(–their) trespasses'.
6. 15   1It 1Sy 1Gr Al '(–your) father'.
6. 18   Al* De 1Sy
6. 25   Al* 1It
6. 32   L 1Gr
7. 6   3Sy 1Cop Clem
7. 16   1Gr
9. 2   D De** 2Gr 1It 1Vg Or Ir Aug 'the sins are forgiven you' for 'your sins are forgiven'.
9. 6   1Gr
9. 16   Al*
9. 18   Si 3Gr 5It Vg Hil
9. 30   Al*
10. 13   1Gr
10. 17   W 1It '(–their) synagogues'.
10. 20   D Epiph Or
10. 24   3It Hil
10. 25   1Gr Clem Epiph '(–his) teacher'. Cf. category 7a above.
10. 32   2Sy
10. 33   1Sy
*11. 2   1Gr

* An asterisk indicates that 'his' is omitted from 'disciples'.

11. 10   1It '(−my) messenger'.
11. 10   1Gr 4Sy '(−your) way'.
11. 20   D 2It 2Sy Aeth
11. 27   Al* 3Gr 1Sy 1Cop Hil
11. 29   1Gr
11. 30   1Gr
12. 9   1Gr '(−their) synagogue'. See category 11a below.
12. 18   Ph 1It
12. 37   Al
12. 44   1It
12. 46   10It Vg '(−his) brothers'. Cf. category 7a above.
12. 48   B*
12. 49   Al* D Si 12Gr 9It Vg Or Epiph '(−his) hand'.
*12. 49   De Vg Epiph
12. 49   1Gr '(−my) mother'.
12. 50   1Gr
13. 25   1Gr 1It 3Sy 1Cop
13. 27   K 12Gr (−σφ)
13. 30   1Sy Aug
*13. 36   3Gr 2It Arm
13. 41   Al F '(−his) angels'.
13. 44   Geo
14. 8   1Gr
*14. 12   4Gr 1Vg. The reference is to John's disciples.
15. 2   1Gr
15. 5   Th Fam 1 12Gr Or
15. 13   1It 1Sy 1Geo Clem
*15. 23   O Si Ph 1It
*15. 32   Al W Th 1Gr 1Geo Hil

Mark

9. 41   1Gr
9. 48   G S V X Om 6+Gr 1It
10. 7   D M* N 1Gr 1It 3Vg
10. 12   4Gr 2It/D Th Fam 13 4Gr 4It Arm
10. 37   2It
10. 42   N Si Fam 1 5Gr 1It
*10. 46   Th
11. 3   It(−1) Vg 1Sy 1Cop 1Geo '(−his) Lord'.
11. 7   4Gr 5It
11. 8   L W
11. 25   D 2Gr

    * An asterisk indicates that 'his' is omitted from 'disciples'.

12. 19   W 𝔓⁴⁵ 2It 1Geo
12. 30   1Gr
*12. 43   W Arm
 13. 15   1It
 13. 27   D L W Ps Fam 1(−1) 6Gr 5It 2Geo Or
 13. 34   2It 1Vg
*14. 12   D 6It Vg 1Geo Arm
 14. 14   A P X Y Ga Th Pi Ph 0116 Ko 8+Gr 4It 2Sy 1Cop Aeth Arm
*14. 32   A Ph Arm
 14. 40   1Gr
 14. 63   1Gr
 15. 20   D
 15. 29   D 2Gr 2It
 15. 34   A E F G K P Ga De Th Pi 059 0112 0192 Famm 1 & 13(−1)
          8+Gr 1It 2Vg 1Cop
*16. 7   2Gr 1It

THE APOCRYPHAL AND PATRISTIC TRADITIONS

Gosp. Ebion. Epiph. Haer. 30. 13. 4 f.; cf. Mt. 3. 4. '(−his) clothing'.
Just. Apol. I. 15. 1; cf. Mt. 5. 28. '(−his) heart'.
Just. Apol. I. 15. 16; cf. Mt. 6. 21. '(−your) treasure'.
Just. Dial. 49. 3; cf. Mt. 3. 12 par. '(−his) grain' (so also Lk.).
Just. Dial. 49. 3; cf. Mt. 3. 12 par. '(−his) barn' (so also Mt.).
Just. Dial. 99. 1; cf. Mk. 15. 34. '(−my) God, (−my) God'.
Just. Dial. 100. 1; cf. Mt. 11. 27. '(−my) father'.
Athen. 11. 1; cf. Mt. 5. 45. '(−your) father'.
Theoph. III. 13; cf. Mt. 5. 32 parr. '(−his) wife'.
II Clem. 6. 2; cf. Mt. 16. 26 '(−his) soul'.

8a   The addition of a noun to a proper name

THE TEXTUAL TRADITION

Matthew

2. 1   reads: 'When Jesus was born in Bethlehem of Judea...' 5It read:
       'When Jesus was born in Bethlehem a city of Judea...' This is
       abbreviated as follows:
2. 1   5It 'Bethlehem+a city'.
2. 5   1It Same.
2. 19 1Sy 'Herod+the king'.
4. 13 2Gr It Vg 'Nazareth+a city'.
4. 13 2Gr Vg 'Capernaum+a city'.
4. 15 2Sy Eph 'Jordan+river'.

   * An asterisk indicates that 'his' is omitted from 'disciples'.

11. 7   7It Vg 'John + the baptist'.
11. 13   1Gr 'until John + the prophet'./Aph Aug + 'the baptist'.
11. 18   Ph 1Gr 'John + the baptist'.
12. 40   5Gr 'Jonah + the prophet'./Aph 'Jonah + the son of Amittai'.
13. 14   2Sy 'Isaiah + the prophet'.
15. 7   6Gr 1It 3Sy 2Cop Same.

Mark

15. 43   1Gr απο Αριμαθαιας + πολεως.

THE APOCRYPHAL AND PATRISTIC TRADITIONS

Gosp. Heb. Jerome, Contra Pelag. III. 2 (see Appendix V. 3); cf. Mt. 18. 21.
   Has Simon for Mt.'s Peter, and adds 'his disciple'.
Pseud. Matt. Lat. 16. 1; cf. Mt. 2. 7. 'Herod + the King'.
Pseud. Matt. Lat. 17. 1; cf. Mt. 2. 16. 'Herod + the King'.
Just. Dial. 51. 3; cf. Lk. 16. 16 par. 'John + the baptist'.

8b The omission of a noun from a proper name

THE TEXTUAL TRADITION

Matthew

1. 18   1Gr '(−his mother) Mary'.
2. 17   W* 'Jeremiah (−the prophet)'.
3. 6   C³ D L Ga Pi Ko(−1) 6+Gr It(−1) Vg Arm Geo Hil 'Jordan
         (−river)'.
8. 17   1Sy 'Isaiah (−the prophet)'. See also category 9b below.
11. 12   3Gr Hil 'John (−the baptist)'.
15. 22   1Gr 'Canaanite (−woman)'.

Mark

15. 22   Al* 2It 1Vg 'Golgotha (−place)'.

THE APOCRYPHAL TRADITION

Protev. Jms. 21. 2; cf. Mt. 2. 3. '(−King) Herod'.

9a The addition of a proper name to a noun or its equivalent or to another proper name

THE TEXTUAL TRADITION

Matthew

1. 22   D 3Gr It(−2) Vg 4Sy Arm Iren 'the prophet + Isaiah'.
1. 24   Al^{cor} 1It 2Cop Aeth 'his wife + Mary'. See also category 11a below.
2. 1   Om 047 5Gr Geo 'Jesus + Christ'.
2. 5   1It (Isaiah)/1Gr 1Cop (Micha)

2. 15 1Sy 'the prophet + Isaiah'.

2. 23 1It Same.

4. 3 1It 'the one tempting + the Devil'. Cf. category 11 a below.

6. 32 Al* 'your father + God'.

8. 14 2Sy '(+ Simon) Peter'.

8. 29 All uncs but Al B C* L Fam 13 2 + Gr 10It Vg 3Sy 2Cop Aeth Arm Geo Got Eus '(+Jesus) son of God'.

9. 27 Si 3Gr '(+Jesus) son of David'. Cf. N 12Gr 1It 1Geo + Lord.

12. 23 8 + Gr Arm 1Geo 'son of David + Christ'.

12. 46 1Vg 'he + Jesus'.

13. 35 Al* Th Fam 13 13Gr 1Vg Aeth 'the prophet + Isaiah'.

13. 55 6It 1Sy 'the carpenter + Joseph'. See also category 11 a below.

14. 1 1Sy 'Jesus + Christ'. Cf. 1Cop 'Jesus + our Lord'.

14. 28 2Sy '(+ Simon) Peter'.

14. 29 1Sy '(+ Simon) Peter'.

15. 15 3Sy '(+ Simon) Peter'.

Mark

9. 12 1Gr 'Elijah + the Thesbite'.

10. 48 Fam 13(− 1) 2Gr '(+Jesus) son of David'. Cf. 4Gr + Lord.

14. 53 A K M W Y Th Pi Fam 13 16 + Gr 2Sy 1Cop Geo Arm Or 'the high priest + Caiaphas'.

14. 61 A K Y Pi 15Gr 1It Vg Arm 'the son of (+ God) the blessed'. Cf. category 11 a below.

15. 1 2Gr '(+ Pontius) Pilate'.

15. 26 1It '(+Jesus) the king of the Jews'.

THE APOCRYPHAL TRADITION

Pseud. Matt. Lat. 16. 2; cf. Mt. 2. 11. 'the child + Jesus'.

Pseud. Thom. 19. 3; cf. Lk. 2. 48. 'his mother + Mary'.

See also Jos. Arim. 3. 4; cf. Mt. 8. 12 'the sons of the kingdom + the children of Abraham and Isaac and Jacob and Moses'.

9b The omission of a proper name from a noun or its equivalent or from another proper name

THE TEXTUAL TRADITION

Matthew

1. 20 Th '(−Joseph) son of David'.

2. 11 1Gr '(− Mary) his mother'.

4. 14 1Gr 'the prophet (− Isaiah)'.

8. 17 1Gr '(− Isaiah) the prophet'.

12. 17 1It 1Cop Same.

12. 39 1Sy 'the prophet (−Jonah)'.

Mark

10. 47 L 10Gr 1It 2Sy Geo '(−Jesus) son of David'.

14. 61   Ga Ph 1Gr 1It '(−the Christ) the Son of the blessed'.

Also

Matt. 14. 3 D 8It Vg Aug '(−Philip) his brother' (Possibly correction of error).

THE APOCRYPHAL AND PATRISTIC TRADITIONS

Pseud. Matt. Lat. 16. 2; cf. Mt. 2. 11. Has 'in his mother's lap' for Mt.'s 'with Mary his mother'.

Just. Apol. 1. 34. 1; cf. Mt. 2. 6. 'My people (−Israel)'.

10a   Other additions of proper names

THE TEXTUAL TRADITION

Matthew

*2. 1   1It 'king + of Judah'/1Cop 'king + of the Jews'.

*3. 7   1Gr 'the baptism + of John'.

*9. 1   2It 'city + of Judea'.

*9. 10   1Cop 'house + of Simon'.

9. 18   2It 'Jairus'.

9. 20   1Gr Per 'coming up from behind + Jesus'.

12. 40   Aph 'Jonah + the son of Amittai'. See also category 8a.

*14. 12   1Geo 'body + of John'.

Mark

*15. 16   2Gr Th M 6 + Gr 'palace + of Caiaphas'.

15. 27   1It (*c*) 'one on his right + by name Zoathan'.

15. 27   1It (*a*) 'one on his left + by name Chammatha'.

*15. 45   3Vg 1Cop 'body + of Jesus'.

15. 47   1Gr + 'and Salome'.

THE APOCRYPHAL TRADITION

Gosp. of the Heb. Origen *In Io.* 2. 6; *Hom. in Ier.* 15. 4 (de Santos, p. 35; H.-S. p. 164). The mountain of Mt. 4. 8 is named Tabor.

Gosp. of the Heb. (H.-S. p. 152). According to a medieval commentary on Mt., the man with the withered hand (cf. Mt. 12. 9 ff.) was named Malchus.

Oxy. Pap. 840 (see Appendix v. 11) mentions 'a certain Pharisaic high priest, Levi by name'.

Gospel of Peter 31; cf. Mt. 17. 62 ff. The Centurion is named Petronius.

Act. Pil. 7. 1; cf. Mk. 5. 25 ff. parr. The woman with the issue of blood is named Bernice.

* See also category 6a.

Act. Pil. 14. 1. Jesus' speech in Mark 16. 15–18 is told in the first person by 'Phinees a priest and Adas a teacher and Angaeus a Levite'. The speech was made from Mount Mamilch.

Jos. of Arim. 1. 4. The testimony of Mt. 26. 61 par. is given by Sarah, the daughter of Caiaphas.

Jos. of Arim. 3. 4; cf. Lk. 23. 43. 'I say to you + Demas.'

Jos. of Arim. 3. 1. The two thieves are named Gestas and Demas.

Act. Pil. 9. 5. The two malefactors are named Dysmas and Gestas.

Act. Pil. 10. 2; cf. Lk. 23. 40. The good malefactor is identified as Dysmas.

Act. Pil. 16. 7. Longinus the soldier pierced Jesus' side (this verse does not quote the Synoptics).

A medieval variant to Mt. 9. 20 (see H.-S. p. 151) names the woman with the issue of blood Mariosa.

Gosp. Heb. (see Appendix v. 7). The names of the three magi were Melchus, Caspar, and Phadizarda.

A medieval comm. on Mt. (see H.-S. p. 152); cf. Mt. 12. 42. The 'queen of the South' is identified as 'Meroe of Aethiopia'.

Medieval comm. on Lk. (see H.-S. p. 142); cf. Lk. 8. 42. 'The daughter' is identified as 'the synagogue, whose name is Mariossa'.

Ibid.; cf. Lk. 11. 31. 'The queen of the South' is identified as 'Meruae'.

**Act. Pil. 1. 1 names ten of the 'chief priests and scribes'.

**Act. Pil. 5. 1. The Egyptian magicians of Ex. 7 are named 'Jannus' and 'Jambres' (as in other late Jewish and Christian literature).

**In Act. Pil. 16. 6 speeches are made by Bouthem the teacher, Jairos the teacher, Rabbi Levi, and Rabbi Isaac.

**Act. Pil. 2. 3–4 names twelve supporters of Jesus among the Jews.

10b Omissions of proper names

THE TEXTUAL TRADITION

Matthew

15. 31   X 1Gr 'the God (−of Israel)'.

Mark

10. 46   1It '(−the son of Timaeus) Bartimaeus'./W 'the son of Timaeus (−Bartimaeus)'.

15. 21   1It '(−and Rufus)'.

16. 1   D 3It omit the three women's names./1Gr omits the first.

THE APOCRYPHAL TRADITION

*Arundel Latin Infancy Gospel 90. Mt. 2. 5. 'Bethlehem (−of Judah)'.

*Act. Pil. 11. 3. Lk. 23. 51. 'a city (−of the Jews)'.

** Not in quotation of Synoptic material.
* See also category 6b.

Act. Pil. 9. 1. Mt. 27. 17. 'which one (—Barabbas or Jesus called Christ)'.

Act. Pil. 11. 3; cf. Lk. 23. 49. The women who had come with Jesus from Galilee are not named. See also 13. 1, 2; cf. Mt. 28. 2 ff., where the women again are mentioned without being named. In neither instance, however, is a verse from the Synoptics quoted which originally contained the names of the women. Nevertheless, the author could have added them by borrowing from another verse.

Act. Pil. 13. 1, 2; cf. Mt. 28. 3 ff. The disciples are mentioned, but not named. The remarks made immediately above also apply here.

Gosp. Pet. 50 f.; cf. Mt. 28. 1//Mk. 16. 1. Pet. has 'Mary Magdalene... took with her women friends', omitting 'the other Mary' (Mt.) and 'Mary the mother of James and Salome' (Mk.).

11a The substitution of a proper name for a noun or pronoun

THE TEXTUAL TRADITION

Matthew

1. 20   reads: 'The angel of the Lord appeared to him, saying...' 1Sy 1Cop Iren read: 'The angel of the Lord appeared to Joseph, saying...' This is abbreviated as follows:

1. 20   1Sy 1Cop Iren 'Joseph' for 'him'.

1. 24   1Sy 1Cop 'Mary' for 'his wife'.

3. 3   1It 1Sy Iren 'the paths of our God' for 'his paths'.

4. 3   1It 'the Devil' for 'the one tempting'. Cf. category 9a above.

6. 33   1It 'God's righteousness' for 'his righteousness'.

8. 5 C^3 L Th^2 Om 3+Gr 1It 2Vg 1Sy 'Jesus' for 'he'.

8. 14   E* Aeth 'Peter's mother-in-law' for 'his mother-in-law'.

* 8. 23   U 047 5Gr 1Sy/1Sy

* 8. 24   1It 1Sy

* 8. 28   2It Vg 1Sy Geo

* 9. 14   1Cop

12. 9   3Gr 'the synagogue of the Jews' for 'their synagogue'.

*12. 15   1Gr

13. 55   1Sy 'Joseph' for 'the carpenter'. See also category 9a above.

14. 11   2Sy 'the head of John' for 'his head'.

14. 12   2It 1Sy 'the disciples of John' for 'his disciples'.

Mark

* 9. 15   D 5It Vg

* 9. 20   1Gr

* 9. 20   1It

*10. 46   1Sy

* An asterisk indicates that the proper name is 'Jesus'.

*10. 52   X Y Ga Th Pi Si Ph Ko(−1) 4+Gr 1Sy Or
*11. 21   M^mg 5Gr 1Geo
*12. 13   1Gr
*13. 3   1Sy
*14. 1   2Gr 1Vg
*14. 3   D 6It Vg 2Cop 1Geo
*14. 10   1Gr 1Sy
*14. 45   N Si 3Gr
*14. 56   Ps
 14. 61   Al* 1Gr Arm 'God' for 'the blessed'. See also category 9a above.
 14. 62   1It 'God' for 'power'.
*15. 16   C³ 4Gr 1It Vg 1Cop
 16. 1   K² M X Fam 13 4+Gr 1It Vg 'Jesus' for 'him'/1Gr has 'the
          body of Jesus'.

THE APOCRYPHAL TRADITION

Gosp. Heb. Ps. Orig. Lat. (see Appendix v. 4); cf. Mt. 19. 16 ff. Has 'Simon'
    for 'his disciples'.
The Jewish Gospel (de Santos, p. 46) variant to Mt. 4. 5 has 'in Jerusalem'
    for 'into the holy city'. (Lk. 4. 9 has 'into Jerusalem'.)
Pseud. Matt. Lat. 17. 2; cf. Mt. 2. 13. Has 'Mary' for 'his mother'.
Pseud. Thom. Lat. 1. 1; cf. Mt. 2. 13. Has 'Mary' for 'his mother'.
Act. Pil. 10. 2; cf. Lk. 23. 40. Has 'Dysmas' for 'the other'.
Act. Pil. 3. 1; cf. Jn. 18. 31. 'to Pilate' for 'to him'.
Pseud. Matt. Lat. 15. 1; cf. Lk. 2. 22. Has 'the purification of Mary' for
    'their purification'.
Pseud. Matt. Lat. 15. 1; cf. Lk. 2. 22. Has 'Joseph took the infant' for
    'they took him'.
Pseud. Matt. Lat. 16. 2; cf. Mt. 2. 11. Has 'to Mary and Joseph' for 'to
    him'.

11b   The substitution of a noun or pronoun for a proper name

THE TEXTUAL TRADITION

Matthew

*15. 1   D 10It Vg Aeth/9Gr Or

Mark

* 9. 4   1It 1Sy
* 9. 5   N Si 1Sy
*10. 50   D Th 3Gr It(−2) Vg

      * An asterisk indicates that the proper name is 'Jesus'.

*11. 33   2Gr 1Sy Aeth
*14. 60   2Gr
 14. 67   Famm 1 & 13(−1) 3Gr 1It 2Sy Geo Arm Eus 'him' for 'Peter'.
 14. 70   2Gr 'him' for 'Peter'.

THE APOCRYPHAL TRADITION

Egerton Pap. 2, Fragm. II, lines 43–59 (de Santos, p. 99); cf. Mt. 22. 17 parr. Has 'pay to the kings' for 'to Caesar'.

Pseud. Thom. 19. 2; cf. Lk. 2. 45. Has 'the city' for 'Jerusalem'.

Nat. Mary 10. 2; cf. Mt. 1. 20. Has 'lead her' for 'take Mary as your wife'.

Act. Pil. 4. 1; cf. Mt. 26. 61 'this temple' for 'temple of God'. Cf. category 6b above.

12a   The substitution of a noun for a pronoun, substantive adjective, or participle

THE TEXTUAL TRADITION

Matthew

 2. 13   reads: 'After they had departed...' C³ D³ 5Gr read: 'After the Magi had departed...' This is abbreviated as follows:
 2. 13   C³ D³ 5Gr 'the Magi' for 'they'.
Cf. 8. 28 1It 'across the sea' for 'to the other side'.
 9. 3   1Geo 'in their hearts' for 'among themselves'.
 9. 18   M* 2Gr 'to the crowds' for 'to them'.
 9. 21   Geo 'in his heart' for 'in himself'.
 10. 5   1Sy 'his disciples' for 'the twelve'.
 12. 15   N 1Cop 'crowds' for 'many'. Cf. category 13a below.
 13. 46   Th 4Gr Arm 'that pearl' for 'it'.
 14. 4   2It 'the wife of your brother' for 'her'. Cf. category 13a below.
 15. 14   D 1It(*d*) 'the blind (men)' for 'them'.

Mark

 9. 16   A C N X Ga Pi Si Ph Ko Fam 13 7+Gr 1It 2Sy Aeth 'the scribes' for 'them'.
 9. 33   3Gr '(his) disciples' for 'them'.
 10. 12   A D N X Y Ga Th Pi Si Ph Ko Famm 1 & 13 12+Gr 10It 3Sy Arm Or 'if a woman divorces' for 'if she divorces'.
 10. 13   A D N W X Y Ga Pi Si Ph Ko Fam 13 7+Gr It Vg 3Sy 1Cop Geo Aeth Arm τοις προσφερουσιν for αυτοις/Th Fam 1 3Gr τοις φερουσιν/1Gr τους προσφεροντας.
 10. 34   2Sy 'in his face' for 'on him'.
 11. 14   1It 'the tree' for 'it'.

 * An asterisk indicates that the proper name is 'Jesus'.

135

11. 18   1Gr 1It 'the people' for 'him'. This effects a substantive change.
12. 5   1Gr 'a slave' for 'another'. See also category 13a.
12. 5   1Gr 'many servants' for 'many others'. See also category 13a.
12. 6   1It 1Geo '(his) son' for 'him'.
12. 7   De 'the son is the heir' for 'this is the heir'.
12. 7   1It 'the son' for 'him'.
12. 28   5Gr 'the Sadducees with him' for 'them'.
14. 4   D Th 1Gr 5It Arm 'his disciples' for 'some'. See also category 6a above.
14. 21   1Sy 1Cop 'better for that man' for 'better for him'.
14. 22   2Gr 1Sy 'his disciples' for 'them'.
14. 23   W Same.
15. 19   2Sy 1Cop 'in his face' for αυτω; see also prep.
16. 1   1Gr 'the body of Jesus' for 'him'./Aeth 'his body'.

THE APOCRYPHAL TRADITION

Pseud. Matt. Lat. 15. 1; cf. Lk. 2. 21. Has 'the child' for Lk.'s 'him'. So also D Vg.
Pseud. Thom. 19. 5; cf. Lk. 2. 51. Has 'obedient to his parents' for 'obedient to them'.
Act. Pil. 3. 1; cf. Jn. 18. 30. 'to the Governor' for 'to him'.
Act. Pil. 9. 1; cf. Mt. 27. 22. 'the Jews' for 'all'.

12b   The substitution of a pronoun for a noun

THE TEXTUAL TRADITION

Matthew

8. 16   1It 2Sy 'them' for 'the spirits'.
13. 25   5Gr 'he' for 'the men'.

Mark

9. 3   D 'someone' for 'fuller' (not cited by Legg).
10. 7   W 'each' for 'man'.
11. 15   A 'in it' for 'in the temple'. Perhaps to avoid repetition.
12. 2   Th 6Gr 'from them' for 'from the tenants'. Perhaps to avoid repetition.
14. 3   1It 'it' for 'the alabaster'.
14. 32   D 1It 'them' for 'his disciples'.
15. 11   Th 2Gr Arm 'who also' for 'and the chief priests'/2Gr Geo 'and these' for 'and the chief priests'. To avoid repetition.
15. 46   1Sy 'in it' for 'in the linen'. Perhaps to avoid repetition.

Just. Apol. I. 15. 12; cf. Mt. 16. 26. Has 'it' for 'his soul'.

Just. Apol. I. 15. 4; cf. Mt. 19. 12. Justin once changes 'eunuchs' to 'some'; twice for ευνουχοι οιτινες he has οι.

II Clem. 5. 4; cf. Mt. 10. 28 par. 'you' for 'the body'. So also Just. Apol. I. 19. 7.

II Clem. 6. 2; cf. Mt. 16. 26 'a certain one' for 'a man'.

13a The addition of a noun to a pronoun, substantive adjective, or substantive participle

THE TEXTUAL TRADITION

Matthew

2. 23   reads: οπως πληρωθη το ρηθεν. 2Sy read: 'So that the word spoken would be fulfilled.' This is abbreviated as follows:

2. 23   2Sy '(+the word) spoken'.

3. 7   1Gr 'many+crowds'.

5. 11   C W Ga De Th Pi Si Ko All minusc 1It 2Sy Arm Geo Or 'evil+ word'/1Sy 'evil+thing'.

8. 27   W 2Gr Hil 'this+man'.

8. 28   8It Vg 1Sy 'two (+men) demoniacs'.

9. 15   9Gr οσον+χρονον.

9. 32   All uncs but Al B Famm 1 & 13(−1) 6+Gr 4It Vg 1Sy Arm Geo Got also 8It Vg 'dumb+man'.

10. 2   1Sy 2Cop Aeth 'the son of Zebedee' for ο του Ζεβεδαιου.

10. 22   5It Vg 'by all+men'./1It 2Vg 'by all+nations'.

11. 8   C L N O P W X Y Ga De Th Pi Si Ph Ko Most minusc 4It 2Vg Sy 2Cop Arm Got 'in soft+garments'.

11. 8   2Cop 'soft+garments'.

12. 15   C D L W X Y Ga De Th Pi Si Ph Ko Most minusc 4It 2Sy 1Cop Arm Geo Eus Or Hil 'many+crowds'. See also 12a above.

13. 19   1Gr 2Sy 'every (+man) bearing'.

14. 4   1It 2Sy 'to have her + (as) wife'. See also 12a above.

15. 34   3Sy Geo 'seven+loaves'.

Mark

9. 19   1Sy 'him+your son'.

9. 35   1Gr 1It 'twelve+disciples'./1It 'twelve+apostles'.

9. 49   5Gr 'all+bread'.

10. 10   D Th 1Gr 4It 1Cop 1Geo 'about this+word'.

10. 17   A K M W Th Pi Fam 13 10+Gr 1Geo 1Sy 1Cop Arm τις πλουσιος for εις.

10. 32   3Gr 'twelve + disciples'.
11. 11   D 13Gr 9It 2Vg 'twelve + disciples'.
12. 5   1Sy 'many other + servants'. See also category 12a.
12. 5   D 5It 1Sy 'another + slave'. Cf. category 13b, Mk. 12. 4; category 12a, Mk. 12. 5.
12. 7   . 1Sy 'this is (+ his son) the heir'.
12. 9   4It 1Cop 'to other + tenants'.
12. 29   A C K M U Pi Si Ph 11 + Gr 4It 'the first + commandment'.
12. 31   1It 'second + commandment'.
12. 32   1Geo 'another + God'.
12. 42   Al 1Gr (one noun added to another) '(+ woman) a widow'.
13. 13   4It 2Vg 'by all + men'./1It 1Vg 'by all + nations'.
14. 17   2It Aeth 'twelve + disciples'.
14. 31   1It 1Sy 1Cop 'all + the disciples'.
15. 38   D 7It 3Vg 'into two + parts'.
15. 47   D 4It 1Cop Arm (noun added to adv.) '(+ the place) where'.
15. 47   W Fam 13 1Gr (noun added to art.) 'Mary the (+ mother) of Jesus'.

THE APOCRYPHAL AND PATRISTIC TRADITIONS

Act. Pil. 4. 1; cf. Mt. 27. 24. 'the blood of this + righteous man'.
Act. Pil. 2. 1; cf. Mt. 27. 19. 'that (*or*, this) righteous + man'.
Theoph. III. 14; cf. Mt. 6. 3. 'your right + hand', 'your left + hand'.

13b   The omission of a noun from a pronoun, adjective, or participle

THE TEXTUAL TRADITION

Matthew

7. 11   L 4It Vg 'good (− gifts)'.
7. 13   1Sy '(− the road) which leads'.
Cf. 9. 20 1Gr 5It 1Vg 'touch (− the hem) of his garment'.
10. 1   1Sy 'twelve (− disciples)'.
12. 36   1Gr 'every idle (− word)'.

Mark

9. 25   1Gr 'the unclean (− spirit)'.
10. 30   2Gr 1It Clem 'in the coming (− age)'.
10. 46   C* 1Gr 'blind (− beggar)'.
12. 4   Al* 1Gr 'another (− slave)'. See also category 13a, Mk. 12. 5.
12. 23   1Gr 2Sy 'they had her (− [as] wife)'.
12. 31   U 1Gr 'another (− commandment)'.

12. 43   W Fam 1 2Gr 7It 1Sy Geo (omit subst. participle from pron.) 'than all (−the ones casting)'.

12. 44   1Sy 'everything...(−all her life)'.

14. 3   1It(d) (Noun omitted from other noun) 'alabaster (−of myrrh) of nard'.

14. 3   D 1Gr 1Sy (as above) 'alabaster of myrrh (−of pure nard)'. D also omits 'very costly'.

14. 8   1Gr 'anointed my (−body)' = 'anointed me'.

14. 12   3Gr 'the first (−day)'.

15. 23   1Gr '(−wine) mixed with myrrh'.

15. 39   0112 1Sy 'this (−man)'.

THE APOCRYPHAL AND PATRISTIC TRADITIONS

Pseud. Thom. 19. 2; cf. Lk. 2. 47. 'all (−the ones hearing him)' (omission of substantive participle).

Gosp. Ebion. Epiph. Haer. 30. 13. 7 f.; cf. Mt. 3. 15. 'all (−righteousness)'.

Just. Apol. 1. 15. 4. Mt. 19. 12. 'not all can receive this (−word)'.

Just. Apol. 1. 15. 2; cf. Mt. 18. 9. 'two (−eyes)'.

14a   The addition of circumstances

THE TEXTUAL TRADITION

Matthew

8. 33   1Gr 'the herdsmen, (+when they saw what had happened), fled'.

Mark

9. 2   W Th 𝔓⁴⁶ Fam 13 4Gr Or add 'and while they (he) were (was) praying' to 'he was transfigured'.

9. 17   At beginning, Gᵐᵍ adds 'at the time a certain man came up to Jesus, kneeling before him, and saying' (similar to the parallel in Mt. 17. 14).

12. 7   N Si 3Gr 'those tenants+when they saw him'/2Gr. Cf. 1It 1Sy + 'when they beheld him'/Th Fam 13 14+Gr 1Sy Geo Arm +'when they beheld him coming'.

12. 9   Text: 'what will the Lord of the vineyard do?'; 1Sy 'when the Lord of the vineyard comes, what will he do?'

14. 13   (W) Th Si Fam 13 5Gr (1Cop) 1Geo Arm (Or) before 'will meet', add 'when you enter (into the city)'.

15. 13   G Fam 13 2Gr 1Sy Arm (omit 'and said') 'they cried out+being excited by the chief priests and said'.

THE APOCRYPHAL TRADITION

Gosp. Heb. Ps. Orig. Lat. (see Appendix v. 4); cf. Mt. 19. 16 ff. Has 'Simon' for 'his disciples' and adds 'who was sitting by him'.

Protev. Jms. 11. 1–2. See Appendix v. 14. Circumstances added.

Pseud. Matt. Lat. 15. 1. After Lk. 2. 22 adds 'when the infant received peritomen'. (According to Ante-Nicene Fathers 34: 'when the infant received perhithomus—perhithomus, that is, circumcision—'.)

Pseud. Matt. Lat. 15. 2; cf. Lk. 2. 28. Add 'and having seen the child'.

Pseud. Matt. Lat. 16. 2; cf. Mt. 2. 11. Has 'sitting in his mother's lap' for Mt.'s 'with Mary his mother'.

Pseud. Matt. Lat. 16. 2; cf. Mt. 2. 12. Before 'warned', adds 'and when they were going to return to King Herod'.

Ps. Thom. Lat. 1. 1; cf. Mt. 2. 13. Adds 'and Jesus was two years old when he went into Egypt'.

Jos. Arim. 2. 4; cf. Mt. 26. 49. 'Hail, Rabbi+it being the evening of the fifth day'.

14b The omission of circumstances

THE TEXTUAL TRADITION

Matthew

13. 4   C omits 'and as he sowed' (in a saying, not narrative).

Mark

9. 9   1Gr omits 'and while they were descending'.
10. 2   D 3It 1Sy omit 'Pharisees coming up'.
10. 32 1It(*k*) omits 'and Jesus was preceding them'.
10. 46 1It(*k*) omits 'and as he was leaving Jericho with his disciples'.
14. 11   D 6It 1Geo Eus 'and (−hearing) they rejoiced'.
14. 18   1Gr omits 'and eating'.
15. 35   C 3Gr omit 'hearing' (De omits 'and some of the bystanders hearing').
16. 1   D 2It 1Gr omit 'and when the sabbath was past' and some or all of the women's names.
16. 2   1It omits 'when the sun is risen'.

THE APOCRYPHAL TRADITION

Nat. Mary 10. 2. Mt. 1. 24. Omits 'when Joseph rose up from sleep'.

15a The addition of explanations

THE TEXTUAL TRADITION

Matthew

5. 18   For 'or one kerea', Aeth Arm have 'quod est unus apex'; Geo has 'solum unum cornu'.
8. 24   After 'waves', 7Gr 5Vg 2Sy add 'for the wind was against them' (from 14. 24).
9. 24   At end, Al* 1Gr 1Cop add 'seeing that she was dead'.

Mark

14. 70   After 'for you are a Galilean' A N X Y Ga De Th Pi Si Ko Fam 13
9+Gr 1It 2Sy 1Cop Aeth Arm add 'and (*or*, for) your speech is
similar', and the like.

16. 3   At end, 2Vg add 'for it was very great'. (These words are from vs.
4. Some MSS have the words in vs. 3, but not in vs. 4. 2Vg have
them in both places.)

THE APOCRYPHAL TRADITION

Nat. of Mary 10. 2; cf. Mt. 1. 20. After 'fear not', adds 'that is, do not have
any suspicion of fornication in the virgin, or think any evil of her, nor
fear'.

Gospel of Peter 10; cf. Mk. 14. 61. 'he held his peace + as though having no
pain.'

Jos. Arim. 2. 3; cf. Mt. 26. 14 ff. Before 'the people' give Judas his money,
it is explained that 'the people did not know that Judas was speaking
about Jesus, for many (*hikanoi*) confessed him to be the Son of God'.

Jos. Arim. 2. 4; cf. Mt. 26. 48 par. 'seize him + for he stole the law and the
prophets'.

15b The omission of explanations

THE TEXTUAL TRADITION

Matthew

2. 20   2Gr omit 'for the ones seeking the life of the child were dead'.
Perhaps omitted by homoeoteleuton.

13. 5   2It 1Sy omit 'on account of not having depth of earth'. (In saying.)

Mark

9. 38   D X W Fam 1(−1) Fam 13 10Gr It(−2) Vg Geo Arm omit 'because he does not follow us'. Perhaps to avoid repetition.

10. 2   1It omits 'tempting him'.

12. 18   1Gr omits 'who say there is no resurrection and ask'.

14. 10   A 'Judas Iscariot (−one of the twelve)'.

14. 70   W 6Gr 1It omit 'for you are a Galilean'. Cf. category 15a above.

15. 15   D 2It omit 'wishing to satisfy the crowd'.

15. 42   1Gr omits 'since it was the day of preparation, that is, the day
before the Sabbath'.

16a The addition of conclusion and result

THE TEXTUAL TRADITION

Matthew

3. 15   At end, 1It adds 'then he baptized him'; 1Sy 'then he permitted
him + to be baptized and Jesus was baptized'.

8. 13   At end, Al C E M N S* U X Th Si Ph Fam 1 13Gr 1It 2Sy Aeth add 'and the centurion turning into his house in that hour found this (his) child (*or*, him) healed'; 1Gr adds 'and the ones who were sent turning into the house found the sick servant healed'.

8. 16   1Gr omits 'many', adds 'and he healed them'.

9. 35   At end, Al* L Ph Fam 13(−1) 12Gr 4It Tat add 'and many followed him'.

15. 27   At end, 4Sy Tat add 'and live'.

Mark

12. 30   At end, A D X Ga Si Ko(−3) Famm 1 & 13 5+Gr It Vg 4Sy Geo Aeth Arm Hil add 'this (is) the first (+and great, 1Gr) commandment'; K U Pi Ph 12+Gr add 'this (is) the first commandment of all'; Euseb Cyp W Th 2Gr add 'this (is) first'.

15. 3   At end, N U W De Th Si Ps Fam 13 16+Gr 2Vg 2Sy Geo Aeth Arm add 'but he answered nothing', and the like.

16 b The omission of conclusion and result

THE TEXTUAL TRADITION

Matthew

4. 24   1It omits 'and he healed them'.

8. 32   1Sy omits 'and they died in the water'.

12. 5   1Gr omits 'and they are guiltless'.

12. 15   1It omits 'and he cured them all'.

Mark

9. 27   W 𝔓⁴⁵ 1Gr 2It 2Sy omit 'and he rose'.

9. 38   See speech omitted.

10. 27   De Ps Fam 1(−1) 14Gr 1It Arm omit 'for all things are possible with God'.

11. 6   1Sy 1Cop omit 'and they left them'.

14. 16   1It omits 'and they prepared the passover'.

15. 32   1Gr 2It omit 'that we may see'.

THE APOCRYPHAL AND PATRISTIC TRADITIONS

Egerton Pap. 2, Fragm. 1, lines 22–41; cf. Jn. 7. 30 (de Santos, p. 98). Lacks 'and no one laid hand upon him'.

Athen. 12. 3; cf. Mt. 5. 46 par. Athen. omits the conclusions of the sayings. See the text, p. 65 above.

17a The addition of emotion

Mark

12. 9   1It 'then the lord (+angered) will come'.
15. 13   See 14a above.

Egerton Pap. 2, Fragm. II, lines 43–59 (de Santos, p. 99); cf. Mt. 22. 17 parr.
Has in addition 'Jesus became angry' (apparently from Mk. 1. 43).
Pseud. Thom. 19. 2; cf. Lk. 2. 45. 'they (+were grieved and) returned'.

17b The omission of emotion

Matthew

9. 8   X Iren omit 'they were afraid'.

Mark

9. 15   1Gr omits 'were greatly amazed, and running'.
10. 21   1Gr omits 'he loved him and'. (Probably by homoeoteleuton, 2Gr
omit 'he loved him and he said to him'.)
10. 32   D K 17Gr 2It 1Vg omit 'and those who followed were afraid';
3It omit 'and...were afraid' (perhaps only to avoid redundancy).
16. 8   1Sy omits 'for trembling and astonishment had them'.

Pseud. Thom. 19. 3; cf. Lk. 2. 48. Has 'coming up' for Lk.'s 'and when
they saw him they were astonished'.

18a The addition of miscellaneous details

Gosp. Heb. Jerome Comm. 1 in Mt. 12. 13 (see Appendix v. 2). The man
with the withered hand was a mason.
Gosp. Heb. Ps. Orig. Lat. (see Appendix v. 4). One of the rich men began
to scratch his head.
The Jewish Gospel (de Santos, p. 47; H.-S. p. 150), variant to Mt. 27. 65.
'And he delivered to them armed men that they might sit over against
the cave and guard it day and night.'
Pap. Oxy. 1. 7, lines 36–41 (de Santos, pp. 90 f.; H.-S. pp. 109 f.). Mt. 5. 14:
'on a mountain'; Pap.: 'on the *akron* of a high mountain'.

Protev. Jms. 12. 3 Mary's age is given as 16.

Protev. Jms. 12. 2; cf. Lk. 1. 39–45. New details added. See Appendix v. 17.

Pseud. Matt. 15. 2; cf. Lk. 2. 25. Simeon's age is given as 112.

Pseud. Matt. 16. 1; cf. Mt. 2. 1. 'to Jerusalem + bringing great gifts'.

Pseud. Thom. Lat. 1. 1; cf. Mt. 2. 13. Adds 'and Jesus was two years old when he went into Egypt'.

*Jos. of Arim. 1. 3 Judas Iscariot was the son of the brother of Caiaphas the priest.

Jos. of Arim. 3. 1 'Gestas on the left, and Demas on the right'.

Act. Pil. 10. 1. The Coptic and Armenian add that Dysmas was placed on the right, Gestas on the left.

Medieval comm. on Luke (see H.-S. p. 151); cf. Lk. 10. 13. The miracles wrought in Chorazin and Bethsaida are numbered in the Gospel of the Hebrews at fifty-three.

Gosp. Pet. 7. 3; cf. Mt. 27. 66. The tomb is sealed with seven seals.

18b The omission of miscellaneous details

THE APOCRYPHAL TRADITION

Ps. Gosp. Matt. Clem. Alex. Strom. iv. 6; cf. Lk. 19. 1 ff. Omits 'and he was rich'.

Protev. Jms. 12. 3; cf. Lk. 1. 24. Omits 'five months'.

Pseud. Matt. Lat. 15. 3; cf. Lk. 2. 36. Omits 'she was of a great age'.

The following summary observations can be made on the basis of these lists.

1. There is an overall tendency to make the subject more explicit rather than less explicit.

2. The same is not true about the direct object. Although more opportunities exist in the Synoptics for omitting a direct object than for adding one, the high number of omissions nevertheless prevents us from drawing any conclusions on this score.

3. The remarks made about the addition of the direct object apply also to the use of the indirect object and similar phrases.

4. There is no clear tendency with regard to the use of prepositional phrases.

5. There is a slight majority of additions of adjectives and adjectival phrases over omissions.

6. There is a clear tendency to add a noun in the genitive case to make a phrase more explicit.

* Not in direct connection with Synoptic material.

7. There is a tendency to add genitive pronouns, except in the writings of Justin, who tends to omit them.

8. There is a slight majority of additions of a noun to a proper name over omissions.

9. In the manuscripts, there is more of a tendency to add proper names to nouns than to omit them.

10. The manuscripts show a clear tendency to make characters and places more explicit by the addition of proper names. The Apocryphal Gospels, as is well known, show a clear tendency to create names for unnamed Gospel characters and to name new characters whom they introduce. They also show some tendency to omit the names of well-known characters.

11. There is a considerable tendency to substitute proper names for nouns and pronouns. The general tendency to add proper names may be observed by noting instances in which the identity of characters mentioned in a verse of the Synoptics is made more explicit in different ways by different groups of manuscripts. Thus at Mt. 13. 55, some manuscripts add 'Joseph' to 'the carpenter', while others substitute 'Joseph' for 'the carpenter'. See categories 9 a and 11a. In the same two categories, see also Mt. 4. 3 and Mk. 14. 61. Also note that in category 11a, the pronoun in Mk. 16. 1 is made more explicit in two different ways.

12. There is a tendency to substitute nouns for pronouns rather than vice versa, except in Justin. The tendency in the manuscripts is the clearer when one considers that some of the instances in which a pronoun is used for a noun apparently result from a desire to avoid repetition.

13. In the MSS there is some tendency to add nouns to pronouns.

14. In the apocryphal literature, there is a tendency to add phrases which indicate circumstances. No tendency is discernible in the MSS.

15, 16, 17. No clear tendency toward adding or omitting explanations, conclusions and results, or emotions can be seen.

18. There is a tendency to add small details of fact. What qualifies as a 'small detail of fact', of course, is sometimes difficult to judge, but the evidence seems to be that new matters of fact creep into the tradition.

It will be noted that there are no categories of numbers or of places as such. The reason is that the evidence to be gained from the sources which were examined was so slight in these two categories that they were not usable. This material, however, is dealt with in other ways. Thus, for example, numbers sometimes appear in 'small details of fact' and in 'circumstances'.

On the whole, then, it seems that there was some tendency to make the tradition more explicit. This tendency was by no means universal, however, and any given passage could become, in certain stages, less explicit. The criterion of explicitness and detail may be applied only 'in bulk'. No one instance can prove anything about the relative antiquity of tradition, but in general the document is later which is more specific and detailed in the ways described in categories 1, 6, 7, 9, 10, 11, 12, 13, 14, 18, and perhaps 5 and 8.

THE EVIDENCE FROM THE SYNOPTIC GOSPELS

We may now turn to the Synoptic Gospels to see how they stand with regard to detail. Before presenting the material itself, it will be well to note more particularly what various scholars have said about details in the Gospels, especially as they bear on the Synoptic problem and on the redactional method of the evangelists.

Bultmann, who probably here represents the majority of scholars, was, as we have seen, of the opinion that the later document is the more detailed.[1] Since many scholars have held Mark to be more detailed, on the whole, than Matthew and Luke,[2] one would expect it to be placed later. It has not been, however. For this reason there is an inconsistency in the position of Bultmann, Dibelius, and, indeed, all who think that the tendency of the tradition is to become more detailed, that Mark is more detailed, and that Mark is the first Gospel.[3]

---

[1] See p. 88 above.

[2] Besides the discussion of the positions of Taylor, Cadbury, and Bussmann above, see, for example, W. C. Allen, *The Gospel according to St Matthew*[3] (The International Critical Commentary), 1912, pp. xvii–xviii.

[3] We may recall that Bultmann's analysis of such literary types as the miracle story and the apophthegm revealed that, in their pure forms, they lacked details. Thus he held details to be secondary elements in these literary forms. (See *Die Geschichte*, pp. 256 ff. [E.T. pp. 241 ff.].) He also held the addition of details to be a universal tendency of tradition and illustrated it from the Synoptic material. (See 'The New Approach', pp. 345 f.) Yet at the same time he recognized that

On this point there are two consistent positions. Vincent Taylor represents one of them. His view is that details are characteristic of early, eye-witness documents; Mark is detailed; Mark is the earliest Gospel and the one closest to the eye-witness period.[1] Cadbury may be roughly put in this same category. He, however, would emphasize what Taylor also will grant, namely, that details are also characteristic of later documents. It is only the intermediate stage of the tradition which lacks details. Mark's details, however, come from stage one of the tradition rather than from stage three.[2]

The other consistent position is that of Bussmann, who, as we have seen, thought details to indicate lateness, held Mark to be the most detailed Gospel, and thus relegated it to last place.[3] W. R. Farmer has also recently shown himself to be of this view. Thus he writes as follows:

Assuming that the Apocryphal Gospel literature was written after the canonical gospels, and since, by comparison, this literature is characterized by a tendency to make the tradition more specific (by the giving of names to persons not named in the canonical Gospel narratives, etc.): *That form of a particular tradition found in the Gospels in which the tradition is more specific is to be adjudged secondary to a form of the same tradition in which the tradition is less specific.*[4]

Using this principle as one of his criteria, Farmer also puts Mark in last place,[5] although he differs from Bussmann in putting Matthew before Luke and in arguing for direct relationships among our Gospels.[6]

The question of consistency of view raises the question of Mark's place in the history of the tradition. Although we cannot have, by the nature of the case, any evidence to support Cadbury's view that the tradition moved in a circle, being first detailed, then not detailed, then detailed again, the view is reasonable enough. On this view, Mark fits into the first stage,

Matthew is often less detailed than Mark. (See *Die Geschichte*, p. 378 [E.T. p. 353].) He seems never to have reconciled his claim that the Synoptic material became more detailed with the statement that Matthew frequently lacks Mark's details, nor to have investigated just how often details are added and omitted in the later Synoptic tradition.

[1] See pp. 91-3 above.   [2] See pp. 93-5 above.
[3] See p. 95 above.
[4] W. R. Farmer, *The Synoptic Problem*, p. 228. The italics are his.
[5] *Ibid.* p. vii and *passim.*   [6] *Ibid.* pp. 202 ff.

and so should be more detailed.[1] On the view of Bussmann and Farmer, however, Mark does not fit into the first stage. Farmer especially makes it clear that he places Mark closer to the Apocryphal Gospels than to the eye-witness period.[2] The question then is quite clear: does Mark fit into the first, eye-witness stage? Nineham, in discussing the view that details show closeness to eye-witness accounts, seems to argue that it does not. Nineham does not entirely discount the possibility that details could go back to the eye-witness stage, but he is struck by the fact that Mark's details, supposedly from such a source, occur in material which is obviously 'from the impersonal tradition of the community'.[3] In Nineham's view, Mark's material is shown to have been passed down by the community, rather than directly communicated by an eye-witness, by its formal characteristics, principally its being comprised of individual pericopes. Thus he writes that

All, or practically all, the material in Mark seems to be of the *pericope* form and so presumably has passed through the formalizing processes of community tradition, just like the similar material in Matthew, Luke and Q.[4]

Nineham could thus argue that Taylor's view of details puts Mark's material earlier than its formal structure does. If Mark's details indicate proximity to an eye-witness source, how does one account for the formal similarity between the Marcan material and the material in Matthew and Luke which is regarded as having been passed down by the community?

It is not our purpose here to solve this problem. We have yet, indeed, to see whether Mark is more detailed than Matthew

---

[1] See, in addition to Taylor, Streeter, *op. cit.* p. 163, and Hawkins, *Horae Synopticae*, p. 126. Both thought that Mark rests upon an eye-witness account.

[2] Farmer, *op. cit.*, pp. 122 f., 130, 134.

[3] D. E. Nineham, 'Eye-witness testimony and the Gospel tradition I', *J.T.S.* IX (1958), 21–2. Nineham also points out two general principles which should be noted before concluding that details prove material to be early. In the first place, 'it is the apocryphal gospels that are richest in such vivid touches and circumstantial detail, and secondly, if the sources of the canonical gospels were to be graded simply on this criterion, the M material would be shown to be at least as close to eye-witness testimony as any other, a surely rather paradoxical conclusion'. He mentions (p. 22) indebtedness to a conversation with H. J. Cadbury for this point.

[4] *Ibid.* p. 20. Nineham quotes V. Taylor (*Formation*, p. 38), in his support: 'With the Gospel of Mark before us it is impossible to deny that the earliest tradition was largely a mass of fragments.' See also Nineham, p. 17.

and Luke, and if so, in what ways. The importance of the problem of Mark's details should, however, now be quite clear. Marcan studies, in my view, have been hampered by the fact that most scholars, following the great German form-critics, have not taken this problem seriously, despite the way in which it was posed by Bussmann. The problem of holding together apparently contradictory facts—Mark's priority, Mark's details, and the general lateness of details—has never really been met, except by those who, like Taylor and Cadbury, explain Mark's details by appeal to its relative closeness to eye-witness accounts. It may be argued, however, that these scholars have not effectively dealt with the problem posed by Nineham, namely, how to account for eye-witness details in material which has been handed down by a community supposedly disinterested[1] in details.[2]

The question of details also bears on Luke's redactional method. Cadbury has offered two solutions to the question of why Luke is less detailed than Mark, though later. Although Cadbury did not offer these answers in response to Bussmann's placing Luke first because of its lack of detail, they serve that purpose very well. In the first place, Cadbury argues that Luke omits foreign names and words because of his literary sensitivity. Cadbury offers considerable evidence that careful writers in Greek avoided foreign words. Josephus did the same. It is part of the same characteristic to apologize for what foreign words are included (as in Lk. 4. 31).[3] Again, Cadbury suggests

---

[1] Cadbury and Taylor agree with Nineham that the community was disinterested in details. See above, pp. 92 ff.

[2] This is not to say that they have not considered the problem. Taylor, it will be recalled, maintains that not all of Mark's material comes from the eye-witness source. That which is most detailed does, however. Thus Taylor would simply deny that the most detailed pericopes in Mark have been anonymously handed down by the community. See, for example, his commentary on Mark, pp. 78 ff., where he distinguishes between material which is 'popular in origin' (the pronouncement stories) and material which 'reached the Evangelist along more personal channels' (the miracle stories). Nineham's challenge is that even material in the second category shows signs of community transmission, principally the pericope form. Cadbury, in contrast to Taylor, regards all of Mark's material as having been passed down by the community. A few details remain in it, however, as somewhat anachronistic elements. See *The making of Luke-Acts*, pp. 83 f. How and why this happened he does not indicate.

[3] *The making of Luke-Acts*, pp. 123–6. For Josephus, see p. 171. Cadbury treats the matter at greater extent in *The style and literary method of Luke* (Cambridge, Mass., 1920), pp. 154 ff. As 'apologies' for foreign words, he lists Lk. 9. 10; 22. 1,

that Luke may omit some things, such as the subject of the verb in Mk. 5. 9, from a desire to avoid repetition, since the same word ('name') occurs earlier in the verse.[1] These two explanations cannot, of course, be expected to account for all the instances in which Luke is less specific than Matthew or Mark, but it will be of interest, in examining the lists which follow, to see in how many cases they apply.

With regard to Matthew's redactional method, we have already observed that Bultmann thought him to have abbreviated Mark by omitting small details.[2] This would presumably be Bultmann's answer to Bussmann's solution of the Synoptic problem: Matthew is less detailed, but it is because he was an abbreviator. We have already seen that the idea that Matthew was an abbreviator is questionable, but it will be of interest to see how consistently he lacks details which are in Mark. Bussmann has met this type of explanation head on, however. He notes that, while Mark has details not in Matthew, Matthew also has some not in Mark and Luke. He comments, 'Wenn diese bei ihm (scil. Matthew) sekundär sind, warum dann nicht auch jene bei Mk?'[3] His discussion of the relationship between Matthew and Mark on the matter of details is of some interest. He notes of Mark that 'er allein mehr bietet in Umschreibungen, erklärenden Zusätzen, [und] die Erzählung nicht wesentlich weiter führenden Erweiterungen'. Then he puts the question,

Why is Mark more precise in such small details (*Angaben*), to name first the most striking, as about *names* and *numbers*, which Matthew appears consistently to pass over, while he either with Mark in contrast to Luke or even by himself alone is at other times richer in quite similar things than the other two?[4]

Bussmann gives lists of names and numbers, showing that, although Matthew laid emphasis on both, he frequently does not have the ones which appear in Mark. 'Thus the conclusion

3; 2. 4; 7. 11; 8. 3; 10. 39; 19. 2. Omissions of barbarous words are found in Luke's parallels to Mk. 3. 17; 10. 46; 11. 10; 12. 42; 14. 32, 36, 43; 15. 22; 15. 34. Luke translates barbarisms in his parallels to Mk. 2. 4 ff.; 3. 18; 4. 15, 21; 5. 41; 6. 8; 12. 41; 9. 5; 10. 51; 12. 14; 15. 15; 15. 39; and the parallel to Mt. 5. 26.
[1] *The style and literary method of Luke*, p. 84.
[2] *Die Geschichte*, p. 378 (E.T. p. 353).
[3] Bussmann, *op. cit.* I, 104.   [4] *Ibid.* pp. 85-6.

follows that Matthew had not yet read those other names in Mark; therefore they are to be charged to the account of an editor.'[1] The burden of Bussmann's argument is seen in this sentence: 'Es fragt sich also wieder, wenn er dieses bringt, obwohl seine Vorlage es nicht hat, warum jenes nicht, wenn er es gelesen hat?'[2]

Bussmann would argue, then, that Matthew had no tendency to omit details, since he adds so many on his own. If we accept this argument, as I am inclined to do, it poses a considerable problem. Either Matthew's relation to Mark is not what it is usually thought to have been, or else his redactional method is not what it is thought to have been. The problem, on the assumption of Mark's direct priority to Matthew, is to find a reasonable explanation of Matthew's redactional method. It really is not good enough to say, with Stanton, that 'we ought not to assume that whatever seems significant to us must have seemed so in another age'. This is the explanation Stanton offers to account for Matthew's paucity of details over against Mark. He goes on to comment that we now prize Mark's details 'as indications that his informant was an eye-witness'.[3]

It is interesting to note that, if one rejects the hypothesis that Matthew was an abbreviator, one encounters the same problem ordinarily encountered by those who wish to place Matthew before Mark. One of the principal arguments against such a view is that Mark's redactional activity, and indeed his purpose in writing, cannot be explained if he followed Matthew. But if one is led not to regard Matthew as an abbreviator, his redactional method becomes difficult to explain on the hypothesis that he used Mark. It was just this consideration which led Bussmann to embrace the view that neither knew the other directly.[4]

[1] *Ibid.* p. 87. The names in Mark which are not in Matthew which Bussmann is unable to imagine Matthew as omitting are those in Mk. 2. 14; 3. 17; 14. 33; 15. 21; 16. 1.

[2] *Ibid.* p. 87. This sentence refers especially to the use of numbers, and the thirty pieces of silver in Mt. 26. 15 in particular. It typifies Bussmann's attitude toward the entire problem, however.

[3] Stanton, *op. cit.* p. 325. See p. 91, n. 3 above.

[4] After investigating the ways in which Mark differs from Matthew and Luke, and especially those instances in which he is more vivid, more precise, more detailed, and more exaggerated, Bussmann concludes (*op. cit.* pp. 100 f., emphasis removed): 'Die bis jetzt besprochenen Abweichungen des Mk von Mt unter

It will now be appropriate to present the material which we have collected which bears on the problem at hand, in order to see if a consistent relationship is to be found.

1′ Subjects in one Gospel but not in another[1]

Matthew

4. 5 reads: 'Then the devil takes him into the holy city.' Lk. 4. 9 reads: 'And he led him into Jerusalem.' This is abbreviated as follows:

4. 5; ctr. Lk. 4. 9 'the devil takes' (Lk.: led).

4. 8; ctr. Lk. 4. 5 'the devil takes' (Lk.: led).

5. 25; ctr. Lk. 12. 58 'lest (+your adversary) hand you over'.

6. 23; ctr. Lk. 11. 34 'your eye is evil'.

8. 4 ('Jesus says') and Lk. 5. 14 ('*he* announced'); ctr. Mk. 1. 44.

8. 22; ctr. Lk. 9. 60.

8. 27; ctr. Lk. 8. 25 (cf. Mk. 4. 41) 'the men marveled'.

8. 31; ctr. Mk. 5. 12 and Lk. 8. 32 'the demons besought'.

8. 34; ctr. Mk. 5. 15 and Lk. 8. 35 'all the city came out'.

9. 2 and Mk. 2. 5; ctr. Lk. 5. 20.

9. 9; ctr. Mk. 2. 14 and Lk. 5. 27 'Jesus saw'.

9. 11; ctr. Mk. 2. 16 and Lk. 5. 30 'your teacher eats'.

9. 19 ('Jesus and his disciples followed'); ctr. Mk. 5. 24 ('he went away').

9. 23; ctr. Mk. 5. 38 and Lk. 8. 51 'Jesus going into'.

9. 24 and Mk. 5. 39; ctr. Lk. 8. 52 'the girl (child) is not dead'.

9. 35; ctr. Mk. 6. 6 'Jesus went about'.

10. 31; ctr. Lk. 12. 7 '*you* are worth'.

11. 10; ctr. Lk. 7. 27 '*I* send'. This is a quotation from Mal. 3. 1. εγω is read there by $\aleph^c$ A Q Γ.

12. 2; ctr. Mk. 2. 24 'your disciples do'.

12. 15; and Mk. 3. 7 ('Jesus departed'); ctr. Lk. 6. 17 ('he stood').

12. 24; ctr. Mk. 3. 22 and Lk. 11. 15 'this one casts out'.

13. 4 and Lk. 8. 5; ctr. Mk. 4. 4 'while *he* was sowing'.

13. 34; ctr. Mk. 4. 33.

14. 16; ctr. Mk. 6. 37 and Lk. 9. 13.

14. 26; ctr. Mk. 6. 49 'the disciples seeing'.

14. 27; ctr. Mk. 6. 50.

14. 35; ctr. Mk. 6. 54 'the men of that place recognizing'.

15. 28; ctr. Mk. 7. 29.

Seitenblick auf L machen die Unmöglichkeit deutlich, dass der Verfasser des ersten Evangeliums das zweite Evangelium in der Form, in der es jetzt abgeschlossen vorliegt, gelesen und benutzt haben kann: es muss ihm in einer kürzeren Gestalt, welche viele kleine Erweiterungen und Änderungen noch nicht enthielt, vorgelegen haben. Damit wäre aber die Urevangeliumshypothese als richtig erwiesen.' [1] Unless otherwise indicated, read '(+Jesus) said'.

15. 32; ctr. Mk. 8. 1 'Jesus calling'.

15. 34; ctr. Mk. 8. 5.

15. 38; ctr. Mk. 8. 9 'the ones eating were'.

16. 5; ctr. Mk. 8. 14 'the disciples forgot'.

16. 6; ctr. Mk. 8. 15.

16. 8; ctr. Mk. 8. 17.

16. 21; ctr. Mk. 8. 31 (cf. Lk. 9. 22) 'Jesus Christ began'.

16. 24; ctr. Mk. 8. 34 and Lk. 9. 23.

17. 1 and Mk. 9. 2; ctr. Lk. 9. 28 'Jesus takes along'.

17. 9; ctr. Mk. 9. 9 'Jesus commanded'.

17. 10; ctr. Mk. 9. 11 'the disciples asked'.

17. 17 and Lk. 9. 41; ctr. Mk. 9. 19.

17. 22; ctr. Mk. 9. 31 and Lk. 9. 43.

18. 7; ctr. Lk. 17. 1 'the scandal comes'. Lk. may be avoiding repetition.

19. 4; ctr. Mk. 10. 6 'the creator made'. But see also Mk. 10. 6, category 6.

19. 20; ctr. Mk. 10. 20 and Lk. 18. 21 'the youth says'.

19. 22; ctr. Mk. 10. 22 and Lk. 18. 23 'the youth hearing'.

19. 25; ctr. Mk. 10. 26 'the disciples were astonished'. Cf. also Lk. 18. 26 'the ones hearing said'.

19. 26 and Mk. 10. 27; ctr. Lk. 18. 27.

19. 26; ctr. Mk. 10. 27 (cf. Lk. 18. 27) '*this* is impossible'.

19. 28 and Mk. 10. 29; ctr. Lk. 18. 29.

20. 25 and Mk. 10. 42; ctr. Lk. 22. 25.

21. 1; ctr. Mk. 11. 1 and Lk. 19. 29 'Jesus sent'.

21. 6 ('the disciples going') and Lk. 19. 32 ('the ones who were sent, going away'); ctr. Mk. 11. 4 ('they went away').

21. 12; ctr. Mk. 11. 15 and Lk. 19. 45 'Jesus entered'.

21. 24 and Mk. 11. 29; ctr. Lk. 20. 3.

21. 35 (cf. Lk. 20. 10); ctr. Mk. 12. 3 'the tenants taking'.

21. 45 f. (chief priests and Pharisees) and Lk. 20. 19 (scribes and chief priests); ctr. Mk. 12. 12.

23. 34; ctr. Lk. 11. 49 '*I* send'.

24. 3 ('the disciples came') and Mk. 13. 3 ('Peter and James and John and Andrew asked'); ctr. Lk. 21. 7 ('they asked').

24. 4 and Mk. 13. 5; ctr. Lk. 21. 8.

24. 20; ctr. Mk. 13. 18 'may (+your flight) not be'.

26. 24 and Mk. 14. 21; ctr. Lk. 22. 22 'the Son of man is handed over'. Lk. perhaps avoids repetition.

26. 26; ctr. Mk. 14. 22 and Lk. 22. 19 'Jesus taking'.

26. 34 and Mk. 14. 30; ctr. Lk. 14. 34.

26. 35; ctr. Mk. 14. 31 'Peter says'.

26. 63; ctr. Mk. 14. 61 'Jesus was silent'.

26. 73; ctr. Mk. 14. 70 '*you* are one of them'. Lk. 22. 59 has '*this one* was with him'.

27. 11; ctr. Mk. 15. 2 and Lk. 23. 3.

27. 15; ctr. Mk. 15. 6 'the governor released'.

27. 22; ctr. Mk. 15. 13 and Lk. 23. 21 '*all* say' (Mk.: cried out; Lk.: shouted out).

27. 47; ctr. Mk. 15. 35 '*this one* calls'.

27. 49; ctr. Mk. 15. 36 'the rest said'. (In Mk., the one who runs up with the sponge also speaks.)

Mark

1. 17; ctr. Mt. 4. 19.

2. 17 and Lk. 5. 31; ctr. Mt. 9. 12.

2. 25 and Lk. 6. 3; ctr. Mt. 12. 3 '*he* hungered'.

3. 5 and Lk. 6. 10; ctr. Mt. 12. 13 'his hand was restored'.

5. 9; ctr. Lk. 8. 30 'my name [is] Legion'. Lk. perhaps avoids repetition.

5. 13; and Lk. 8. 33; ctr. Mt. 8. 32 'the unclean spirits (Lk.: the demons) went out'.

6. 27; ctr. Mt. 14. 10 'the king sending'.

6. 28; ctr. Mt. 14. 11 'the girl gave' (Mt.: brought).

6. 45; ctr. Mt. 14. 22 '*he* dismisses'.

7. 14; ctr. Mt. 15. 10 '*all* hear'.

8. 29; ctr. Mt. 16. 15 and Lk. 9. 20 '*he* asked', etc.

10. 2; ctr. Mt. 19. 3 'a man to divorce' (subj. of inf.).

10. 18 and Lk. 18. 19; ctr. Mt. 19. 17.

10. 39; ctr. Mt. 20. 23.

10. 51; ctr. Mt. 20. 32 and Lk. 18. 40.

10. 51; ctr. Mt. 20. 33 and Lk. 18. 41 'the blind man said'.

11. 33 and Lk. 20. 8; ctr. Mt. 21. 27 'Jesus says'.

12. 17; ctr. Mt. 22. 21 and Lk. 20. 25.

12. 35; ctr. Lk. 20. 41 'how do (+the scribes) say'.

13. 2; ctr. Mt. 24. 2 and Lk. 21. 5. But see also Mt. 24. 1.

13. 19; ctr. Mt. 24. 21 'those days will be'.

14. 16 (cf. Mt. 26. 19); ctr. Lk. 22. 13 'the disciples went out'.

14. 18; ctr. Mt. 26. 21.

15. 5; ctr. Mt. 27. 14 'Jesus answered'.

15. 10; ctr. Mt. 27. 18 'the chief priests handed over'.

15. 14; ctr. Mt. 27. 23 and Lk. 23. 22 'Pilate said'.

Luke

4. 6; ctr. Mt. 4. 9 'the devil said'.

4. 7; ctr. Mt. 4. 9 '*you* worship'.

5. 18; ctr. Mk. 2. 3 and Mt. 9. 2 'men bore'.

6. 3; ctr. Mt. 12. 3 and Mk. 2. 25.

6. 7; ctr. Mk. 3. 2 (cf. Mt. 12. 10) 'the scribes and Pharisees watched'.

6. 9; ctr. Mk. 3. 4.

6. 23; ctr. Mt. 5. 12 *b* 'their fathers did (Mt.: persecuted)'.

8. 13; ctr. Mt. 13. 21 and Mk. 4. 17 '*these* have root'.

8. 30; ctr. Mk. 5. 9 'Jesus asked'.

8. 37; ctr. Mt. 8. 34 and Mk. 5. 17 'all the multitude, etc. asked (Mt. and Mk.: besought) him'.

8. 49; ctr. Mk. 5. 35 'a certain one comes'.

8. 54; ctr. Mt. 9. 25 and Mk. 5. 41 '*he*, seizing her hand'.

8. 56; ctr. Mk. 5. 42 'her parents were amazed'.

9. 24; ctr. Mt. 16. 25 and Mk. 8. 35 '*this one* will save'. See also casus pendens.

10. 24; ctr. Mt. 13. 17 '*you* see'.

11. 17; ctr. Mt. 12. 25 '*he* said'.

11. 33; ctr. Mt. 5. 15 'no one lights'.

17. 6; ctr. Mt. 17. 20 'the Lord said'.

18. 39; ctr. Mt. 20. 31 and Mk. 10. 48 '*he* cried out'.

19. 38; ctr. Mt. 21. 9 and Mk. 11. 9 'blessed is (+ the king) who comes'.

20. 19 (cf. Mt. 21. 45 f.); ctr. Mk. 12. 12 'the scribes and the chief priests sought'.

20. 22; ctr. Mt. 22. 17 and Mk. 12. 14 'lawful (+ for us) to give' ((subj. of inf.).

20. 33; ctr. Mt. 22. 28 and Mk. 12. 23 'the woman becomes'.

21. 9; ctr. Mt. 24. 6 and Mk. 13. 7 'it is necessary (+ for these things) to happen' ((subj. of inf.).

21. 31; ctr. Mt. 24. 33 and Mk. 13. 29 'the kingdom of God is near'.

23. 22; ctr. Mt. 27. 23 and Mk. 15. 14 '*this one* did'.

Summary

Mt. more explicit than Mk. 49 times.	Mt:Mk::49:23
Mt. more explicit than Lk. 38 times.	Mt:Lk::38:26
Mk. more explicit than Mt. 23 times.	Mk:Lk::21:24
	Omitting 'Jesus'
Mk. more explicit than Lk. 21 times.	Mt:Mk::25:13
Lk. more explicit than Mt. 26 times.	Mt:Lk::19:22
Lk. more explicit than Mk. 24 times.	Mk:Lk::9:19

2′ Direct objects in one Gospel but not in another

Matthew

4. 5 reads: τότε παραλαμβάνει αὐτὸν ὁ διάβολος...καὶ ἔστησεν αὐτὸν ἐπὶ τὸ πτερύγιον τοῦ ἱεροῦ. Lk. 4. 9 reads: ἤγαγεν δὲ αὐτὸν...καὶ ἔστησεν ἐπὶ τὸ πτερύγιον τοῦ ἱεροῦ. This is abbreviated as follows:

4. 5; ctr. Lk. 4. 9 'he stood + him'.

4. 23; ctr. Mk. 1. 39 and Lk. 4. 44 'preaching + the Gospel of the kingdom'.

7. 26; ctr. Lk. 6. 49 'hearing (+ these words of mine) and not doing (+ them)'. (Lk. may be avoiding repetition. See his vs. 47.)

8. 3 and Lk. 5. 13; ctr. Mk. 1. 41 'touched + him'.

8. 4 ('offer the gift which') and Mk. 1. 44 ('offer...that which'); ctr. Lk. 5. 14 ('offer just as').

8. 33; ctr. Mk. 5. 14 and Lk. 8. 34 'they announced + all things', etc.

10. 39; ctr. Lk. 17. 33 'the one losing + his life'. (Lk. may be avoiding repetition.)

14. 1 and Lk. 9. 7; ctr. Mk. 6. 14 'Herod heard + Jesus' fame' (Lk.: 'all that had happened').

21. 9; ctr. Mk. 11. 9 'the ones going before + him'.

22. 19; ctr. Mk. 12. 16 'they brought + a denarius'. (Mk. may be avoiding repetition. See his vs. 15.)

26. 23; ctr. Mk. 14. 20 'dipping + the hand'. (See also 'the hand' in Lk. 22. 21.)

Mark

1. 14; ctr. Mt. 4. 17 'preaching + the Gospel of God'.

1. 44; ctr. Mt. 8. 4 and Lk. 5. 14 'say + nothing'.

2. 8; ctr. Lk. 5. 22 'debate + these things'.

2. 16; ctr. Mt. 9. 11 'seeing + that he eats with the sinners and tax-collectors'.

3. 2; ctr. Lk. 6. 7 (cf. Mt. 12. 10) 'heal + him'.

5. 14; ctr. Mt. 8. 33 and Lk. 8. 34 'the ones pasturing + them'.

5. 36; ctr. Lk. 8. 50 'overhearing (Lk.: hearing) + the word spoken'.

6. 28; ctr. Mt. 14. 11 'gave (+ it) to the girl'.

6. 28; ctr. Mt. 14. 11 'gave (Mt.: brought) (+ it) to her mother'.

6. 56; ctr. Mt. 14. 36 'touched + him'.

7. 14; ctr. Mt. 15. 10 'hear + me'.

9. 39; ctr. Lk. 9. 50 'do not prevent + him'.

10. 32; ctr. Mt. 20. 17 and Lk. 18. 31 'to say + what was about to happen to him'.

10. 34 ('they will scourge (+ him) and kill') and Lk. 18. 33 ('having scourged, they will kill + him'); ctr. Mt. 20. 19.

10. 36; ctr. Mt. 20. 21 'what do you want + me to do for you'.

11. 2 and Lk. 19. 30; ctr. Mt. 21. 2 'loose + it'.

13. 23; ctr. Mt. 24. 25 'I have foretold + all things'.

14. 58; ctr. Mt. 26. 61 'build + another'.

Luke

4. 31; ctr. Mk. 1. 21 'teaching + them'.

7. 9; ctr. Mt. 8. 10 'hearing + these things'.

7. 9; ctr. Mt. 8. 10 'he marveled + at him'.

7. 33; ctr. Mt. 11. 18 'neither eating (+ bread) nor drinking (+ wine)'.

8. 5; ctr. Mt. 13. 3 and Mk. 4. 3 'to sow + his seed'.

9. 34; ctr. Mt. 17. 5 'saying + these things'.

Summary

Mt. more explicit than Mk. 7 times.	Mt:Mk::7:14
Mt. more explicit than Lk. 6 times.	Mt:Lk::6:7
Mk. more explicit than Mt. 14 times.	Mk:Lk::8:4
Mk. more explicit than Lk. 8 times.	
Lk. more explicit than Mt. 7 times.	
Lk. more explicit than Mk. 4 times.	

3′ Indirect objects and equivalent πρός phrases in one Gospel but not in another[1]

Matthew

9. 2 reads: καὶ ἰδοὺ προσέφερον αὐτῷ παραλυτικὸν κ.τ.λ. Mk. 2. 3 reads: καὶ ἔρχονται φέροντες πρὸς αὐτὸν παραλυτικὸν κ.τ.λ. Lk. 5. 18 reads: καὶ ἰδοὺ ἄνδρες φέροντες... ἄνθρωπον κ.τ.λ. This is abbreviated as follows:

9. 2 and Mk. 2. 3; ctr. Lk. 5. 18 'bearing + to him'.

9. 2 and Mk. 2. 5; ctr. Lk. 5. 20 'said + to the paralytic'.

12. 2 and Mk. 2. 24; ctr. Lk. 6. 2.

14. 17 and Mk. 6. 37; ctr. Lk. 9. 13.

17. 17 and Mk. 9. 19; ctr. Lk. 9. 41 'bring + to me'. (Lk. has 'here'.)

17. 20; ctr. Lk. 17. 6.

18. 7; ctr. Lk. 17. 1 'woe + to the man'.

19. 3; ctr. Mk. 10. 2 'came up + to him'.

19. 20 and Mk. 10. 20; ctr. Lk. 18. 21.

19. 23 and Mk. 10. 23; ctr. Lk. 18. 24 'said + to his disciples'.

19. 26 and Mk. 10. 27; ctr. Lk. 18. 27.

19. 27 and Mk. 10. 28; ctr. Lk. 18. 28.

19. 28 and Lk. 18. 29; ctr. Mk. 10. 29.

20. 33 and Mk. 10. 51; ctr. Lk. 18. 41.

21. 2 and Mk. 11. 2; ctr. Lk. 19. 30.

21. 2; ctr. Mk. 11. 2 and Lk. 19. 30 'lead (Mk.: bring) + to me'.

21. 6; ctr. Mk. 11. 6.

21. 23 and Mk. 11. 27; ctr. Lk. 20. 1 'they come up + to him'.

21. 25; ctr. Mk. 11. 31 and Lk. 20. 5.

21. 27 and Mk. 11. 33; ctr. Lk. 20. 7 'answering + to Jesus'.

21. 33; ctr. Mk. 12. 1 'set a hedge + to it'.

21. 37 and Mk. 12. 6; ctr. Lk. 20. 13 'sent + to them'.

21. 40 ('do + to those tenants') and Lk. 20. 15 ('do + to them'); ctr. Mk. 12. 9.

[1] Unless otherwise noted, a verb of saying is followed by 'to him' and the like.

157

22. 19; ctr. Mk. 12. 16 'brought + to him'. Perhaps Mk. is avoiding repetition. See his vs. 15.

22. 23 and Mk. 12. 18; ctr. Lk. 20. 27 'they came + to him'.

24. 2 and Mk. 13. 2; ctr. Lk. 21. 5.

24. 4 and Mk. 13. 5; ctr. Lk. 21. 8.

24. 45; ctr. Lk. 12. 42 'to give + to them'.

26. 10; ctr. Mk. 14. 6.

26. 34 and Mk. 14. 30; ctr. Lk. 22. 34.

26. 35 ('Peter says to him'); ctr. Mk. 14. 31 ('he spoke').

26. 40 and Lk. 22. 45; ctr. Mk. 14. 37 'comes + to the disciples'.

26. 45; ctr. Mk. 14. 41 'he comes + to the disciples'.

26. 58 and Mk. 14. 54; ctr. Lk. 22. 54 'followed + him'.

26. 64; ctr. Mk. 14. 62.

26. 68; ctr. Mk. 14. 65 and Lk. 22. 64 'prophesy | to us'.

26. 69; ctr. Mk. 14. 66 'came + to him'.

27. 14; ctr. Mk. 15. 5.

Mark

1. 40; ctr. Mt. 8. 2 'coming + to him'.

1. 40; ctr. Mt. 8. 2 and Lk. 5. 12.

1. 41; ctr. Mt. 8. 3 and Lk. 5. 13.

2. 9; ctr. Mt. 9. 5 and Lk. 5. 23 'to say + to the paralytic'.

2. 17 and Lk. 5. 31; ctr. Mt. 9. 12.

4. 11; ctr. Mt. 13. 11 and Lk. 8. 10.

4. 35 and Lk. 8. 22; ctr. Mt. 8. 18.

4. 41 and Lk. 8. 25; ctr. Mt. 8. 27.

5. 9; ctr. Lk. 8. 30.

5. 19; ctr. Lk. 8. 39.

5. 19; ctr. Lk. 8. 38.

5. 34 and Lk. 8. 48; ctr. Mt. 9. 22.

5. 39; ctr. Mt. 9. 23 and Lk. 8. 52.

5. 41; ctr. Lk. 8. 54.

6. 39 ('he commanded to them') and Lk. 9. 14 ('he said to his disciples'); ctr. Mt. 14. 19 ('ordering').

7. 18; ctr. Mt. 15. 16.

7. 28; ctr. Mt. 15. 27.

8. 1; ctr. Mt. 15. 32.

8. 17; ctr. Mt. 16. 8.

8. 27; ctr. Mt. 16. 13 and Lk. 9. 18.

8. 28; ctr. Mt. 16. 14 and Lk. 9. 19.

8. 29; ctr. Mt. 16. 16 and Lk. 9. 20.

9. 12; ctr. Mt. 17. 11.

9. 19; ctr. Mt. 17. 17 and Lk. 9. 41.

9. 36 and Lk. 9. 48; ctr. Mt. 18. 3.

9. 38; ctr. Lk. 9. 49.

10. 14; ctr. Mt. 19. 14 (cf. Lk. 8. 16).

10. 26; ctr. Mt. 19. 25 and Lk. 18. 26.

10. 34; ctr. Mt. 20. 19 (cf. Lk. 18. 32) 'mock + at him'.

10. 38; ctr. Mt. 20. 22.

10. 42 and Lk. 22. 25; ctr. Mt. 20. 25.

10. 51 ('and answering him Jesus said') and Lk. 18. 40 ('he asked him');
ctr. Mt. 20. 32 ('and he said').

11. 6; ctr. Lk. 19. 34.

11. 7 and Lk. 19. 35; ctr. Mt. 21. 7 'they bring (Mt. and Lk.: led) ... + to
Jesus'.

11. 17; ctr. Mt. 21. 13 and Lk. 19. 46 'a house of prayer + for all people'.

11. 28 and Lk. 20. 2; ctr. Mt. 21. 23.

12. 4; ctr. Mt. 21. 36 and Lk. 20. 11 'he sent + to them'.

12. 14 and Lk. 20. 21; ctr. Mt. 22. 16.

12. 15 and Lk. 20. 23; ctr. Mt. 22. 18.

12. 16; ctr. Mt. 22. 21 and Lk. 20. 24.

12. 43; ctr. Lk. 21. 3.

14. 4; ctr. Mt. 26. 8 'indignant + to themselves'. ?

14. 13 and Lk. 22. 10; ctr. Mt. 26. 18.

14. 15; ctr. Lk. 22. 12 'prepare + for us'.

14. 20; ctr. Mt. 26. 23.

15. 2 and Lk. 23. 3; ctr. Mt. 27. 11.

15. 14 and Lk. 23. 22; ctr. Mt. 27. 23.

15. 31; ctr. Mt. 27. 41 'mocking + to one another'.

Luke

5. 20; ctr. Mt. 9. 2 and Mk. 2. 5 'are forgiven + to you'.

7. 9; ctr. Mt. 8. 10 'following + him'.

9. 50; ctr. Mk. 9. 39.

13. 25; ctr. Mt. 25. 12.

22. 6; ctr. Mt. 26. 16 and Mk. 14. 11 'hand over + to them'.

22. 11; ctr. Mt. 26. 18 and Mk. 14. 14.

Summary

Mt. more explicit than Mk. 16 times.	Mt:Mk::16:40
Mt. more explicit than Lk. 25 times.	Mt:Lk::25:20
Mk. more explicit than Mt. 40 times.	Mk:Lk::40:7
Mk. more explicit than Lk. 40 times.	
Lk. more explicit than Mt. 20 times.	
Lk. more explicit than Mk. 7 times.	

4' Prepositional phrases in one Gospel but not in another

Matthew

3. 11 reads: 'I baptize you with water unto repentance.' Mk. 1. 8 and Lk.
   3. 16 read: 'I baptize you with water.' This is abbreviated as follows:
3. 11; ctr. Mk. 1. 8 and Lk. 3. 16 'I baptize you + unto repentance'. But
   see also Mk. 1. 4 and Lk. 3. 3, 'a baptism of repentance unto forgiveness of sins'.
4. 8; ctr. Lk. 4. 5 'he takes him (Lk.: led him) + into a very high mountain'.
4. 21; ctr. Mk. 1. 19 + 'with Zebedee their father'.
5. 32 and 19. 9; ctr. Mk. 10. 11 and Lk. 16. 18 + 'apart from a reason of
   unchastity', etc.
8. 24 (+ 'in the sea') and Lk. 8. 23 (| 'upon the lake'); ctr. Mk. 4. 37,
8. 32 ('died + in the water') and Mk. 5. 13 ('were drowned + in the sea');
   ctr. Lk. 8. 33 ('drowned').
9. 2 and Lk. 5. 18; ctr. Mk. 2. 3 + 'on a bed'.
9. 3 ('they said + to themselves') and Mk. 2. 6 ('debating + in their hearts');
   ctr. Lk. 5. 21 ('they debated saying').
9. 21; ctr. Mk. 5. 28 'she said + to herself'.
10. 39; ctr. Lk. 17. 33 + 'for my sake'.
12. 1; ctr. Mk. 2. 23 and Lk. 6. 1 + 'in that time'.
12. 45; ctr. Lk. 11. 26 'taking + with himself'.
13. 1; ctr. Mk. 4. 1 + 'in that day'.
13. 21 and Mk. 4. 17; ctr. Lk. 8. 13 'root + in himself' (Mk.: themselves).
14. 6; ctr. Mk. 6. 22 + 'in the midst'.
14. 23; ctr. Mk. 6. 46 + 'by himself'.
14. 26; ctr. Mk. 6. 49 'they cried out + from fear'. But see also Mk. 6. 50,
   Explanations.
15. 38; ctr. Mk. 8. 9 + 'apart from women and children'.
16. 8; ctr. Mk. 8. 17 'debate + among yourselves'.
17. 1 and Mk. 9. 2; ctr. Lk. 9. 28 + 'by himself'.
17. 5; ctr. Mk. 9. 7 and Lk. 9. 35 + 'in whom I am well pleased'.
18. 1 (cf. Lk. 9. 46); ctr. Mk. 9. 34 'who is greater + in the kingdom of the
   heavens'. Lk. has 'greater + of them'.
20. 17; ctr. Mk. 10. 32 'taking the twelve + *kat' idian*'.
20. 23; ctr. Mk. 10. 40 'prepared + by my father'.
21. 17; ctr. Mk. 11. 11 'he went + out of the city'. (But see also Mk. 11. 19.)
21. 19; ctr. Mk. 11. 13 'found nothing + in it'.
21. 33; ctr. Mk. 12. 1 'dug + in it'.
22. 23; ctr. Mk. 12. 18 and Lk. 20. 27 + 'in that day'.
22. 25; ctr. Mk. 12. 20 and Lk. 20. 29 'there were + among us'.
23. 39; ctr. Lk. 13. 35 'see me + from now'.
24. 3 and Mk. 13. 3; ctr. Lk. 21. 7 + 'by himself'.

24. 33 and Mk. 13. 29; ctr. Lk. 21. 31 'near + upon the gates'.

24. 44; ctr. Lk. 12. 40 + 'on account of this'.

26. 29; ctr. Mk. 14. 25 'I drink it + with you'.

26. 31; ctr. Mk. 14. 27 + 'in me in this night'.

26. 33; ctr. Mk. 14. 29 'scandalized + at you'.

26. 38; ctr. Mk. 14. 34 'watch + with me'.

26. 40; ctr. Mk. 14. 37 'watch + with me'.

26. 42; ctr. Mk. 14. 39 'again + for the second time'. Note redundancy.

26. 55; ctr. Mk. 14. 48 and Lk. 22. 52 + 'in that hour'.

26. 70; ctr. Mk. 14. 68 and Lk. 22. 57 'he denied + before all'.

26. 72; ctr. Mk. 14. 70 'denied + with an oath'.

27. 1; ctr. Mk. 15. 1 (cf. Lk. 22. 66) 'counsel + against Jesus'.

27. 27; ctr. Mk. 15. 16 'gathered (Mk.: called together) + before him'.

27. 42; ctr. Mk. 15. 32 'believe + upon him'.

27. 48; ctr. Mk. 15. 36 'one + of them'.

Compare also:

8. 16; ctr. Mk. 1. 34 (see Lk. 4. 41) 'he cast out spirits (Mk.: many demons) + with a word' (λογῳ).

10. 14 ('out of that house or city') and Lk. 9. 5 ('from that city'); ctr. Mk. 6. 11 (εκειθεν).

14. 13 and Mk. 6. 33; ctr. Lk. 9. 11 + 'on foot' (πεϩη).

19. 1 ('from Galilee'); ctr. Mk. 10. 1 (εκειθεν).

Mark

1. 20; ctr. Mt. 4. 22 + 'with the hirelings'.

1. 44 and Lk. 5. 14; ctr. Mt. 8. 4 'offer + concerning your cleansing'.

2. 13; ctr. Lk. 5. 27 'he went out + beside the sea'.

2. 20 and Lk. 5. 35; ctr. Mt. 9. 15 'then they shall fast + in those day(s)'. Mt. may be avoiding redundancy.

2. 26; ctr. Mt. 12. 4 and Lk. 6. 4 + 'when Abiathar was high priest'.

3. 5; ctr. Lk. 6. 10 + 'with anger'.

3. 6; ctr. Mt. 12. 14 + 'with the Herodians'.

3. 7 (+ 'with his disciples') and Lk. 6. 17 (+ 'with them'); ctr. Mt. 12. 15.

3. 7; ctr. Mt. 12. 15 'he departed + to the sea'. But Mt. has *ekeithen*.

4. 1; ctr. Mt. 13. 2 'to sit + on the sea'.

4. 1; ctr. Mt. 13. 2 'crowd was + at the sea'.

4. 38; ctr. Mt. 8. 25 'he was sleeping + in the stern, on the cushion'.

5. 6; ctr. Lk. 8. 28 'see Jesus + from afar'.

5. 14 and Lk. 8. 34; ctr. Mt. 8. 33 + 'and in the fields'.

5. 19; ctr. Lk. 8. 39 + 'to your own'.

5. 20; ctr. Lk. 8. 39 'to preach + in the Decapolis'.

5. 27; ctr. Mt. 9. 20 and Lk. 8. 44 + 'coming + in the crowd'.

6. 11 and Lk. 9. 5; ctr. Mt. 14. 14 + 'unto a witness against them'.

161

DETAIL AND THE TENDENCY OF THE TRADITION

6. 45; ctr. Mt. 18. 22 + 'to Bethsaida'.

6. 50; ctr. Mt. 14. 27 'he spoke + with them'.

6. 55; ctr. Mt. 14. 35 'they brought + upon pallets'.

8. 3; ctr. Mt. 15. 32 + 'to their house'.

8. 10; ctr. Mt. 15. 39 + 'with his disciples'.

8. 13; ctr. Mt. 16. 4 'departed + to the other side'.

8. 27; ctr. Mt. 16. 13 and Lk. 9. 18 + 'in the road'.

8. 38; ctr. Lk. 9. 26 + 'in this adulterous and sinful generation'.

9. 8; ctr. Mt. 17. 8 + 'with them'.

9. 17 and Lk. 9. 38; ctr. Mt. 17. 14 + 'out of (Lk.: from) the crowd'.

10. 1; ctr. Mt. 5. 32 and Mt. 19. 9 and Lk. 16. 18 'commits adultery + against her'.

10. 20 and Lk. 18. 21; ctr. Mt. 19. 20 + 'from youth'.

10. 29; ctr. Mt. 19. 29 and Lk. 18. 29 + 'for the sake of the Gospel'.

10. 30 and Lk. 18. 30; ctr. Mt. 19. 29 'receive + in this time'.

10. 52; ctr. Mt. 20. 34 and Lk. 18. 43 'followed him + in the road'.

11. 2; ctr. Lk. 19. 30 'entering + into it'.

11. 11; ctr. Mt. 21. 17 + 'with the twelve'.

11. 23; ctr. Mt. 21. 21 'does not doubt + in his heart'.

12. 2; ctr. Mt. 21. 34 (see Lk. 20. 10) 'receive + from the tenants'.

12. 17 and Lk. 20. 26; ctr. Mt. 22. 22 'marvelling + at him' (Lk.: at his answer).

12. 26 (cf. Lk. 20. 37); ctr. Mt. 22. 31 'read + in the book of Moses, at the bush' (Lk.: 'Moses showed at the "bush"').

13. 3; ctr. Mt. 24. 3 + 'opposite the temple'.

14. 33; ctr. Mt. 26. 37 + 'with him'.

14. 49 and Lk. 22. 53; ctr. Mt. 26. 55 'I was + with you'. (Mk. and Lk. have different Greek.)

14. 60; ctr. Mt. 26. 62 'rising up + in the midst'.

14. 72; ctr. Mt. 26. 74 and Lk. 22. 60 'the cock crew + for the second time'.

15. 24; ctr. Mt. 27. 35 and Lk. 23. 34 'cast lots + for them'. Mk. also has + 'who should take what'.

Compare also:

2. 8; ctr. Mt. 9. 4 and Lk. 5. 22 'Jesus knew + in his spirit' (τῷ πνεύματι αὐτοῦ).

5. 7 and Lk. 8. 28; ctr. Mt. 8. 29 'cried out + with a loud voice' (φωνῇ μεγάλῃ).

Luke

4. 5; ctr. Mt. 4. 8 + 'in a moment of time'.

4. 14; ctr. Mt. 4. 12 and Mk. 1. 14 + 'in the power of the Spirit'. But agreement is scant.

4. 16; ctr. Mt. 13. 54 and Mk. 6. 1 + 'according to his custom'.

5. 32; ctr. Mt. 9. 13 and Mk. 2. 17 'sinners + unto repentance'.

6. 23; ctr. Mt. 5. 17 'rejoice + in that day'.

8. 15; ctr. Mt. 13. 23 and Mk. 4. 20 + 'in a beautiful and good heart'.

8. 33; ctr. Mt. 8. 32 and Mk. 5. 13 'going out + from the man'.

8. 35; ctr. Mk. 5. 15 + 'at the feet of Jesus'.

8. 39; ctr. Mk. 5. 20 'he went away + through all the city'. But see Mk. 5. 20, same category.

9. 18; ctr. Mt. 16. 13 and Mk. 8. 27 + 'alone' (*kata monas*).

9. 23; ctr. Mt. 16. 24 and Mk. 8. 34 + 'daily' (*kath' hēmeran*).

9. 45; ctr. Mk. 9. 32 'asked him + concerning this word'.

12. 3; ctr. Mt. 10. 27 'you said + in private rooms'.

20. 19; ctr. Mt. 21. 46 and Mk. 12. 12 + 'in that very hour'.

21. 4; ctr. Mk. 12. 44 'they cast + unto the gifts'.

22. 6; ctr. Mt. 26. 16 and Mk. 14. 11 'betray him + apart from the crowd'.

22. 10; ctr. Mk. 14. 13 'follow him + into the house'.

22. 39; ctr. Mt. 26. 30 and Mk. 14. 26 'he went + according to custom'.

22. 45; ctr. Mt. 26. 40 and Mk. 14. 37 'sleeping + from sorrow'.

23. 26; ctr. Mt. 27. 32 and Mk. 15. 21 'bear the cross + behind Jesus'.

Also compare:

3. 22; ctr. Mt. 3. 16 and Mk. 1. 10 'spirit comes down + bodily' (σωματικῷ).

Summary

Mt. more detailed than Mk. 38 times.	Mt:Mk::38:40
Mt. more detailed than Lk. 20 times.	Mt:Lk::20:27
Mk. more detailed than Mt. 40 times.	Mk:Lk::23:21
Mk. more detailed than Lk. 23 times.	
Lk. more detailed than Mt. 27 times.	
Lk. more detailed than Mk. 21 times.	

5′ Adjectives and adjectival clauses in one Gospel but not in another

Matthew

5. 39 reads: 'Whoever strikes you upon the right cheek...' Lk. 6. 29 reads: 'To the one striking you upon the cheek...' This is abbreviated as follows:

5. 39; ctr. Lk. 6. 29 'the (+ right) cheek'.

6. 27; ctr. Lk. 12. 25 '(+ one) cubit'.

7. 24; ctr. Lk. 6. 48 '(+ wise) man'.

7. 26; ctr. Lk. 6. 49 '(+ foolish) man'.

8. 26 and Mk. 4. 39; ctr. Lk. 8. 24 '(+ great) calm'.

9. 8; ctr. Mk. 2. 12 and Lk. 5. 26 'God + who gave such authority to men'.

10. 20 ('the spirit...which speaks in you'); ctr. Mk. 13. 11 ('the spirit').

17. 1 and Mk. 9. 2; ctr. Lk. 9. 28 '(+high) mountain'.

17. 5; ctr. Mk. 9. 7 and Lk. 9. 34 '(+bright) cloud'.

17. 17 and Lk. 9. 41; ctr. Mk. 9. 19 'faithless (+and perverse) generation'.

20. 30; ctr. Mk. 10. 46 and Lk. 18. 35 '(+two) blind men'.

21. 19; ctr. Mk. 11. 13 '(+one) fig tree'. See Mk. 11. 13 below.

21. 24 and Mk. 11. 29; ctr. Lk. 20. 3 '(+one) word'.

21. 33; ctr. Mk. 12. 1 and Lk. 20. 9 'a man+who was a householder'.

21. 41; ctr. Mk. 12. 9 and Lk. 20. 16 'tenants+who will give him the fruits in their seasons'.

24. 15; ctr. Mk. 13. 14 'the abomination of desolation+spoken of by Daniel the prophet'.

24. 21 and Lk. 21. 23; ctr. Mk. 13. 19 '(+great) tribulation'.

24. 24; ctr. Mk. 13. 22 '(+great) signs'.

24. 48; ctr. Lk. 12. 45 'that (+evil) servant'.

26. 15; ctr. Mk. 14. 11 and Lk. 22. 5 '(+thirty) silver pieces'. See also category 18.

27. 59; ctr. Mk. 15. 46 and Lk. 23. 53 '(+clean) linen shroud'.

27. 60; ctr. Mk. 15. 46 and Lk. 23. 53 '(+his new) tomb'.

27. 60; ctr. Mk. 15. 46 '(+great) stone'.

Mark

3. 22 ('the scribes who came down from Jerusalem'); ctr. Mt. 12. 24 ('the Pharisees') and Lk. 11. 15 ('certain ones').

4. 31; ctr. Mt. 13. 32 'all the seeds+which are upon the earth'.

5. 7 and Lk. 8. 28; ctr. Mt. 8. 29 'the (+highest) God'.

6. 2; ctr. Mt. 13. 54 'mighty works+such as happen through his hands'.

6. 2; ctr. Mt. 13. 54 'wisdom+which is given to this one'.

6. 6; ctr. Mt. 9. 35 'the villages+round about'.

6. 36 and Lk. 9. 12; ctr. Mt. 14. 15 'villages+round about'.

6. 39; ctr. Mt. 14. 19 '(+green) grass'.

7. 23; ctr. Mt. 15. 20 '(+evil) things'.

8. 38 and Lk. 9. 26 ('the holy angels'); ctr. Mt. 16. 27 ('his angels').

9. 3; ctr. Mt. 17. 2 and Lk. 9. 29 'white+which a fuller upon the earth is not able thus to whiten'.

9. 38; ctr. Lk. 9. 49 +'who does not follow you'.

11. 2 and Lk. 19. 30; ctr. Mt. 21. 2 'a colt+on which no one has ever sat'.

11. 13; ctr. Mt. 21. 19 'a fig tree+having leaves'. But Mt. has '(+one) fig tree'.

12. 36 ('the Holy Spirit'); ctr. Mt. 22. 43 ('the spirit'). See Kittel, E.T., I, 103.

12. 42; ctr. Mt. 21. 2 'two lepta+which is a quadrans'.

13. 11 ('the Holy Spirit'); ctr. Mt. 10. 20 ('the spirit of your Father'). Cf. add. of genitive noun. Cf. Kittel as above. Cf. Mt. 10. 20, same category.

13. 19; ctr. Mt. 24. 21 +'which God created'.

13. 20; ctr. Mt. 24. 22 'the elect + whom he chose'.

14. 71; ctr. Mt. 26. 74 'this (Mt.: the) man + whom you mention'.

15. 7; ctr. Mt. 27. 16 'Barabbas + who had committed murder in the insur-
rection'. (See also Lk. 23. 19.)

15. 21 and Lk. 23. 26; ctr. Mt. 27. 32 'Simon + [who was] coming from the
field'.

15. 39; ctr. Mt. 27. 54 and Lk. 23. 47 'the centurion + who stood in front of
him'.

15. 40; ctr. Mt. 27. 56 'James + the less'.

15. 42; ctr. Lk. 23. 54 'day of preparation + which is the day before the
Sabbath'.

Luke

3. 22; ctr. Mk. 1. 10 'the (+ Holy) Spirit'. Mt. 3. 16 has 'the Spirit of God'.
See gen. noun.

5. 37; ctr. Mk. 2. 22 'the (+ new) wine'.

6. 6; ctr. Mt. 12. 10 and Mk. 3. 1 '(+ his right) hand'.

8. 26; ctr. Mt. 8. 28 and Mk. 5. 1 'country of the Gerasenes + which is
opposite Galilee'.

8. 42; ctr. Mt. 9. 18 and Mk. 5. 21 '(+ only) daughter'.

12. 1; ctr. Mt. 16. 6 and Mk. 8. 15 'the leaven + which is hypocrisy'. (Also
explanatory.)

22. 20; ctr. Mt. 26. 28 and Mk. 14. 24 '(+ new) covenant'.

22. 50; ctr. Mt. 26. 51 and Mk. 14. 47 'his (+ right) ear'.

23. 53; ctr. Mt. 27. 60 and Mk. 15. 46 'tomb hewn of rock, + in which
no one had yet been laid'. (Perhaps from reverence.)

Summary

Mt. more explicit than Mk. 15 times.   Mt:Mk::15:23
Mt. more explicit than Lk. 16 times.   Mt:Lk::16:12
Mk. more explicit than Mt. 23 times.   Mk:Lk::8:11
Mk. more explicit than Lk. 8 times.
Lk. more explicit than Mt. 12 times.
Lk. more explicit than Mk. 11 times.

6′ Genitive nouns in one Gospel but not in another

Matthew

3. 1 reads: 'John the Baptist appeared preaching in the desert of Judea.'
Mk. 1. 4 reads: 'John the baptizer appeared in the desert.' Lk. 3. 2
reads: 'The word of God came upon John...in the desert.' This is
abbreviated as follows:

3. 1; ctr. Mk. 1. 4 and Lk. 3. 2 'desert + of Judea'.

3. 16; ctr. Mk. 1. 10 'spirit + of God'. (Lk. 3. 22 has 'the Holy Spirit'.)

6. 28; ctr. Lk. 12. 27 'lilies + of the field'.

9. 23 and Mk. 5. 38; ctr. Lk. 8. 51 'the house of the ruler' (Mk.: ruler of the synagogue).

13. 19 and Lk. 8. 11; ctr. Mk. 4. 14 'the word + of the kingdom' (Lk.: of God).

21. 23; ctr. Mk. 11. 27 and Lk. 20. 1 'the elders + of the people'.

21. 34; ctr. Mk. 12. 2 and Lk. 20. 10 'time + of fruit'.

22. 16 and Mk. 12. 14 'face + of man', cf. Lk. 20. 21.

24. 30; ctr. Mk. 13. 26 and Lk. 21. 27 'clouds + of heaven'.

26. 31; ctr. Mk. 14. 27 'the sheep + of the shepherd'. So LXX A of Zech. 13. 7.

26. 47; ctr. Mk. 14. 43 'elders + of the people'.

26. 56; ctr. Mk. 14. 49 'the writings + of the prophets'.

26. 58 and Mk. 14. 54; ctr. Lk. 22. 55 'the courtyard + of the high priest'.

27. 1 and Lk. 22. 66; ctr. Mk. 15. 1 'elders + of the people'.

27. 27; ctr. Mk. 15. 16 'the soldiers + of the governor'.

Mark

1. 28; ctr. Lk. 4. 37 'the surrounding region + of Galilee'.

5. 1; ctr. Mt. 8. 28 'the other side + of the sea'.

7. 21; ctr. Mt. 15. 19 'the heart + of men'.

8. 19; ctr. Mt. 16. 9 'baskets + of fragments'.

10. 6; ctr. Mt. 19. 4 'the beginning + of creation'. See Mt. 19. 4, category 1'.

11. 22; ctr. Mt. 21. 21 'have faith + in God' (obj. gen.).

14. 4; ctr. Mt. 26. 8 'destruction + of the ointment'.

14. 66; ctr. Mt. 26. 69 and Lk. 22. 56 'a maid + of the high priest'.

Luke

6. 45; ctr. Mt. 12. 35 'the treasury + of the heart'.

8. 5; ctr. Mt. 13. 4 and Mk. 4. 4 'birds + of the heaven'.

8. 22; ctr. Mt. 8. 18 and Mk. 4. 35 'the other side + of the lake'.

9. 20; ctr. Mk. 8. 29 'the Christ + of God'. See also Mt. 16. 16, category 8' below.

12. 30; ctr. Mt. 6. 32 τὰ ἔθνη + τοῦ κόσμου. There is a substantive difference: τὰ ἔθνη means 'gentiles' in Mt., but 'nations' in Lk.

22. 11; ctr. Mk. 14. 14 'to the householder + of the house'. (Mt. 26. 18: to him.)

22. 69; ctr. Mt. 26. 64 and Mk. 14. 62 'power + of God'.

Summary

Mt. more explicit than Mk. 11 times.   Mt:Mk::11:7

Mt. more explicit than Lk. 8 times.   Mt:Lk::8:5

Mk. more explicit than Mt. 7 times.   Mk:Lk::5:7

Mk. more explicit than Lk. 5 times.

Lk. more explicit than Mt. 5 times.

Lk. more explicit than Mk. 7 times.

7′ Genitive pronouns in one Gospel but not in another

Matthew

3. 12 reads: 'his wheat'. Lk. 3. 17 reads: 'wheat'. This is indicated as follows:

3. 12; ctr. Lk. 3. 17 'his wheat'.

4. 21; ctr. Mk. 1. 19 'their nets'.

6. 25; ctr. Lk. 12. 22 'your soul', 'your body'.

7. 9; ctr. Lk. 11. 11 'his son'.

7. 11; ctr. Lk. 11. 13 'your father'.

7. 24; ctr. Lk. 6. 48 'his house'.

7. 26; ctr. Lk. 6. 49 'his house'.

9. 18; ctr. Mk. 5. 23 'your hand'.

10. 17; ctr. Mk. 13. 9 and Lk. 21. 12 'their synagogues'.

10. 35; ctr. Lk. 12. 53 'his father', 'her mother', 'her mother-in-law'. See
  Mic. 7. 6, where the genitive pronoun is used.

12. 9; ctr. Mk. 3. 1 and Lk. 6. 6 'their synagogue'.

12. 13 and Lk. 6. 10; ctr. Mk. 3. 5 'your hand'.

13. 54; ctr. Mk. 6. 2 'their synagogue'.

15. 32; ctr. Mk. 8. 1 'his disciples'.

16. 27 ('his angels'); ctr. Mk. 8. 38 and Lk. 9. 26 ('the holy angels').

19. 3; ctr. Mk. 10. 2 'his wife'.

21. 34; ctr. Mk. 12. 2 and Lk. 20. 10 'his servant(s)'.

22. 24; ctr. Mk. 12. 19 and Lk. 20. 28 'his wife'.

24. 31; ctr. Mk. 13. 27 'his angels'.

26. 39; ctr. Mk. 14. 36 and Lk. 22. 42 'my father'. Mk. has 'Abba, Father'.

27. 32 and Mk. 15. 21; ctr. Lk. 23. 26 'his cross'.

27. 60; ctr. Mk. 15. 46 and Lk. 23. 53 '(+his new) tomb'.

Mark

1. 7 and Lk. 3. 16; ctr. Mt. 3. 11 'his sandals'. See Semitic wording.

1. 23; ctr. Lk. 4. 33 'their synagogue'.

1. 41; ctr. Mt. 8. 3 and Lk. 5. 13 'his hand'.

2. 15 and Lk. 5. 29; ctr. Mt. 9. 10 'his house'.

3. 31; ctr. Mt. 12. 46 and Lk. 8. 19 'his mother'.

6. 4 and Lk. 4. 24; ctr. Mt. 13. 57 'his fatherland'.

6. 29; ctr. Mt. 14. 12 'his body'.

6. 35; ctr. Mt. 14. 15 'his disciples'.

6. 45; ctr. Mt. 14. 22 'his disciples'.

8. 4; ctr. Mt. 15. 33 'his disciples'.

8. 6; ctr. Mt. 15. 36 'his disciples'.

10. 20; ctr. Lk. 18. 21 'my youth'.

10. 42; ctr. Mt. 20. 25 'their great ones'.

11. 1; ctr. Mt. 21. 1 and Lk. 19. 29 'his disciples'.

11. 7 and Lk. 19. 35; ctr. Mt. 21. 7 'their garments'.
12. 44; ctr. Lk. 21. 4 'her life'.
14. 12; ctr. Mt. 26. 17 'his disciples'.
14. 32; ctr. Mt. 26. 36 'his disciples'.
15. 27; ctr. Mt. 27. 38 'his left'.

Luke

3. 17; ctr. Mt. 3. 12 'his granary'.
6. 6; ctr. Mt. 12. 10 and Mk. 3. 1 '(+his right) hand'.
11. 34; ctr. Mt. 6. 22 'your eye'.
22. 66; ctr. Mk. 15. 1 'their Sanhedrin'. Mk. has 'the whole Sanhedrin'.

Summary

Mt. more explicit than Mk. 14 times.   Mt:Mk::14:16
Mt. more explicit than Lk. 15 times.   Mt:Lk::15:7
Mk. more explicit than Mt. 16 times.   Mk:Lk::7:3
Mk. more explicit than Lk. 7 times.
Lk. more explicit than Mt. 7 times.
Lk. more explicit than Mk. 3 times.

8′ The use of a noun with a proper name in one Gospel but not in another

Matthew

4. 18 reads: 'He saw two brothers, Simon the one called Peter and Andrew his brother.' Mk. 1. 16 reads: 'He saw Simon and Andrew the brother of Simon.' This is abbreviated as follows:
4. 18; ctr. Mk. 1. 16 'he saw (+two brothers), Simon, (+the one called Peter), and Andrew'.
4. 21; ctr. Mk. 1. 19 'he saw (+two other brothers), James...and John'. Note Mt.'s redundancy: 'two other brothers...John his brother.'
10. 2 and Mk. 3. 17; ctr. Lk. 6. 14 'John+his brother', and the like.
10. 2 and Mk. 3. 17; ctr. Lk. 6. 13 'James+the (son) of Zebedee'.
10. 2 and Lk. 6. 14; ctr. Mk. 3. 18 'Andrew+his brother'.
10. 3; ctr. Mk. 3. 18 and Lk. 6. 15 'Matthew+the tax-collector'.
11. 11; ctr. Lk. 7. 28 'John+the Baptist'.
12. 39; ctr. Lk. 11. 29 'Jonah+the Prophet'.
16. 16; ctr. Mk. 8. 29 'the Christ+the Son of the living God'. Cf. Lk. 9. 20, 'the Christ of God'.
17. 1; ctr. Mk. 9. 2 and Lk. 9. 28 'John+his brother'.
23. 35; ctr. Lk. 11. 51 'Zachariah+the son of Barachiah'.
27. 2; ctr. Mk. 15. 1 and Lk. 23. 1 'Pilate+the governor'.

168

Mark

2. 14; ctr. Lk. 5. 27 (cf. Mt. 9. 9) 'Levi + the (son) of Alphaeus'. But Lk. has 'tax-collector, Levi by name'.

5. 37; ctr. Lk. 8. 51 'John + the brother of James'.

15. 21; ctr. Mt. 27. 32 and Lk. 23. 26 'Simon the Cyrene + the father of Alexander and Rufus'.

Luke

4. 31; ctr. Mk. 1. 21 'Capernaum + a city of Galilee'.

7. 33; ctr. Mt. 11. 18 'John + the Baptist'.

23. 51; ctr. Mt. 27. 57 and Mk. 15. 43 'Arimathea + a city of the Jews'.

Summary

Mt. more explicit than Mk. 7 times.	Mt:Mk::7:1
Mt. more explicit than Lk. 8 times.	Mt:Lk::8:2
Mk. more explicit than Mt. 1 time.	Mk:Lk::5:3
Mk. more explicit than Lk. 5 times.	
Lk. more explicit than Mt. 2 times.	
Lk. more explicit than Mk. 3 times.	

9′ The use of a proper name with a noun or with another proper name in one Gospel but not in another

Matthew

16. 16 reads: 'And answering, Simon Peter said...' Mk. 8. 29 reads: 'Answering, Peter says to him...' Lk. 9. 20 reads: 'And Peter answering said...' This is abbreviated as follows:

16. 16; ctr. Mk. 8. 29 and Lk. 9. 20 '(+ Simon) Peter'.

26. 57; ctr. Mk. 14. 53 (cf. Lk. 22. 54) '(+ Caiaphas) the high priest'.

Mark

1. 20; ctr. Mt. 4. 22 'their father + Zebedee'.

5. 7 and Lk. 8. 28; ctr. Mt. 8. 29 '(+ Jesus) son of God'.

6. 17; ctr. Mt. 14. 3 'his brother + Philip'.

10. 47 and Lk. 18. 37; ctr. Mt. 20. 30 'Jesus + the Nazarene', and the like.

16. 6; ctr. Mt. 28. 5 'Jesus + the Nazarene'.

Summary

Mt. more explicit than Mk. 2 times.	Mt:Mk::2:5
Mt. more explicit than Lk. 1 time.	Mt:Lk::1:2
Mk. more explicit than Mt. 5 times.	
Mk. more explicit than Lk. 0.	
Lk. more explicit than Mt. 2 times.	
Lk. more explicit than Mk. 0.	

10′ Other instances of proper names in one Gospel but not in another

Matthew

3. 13 ('to the Jordan') and Mk. 1. 9 ('in the Jordan'); ctr. Lk. 3. 21.

10. 2 and Mk. 3. 17; ctr. Lk. 6. 13 'James + the son of Zebedee'.

10. 15 ('Sodom and Gomorrah'); ctr. Lk. 10. 12 ('the Sodomites').

15. 21; ctr. Mk. 7. 24 'Tyre + and Sidon'.

16. 4 and 12. 39 and Lk. 11. 29; ctr. Mk. 8. 12 + 'except the sign of Jonah'.

16. 14; ctr. Mk. 8. 28 and Lk. 9. 19 '(+ Jeremiah) or one of the prophets'.

23. 35; ctr. Lk. 11. 51 'Zachariah + the son of Barachiah'.

26. 3; ctr. Mk. 14. 1 and Lk. 22. 2 + 'the high priest called Caiaphas'.

26. 25 ('Judas who betrayed him'); ctr. Lk. 22. 23 ('they'). But there is no verbatim agreement between the two verses, despite the similarity of content.

26. 68; ctr. Mk. 14. 65 and Lk. 22. 64 'prophesy + Christ'.

Mark

1. 9; ctr. Mt. 3. 13 'from (+ Nazareth of) Galilee'.

1. 29; ctr. Mt. 8. 14 and Lk. 4. 38 + 'and Andrew with James and John'.

2. 14; ctr. Mt. 9. 9 and Lk. 5. 27 'Levi (Mt.: 'Matthew') + the son of Alphaeus'.

2. 26; ctr. Mt. 12. 4 and Lk. 6. 4 + 'while Abiathar was high priest'. See also category 4′.

3. 17; ctr. Mt. 10. 2 and Lk. 6. 14 + 'and he gave to them the name Boanerges, that is, Sons of Thunder'.

5. 22 and Lk. 8. 41; ctr. Mt. 9. 18 + 'Jairus by name'.

6. 45; ctr. Mt. 14. 22 'to the other side + toward Bethsaida'.

7. 31 (Tyre, Sidon, the sea of Galilee, the Decapolis); ctr. Mt. 15. 29 (the Sea of Galilee).

8. 27 and Mt. 16. 13; ctr. Lk. 9. 18 + 'Caesarea Philippi'.

10. 46; ctr. Mt. 20. 30 and Lk. 18. 35 + 'the son of Timaeus, Bartimaeus'.

11. 1 and Lk. 19. 29 ('Bethphage and Bethany'); ctr. Mt. 21. 1 ('Bethphage').

14. 37; ctr. Mt. 26. 40 and Lk. 22. 46 'he says to Peter, + Simon'.

15. 21; ctr. Mt. 27. 3 and Lk. 23. 26 + 'the father of Alexander and Rufus'.

16. 1 ('Salome') and Lk. 24. 10 ('Joanna'); ctr. Mt. 28. 1. Mark also has 'Salome' in 15. 40, where Mt. 27. 56 has 'the mother of the sons of Zebedee'. Luke does not list the women's names in his parallel, 23. 49.

16. 7; ctr. Mt. 28. 7 'say to his disciples + and to Peter'.

Luke

3. 2; ctr. Mt. 3. 1 and Mk. 1. 4 'John + the son of Zachariah'.

4. 31; ctr. Mk. 1. 21 'Capernaum + a city of Galilee'.

22. 34; ctr. Mt. 26. 34 and Mk. 14. 30 'I say to you, + Peter'.

Summary

Mt. more detailed than Mk. 4 times.	Mt:Mk::4:14
Mt. more detailed than Lk. 9 times.	Mt:Lk::9:5
Mk. more detailed than Mt. 14 times.	Mk:Lk::10:4
Mk. more detailed than Lk. 10 times.	
Lk. more detailed than Mt. 5 times.	
Lk. more detailed than Mk. 4 times.	

11′ The appearance of a proper name in one Gospel where a noun or pronoun appears in another

Matthew

3. 7 ('seeing many of the Pharisees and Sadducees'); ctr. Lk. 3. 7 ('he said to the crowd').

12. 1 ('Jesus'); ctr. Mk. 2. 23 and Lk. 6. 1 ('he').

12. 24 ('the Pharisees') and cf. Mk. 3. 22 ('the scribes who came down from Jerusalem'); ctr. Lk. 11. 15 ('certain ones').

14. 10 ('John'); ctr. Mk. 6. 27 ('him').

15. 1 ('they came to Jesus'); ctr. Mk. 7. 1 ('they gathered together to him').

15. 15 ('Peter'); ctr. Mk. 7. 17 ('his disciples').

Cf. 19. 1 ('from Galilee'); ctr. Mk. 10. 1 ('from there').

24. 1 ('Jesus'); ctr. Mk. 13. 1 ('he').

26. 4 ('Jesus'); ctr. Mk. 14. 1 and Lk. 22. 2 ('him').

26. 6 ('Jesus'); ctr. Mk. 14. 3 ('he').

26. 17 ('Jesus'); ctr. Mk. 14. 12 ('him').

26. 40 and Mk. 14. 37 ('Peter'); ctr. Lk. 22. 46 ('them').

26. 49 and Lk. 22. 47 ('Jesus'); ctr. Mk. 14. 45 ('him').

26. 50 ('on Jesus'); ctr. Mk. 14. 46 ('on him').

26. 57 and Mk. 14. 53 ('Jesus'); ctr. Lk. 22. 54 ('him'). But the agreement is not high.

26. 69 ('with Jesus the Galilean') and Mk. 14. 67 ('with the Nazarean, Jesus'); ctr. Lk. 22. 56 ('with him').

26. 71 ('with Jesus the Nazarean'); ctr. Mk. 14. 69 and Lk. 22. 58 ('of them').

27. 22 ('Jesus'); ctr. Mk. 15. 12 ('whom').

27. 27 ('Jesus'); ctr. Mk. 15. 16 ('him').

27. 55 ('they followed Jesus'); ctr. Mk. 15. 41 and Lk. 23. 49 ('they followed him').

Mark

1. 16 ('the brother of Simon'); ctr. Mt. 4. 18 ('his brother').

1. 30 and Lk. 4. 38 ('Simon's mother-in-law'); ctr. Mt. 8. 14 ('his mother-in-law').

1. 36 ('Simon and those with him'); ctr. Lk. 4. 42 ('the crowds').
2. 1 ('into Capernaum'); ctr. Mt. 9. 1 ('into his own city').
3. 17 ('the brother of James'); ctr. Mt. 10. 2 ('his brother').
5. 20 ('he departed and began to preach in the Decapolis'); ctr. Lk. 8. 39 ('he went throughout all the city preaching').
6. 18 ('to Herod'); ctr. Mt. 14. 4 ('to him').
6. 20 ('Herod feared John'); ctr. Mt. 14. 5 ('he feared the crowd').
9. 4 ('speaking to Jesus'); ctr. Mt. 17. 3 ('with him') and Lk. 9. 30 ('to him').
10. 41 ('James and John'); ctr. Mt. 20. 24 ('the two brothers').
11. 21 ('Peter'); ctr. Mt. 21. 20 ('the disciples').
11. 33 and Lk. 20. 8 ('Jesus'); ctr. Mt. 21. 27 ('*he*').
13. 3 ('Peter and James and John and Andrew'); ctr. Mt. 24. 3 ('the disciples') and Lk. 21. 7 (subject understood, referring back to 'certain ones' in vs. 5).
14. 33 ('James and John'); ctr. Mt. 26. 37 ('the two sons of Zebedee'). It is not clear that Mark is actually more explicit than Matthew here.
14. 60 ('Jesus'); ctr. Mt. 26. 62 ('him').
15. 1 ('Jesus'); ctr. Mt. 27. 2 ('him'). But see 'against Jesus', Mt. 27. 1.
15. 2 and Lk. 23. 3 ('Pilate'); ctr. Mt. 27. 11 ('the governor').
15. 5 ('Pilate'); ctr. Mt. 27. 14 ('the governor').
15. 47 ('Mary the mother of Joses'); ctr. Mt. 27. 61 ('the other Mary').
16. 1 and Lk. 24. 10 ('Mary the mother of James'); ctr. Mt. 28. 1 ('the other Mary').

Luke

4. 9 ('into Jerusalem'); ctr. Mt. 4. 5 ('into the holy city').
4. 16 ('into Nazareth'); ctr. Mt. 13. 54 and Mk. 6. 1 ('into his homeland').
8. 41 ('the feet of Jesus'); ctr. Mk. 5. 22 ('his feet').
8. 45 ('Peter'); ctr. Mk. 5. 31 ('his disciples').
9. 10 ('Bethsaida'); ctr. Mt. 14. 13 and Mk. 6. 32 ('desert place'). Luke has 'desert place' in 9. 12.
22. 8 ('he sent Peter and John'); ctr. Mk. 14. 13 ('he sends two of his disciples'). Matthew lacks the sentence.

Summary

Mt. more explicit than Mk. 15 times.
Mt. more explicit than Lk. 9 times.
Mk. more explicit than Mt. 18 times (with two doubtful).
Mk. more explicit than Lk. 8 times.
Lk. more explicit than Mt. 7 times.
Lk. more explicit than Mk. 6 times.
Mt:Mk::15:18(16)   Omitting 'Jesus':

Mt:Lk::9:7   Mt:Mk::3:14(13)
Mk:Lk::8:6   Mt:Lk::3:6
                    Mk:Lk::5:4

12′ The appearance of a noun in one Gospel where a pronoun appears in another

Matthew

9. 14 and Mk. 2. 18 ('your disciples'); ctr. Lk. 5. 33 ('yours').

9. 37 ('the disciples'); ctr. Lk. 10. 2 ('them'). But see also 'seventy others', Lk. 10. 1.

Cf. 10. 14 ('out of that house or city') and Lk. 9. 5 ('from that city'); ctr. Mk. 6. 11 ('from there').

12. 13 and Mk. 3. 5 ('the man'); ctr. Lk. 6. 10 ('him').

12. 48 ('to the one speaking to him'); ctr. Mk. 3. 33 and Lk. 8. 21 ('to them'). (Subst. ptcple. for pron.)

13. 34 ('to the crowds'); ctr. Mk. 4. 33 ('to them').

14. 15 and Lk. 9. 12 ('the crowd(s)'); ctr. Mk. 6. 36 ('them').

14. 19 ('the crowds to recline'); ctr. Mk. 6. 39 ('all to recline').

14. 19 and Mk. 6. 41 ('the loaves'); ctr. Lk. 9. 16 ('them').

14. 19 and Lk. 9. 16 ('the crowd(s)'); ctr. Mk. 6. 41 ('them').

14. 23 ('dismissing the crowds'); ctr. Mk. 6. 46 ('taking leave of them').

15. 39 ('the crowds'); ctr. Mk. 8. 9 ('them').

16. 20 ('the disciples'); ctr. Mk. 8. 30 and Lk. 9. 21 ('them').

16. 21 ('to show his disciples'); ctr. Mk. 8. 31 ('to teach them').

16. 24 ('his disciples') and Mk. 8. 34 ('the crowd with his disciples'); ctr. Lk. 9. 23 ('all').

17. 14 ('a man') and Lk. 9. 38 ('a man from the crowd'); ctr. Mk. 9. 17 ('one out of the crowd').

21. 7 and Mk. 11. 7 ('the colt'); ctr. Lk. 19. 35 ('it').

21. 35 ('his slaves'); ctr. Mk. 12. 3 and Lk. 20. 10 ('him').

21. 38 ('seeing the son'); ctr. Lk. 20. 14 ('seeing him').

21. 40 ('to those tenants'); ctr. Lk. 20. 15 ('to them'). See also Mk. 12. 9, same category.

26. 8 ('the disciples were indignant'); ctr. Mk. 14. 4 ('some were indignant').

26. 10 ('the woman'); ctr. Mk. 14. 6 ('her').

26. 26 ('the disciples'); ctr. Mk. 14. 22 and Lk. 22. 19 ('them').

26. 55 ('to the crowds') and Lk. 22. 52 ('to those who had come out against him, the chief priests and captains of the temple and elders'); ctr. Mk. 14. 48 ('to them').

27. 15 ('the crowd'); ctr. Mk. 15. 6 ('them').

28. 5 ('the women'); ctr. Mk. 16. 6 ('them').

Mark

1. 34 ('the demons to speak'); ctr. Lk. 4. 41 ('them').
2. 18 ('the disciples of the Pharisees'); ctr. Lk. 5. 33 ('the ones of the Pharisees').
4. 33 ('the word'); ctr. Mt. 13. 34 ('all these things').
5. 36 ('to the ruler of the synagogue'); ctr. Lk. 8. 50 ('to him').
5. 41 ('the hand of the child'); ctr. Mt. 9. 25 and Lk. 8. 54 ('her hand').
6. 18 ('the wife of your brother'); ctr. Mt. 14. 4 ('her').
7. 11 ('a man'); ctr. Mt. 15. 5 ('whoever').
8. 12 ('this generation'); ctr. Mt. 16. 4 and Lk. 11. 29 ('it').
9. 25 and Lk. 9. 42 ('the unclean spirit'); ctr. Mt. 17. 18 ('him'). In Mt., apparently the pronoun applies to the boy, which seems rather harsh.
9. 31 and Lk. 9. 43 ('his disciples'); ctr. Mt. 17. 22 ('them').
12. 2 and Lk. 20. 10 ('the fruit of the vineyard'); ctr. Mt. 21. 34 ('its fruits').
12. 9 and Lk. 20. 16 ('destroy the tenants'); ctr. Mt. 21. 41 ('destroy them'). See Mt. 21. 40, same category.
13. 2 ('these great buildings'); ctr. Mt. 24. 2 ('all these things') and Lk. 21. 6 ('these things').
14. 5 ('more than three hundred denarii'); ctr. Mt. 26. 9 ('much').
14. 14 and Lk. 22. 11 ('householder'); ctr. Mt. 26. 18 ('him').

Luke

9. 41 ('your son'); ctr. Mt. 17. 17 and Mk. 9. 19 ('him').
12. 24 ('the birds'); ctr. Mt. 6. 26 ('they').
19. 35 ('the colt'); ctr. Mt. 21. 7 ('them') and Mk. 11. 7 ('it').
20. 9 ('to the people'); ctr. Mk. 12. 1 ('to them').

Summary

Mt. more explicit than Mk. 18 times.   Mt:Mk::18:12
Mt. more explicit than Lk. 12 times.   Mt:Lk::12:9
Mk. more explicit than Mt. 12 times.   Mk:Lk::11:7
Mk. more explicit than Lk. 11 times.
Lk. more explicit than Mt. 9 times.
Lk. more explicit than Mk. 7 times.

13′ The use of a noun with a pronoun in one Gospel where only a pronoun appears in another

Matthew

8. 4 reads: καὶ προσένεγκον τὸ δῶρον ὃ προσέταξεν Μωϋσῆς κ.τ.λ. Mk. 1. 44 reads: καὶ προσένεγκε...ἃ προσέταξεν Μωϋσῆς κ.τ.λ. This is abbreviated as follows:
8. 4; ctr. Mk. 1. 44 '(+ the gift) which'.

8. 19 ('one scribe'); ctr. Lk. 9. 57 ('a certain one'). See also *heis* and *tis*, below.

12. 35; ctr. Lk. 6. 45 'and the evil + man'. Lk. may avoid repetition here: he had just written 'good man'.

21. 9 ('the crowd which went before'); ctr. Mk. 11. 9 ('the ones going before').

21. 41; ctr. Mk. 12. 9 and Lk. 20. 16 'to other + tenants'.

26. 35; ctr. Mk. 14. 31 'all + the disciples'.

26. 56; ctr. Mk. 14. 50 'all + the disciples'.

27. 44; ctr. Mk. 15. 32 '(+ the thieves) who were crucified with him'.

Mark

10. 46; ctr. Mt. 20. 30; Lk. 18. 35 'a blind + beggar'. But note Lk. 18. 35, 'begging'.

12. 43; ctr. Lk. 21. 3 'all + the ones casting into the treasury'. (Subst. ptcple.)

14. 5; ctr. Mt. 26. 9 'this + ointment'.

14. 12; ctr. Mt. 26. 17 'the first + day'. (Lk. 22. 7 has only 'the day'.)

14. 18; ctr. Mt. 26. 21 'one of you + the one eating with me'. (Subst. ptcple.)

14. 20; ctr. Mt. 26. 23 '(+ one of the twelve), who dips'.

15. 39 and Lk. 23. 47; ctr. Mt. 27. 54 'this + man'.

Luke

4. 36; ctr. Mk. 1. 27 'this + word'.

5. 18 ('a man who was paralyzed'); ctr. Mt. 9. 2 and Mk. 2. 3 ('a paralytic').

7. 9 ('the crowd following him'); ctr. Mt. 8. 10 ('the ones following him').

7. 25; ctr. Mt. 11. 8 'soft + garments'.

18. 18 ('a certain ruler'); ctr. Mt. 19. 16 and Mk. 10. 17 ('one').

22. 20; ctr. Mt. 26. 28 and Mk. 14. 24 'this + cup'.

Summary

Mt. more explicit than Mk. 6 times.	Mt:Mk::6:6
Mt. more explicit than Lk. 3 times.	Mt:Lk::3:6
Mk. more explicit than Mt. 6 times.	Mk:Lk::2:4
Mk. more explicit than Lk. 2 times.	
Lk. more explicit than Mt. 6 times.	
Lk. more explicit than Mk. 4 times.	

14′ The use of a phrase indicating circumstance in one Gospel but not in another

Matthew

4. 12 reads: 'When he heard that John had been arrested, he departed into Galilee.' Mk. 1. 14 reads: 'And after John was arrested, Jesus went into Galilee.' Lk. 4. 14–15 reads: 'And Jesus returned in the power of the spirit into Galilee.' This is abbreviated as follows:

4. 12 and Mk. 1. 14; ctr. Lk. 4. 14 + 'when he heard that John was arrested', and the like.

9. 12 and Mk. 2. 17; ctr. Lk. 5. 31 '(+ when he heard), he said'.

12. 15; ctr. Mk. 3. 7 '(+ when he knew), he departed'.

13. 1; ctr. Mk. 4. 1 + 'Jesus went out of the house and sat'.

16. 5; ctr. Mk. 8. 14 + 'when his disciples came to the other side'.

17. 5 and Lk. 9. 34; ctr. Mk. 9. 7 + 'while he was saying these things'.

[19. 22 and Lk. 18. 23 ('when he heard'); ctr. Mk. 10. 22 ('being sad').] See category 17′, Mk. 10. 22.

19. 25; ctr. Mk. 10. 26 and Lk. 18. 26 + 'when they heard'.

21. 38 (+ 'when they saw the son') and Lk. 20. 14 (+ 'when they saw him'); ctr. Mk. 12. 7.

21. 40; ctr. Mk. 12. 9 and Lk. 20. 15 + 'when he comes'.

21. 45; ctr. Mk. 12. 12 and Lk. 20. 19 + 'when the chief priests and the Pharisees heard'.

22. 22; ctr. Mk. 12. 17 and Lk. 20. 26 + 'when they heard'.

26. 8; ctr. Mk. 14. 4 + 'when they saw'.

26. 10; ctr. Mk. 14. 6 + 'when he knew'.

27. 32 (+ 'while they were going out') and Lk. 23. 26 (+ 'as they led him away'); ctr. Mk. 15. 21.

27. 34 ('when he tasted, he did not want to drink'); ctr. Mk. 15. 23 ('but he did not take').

Mark

1. 21; ctr. Lk. 4. 31 + 'entering the synagogue'.

1. 33; ctr. Mt. 8. 16 and Lk. 4. 40 + 'and all the city was gathered at the door'.

2. 2; ctr. Mt. 9. 1 + 'And many were gathered together, so that there was no longer room for them, not even about the door, and he was preaching the word to them'. See also Lk. 5. 17, which gives an explicit setting.

2. 6 ('they were sitting there debating') and Lk. 5. 21 ('they began to debate'); ctr. Mt. 9. 3.

2. 13 ('and he went out again by the sea, and all the crowd came to him, and he taught them'); ctr. Mt. 9. 9 ('from there') and Lk. 5. 27 ('after these things').

2. 18; ctr. Mt. 9. 14 and Lk. 5. 33 +'now the disciples of John and the Pharisees were fasting'. This perhaps should be listed in category 15.

3. 32 ('and a crowd was sitting around him') and Lk. 8. 19 ('they could not reach him for the crowd'); ctr. Mt. 12. 46.

4. 10; ctr. Mt. 13. 10 and Lk. 8. 9 +'when he was alone'.

4. 36; ctr. Mt. 8. 23 and Lk. 8. 23 +'other boats were with him'. Perhaps this should be listed in category 18.

5. 3–5 and Lk. 8. 27 b, 29 b; ctr. Mt. 8. 28. The circumstances of the demoniac are explained in Mark and Luke.

5. 6 and Lk. 8. 28; ctr. Mt. 8. 29 +'when he saw Jesus'.

5. 22; ctr. Mt. 9. 18 and Lk. 8. 41 +'when he saw him'.

5. 24 ('and a large crowd followed him and pressed around him') and similarly Lk. 8. 42 b; ctr. Mt. 9. 19.

5. 27; ctr. Mt. 9. 20 and Lk. 8. 43 +'when she heard the things about Jesus'.

6. 2 ('the Sabbath having come') and Lk. 4. 16 ('on the day of the Sabbath'); ctr. Mt. 13. 54.

6. 16; ctr. Lk. 9. 9 '(+when he heard), Herod said'.

6. 29; ctr. Mt. 14. 12 '(+when they heard), the disciples came'.

6. 31 b; ctr. Mt. 14. 13 and Lk. 9. 10 +'for many were coming and going and they had no leisure even to eat'. Cf. also Mk. 1. 33; 2. 1 f.; 3. 9; and especially 3. 20.

6. 54; ctr. Mt. 14. 34 +'when they got out of the boat'.

7. 2; ctr. Mt. 15. 1 +'when they saw that some of his disciples ate with defiled—that is, unwashed—hands'.

7. 17; ctr. Mt. 15. 15 +'when he went into a house from the crowd'. See 6. 31 above.

7. 24; ctr. Mt. 15. 21 +'and entering a house he wanted no one to know, but he was not able to hide'. Cf. Mk. 1. 45; 9. 30.

7. 25; ctr. Mt. 15. 22 +'having heard about him'.

8. 1; ctr. Mt. 15. 32 +'in those days when again there was a great crowd and they had nothing to eat'.

8. 33; ctr. Mt. 16. 23 +'when he saw his disciples'.

10. 14; ctr. Mt. 19. 14 and Lk. 18. 16 '(+when he saw), he said.'

10. 17; ctr. Mt. 19. 16 and Lk. 18. 18 +'while he was going out in the road'.

10. 32; ctr. Mt. 20. 17 +'and Jesus was going before them'.

11. 2 and Lk. 19. 30; ctr. Mt. 21. 2 '(+when you enter), you will find'.

12. 37 b ('and the great crowd was hearing him gladly') and Lk. 20. 45 ('when all the people were hearing'); ctr. Mt. 23. 1.

12. 43; ctr. Lk. 21. 3 '(+and calling his disciples), he said'.

14. 11; ctr. Lk. 22. 5 '(+when they heard), they rejoiced'.

14. 54; ctr. Mt. 26. 58 and Lk. 22. 55 +'warming himself at the fire'. But see also Lk. 22. 56.

14. 67; ctr. Mt. 26. 69 +'and when she saw Peter warming himself'. See also Lk. 22. 56 'when she saw him'.
15. 32; ctr. Mt. 27. 42 '(+that we may see) and believe'. (That is, 'when we see...')

Luke

3. 15; ctr. Mt. 3. 11 and Mk. 1. 7 +'and as the people were in expectation, and all men questioned in their hearts concerning John, whether perhaps he were the Christ'.
4. 2 ('when they were completed'); ctr. Mt. 4. 2 ('afterward').
5. 12; ctr. Mt. 8. 2 and Mk. 1. 40 +'when he saw Jesus'.
6. 6; ctr. Mt. 12. 9 and Mk. 3. 1 +'it happened on another Sabbath'.
6. 8; ctr. Mt. 12. 10 and Mk. 3. 2 +'but he knew their thoughts'.
8. 34; ctr. Mt. 8. 33 and Mk. 5. 14 'the herdsmen+when they saw'.
9. 18; ctr. Mt. 16. 13 and Mk. 8. 27 +'while he was praying'. Matthew and Mark have 'Jesus went into Caesarea Philippi', and the like. See category 10 above.
9. 33; ctr. Mt. 17. 4 and Mk. 9. 5 +'and it happened while they were departing from him'.
9. 42 (see also Mk. 9. 20); ctr. Mt. 17. 17 +'while he was coming, the demons tore him and convulsed him'.
18. 15; ctr. Mt. 19. 13 and Mk. 10. 13 '(+when they saw), they rebuked'.
18. 22; ctr. Mt. 19. 21 and Mk. 10. 21 '(+when he heard), he said'.
18. 24; ctr. Mt. 19. 23 +'when he saw him'. See also Mk. 10. 23, additional action, in chapter II above ('looking around').
18. 40; ctr. Mt. 20. 32 +'when he drew near'. See also Mk. 10. 50, additional scene, in chapter II above.
19. 36; ctr. Mt. 21. 8 and Mk. 11. 8 +'as he was going'.
19. 37; ctr. Mt. 21. 8 and Mk. 11. 8 +'as he was drawing near to the descent of the Mount of Olives'.
19. 47; ctr. Mt. 21. 13 and Mk. 11. 18 +'and he was teaching daily in the temple'. But see also Mk. 11. 18 +'they heard'.
22. 45; ctr. Mt. 26. 40 and Mk. 14. 37 '(+and when he rose from prayer), he came'.
22. 60; ctr. Mt. 26. 74 and Mk. 14. 72 '(+while he was yet speaking), the cock crew'.

Summary

Mt. more explicit than Mk. 13 times.   Mt:Mk::13:31
Mt. more explicit than Lk. 6 times.   Mt:Lk::6:27
Mk. more explicit than Mt. 31 times.   Mk:Lk::17:17
Mk. more explicit than Lk. 17 times.
Lk. more explicit than Mt. 27 times.
Lk. more explicit than Mk. 17 times.

15′ Explanations in one Gospel but not in another

Matthew

9. 21 and Mk. 5. 28; ctr. Lk. 8. 44 +'For she said, "If only I touch his garment, I shall be saved"'. (See also new speech.)

21. 46; ctr. Mk. 12. 12 and Lk. 20. 19 +'since they held him as a prophet'.

22. 38; ctr. Mk. 12. 31 and Lk. 10. 27 +'This is the great and first commandment'.

Mark

2. 15; ctr. Mt. 9. 10 and Lk. 5. 29 +'For they were many, and they followed him'.

3. 30; ctr. Mt. 12. 32 +'Because they said, "He has an unclean spirit"'.

4. 14 ('the sower sows the word') and Lk. 8. 11 ('the seed is the word of God'); ctr. Mt. 13. 19.

5. 8 (+'for he had said, "Unclean spirit, come out of the man"') and Lk. 8. 29 (similarly, but indirect discourse); ctr. Mt. 8. 29.

6. 14; ctr. Mt. 14. 1 and Lk. 9. 7 +'for his name had become known'.

6. 17; ctr. Mt. 14. 3 'on account of the wife of his brother + because he married her'.

6. 50; ctr. Mt. 14. 26 +'For they all saw him and were terrified'. (But cf. Mt. 14. 26 +'from fear'.)

6. 52; ctr. Mt. 14. 33 +'For they did not understand about the loaves, but their hearts were hardened'.

7. 3 f.; ctr. Mt. 15. 1 + The Pharisees and all the Jews do not eat without washing, etc.

7. 19; ctr. Mt. 15. 17 +'cleansing all foods'.

8. 3; ctr. Mt. 15. 32 +'and some of them have come from afar'. (This could be classified in category 17.)

9. 6 ('for he did not know what he should answer, for they were afraid'), cf. Lk. 9. 33 ('not knowing what he said'); ctr. Mt. 17. 4.

11. 18; ctr. Lk. 19. 47 +'for they feared him'.

14. 12 (+'when they sacrificed the Passover') and Lk. 22. 7 (+'on which the Passover lamb had to be sacrificed'); ctr. Mt. 26. 17.

15. 16 ('into the palace, which is the praetorium'); ctr. Mt. 27. 27 ('into the praetorium').

[16. 4; ctr. Mt. 28. 2 and Lk. 24. 2. Mk. explains that the stone was 'very large'.]

Luke

8. 37; ctr. Mt. 8. 34 and Mk. 5. 17 +'because they were seized with great fear'.

8. 53; ctr. Mt. 9. 24 and Mk. 5. 40 'And they laughed at him + knowing that she was dead'.

20. 38; ctr. Mt. 22. 32 and Mk. 12. 27 + 'for all live to him'.

22. 3; ctr. Mt. 26. 14 and Mk. 14. 10 + 'Satan entered Judas'.

Summary

Mt. more explicit than Mk. 2 times.	Mt:Mk::2:15
Mt. more explicit than Lk. 3 times.	Mt:Lk::3:8
Mk. more explicit than Mt. 15 times.	Mk:Lk::5:4
Mk. more explicit than Lk. 5 times.	
Lk. more explicit than Mt. 8 times.	
Lk. more explicit than Mk. 4 times.	

16′ Conclusions and results mentioned in one Gospel but not in another

Matthew

7. 12 reads: 'So whatever you wish that men would do to you, do so to them; for this is the law and the prophets.' Lk. 6. 31 reads: 'And as you wish that men would do to you, do so to them.' This is abbreviated as follows:

7. 12; ctr. Lk. 6. 31 + 'for this is the law and the prophets'.

9. 22; ctr. Mk. 5. 34 and Lk. 8. 48 + 'and the woman was saved from that hour'.

9. 26; ctr. Mk. 5. 43 and Lk. 8. 56 + 'and this report went out into all that land'.

15. 20; ctr. Mk. 7. 23 'These are what defile a man + but to eat with unwashed hands does not defile a man'.

16. 12; ctr. Mk. 8. 21 + 'Then they understood that he did not say to beware of the leaven of bread', etc.

17. 13; ctr. Mk. 9. 13 + 'Then the disciples understood that he spoke to them about John the Baptist'.

19. 15 ('and placing his hands upon them he went away from there') and Mk. 10. 16 ('and taking them in his arms he blessed them, placing his hands upon them'); ctr. Lk. 18. 17.

27. 58b; ctr. Lk. 23. 52 + 'then Pilate commanded it to be given'. See also Mk. 15. 44-5, in the category on new scenes.

Mark

1. 45 ('but going out he began to preach many things', etc.) and Lk. 5. 15 f. ('but so much the more the report went out concerning him', etc.); ctr. Mt. 8. 4.

2. 12 ('and immediately took up the pallet') and similarly Lk. 5. 25; ctr. Mt. 9. 7.

3. 4; ctr. Lk. 6. 9 +'and they were silent'.
4. 39 ('and the wind ceased') and Lk. 8. 24 ('and they stopped'); ctr. Mt. 8. 26.
5. 20; ctr. Lk. 8. 39 +'and all marveled'.
6. 40 ('so they sat down in groups, by hundreds and by fifties') and similarly Lk. 9. 15; ctr. Mt. 14. 19. Perhaps this should be listed in category 18'.
11. 6; ctr. Mt. 21. 6 and Lk. 19. 34 +'and they let them'.
14. 40; ctr. Mt. 26. 43 +'and they did not know what to answer him'.

Luke

3. 18; ctr. Mt. 3. 12 +'So, with many other exhortations, he evangelized the people'.
9. 43; ctr. Mt. 17. 18 and Mk. 9. 27 +'and all were astonished at the majesty of God'.
20. 26; ctr. Mt. 22. 21 and Mk. 12. 17 +'And they were not able to catch him by a word in the presence of the people'.
20. 26 ('Marvelling+they were silent') and Mt. 22. 22 ('leaving him they departed'); ctr. Mk. 12. 17. See also Chap. II, Category 6', Mt. 22. 22.

Summary

Mt. is more detailed than Mk. 6 times.	Mt:Mk::6:6
Mt. is more detailed than Lk. 5 times.	Mt:Lk::5:7
Mk. is more detailed than Mt. 6 times.	Mk:Lk::4:3
Mk. is more detailed than Lk. 4 times.	
Lk. is more detailed than Mt. 7 times.	
Lk. is more detailed than Mk. 3 times.	

17' Emotions mentioned in one Gospel but not in another

Matthew

14. 26 reads: 'They were terrified, saying, "It is a ghost!" And they cried out from fear.' Mk. 6. 49 reads: 'They thought that it was a ghost, and cried out.' This is abbreviated as follows:
14. 26; ctr. Mk. 6. 49 'they cried out+from fear'. Cf. Mk. 6. 50, category 15'.
19. 25 and Mk. 10. 26; ctr. Lk. 18. 26 'they were greatly astonished'.
20. 34; ctr. Mk. 10. 52 and Lk. 18. 42 +'feeling compassion'.
27. 54; ctr. Mk. 15. 39 and Lk. 23. 47 'they feared exceedingly'.

Mark

1. 41; ctr. Mt. 8. 3 and Lk. 5. 13 +'feeling compassion'.
3. 5; ctr. Lk. 6. 10 +'with wrath, grieved at the hardness of their hearts'.
5. 42 ('and immediately they were amazed with a great amazement') and Lk. 8. 56 ('and her parents were amazed'); ctr. Mt. 9. 25.

6. 6; ctr. Mt. 13. 58 '(+he marveled) on account of their unbelief'.
6. 51; ctr. Mt. 14. 32 +'and they were very exceedingly amazed in them-
    selves'.
8. 12; ctr. Mt. 16. 1 +'he groaned in his spirit'.
10. 14; ctr. Mt. 19. 14 and Lk. 18. 16 +'he was indignant'.
10. 21; ctr. Mt. 19. 21 and Lk. 18. 22 + 'he loved him'.
10. 22 ('being sad'); ctr. Mt. 19. 22 and Lk. 18. 23 ('hearing'). Cf. cate-
    gory 14', Mt. 19. 22.
10. 24; ctr. Mt. 19. 23 and Lk. 18. 24 +'and his disciples were amazed at his
    words'.
10. 32; ctr. Mt. 20. 17 +'they were amazed, and the ones following were
    afraid'.
11. 18; ctr. Lk. 19. 47 +'for they feared him'.
14. 11 and Lk. 22. 5; ctr. Mt. 26. 15 +'they rejoiced'.

Luke

6. 11; ctr. Mt. 12. 14 and Mk. 3. 6 +'they were filled with fury'.
8. 37; ctr. Mt. 8. 34 and Mk. 5. 17 'they asked him to depart+because they
    were seized with a great fear'. Cf. category 15'.

Summary

Mt. more detailed than Mk. 3 times.	Mt:Mk::3:11
Mt. more detailed than Lk. 3 times.	Mt:Lk::3:4
Mk. more detailed than Mt. 11 times.	Mk:Lk::8:2
Mk. more detailed than Lk. 8 times.	
Lk. more detailed than Mt. 4 times.	
Lk. more detailed than Mk. 2 times.	

18' The presence of miscellaneous details in one Gospel but not in another

Matthew

26. 3; ctr. Mk. 14. 1 and Lk. 22. 2 +The enemies of Jesus gathered 'in the
    palace of the high priest, who was called Caiaphas'.
26. 15; ctr. Mk. 14. 11 and Lk. 22. 5 '(+thirty) silver pieces'.

Mark

2. 3; ctr. Mt. 9. 2 and Lk. 5. 18 +'borne by four'.
4. 38; ctr. Mt. 8. 24 and Lk. 8. 23 +'in the stern, on the cushion'. See also
    category 4'.
5. 13; ctr. Mt. 8. 32 and Lk. 8. 33 +'about two thousand'.
5. 26 (+'who had suffered much under many physicians' etc.) and Lk.
    8. 43 (+'who was not able to be healed by anyone'); ctr. Mt. 9. 20.

5. 42 and Lk. 8. 42; ctr. Mt. 9. 18–26. Mk. and Lk. tell us that the girl was twelve years old.

6. 7; ctr. Mt. 10. 8 and Lk. 9. 2 + 'he sent them out two by two'.

6. 23; ctr. Mt. 14. 7 + 'until half of my kingdom'.

6. 37; ctr. Mt. 14. 17 and Lk. 9. 13 + 'two hundred denarii worth of bread'.

6. 48; ctr. Mt. 14. 25 + 'and he wanted to pass by them'.

8. 14; ctr. Mt. 16. 5 + 'and they had only one loaf with them in the boat'.

9. 10; ctr. Mt. 17. 9 + 'and they kept the saying to themselves, questioning what the rising from the dead meant'.

10. 10; ctr. Mt. 19. 9 The disciples ask Jesus about his saying on marriage + 'in the house'. Cf. category 14', Mk. 7. 17.

11. 16; ctr. Mt. 21. 12 + 'and he did not permit anyone to carry a vessel through the temple'.

14. 5 ('three hundred denarii'); ctr. Mt. 26. 9 ('much').

14. 13 (Jesus sends two of the disciples) and Lk. 22. 7 (he sends Peter and James); ctr. Mt. 26. 17–18 (it is not said who is sent).

14. 30; ctr. Mt. 26. 34 and Lk. 22. 34 and Mk. 14. 72; ctr. Mt. 26. 75 and Lk. 22. 61 'before the cock crows + twice'.

15. 25; ctr. Mt. 27. 36 and Lk. 23. 34 + 'It was the third hour, and they crucified him'.

Luke

9. 38; ctr. Mt. 17. 15 and Mk. 9. 17 The epileptic is the father's *only* child. Cf. Lk. 8. 42, category 5'.

Summary

Mt. more detailed than Mk. 2 times.	Mt:Mk::2:17
Mt. more detailed than Lk. 2 times.	Mt:Lk::2:4
Mk. more detailed than Mt. 17 times.	Mk:Lk::7:1
Mk. more detailed than Lk. 7 times.	
Lk. more detailed than Mt. 4 times.	
Lk. more detailed than Mk. 1 time.	

We may make the following summary comments:[1]

1. Matthew is clearly the most specific Gospel in the category of making the subject of a sentence or clause explicit. It is more explicit when compared with Luke as well as with Mark. Luke is slightly more explicit than Mark, but perhaps the difference is not large enough to be significant. This evidence is compatible with the usual solution to the synoptic problem. It is interesting

---

[1] We may recall that the analysis of the post-canonical tradition indicated that the categories numbered 1, 6, 7, 9, 10, 11, 12, 13, 14, 18, and, to a lesser degree, 5 and 8, are useful for evaluating relative antiquity.

to note the figures which result when the instances in which 'Jesus' is the subject are eliminated. The relationship between Matthew and Mark is not appreciably altered. The relationships of Matthew and Mark with Luke are altered, however. It appears that Luke had little or no interest in mentioning Jesus as the subject of a sentence. He very seldom does so where either Matthew or Mark does not, and frequently does not do so where Matthew or Mark does. It might be suggested that Luke wished to avoid too frequent repetition of the same name, even when it was the name of the central figure.

2. Mark makes the direct object explicit more often than do Matthew and Luke. Luke and Matthew are approximately equal. This category did not appear significant for the relative dating of documents, however.

3. In making the indirect object explicit, Mark is also the most detailed of the Gospels. Matthew is somewhat more detailed than Luke.

4. Matthew appears slightly less detailed than either Mark or Luke in the use of non-adjectival prepositional phrases. Mark and Luke are about the same.

5. In the category of adjectives and adjectival phrases, the relationships are unusually confused. Luke is less detailed than Matthew, but slightly more detailed than Mark. Matthew is much more detailed than Luke, but less detailed than Mark. No clear redactional method appears here.

6. In the category of the addition of nouns in the genitive, which is of some value in determining relative antiquity, we see that Matthew is more detailed than Mark and Luke and that Luke is more detailed than Mark. This accords with the two-document hypothesis.

7. With regard to the addition of genitive pronouns, which is also a 'useful' category, the only clear observation to be made is that Luke is less detailed than Matthew and Mark. Mark is slightly more detailed than Matthew, but the difference is not large enough to be of significance. It may be that here Luke should be compared with Justin, who showed a tendency to omit the genitive pronoun.

8. Matthew adds a noun to a proper name far oftener than Mark and Luke, but it is doubtful if much significance attaches to this.

9. Mark is more explicit than Matthew in adding proper names to nouns and to other proper names.

10. In the category of other additions of proper names, Mark is clearly the most detailed and Luke the least. It is doubtful that the absence from Luke of proper names which are in Matthew and Mark can be attributed to a wish to avoid foreign words. The author of Luke can hardly have considered Caesarea Philippi barbaric (the Latin word Caesar was probably not offensive to his readers: Caesar is used 10 times and Caesarea 15 times in Acts). On the other hand, some words which are clearly barbaric are peculiar to his Gospel: see Nazareth and Bethsaida in category 11' above, and note Joanna in category 10' under Mk. 16. 1. It may be that he had other reasons for avoiding proper names, but on the basis of this list the Gospel of Luke appears to be earlier than the Gospels of Matthew and Mark, while Mark appears to be the latest of the three.

We should also note that 'Jairus' in Mk. 5. 22 is not read by D and 5 MSS of the Old Latin. It may be thought to be a later addition, derived from Luke. See Taylor's discussion in *The Gospel according to St Mark, ad loc.*

11. There seemed to be a clear tendency in the post-canonical material to substitute proper names for nouns or pronouns. Somewhat surprisingly, there are no clear differences among our Gospels at this point. If the two doubtful instances in Mark (14. 33 and 15. 1) are discounted, Matthew and Mark are almost equal in this respect. Mark and Luke are equal, as are Matthew and Luke. We should note, however, that in most of the instances in which Matthew has a proper name where Mark or Luke has a noun or pronoun, the proper name is 'Jesus'. As we saw in category 1 above, Matthew has a clear tendency to name Jesus explicitly. If we subtract from the entire list all the instances of the naming of Jesus, we see that Mark and Luke are both considerably more explicit than Matthew in mentioning other names than that of Jesus. On the same basis, Luke is slightly more explicit than Mark. It is doubtful if this distinction provides any positive results, however. The manuscripts show the tendency to use the name 'Jesus', while the Apocryphal Gospels show the tendency to make other names explicit.

We should also note that there is one instance in which Matthew names a disciple where Mark has only 'disciples', two instances in which Mark is more explicit than Matthew (in one of them he is also more explicit than Luke), and one instance in which Luke is more explicit than Mark. No clear redactional method is apparent here.

12. Matthew has a noun where Mark and Luke have pronouns more often than either has a noun where Matthew has a pronoun. Luke is somewhat less explicit on this score than Mark. One may once again wish to compare Luke with Justin, who here went against the more common tendency. It is noteworthy, however, that Matthew and Mark are closer together than might have been expected.

13. In the addition of nouns to pronouns, some tendency for which existed in the post-canonical material, Luke is more explicit than Matthew and Mark. Matthew and Mark are equal.

14. The addition of circumstances was clearly seen in the Apocryphal Gospels. In this respect both Mark and Luke, while balanced with each other, are overwhelmingly more detailed than Matthew. We should note that in this category the collection of evidence constitutes a difficulty, since the arrangement of a pericope in one Gospel may cause that writer to add circumstances which the other does not find necessary. I have not used information from the introductions to pericopes when the introductions differed because of a difference in setting. Also, introductions in which there is very scant verbatim agreement have not been used. The passages in which circumstances are mentioned which have not been used are Mk. 1. 9 parr.; 1. 14 parr.; 5. 21 parr.; 9. 30 parr. (where each evangelist gives a different circumstance); 11. 27 parr. (as 9. 30); 12. 28 parr.; Mt. 8. 1//Lk. 5. 12; Mt. 8. 18//Lk. 9. 57; Mt. 13. 53//Mk. 6. 1; Mt. 14. 13 ('when Jesus heard')//Mk. 6. 30 and Lk. 9. 10 (the return of the disciples); Lk. 8. 4; 8. 22; 19. 28.

15, 16, 17. In categories 15 and 17, Matthew is the least explicit and Mark the most, while in 16 they are even. Our post-canonical evidence did not indicate that these were significant categories, however.

18. In the matter of small details of fact, Mark is very much more detailed than Matthew and considerably more detailed

than Luke. Luke is also somewhat more detailed than Matthew. It is primarily to this category and the category of new names that scholars point in discussing Mark's details. We have seen it to be a tendency of the post-canonical tradition to admit new matters of fact.

Dealing only with the significant categories, we may make certain distinctions. There are, in the first place, two categories which support Mark's priority to Matthew and Luke.

Category 1 (subjects) gives evidence for aligning the Gospels in the order Mark, Luke, Matthew.

Category 6 (genitive nouns) supports the same order.

In Category 12 (nouns for pronouns) Matthew also appears secondary to Mark, although Luke appears prior to both. Matthew and Mark are close together.

Category 8 (nouns added to proper names), although not one of the stronger categories, indicates that Matthew is secondary both to Mark and Luke. No significant difference appears between Mark and Luke.

Three categories support Matthew's priority.

Category 9 supports Matthew's priority to Mark, although the number of passages in this category is not large enough to permit a very firm conclusion.

Category 14 (circumstances) supports Matthew's priority to Mark and Luke, but does not distinguish between Mark and Luke.

Category 18 (miscellaneous details) supports the order Matthew, Luke, Mark.

There are three categories in which Luke appears prior to Matthew and Mark. It is noteworthy, however, that in two of them—categories 7 and 12—he agrees with Justin, who at these points departed from the general tendency. It may be argued in both cases that Luke's apparent priority is to be explained by his redactional method.

Category 12 (nouns for pronouns), as we have seen, supports the order Luke, Mark, Matthew.

Category 7 (genitive pronouns) supports Luke's priority, but is indecisive for the relation of Matthew to Mark.

Category 10 (proper names) also favors Luke's priority to Matthew and Mark and Matthew's priority to Mark. It may be that some will wish to account for Luke's lack of proper names by citing Cadbury's evidence on the avoidance of foreign words. For reasons given above, however, I am not persuaded on this point. The evidence of this category seems to have been strongly influential on Bussmann, who argued that Luke, having the fewest proper names, represented the earliest form of G, the source which, according to Bussmann, lay behind our Synoptics.

Category 13 (nouns added to pronouns), however, argues for Luke's being later than Matthew and Mark. It is indecisive for the relation of Matthew to Mark.

We have already seen that category 11 (proper names for nouns or pronouns) reveals no decisive differences among the three Gospels.

The simple priority of any one Gospel to the others cannot be demonstrated by the evidence of this chapter. It is clear, rather, that the questions which finally emerge from this section concern redactional method and the relation of Mark to the eye-witness period. The categories which argue for Matthew's priority to Mark are just those which some would explain as containing material which Mark owes to his eye-witness source. Matthew, in this view, found such evidences of the eye-witness period unnecessary and omitted them. Those who cannot place Mark's material so early in the stream of the tradition or who do not agree that eye-witness tradition was detailed, however, should be moved, on the basis of this evidence, to question Mark's absolute priority to Matthew and Luke. A consideration of categories 1 and 6, and to a somewhat lesser extent 8 and 12, should also make one hesitate to confirm Matthew's absolute priority to Mark.

It is also important to note in this regard that the significant categories 7 and 13 offered no decisive evidence for the relation of Matthew and Mark.

I am inclined to account for Luke's appearance of priority in categories 7 and 12 as the result of his redactional activity, especially since in each case he agrees with Justin. Category 10 remains as favoring Luke's priority, however.

In summary, we must conclude that the principal lesson to be learned from the study of details is that of caution. It is clear that the criterion of detail should not be used too quickly to establish the relative antiquity of one document to another.

Nevertheless, there do seem to be fairly clear tendencies in the material as a whole on this point. The post-canonical tradition tended to become more detailed in several ways: by adding subjects, nouns in the genitive, genitive pronouns, and proper names to nouns; by supplying proper names where they had not previously been and substituting proper names for nouns and pronouns; by adding nouns to pronouns; by noting the circumstance or occasion of an event; and by adding miscellaneous factual details. The evidence from the post-canonical tradition cannot be applied to the Synoptics as neatly as one might wish, but that does not necessarily invalidate the evidence—to the contrary! Further, even if this evidence cannot decisively establish one solution to the Synoptic problem over against another, it should prove useful in any discussion of the redactional method of the evangelists.

CHAPTER IV

DIMINISHING SEMITISM
AS A POSSIBLE TENDENCY OF
THE TRADITION

INTRODUCTION

It is a widely accepted canon of New Testament scholarship that
Semitic coloring in a Gospel narrative usually indicates a fairly
early tradition. A section of the Gospel narrative which contains frequent Semitisms is often described as 'very early' or
even 'authentic'.[1] This canon is employed for proving both
relative and absolute antiquity. Scholars of all persuasions have
used it so. Without wishing to belabor an obvious point, we
may take a few examples.

The distinction of 'Semitic' from 'Hellenistic' is fundamental to the German form critics, especially Bultmann. He
speaks of the 'enormous distinction which existed between
Palestinian and Hellenistic Christianity' as having been
established by the work of Bousset and Heitmüller.[2] The way
in which this distinction is employed is indicated when he says
that

[1] See the discussion of Jeremias' view of Mk. 4. 11–12, below, p. 193 and n. 2.
We may also cite Vincent Taylor, *The Gospel according to St Mark*, p. 392. He
characterizes the narrative in Mk. 9. 3–8, in which there are several possible
Semitisms and in which there is 'a relative infrequency of characteristic Markan
words', as 'primitive and Palestinian in origin'. See also Max Wilcox, *The
Semitisms of Acts* (Oxford, 1965), p. 184. The 'protruding Semitisms' in certain
portions of Acts 'are also a sign to us of the authenticity and antiquity of the
material enshrined'.

[2] *Die Erforschung*, p. 11 (E.T. p. 17). See also 'The New Approach', pp. 360–1,
where he states that Bousset 'showed that primitive Palestinian Christianity was
very different from Hellenistic Christianity. The former remained within the
limits of Judaism and regarded itself as the true Israel; its piety was eschato-
logical and it awaited Jesus as the coming Son of Man. Primitive Hellenistic
Christianity, on the other hand, was a religion of cult, in the center of which
stood Jesus Christ as the "Lord" who communicated his heavenly powers in the
worship and the sacraments of the community. It goes without saying that the
recognition of this difference is of great importance in the analysis of the synoptic
tradition. It means that the elements of cult religion contained in the Synoptic
Gospels are secondary, coming from Hellenistic sources.'

190

This is so wrong
see, e.g., Hage!

since our gospels arose out of Greek Christianity, the distinction provides us with a criterion which frequently enables us to determine whether this or that feature belongs to the older tradition or was composed later.[1]

It is true that Bultmann recognized that in Palestine there was a piety similar to that of Hellenism. The similarity, he thought, came from the influence of Iranian-Babylonian ideas on both Judaism and Hellenism.[2] In actual practice, however, he distinguished sharply between Palestinian and Hellenistic Christianity, regarding traditions which represent the former as earlier than those which represent the latter. The distinction is frequently made in his *History of the Synoptic Tradition*. Thus, for example, in discussing Mk. 12. 35-7 he says that the passage must come either from a section of the primitive Church *or* from the Hellenistic Church.[3] The primitive Church could not be Hellenistic, nor the Hellenistic Church primitive.

Dibelius was basically of the same view. After noting Christianity's origin in the 'farmer culture' of Galilee, he comments that 'eine völlig andere Lage entsteht, als das Christentum in die hellenistische Welt eintritt'.[4] The distinction between Hellenistic and Palestinian Christianity remains of major significance 'even when we today reckon more strongly with Hellenistic influences already in Palestine'.[5]

The acceptance among the form critics of this distinction and its consequences for the determination of antiquity of tradition may also be seen in Kundsin's article, 'Primitive Christianity in the Light of Gospel Research'. Kundsin says that the consideration which is 'of the greatest importance in determining the age and origin of the tradition' is that 'the earliest phase of the common tradition presupposes the land and the speech of *Palestine* . . .'.[6]

This general position is followed by most scholars regardless of general persuasion. Vincent Taylor, in his commentary on Mark, presents a judicious statement of this view. Following an

---

[1] *Die Erforschung*, p. 12 (E.T. p. 18).
[2] *Ibid.*; cf. also 'The New Approach', pp. 361 f., where he mentions the possible influence of 'oriental-syncretistic conceptions' upon the preaching of Jesus and his first followers.
[3] *Die Geschichte*, p. 146 (E.T. p. 137).
[4] 'Zur Formgeschichte', p. 215. [5] *Ibid.* p. 216.
[6] Karl Kundsin, 'Primitive Christianity in the Light of Gospel Research', *Form Criticism* (ed. by F. C. Grant), p. 94.

analysis of Markan Semitisms, he concludes that, although Mark was probably not written in Aramaic, 'its sayings and many of its narratives stand near Semitic tradition'. He then gives his judgement of the significance of this.

> We cannot adopt without critical scrutiny the principle that the presence of an Aramaic element or atmosphere in Mark's Greek guarantees, without more ado, the historical character of what is recorded, for the possibility of mistakes and misunderstandings exists even in the higher waters of the stream of Gospel tradition. But we can certainly conclude that a Gospel so deeply coloured by Semitic usages must, in the main, bear a high historical value.[1]

It is especially important to note that, while Semitisms may not prove the historical authenticity of a certain tradition, they at least prove it to be fairly early ('in the higher waters . . .'). In the body of the commentary Semitisms are frequently remarked, often with the inference that they indicate a relatively early tradition.[2]

Perhaps the two best-known contemporary advocates of employing Semitisms as a test for antiquity are Joachim Jeremias and Matthew Black. Both scholars work on the assumption that Semitisms indicate antiquity. Thus Professor Black is inclined to give to Codex D a great deal more value than most scholars would, because of its Semitisms. 'The fact', he says, 'that D stands nearer the underlying Aramaic tradition is of the greatest importance; in Luke it is the more primitive type of text.'[3] Although Black is not of the opinion that our Gospels were originally written in Aramaic, he does think that they had, in part at least, Aramaic sources.[4] His argument is that a manuscript (such as D) which has Semitisms not in other manuscripts derived its Semitisms from the Aramaic sources of the Gospels. Thus, in discussing the 'alleged "Syriacisms" in D', he states that they may not be 'Syriacisms' at all. 'They may be Aramaisms and come from the Aramaic *sources* and *background* of the Gospels' (my italics).[5] The assumption is that a scribe would not on his own invent 'Aramaisms' (that is, that the tradition did not tend to become more Semitic), and so must

---

[1] *The Gospel according to St Mark*, p. 65.
[2] See, for example, pp. 326, 349, and especially 392.
[3] *An Aramaic approach*[2], p. 29 (3rd ed. p. 31).
[4] *Ibid.* p. 206 (3rd ed. p. 271).   [5] *Ibid.* p. 30 (3rd ed. p. 33).

have derived from a primitive source any Aramaisms which he records which are not in other manuscripts.[1] Aramaisms, in other words, represent a 'throwback' to an early stage of the tradition.

Jeremias also thinks that Semitisms indicate antiquity. For example, in discussing Mk. 4. 11–12 he notes three Semitic usages and the agreement of the quotation of Is. 6. 9 f. with the Targum. On this basis he is able to state that 'we may assume with certainty that Mk. 4. 11–12 is a very early logion'.[2] What is common to all these scholars, and to many others whom we might name,[3] is that they see a positive relationship between Semitisms and the antiquity of tradition. The one indicates the other. It is our task to examine this criterion.

Before carrying the discussion farther, however, we must define the topic. We may use the terms Semitism and Semitic in a general sense to refer to the presence in the Gospel traditions of grammar, syntax, language, and ideas which seem to be influenced by Semitic patterns of speech or by the historical situation of first-century Palestine. It is clear that we may make a basic distinction between Semitisms of form and Semitisms of content. The term formal Semitisms refers to the way in which something is said. The term Semitisms of content refers to what is said. Semitisms of content are seldom dealt with as such, and the word Semitisms usually refers to formal Semitisms. It is used so here. To catalogue Semitisms of content would require greater historical knowledge than is available to me and would of necessity involve a great number of subjective and perhaps

[1] Black does not account for how this could have happened. He seems persuaded that Aramaisms indicate primitive tradition, but does not give a clear statement of why this is so or of how Aramaisms which crop up in late documents could have arrived there. (See also Appendix I, pp. 286 ff. below.) This is a weak point in an otherwise excellent book. One might have expected Black to argue that the Gospels, when first composed, contained more Semitisms than later manuscripts reveal and that a manuscript containing numerous Semitisms is closer to the autograph than those which do not. But this does not seem to be his argument.

[2] *The parables of Jesus*[2], p. 15. Jeremias quotes with approval the conclusion which T. W. Manson (*The teaching of Jesus*, p. 77) drew from the agreement between Mark's quotation of Is. 6. 9 and the Targum: the agreement 'creates a strong presumption in favour of [the] authenticity' of the passage in Mark.

[3] For example, see the statement of H. E. W. Turner, *Historicity and the Gospels* (London, 1963), pp. 77 f.: 'In general terms, the closer the approximation of a passage in the Gospels to the style and idiom of contemporary Aramaic, the greater the presumption of authenticity.'

ill-informed judgements. Such matters would have to be decided as whether the apocryphal scenes of the trial before the
Sanhedrin are nearer or farther from first-century Jewish
practice than the scenes in the canonical Gospels. Although it
is not impossible to reach a decision on this score, this kind of
investigation, multiplied many times, lies beyond the scope of
this study. It also lies beyond the work of most scholars who
have used Semitisms as a criterion of antiquity. For this reason
the limitation of this study to formal Semitisms is both justifiable and advisable.

Enough has already been said to indicate how formal
Semitisms are used to establish the antiquity of Gospel traditions. At first blush the assumption that the more Semitic the
earlier seems so reasonable that no reason may be seen for
questioning it. Jesus was a Jew, as were the first Christians;
Christianity moved from Judaism into the Graeco-Roman
world; therefore Semitic elements are carry-overs from
Christianity's birthplace, while Hellenistic elements are later
additions. But now it is becoming ever more widely recognized
that this neat picture is so inadequate as to earn the adjective
'false'. Why this is so may be indicated by two generalizations.
In the first place, it is no longer possible to distinguish so sharply
between Judaism and Hellenism: by the first century there had
already been considerable interpenetration. In the second
place, we cannot think of Christianity as progressing uniformly
from Judaism to Hellenism. It is not necessary to review here
the arguments and evidence which have been brought forward
by several scholars to support the first generalization. The
publication of the Dead Sea Scrolls and the work of E. R.
Goodenough[1] provide us with abundant materials to see elements quite at home in Judaism which not too many years ago
would have been called Hellenistic and non-Jewish. Professor
Lieberman has also pointed to the agreement of the way of life
presupposed in the Rabbinic materials with that present in the
Gentile countries.[2]

---

[1] *Jewish symbols in the Greco-Roman period* (12 vols.; New York, 1953 and subsequent
years).
[2] Saul Lieberman, *Hellenism in Jewish Palestine*[2] (New York, 1962). See also his
Greek in Jewish Palestine (New York, 1942) and 'How much Greek in Jewish
Palestine', *Biblical and Other Studies*, ed. Alexander Altmann (Cambridge,
Massachusetts, 1963), pp. 123–41. The falsity of a sharp distinction between

The second generalization—that we can no longer think of a straight progression of Christianity from Judaism to Hellenism—is subject to attack on the grounds that no one ever thought in that way. It is perfectly true that this picture of Christianity[1] has seldom, if ever, been seriously defended by a scholar. But this picture seems to lie undefended—indeed, undetected—in the background of many statements about the significance of Semitisms. The whole idea that Semitisms indicate some degree of antiquity—seen in the quotations given above—really depends on such a picture. The conception of early Christianity as progressing from Judaism to Hellenism is seen quite clearly on the same page of Vincent Taylor's commentary from which we have already quoted. He speaks of the 'high historical value' of a Gospel 'so deeply coloured by Semitic usages', in contrast to 'corruptions' caused by 'the impact of Hellenistic influences'.[2] Here the underlying conception seems to be that Christianity was originally born in a 'pure' Judaism but later progressed to a 'corrupting' Hellenism. It almost seems to be that the Judaic period as a whole preceded the period in which Hellenistic influences came to be felt, so that anything from the Judaic period is temporally earlier than anything showing Hellenistic influence. This conception also seems to have influenced the other scholars whom we have cited above. Such a

Hellenism and Judaism has also been argued by David Daube in 'Rabbinic methods of interpretation and Hellenistic rhetoric', *HUCA*, xxii (1949), 239–64 and *The New Testament and Rabbinic Judaism*; see p. ix; by W. D. Davies in *Paul and Rabbinic Judaism*[2] (London, 1958), pp. 1–16 and 'Paul and Judaism', *The Bible in modern scholarship*, ed. J. Philip Hyatt (Nashville, 1965), pp. 178–87; and by Morton Smith, 'Palestinian Judaism in the first century', *Israel: its role in civilization*, ed. Moshe Davis (New York, 1956), pp. 67–81.

[1] A picture of Christianity as progressing from Judaism to Hellenism might easily be acquired through a careless reading of Acts. Acts shows how the Gospel spread from Jerusalem to the rest of Judea, to Samaria, and to the uttermost parts of the earth (1. 8). The uttermost parts, however, lie mostly to the west, and the book ends with Paul in Rome: the culmination of the early Christian movement. Acts does not tell the story of Christianity's spread south and east, but of its movement west. Even so, we may learn that Christianity was established in Damascus (9. 10) and that the earliest Church contained 'Hellenists' as well as 'Hebrews' (6. 1). Acts itself, in other words, shows that the story of Christianity's spread to the west is not the whole story and that Judaic and Hellenistic Christianity existed at the same time. W. D. Davies, *Christian Origins and Judaism* (Philadelphia, 1962), p. 196, observes that 'it is extremely difficult to reach a point in the early Church when Jews and Gentiles were not involved'.

[2] *The Gospel according to St Mark*, p. 65.

conception seems to be reflected in the following statement by Cadbury:

The gospel was transferred not only from Aramaic to Greek—but from Palestine to Europe, and from Jews to Gentiles. This involved a change in linguistic, geographical, racial and cultural background...[1]

The word *transferred* indicates that the gospel left one milieu and entered the other. This eventually happened, but it entered Europe long before it left Palestine. The word *transfer* connotes a simultaneous leaving and entry. No doubt Cadbury actually does not think that the gospel left Palestine when it entered Europe, but that notion springs up here. It seems to lie hidden under the thinking of many scholars.

Once the matter is stated thus baldly, of course, most knowledgeable scholars will characterize such a picture as a gross exaggeration. The *continuing* relationship of Christianity and Judaism, emphasized by W. D. Davies in his recent book, *The Sermon on the Mount*,[2] is now apparent to most scholars. It takes only a moment's reflection to realize that a considerable amount of the material in the New Testament reflects the growing tension and the evolving relationship between Judaism and Christianity.[3] But the consequence of this reflection is that traditions reflecting a Semitic milieu could have entered the Christian tradition long after the first few years.[4] This conclusion is reinforced by the consideration that many second and third generation Christians were Semites. Despite the picture which one might gain from Acts, Christianity moved east as well as west. It also, of course, became fairly strong in Syria. And Palestinian Christianity by no means perished at the crucifixion. Even if it be thought that a certain tradition represents a Palestinian milieu before A.D. 70, it by no means follows that it must be earlier than any Hellenistic tradition. Paul's letters show us that the mission toward the West gained a wide

---

[1] H. J. Cadbury, *The making of Luke-Acts*, pp. 27 f.

[2] Cambridge, 1964.

[3] For example, note the passages in which Jewish persecution of Christians is mentioned, such as Mt. 10. 17, and those in which Christians are threatened with expulsion from the synagogue, Jn. 9. 22; 12. 42; 16. 2. Other passages showing the developing relation between Christianity and Judaism are discussed by Davies, *ibid.*, especially pp. 286 ff.

[4] The possibility of the re-Judaization of material is also pertinent here. On this, see Appendix IV.

enough range to permit the development ('corruption', some would say) of traditions on Gentile soil before A.D. 70.

Thus we see that, in general terms, the idea that Semitisms indicate early tradition is questionable on two grounds. In the first place, it is not possible to distinguish as sharply as some have between Hellenism and Judaism. In the second place, the idea that Christianity encountered Hellenism only after it left Judaism is erroneous. Its close relation to Judaism continued for years after the Gentile mission was well under way.

One scholar who has presented a view quite different from the one we have been considering is Morton Smith. He argues that far from there having been a progression of Christianity from Judaism to Hellenism, just the reverse was the case. Smith speaks of 'a progressive Judaizing of Christianity after Jesus' death'.[1] His position contains four points. (1) Smith notes that only in John is Jesus called a Jew (4. 9). An emphasis on Jesus' Jewishness is also found in Jn. 4. 22 and 18. 35. This emphasis was motivated by the theological requirement to show that Jesus was rejected by his own (Jn. 1. 11). Thus Smith concludes that emphasis on the Jewishness of Jesus was a relatively late development.[2] (2) John contains sentences 'which look as if they had been translated from the Aramaic'. Further, in John one finds Jesus arguing 'in the forms used by the rabbis'. Smith suggests that it is not altogether satisfactory either to assign these elements to an early source which was later worked over by the final evangelist or to assign John as a whole to an early date. It is not necessary to equate Aramaic influence on John's Greek or rabbinic forms of argument in his Gospel with an early date. Neither Aramaic forms of expression nor 'the simpler forms of argument which appear...in rabbinic litera-

---

[1] Morton Smith, 'The Jewish Elements in the Gospels', *The Journal of Bible and Religion*, XXIV (1956), 95. For the idea of re-Judaizing, compare the following statement by Bultmann, *Die Geschichte*, p. 378 (E.T. p. 353): 'Such abbreviations [of Mark's details by Matthew] have deprived the miracle stories of their purity of form without of course changing them into another literary genus. Dibelius believes: they were dematerialized, christologized. [Here Bultmann refers to *Die Formgeschichte*, p. 55.] I think it fits the facts better to say: they are less Hellenistic; in this editorial work Matthew's Jewish-Christian quality is brought to light.'

[2] *Ibid.* pp. 91 f. Smith sees the emphasis on the Jewishness of Jesus as a counterpart to the emphasis on the distinction between Judaism and Christianity which is also made in John.

ture' have been proved to be 'the peculiar property of Judaism; they may have been widespread among Gentiles in Palestine and Syria'. Smith continues:

No one would deny that throughout this area, during the first century, a great deal of argument went on between Jews and Christians. Argument supposes a common language and common forms of reasoning. So in the case of John, while some details are almost certainly Jewish, a great deal may have been derived both by the Gospel and by rabbinic literature from the common environment.[1]

(3) Many of the teachings attributed to Jesus could have been borrowed from contemporary Judaism. Jesus himself may have had a more distinctive teaching than some of the Gospel materials indicate. Smith observes with regard to such sayings as the 'Golden Rule' (Mt. 7. 12; the negative form appears in Tobit 4. 15 and Shabbath 31 a) that 'good sayings went about the ancient world looking for good fathers, and it often happened that they found several'.[2] Jewish teaching material could have been attributed to Jesus at a later date.[3] (4) Even the debates between Jesus and various Jewish groups may be the result of a concern on the part of Christians to defend Christianity against Judaism and to show points of agreement and disagreement between the mother faith and the evolving new one. Jesus himself may not have been so concerned to answer Jewish criticism. The collection of material in Mk. 11. 27–12. 34 shows how Christianity set itself apart from other Jewish groups. The collection was

made to serve the interests of the early Church, at a time when the Church was still one among the sects of Judaism and concerned to define its position vis-à-vis the other Jewish groups.[4]

These four points Smith takes to support the view that Christianity was progressively Judaized after Jesus' death.[5]

It is not our purpose to evaluate Smith's position in detail. It is clear, however, that there is a basic agreement between

---

[1] *Ibid.* p. 92.   [2] *Ibid.* p. 94.
[3] *Ibid.* p. 95. From another point of view, E. Stauffer, *Jesus and his story*, E.T. by Dorothea M. Barton (London, 1960), emphasizes the dissimilarity of Jesus' teaching and traditional Judaism. See especially the section 'Jesus' break with the Torah', pp. 67–9.
[4] *Ibid.* p. 95.
[5] See the summary on p. 95.

his position and the points we have already made against the view that Semitic coloring indicates antiquity. For our present purpose it is sufficient to point out that there is not necessarily a positive correlation between Semitisms and antiquity. An early tradition could have Hellenistic coloring[1] while a late one could have Semitic coloring.[2]

But even though it is so that an individual Semitism does not *prove* antiquity, are not traditions which smack linguistically of the speech of Palestine more likely to be closer to the original Aramaic traditions than those which do not? Is it not more probable that linguistic Semitisms in the Greek of the New Testament are remnants of the original language which have not yet been removed than that an original Greek translation relatively free from Semitisms was made, but that Semitisms were then re-introduced into the Greek? The position represented by the question is a strong one, and it would be impossible completely to invalidate it. There is, however, a certain body of evidence which goes in the opposite direction and which indicates, perhaps against all expectation, that linguistic Semitisms were sometimes introduced into the Greek tradition. Before listing the evidence to see just where the balance of probability lies, however, we must first discuss certain other points. We take first the matter of Septuagintalisms.

It is frequently granted that Hebraisms, in contradistinction to Aramaisms, could have been introduced into the tradition. Hebraisms, it is sometimes said, could have been used in imitation of the Hebraic Greek of the Septuagint ('Septuagintalisms'),[3] but Aramaisms indicate the influence of the language

[1] In an examination of the problem of the language of Jesus ('The Language Milieu of First-Century Palestine: Its Bearing on the Authenticity of the Gospel Tradition', *JBL*, LXXXIII (1964), 404–8), Robert Gundry argues that 'the absence of Semitisms does not lessen the possibility of authenticity.' See p. 408.

[2] H. F. D. Sparks, 'Some observations on the Semitic background of the New Testament', *Bulletin of Studiorum Novi Testamenti Societas*, II (1951), 33–43, gives an excellent review of the possible sources of Semitic influence on the language of the New Testament. He cites examples of definitely secondary Semitic influence. Cf. also Cadbury, *The making of Luke-Acts*, p. 74.

[3] I use the term Septuagintalism to indicate any usage which, because of its frequent occurrence in the Septuagint, may be thought to have been borrowed from that source when it occurs in the work of a Christian writer. Klaus Beyer, in his important work *Semitische Syntax im Neuen Testament* (Göttingen, 1962), adopts a different definition. He defines Septuagintalisms as constructions, 'die wegen falscher Verwendung hebräischer Sprachmittel nicht Hebraismen sein

of Jesus.[1] Now it seems quite clear that some people did write Greek in imitation of the LXX. This would have been no more impossible at that time than it would be today for someone well acquainted with the King James Version of the Bible to write 'biblical English'. Such an attempt might not deceive a real expert in seventeenth-century English, but it could well be a reasonably good imitation. It is relatively easy to impart something of the flavor of King James English to modern speech without making a real effort at imitation. This can be done by simply using thou, thee, and the like for the second person pronouns and the verb endings -est and -eth. Precisely the same thing is true of the Greek of the LXX. By imitating some of its most obvious peculiarities a biblical flavor could be imparted to later writings. It would have been no more necessary for an ancient author to think that he was writing canonical literature in order for him to use Septuagintalisms than it is for a modern to think that he is doing so when he speaks King James English in Church. One need only be dealing with holy matters to use the language associated with religious subjects.

The New Testament writer who is frequently mentioned as imitating the style of the LXX is Luke.[2] We may take as an example a sentence pattern with which Luke introduces many of his Gospel narratives. The pattern is exemplified by Lk. 5. 1:
Ἐγένετο δὲ ἐν τῷ τὸν ὄχλον ἐπικεῖσθαι αὐτῷ καὶ ἀκούειν τὸν λόγον τοῦ θεοῦ, καὶ αὐτὸς ἦν ἑστὼς κ.τ.λ. The pattern is ἐγένετο (introduced by either καί or δέ), an adverbial phrase indicating time (frequently ἐν with the articular infinitive in Luke), and the main verb, usually, but not always, introduced by καί. A similar pattern may be seen in such places as Lk. 5. 17; 8. 1, 22; 9. 28; 9. 51; 14. 1; 17. 11; 19. 15; cf. also 22. 24.

könnten' (see p. 11). Our definition will describe Hebraisms which appear in the Septuagint as Septuagintalisms. Wilcox, *op. cit.* p. 184, uses the definition of Septuagintalism which is adopted here. He distinguishes between 'Semitic-looking' expressions which may be Septuagintalisms and 'Semitisms proper' which cannot be explained as Septuagintalisms.
[1] See, for example, Dalman, *The words of Jesus*, pp. 37–42. He concludes (p. 42) that 'the thesis is justified that the fewer the Hebraisms, the greater the originality'. See further the discussion on the language of Jesus below.
[2] See, for example, H. St John Thackeray, *A grammar of the Old Testament in Greek* (Cambridge, 1909), pp. 50 f.; H. J. Cadbury, *The making of Luke-Acts*, pp. 122 f., 221 ff.; Dalman, *The words of Jesus*, pp. 37 ff.; H. F. D. Sparks, 'The Semitisms of St Luke's Gospel', *J.T.S.* XLIV (1943), 129–38.

200

The pattern without the final καί is found in 9. 18; 11. 1; 18. 35. The significant thing is that the very same construction appears in certain portions of the LXX, but not in ordinary Greek.[1] In I Kndms. (I Sam.) 4. 1, for example, we read: καὶ ἐγενήθη ἐν ταῖς ἡμέραις ἐκείναις καὶ συναθροίζονται ἀλλόφυλοι εἰς πόλεμον ἐπὶ ᾽Ισραήλ. 'And it happened in those days, and the Philistines gather(ed) for war on Israel.' Similar constructions may be seen in I Kndms. 8. 1; 9. 26; 11. 1; 23. 6; 24. 2; 30. 1. Here, then, we seem clearly to have a conscious echo of the Hebraic Greek of the LXX.[2]

The author of the third Gospel, however, is by no means the only Greek writer to employ usages characteristic of the LXX. We may briefly give one or two examples from the apocryphal literature. It is characteristic of Hebrew, and consequently of much of the LXX, that the verb of a sentence regularly precedes the subject. This sentence order is quite proper in ordinary Greek, but it occurs there with nothing like the regularity with which it occurs in Greek influenced by Hebrew. In the first seven chapters of the Protev. Jms., I have counted 66 instances in which the verb precedes the subject and 23 in which the subject precedes the verb. This proportion (when taken together with other Semitic elements in the Greek of the

---

[1] See the discussion in Thackeray, op. cit. pp. 50f. He gives tables of the occurrence of constructions with ἐγένετο. The constructions ἐγένετο ἦλθε and ἐγένετο καὶ ἦλθε are both Hebraisms. Only the form ἐγένετο ἐλθεῖν has Greek parallels. Thackeray notes that in the Gospel of Luke the author used the first construction twice as often as the second and the second twice as often as the third. In Acts he used only the third. See also the discussions by Beyer, op. cit. pp. 29–62, and by M. Johannessohn, 'Das biblische καὶ ἐγένετο und seine Geschichte', Zeitschrift für vergleichende Sprachforschung, LIII (1925), 161–212.

[2] This is reinforced by Beyer's observation (op. cit. p. 30) that וַיְהִי followed by a temporal phrase occurs most often in the older Hebrew books, but, under Aramaic influence, declines in usage in later Hebrew. He also comments (p. 30 n. 6) that in the New Testament the usage appears to be a 'stylistic device'. It is then somewhat curious that on p. 60 he lists several occurrences of the usage which may be understood as 'translations from a Hebrew original (Vorlage)'. On his definition of Septuagintalisms, Beyer must count many occurrences of our phrase Hebraisms rather than Septuagintalisms, but he nevertheless recognizes that Luke's use of the phrase depends on the usage of the LXX. See p. 297. M. H. Segal, A grammar of Mishnaic Hebrew (Oxford, 1958), p. 72, observes that 'the Consecutive Tenses have practically disappeared from' Mishnaic Hebrew. He does not attribute this altogether to Aramaic influence, however; see p. 73.

Another clear Septuagintalism in Luke is the use of προστιθέναι followed by the infinitive to indicate repeated action (as in Lk. 20. 11, 12). On this, see Thackeray, op. cit. pp. 52 f.

book) seems to indicate at least a 'secondary Semitic' influence
—in other words, the influence of the LXX. We may also refer
to the introductory ὀρθίσαντες ('having risen up early') of
Act. Pil. 12. 2; 15. 4 *bis*; etc. This verb is used about 57 times
in the LXX and once in the N.T., but apparently nowhere else
in Greek literature. It may safely be regarded as a Septuagintalism (cf. the introductory ἀνέστη in Act. Pil. 15. 1; etc.).[1]
Several other examples could be given, but it is now clear that
Greek authors could and did borrow elements of Hebraic
Greek from the LXX.[2]

The conclusion to be drawn from this is that Hebraisms in
the Gospel tradition which may be paralleled more or less
extensively in the LXX prove nothing about the antiquity of
the traditions in which they occur.[3] It is true that some linguistic Hebraisms could be hold-overs from a Semitic original,
but none need be, and some could not be, since they reflect
classical rather than contemporary Hebrew.[4]

Most of the scholars who use linguistic Semitisms to establish
the antiquity of the traditions in which they occur, however,
are careful to speak of Aramaisms rather than Hebraisms.
Doubtless one reason for this is that they are perfectly aware of
what we have just been emphasizing: that Hebraisms could
very well come from the LXX. But they also do so because they

---

[1] The verb usually translates the hiph'il of שָׁכַם in the LXX. The one New Testament occurrence is at Lk. 21. 38. Liddell and Scott list no appearances of
ὀρθρίζω (ὀρθίζω) outside the Old and New Testaments. In the LXX the introductory participle, used in the Act. Pil., is frequently used, as is the introductory
third person form of the verb.

[2] We have only investigated Septuagintalisms, but it must be remembered that
Greek Targums and certain of the pseudepigraphical books were also sources
from which a Greek-speaking person could have learned Semitic idiom. See also
the statement by Nigel Turner, p. 205 below. Turner takes into account the
influence not only of the LXX, but also of the synagogues of the Dispersion.

[3] Some scholars (see also p. 203 and nn. 2 and 3 below) think that Jesus spoke
(late) Hebrew and argue that Hebraisms do indicate antiquity. This is the view
of R. L. Lindsay ('A modified two-document theory of the Synoptic dependence
and interdependence', *Nov. Test.*, VI (1963), 239–63). Although he thinks that
Matthew is the third Gospel (Luke is placed first), he is nevertheless of the
opinion that Matthew's Hebraic style shows him frequently to have retained the
earliest tradition. See pp. 245, 247, 255.

[4] The question of whether or not Semitisms indicate a Semitic *Grundschrift* or the
influence of the Septuagint also arises in the study of the Testaments of the
Twelve Patriarchs. Most recently, see M. de Jonge, 'Christian influence in the
Testaments of the Twelve Patriarchs', *Nov. Test.* IV (1960), 184–6.

are persuaded that the language of Jesus and his disciples was Aramaic. Aramaisms, therefore, are taken to reflect a tradition lying very close to the source of the tradition.

The study of Aramaisms is a very delicate one, and it immediately involves us in very difficult questions, most of which can only be mentioned. There is in the first place the initial assumption, namely, that Jesus and the disciples predominantly spoke Aramaic.[1] This assumption has been questioned by several scholars, who emphasize either the probability that at least certain of Jesus' teachings (for example, disputes with Pharisees)[2] were in Hebrew[3] or that he may sometimes have taught in Greek.[4] The whole question of how thoroughly trilingual Palestine was in the first century still awaits solution. But there should no longer be any doubt that it was tri-lingual to a certain extent.[5] It still seems safe to conclude, however, that at least a significant proportion of the earliest Christian traditions was first formulated in Aramaic. This certainly justifies a search for the Aramaic background of the Gospel materials.

A second problem related to this program is that, even if Jesus and his disciples did predominantly speak Aramaic, they were not the last generation to do so. It is to this factor that Morton Smith is referring when he points out that Judaism had no monopoly on the Aramaic language. The Christian

---

[1] Fundamental is still the work of G. Dalman. See *Die Worte Jesu*[2] (Leipzig, 1930), E.T. of the first edition by D. M. Kay (Edinburgh, 1902), and *Jesus-Jeschua* (Leipzig, 1922), E.T. by Paul Levertoff (London, 1929). See also J. Jeremias, *The parables of Jesus*[2], p. 25; C. F. Burney, *The poetry of Our Lord* (Oxford, 1925); and Black, *An Aramaic approach*.

[2] T. W. Manson, *The teaching of Jesus* (Cambridge, 1935), pp. 46 ff. Black, *op. cit.* p. 14, agrees.

[3] See I. Rabinowitz, '"Be opened" = 'Εφφαθά (Mark 7. 34): Did Jesus Speak Hebrew?' *Z.N.T.W.* LIII (1962), 229–38; Jehoshua Grintz, 'Hebrew as the Spoken and Written Language in the Last Days of the Second Temple', *J.B.L.* LXXIX (1960), 32 ff. See also the article by Lindsay cited above (p. 202 n. 3).

[4] See B. H. Thompson, 'To what extent did Jesus use Greek?', *Religion in Life*, XXXII (1962/3), 103–15; A. W. Argyle, 'Did Jesus speak Greek?', *Exp. Times*, LXVII (1955/6), 92 f., 383. On the whole question, see Matthew Black, 'The recovery of the language of Jesus', *N.T.S.* III (1956/7), 305 f.

[5] We may once again refer to the article by Gundry cited above, where the evidence and the literature are referred to. See also Manson, *op. cit.* pp. 46 ff., who observes that Latin must also have been in some use in Palestine. That a language was known in Palestine does not necessarily imply that Jesus used it in his teaching. Manson thinks that Jesus used Latin not at all and Greek but seldom: he may have spoken Greek before Pilate. Cf. also Black, *Aramaic approach*, p. 13 (3rd ed. p. 15).

tradition could have acquired even linguistic Aramaisms from places other than the original form of the tradition.[1] It is not intrinsically improbable that many of the Christians who handed down traditions in such churches as the one in Syrian Antioch were bilingual and may have introduced Aramaisms into the Greek tradition.[2] Whether there is any evidence that such things actually happened we shall consider below.[3]

A further complication is the possibility, recently resurrected, that Greek flavored with Semitisms may indicate not Aramaic sources but only the use of Jewish Greek.

The old idea that biblical Greek was a special Jewish Greek, a 'language of the Holy Spirit', was successfully combatted by Deismann, whose views received powerful support from Moulton. According to Deissmann, the linguistic unity of the Greek Bible 'rests solely on the historical circumstance that all these texts are late-Greek' (*Bible Studies*[2], E.T. by A. Grieve [Edinburgh, 1909], p. 66) The Semitic Greek of the Septuagint was neither spoken nor written either before or after the translation was made (p. 67). Judaeo-Greek 'was never an actual living language at all' (p. 69). Deissmann, of course, was combatting the idea of a specially inspired language through which God communicated to his people. Now some scholars are arguing on strictly linguistic grounds that biblical Greek is distinguishable from ordinary koine, largely because of direct and indirect Semitic influences on it. For the history of the question, see also Black, *Exp. Times*, LXXVII (1965), 20.

Nigel Turner, while not denying the 'possibility that Aramaic documents lay behind the New Testament books', argues that there existed 'a living dialect of Jewish Greek'.[4] This dialect was used not only by the New Testament writers (including

---

[1] H. E. W. Turner, *op. cit.* p. 78, is unpersuaded by this consideration. 'If for a relatively brief period Aramaic was the predominant language of some centres of the Christian Church, this fact does not appear to weaken materially the significance of this criterion for the assessment of Gospel material.'

[2] Cf. Black, *Aramaic approach*, p. 15 (3rd ed. p. 17).

[3] We may indicate in advance that there will be *some* evidence for the introduction of Semitisms. The question will be how much evidence there is. Beyer, in introducing his study, points to the addition of Semitisms: 'Naturally the manuscripts and not any one textus receptus are employed as the basis [of the study]; thus variant readings which, on account of their poor attestation, can have no prospect of originality are also considered. This is so because they show how, during the later transmission of the New Testament, Semitic constructions originate which are partially yet visible; thus caution is necessary.' *Op. cit.*, p. 10.

[4] Nigel Turner, 'Second thoughts: VII. Papyrus finds', *Exp. Times*, LXXVI (1964), 45.

those whom no one thinks to have been influenced directly by Aramaic), but also by the translators of the LXX and other Greek versions of the Old Testament, by the Apostolic Fathers, and by the authors of various of the Pseudepigrapha. This dialect differs both from the popular papyri and from the literary koine.[1] The argument applies both to vocabulary and syntax. Concerning the latter, Turner writes that 'the Greek Bible and the synagogues of the Dispersion powerfully influenced the idiom of Grecian Jews everywhere. That is why we have met so many "Semitisms" in the papyrus finds.'[2]

Turner's conclusions are also stated in the third volume of Moulton's grammar. We may quote them at length.

Biblical Greek is a unique language with a unity and character of its own. It does not follow that if a construction occurs as frequently in the epistles as in the gospels it will be less likely to have a Semitic origin, for direct translation is not the only possible medium of Semitic influence. When the LXX was established its idioms powerfully influenced free compositions of Biblical Greek. The idiosyncrasies of Biblical Greek syntax are shared in varying degrees by almost all the NT writers, whether they were translating or not. There is a family likeness among these Biblical works, setting them apart from the papyri and from contemporary literary Greek, although the books with Semitic sources may have these features to an especial degree.[3]

The effect of Turner's work upon our study is simply to suggest one more possible way of accounting for Semitisms in the Gospel tradition.[4] We have still to see how much tendency existed toward making the Gospel tradition more Semitic.

The final problem in the search for Aramaisms which we shall mention is the difficulty of ascertaining just what is and is not a true Aramaism. Many usages characteristic of Aramaic are also characteristic of Hebrew.[5] These are of relatively little value to the Aramaist, for they may frequently be paralleled

[1] *Ibid.* p. 46.   [2] *Ibid.* p. 47.
[3] *A grammar of New Testament Greek*, III (Edinburgh, 1963), pp. 4–5.
[4] Cf. also N. Turner, 'The unique character of biblical Greek', *V.T.* v (1955), 208–13. Matthew Black ('Second thoughts: IX. The Semitic element in the New Testament', *Exp. Times*, LXXVII (1965), 20–3) indicates that he shares this view. Black also gives further references. See especially N. Turner's article on the language of the New Testament in the revised edition of Peake's *Commentary*, pp. 659–62 (and compare Moulton's article in the first edition, pp. 591–3); H. S. Gehman, *V.T.* I (1951), 81–90 and *V.T.* III (1953), 141–8; Peter Katz, *Welt des Orients*, II (1954–9), 267–73.
[5] Cf. Black, *Aramaic approach*, p. 31 (3rd ed. p. 34).

extensively in the LXX. Still other 'Aramaisms' may be paralleled in the non-literary Greek papyri, while others are as characteristic of Latin as of Aramaic. Matthew Black, in his book on Aramaisms in the Gospels and Acts, has given a judicious analysis of the probabilities of genuine Aramaic influence when the Greek of the New Testament contains a construction which can be paralleled in Aramaic. An even more detailed analysis of the probabilities of Semitic influence on certain constructions in the New Testament is given by Klaus Beyer in the work previously mentioned. The point of these investigations is to ascertain which usages which appear in the New Testament are sufficiently rare elsewhere in Greek literature and sufficiently common in Aramaic that they may be confidently attributed to direct Aramaic influence. A careful perusal of Professor Black's discussions on this score reveals that hardly any of the Aramaisms he discusses are totally foreign to Greek. Several more are sufficiently rare in Greek to make Aramaic influence likely, especially if the usage occurs frequently in some particular portion of the Gospel material. Others are common enough in Greek to make the appeal to Aramaic problematical.[1]

It is clearly beyond the scope of this book to try to decide which usages occur so often in Aramaic and so seldom in Greek that they may properly be considered Aramaisms. We have had to be content to rely here on the work of others. I have used primarily the works of Black and of Beyer,[2] and have also referred to discussions by Jeremias,[3] Torrey,[4] Dalman,[5]

[1] We should quote here at length Black's considered opinion on this issue (see 'Second Thoughts', p. 21): 'It is only very rarely possible to determine on the basis of a Greek Semitism whether it is the result of Hebrew or Aramaic influence; whether we are dealing with Septuagint influence or source or translation phenomena. For the sayings and teaching of Jesus, however, there is little doubt that the bulk of Semitisms are translation phenomena, and have arisen in the process of translating and paraphrasing the *verba ipsissima* of Jesus. We can be sure of this, not only on the *a priori* ground that Jesus spoke Aramaic, but from those few distinctive Aramaisms which are to be detected in the translation Greek of the Gospels. In this connexion I have seen no reason to change the conclusions which I reached in my *Aramaic Approach*..., that an Aramaic tradition (oral or written) lies behind the sayings of Jesus (in the Fourth Gospel as well as in the Synoptics), and possibly in the tradition of the words of the Baptist, and the speeches in Acts.'

[2] As cited above.   [3] *The parables of Jesus.*
[4] C. C. Torrey, *Our translated Gospels* (New York, 1936).
[5] *The words of Jesus.*

Howard,[1] and Hawkins.[2] Other scholars have sometimes compiled lists of certain of the phenomena with which we deal in this chapter. My procedure has been to compile lists independently and to check them against any others available (which have varied in quality from very accurate to very inaccurate). This procedure should result in a high degree of accuracy. Even so, I do not suppose that the lists which follow are perfectly complete and accurate; here as elsewhere they are as accurate as I could make them. The other lists used are these: Wernle's list of parataxis in Mark where Matthew and Luke have a subordinating participle;[3] Hawkins's list of historic presents;[4] Doeve's list of instances of casus pendens;[5] Hawkins's list of instances in which Luke and Matthew have δέ for Mark's καί;[6] Turner's list of asyndeta in Mark;[7] and the lists by Black and Beyer on several points. The works by Hawkins, Black, Beyer, and Turner maintain an extraordinarily high level of accuracy.

On the basis of the work of the Semitic scholars mentioned above I have organized the lists which follow. Some suggested Aramaisms, such as the ethical dative,[8] have not been included because of lack of evidence in the post-canonical tradition. The last category is something of a catch-all, but principally includes instances of Semitic-like syntax.[9] The other categories should be clear to those who have some knowledge of the subject, but the way in which two of them are used requires special explanation.

The study of Aramaisms has sometimes been linked to the more general study of grammatical and syntactical infelicities.[10] The argument is that the natural tendency was to improve the Greek, so that all constructions which do not qualify as good Greek—whether Aramaisms or not—would have been changed.

---

[1] W. F. Howard, 'Semitisms in the New Testament', pp. 413–85 of *A grammar of New Testament Greek*, II (by J. H. Moulton and W. F. Howard) (Edinburgh, 1956).
[2] *Horae Synopticae*[2] (Oxford, 1909).
[3] Paul Wernle, *Die synoptische Frage* (Tübingen, 1899), pp. 22 f., 150 f.
[4] Hawkins, *op. cit.* pp. 144 ff.   [5] J. W. Doeve, *op. cit.* p. 74 n. 1.
[6] Hawkins, *op. cit.* p. 150.
[7] C. H. Turner, 'Marcan usage', *J.T.S.* XXVIII (1926/7), 15–18.
[8] See Black, *An Aramaic approach*[2], pp. 75 ff. (3rd ed. pp. 101 ff.).
[9] Primarily those listed by Beyer.
[10] See, for example, Hawkins, *op. cit.* pp. 131–8 and n. 2 to p. 131.

It is difficult to decide what standards of 'good Greek' were usual in the first century. We have not, therefore, attempted to deal with the question of whether a tendency existed in general to improve the language of the Gospel material. One of the categories below may touch on this question, however. It is the use of the historic present. As we shall see below, the historic present has sometimes been taken to represent Aramaic usage, but more often is taken as a vernacularism which careful writers would have avoided. It will in either case prove interesting to see how it was handled in the post-canonical material.

Only one other category requires special mention: the first, καί parataxis. I have not attempted to distinguish between parataxis permissible in good Greek and that not to be found in good Greek. In the first place, the distinction is difficult to make. But more important is another consideration. The significant thing seems to be the way in which καί is overworked, not only in Mark but also in other documents with which we deal. Many of the uses of καί are proper enough Greek, but I thought it best to include even these, in order to show the extent to which the 'καί style'[1] predominates in certain of our sources. Thus every instance of 'parataxis' listed is not non-Greek parataxis (if there really be any such thing). Nevertheless, as far as I can determine, the proportion of changes to and from καί which is found in our lists would be about the same if only instances of 'non-Greek' parataxis were considered.

It should be especially emphasized at this point that the lists which follow depend upon accepting modern critical versions of the New Testament as offering, by and large, the authentic text. If one were to follow Kilpatrick in systematically applying the principle that the least grammatical reading is the earliest (because of the supposed tendency of the scribes to improve the Greek), he would find very few instances, if any, in which a more Semitic reading arose in the course of transmission.[2] The Semitic readings, regardless of what manuscripts support them, would be judged authentic. Similarly, Kilpatrick would presumably judge the historic presents in list 4a below to

---

[1] The phrase is de Strycker's, *op. cit.* p. 293.
[2] See especially 'The Greek New Testament text of today and the *Textus Receptus*', *Essays in Memory of G. H. C. Macgregor*, pp. 189–208, and 'Atticism and the text of the Greek New Testament', *Festschrift für Josef Schmid*. The latter was unfortunately not available to me.

be generally authentic, although they are here counted as being later changes. On the basis of his knowledge of the preferences of the later Greek grammarians and a consideration of the historic presents which are in Mark but not in Matthew and Luke, Kilpatrick maintains that 'where our manuscripts vary between the present historic and a past tense, other things being equal, the present is likely to be original and the past tense a correction to literary *Koine*'.[1] Differing with Westcott and Hort and Nestle, he considers the historic presents at Mk. 10. 51; 12. 16, 43, which are read by representatives of the koine text-type (see 4a below), to be examples of the koine's having maintained the authentic reading.[2] To put the difference clearly: Professor Kilpatrick assumes the validity of certain principles and judges readings on the basis of them, while I assume the general validity of the modern critical editions of the New Testament and attempt to test the principles. Both methods are subject to criticism, but one must begin somewhere. The modern critical texts were the only possible starting point for the present study. We have, however, the advantage of examining the evidence in the patristic and apocryphal traditions in addition to the manuscript evidence. The apocryphal material, especially, is seldom suspected of harboring authentic readings. If Semitic readings prove to be more or less common there, it will be very difficult to argue that such readings are the authentic ones.

THE EVIDENCE FROM THE POST-CANONICAL TRADITION

1a The change of other conjunctions to καί[3]

THE TEXTUAL TRADITION

Matthew

3. 16 reads: βαπτισθεὶς δὲ ὁ ᾽Ιησοῦς. C³ D^suppl L P W Ga Si Ko 10+Gr 9It 4Sy Aeth Arm Hip Hil read: καὶ βαπτισθεὶς ὁ ᾽Ιησοῦς. This is abbreviated as follows:

3. 16 C³ D^suppl L P W Ga Si Ko 10+Gr 9It 4Sy Aeth Arm Hip Hil

4. 18 L 1Gr

8. 1 Z

8. 8 All uncs. but Al* B Most minusc. It Vg 1Sy 1Cop Aeth[4]

---

[1] 'The Greek New Testament text', p. 198.   [2] *Ibid.* p. 199.
[3] Unless otherwise noted, the change is from *de* to *kai*.
[4] *Kai* is accepted by the U.B.S. text.

10. 33 W 2Sy Arm 1Geo
12. 39 1Gr
13. 5 1Gr 2Sy Arm Geo
13. 27 Ga 2Gr 2Sy 1Geo (here *kai* serves to break a string of *de*'s). Cf. category 3a below.
14. 13 C W X Ga De Si 0106 Ko 1Cop Aeth Arm
14. 27 2Gr It(−3) 3Sy Aeth Arm
14. 31 3Gr It(−3) Vg 2Sy Aeth Arm 1Geo. Cf. category 3a below.
15. 34 1Gr

Mark

9. 19 D W Th 𝔓⁴⁵ Famm 1 & 13 5Gr It(−3) 1Sy 1Cop Aeth
9. 25 D It Vg 2Sy 2Cop
10. 5 A D N W X Y Ga Pi Si Ph Ko Most minusc. 2It
10. 32 A C² N X Ga Pi Si Ph Ko(−1) 5+Gr 3It Vg 2Sy Geo also Fam 13 1Gr 1It
12. 17 A N W X Ga Pi Si Ph Ko 𝔓⁴⁵ Famm 1 & 13 5+Gr 1Sy Geo Aeth
13. 5 D G W Th Famm 1 & 13 6Gr 8It Vg Geo Aeth
13. 18 D 5It Aeth. Cf. category 3a below.
14. 11 A 1Sy Aeth
14. 47 W Fam 1(−1) Geo Arm also D 5It 1Sy
14. 61 1Gr
14. 64 W Th Famm 1 & 13 3Gr(inc. 565,700) 4It 1Sy 1Cop 1Geo
15. 2 D 2It Aeth. Cf. category 3a below.
15. 23 D Fam 1 It Vg 1Sy Aug
15. 36 D Th 4Gr It(−1) 1Vg 1Sy Geo Aeth Arm

THE APOCRYPHAL AND PATRISTIC TRADITIONS

Mt. 3. 4 reads: Αὐτὸς δὲ ὁ Ἰωάννης εἶχεν. The Gospel of the Ebionites, according to Epiphanius, *Refutation of All the Heresies* 30. 13. 4 f., reads: καὶ εἶχεν ὁ Ἰωάννης. This is abbreviated as follows:

Gosp. Ebion. Epiph. Haer. 30. 13. 4 f.; cf. Mt. 3. 4.
Ibid.; cf. Mt. 3. 4*b*.
Protev. Jms. 11. 3; cf. Lk. 1. 38.
Protev. Jms. 14. 2; cf. Mt. 1. 24.
Protev. Jms. 21. 2; cf. Mt. 2. 3.
Protev. Jms. 21. 2; cf. Mt. 2. 8.
Act. Pil. 10. 1; cf. Lk. 23. 34.
Act. Pil. 10. 1; cf. Lk. 23. 35.
Act. Pil. 11. 1; cf. Lk. 23. 45.
Act. Pil. 11. 1; cf. Lk. 23. 46.
Act. Pil. 13. 1; cf. Mt. 28. 4.
Act. Pil. 13. 1; cf. Mt. 28. 5.

1b The change of καί to other conjunctions[1]

THE TEXTUAL TRADITION

Matthew

9. 4   Th 2Gr 1It 1Cop Aeth Arm
9. 9   2Gr. Cf. category 3a below.
9. 26   1Gr 1Cop
10. 39   D 1It(*d*) 1Cop Aeth

Mark

9. 5   2Gr
9. 7   N Si 3Gr
9. 9   A W X Y Ga Th Pi Ph Ko Famm 1 & 13 6+Gr 1It 1Sy 1Cop
9. 33   1Gr 1Cop
10. 2   W Th 2Gr 1Cop Arm
10. 42   A N X Y Ga Pi Si Ko Fam 13 6+Gr 4It Vg 1Sy Geo 1Cop also
         Fam 1(−1) 2Gr W 1Gr
10. 49   D 1Gr(565)
10. 51   Th 1Gr(565)
10. 52   Al* A C D W X Y Ga Th Pi Si Ph Ko Most minusc. It(−1) Vg
         1Sy 2Cop
11. 4   A C W X Y Ga Pi Si Ph Ko 4+Gr 1Sy 1Cop 1Geo (*de*)/Fam 1
         Fam 13 5Gr (*oun*). Cf. categories 2b and 3a below.
11. 5   W X Si Famm 1(−1) and 13(−1) 2Gr 1Cop
11. 8   A D N W X Y Ga Th Pi Si Ph Ko Famm 1 & 13 6+Gr It(−2) Vg
         2Sy 1Cop Aeth
11. 13   0188 1Gr(565) 2It Or
11. 14   0188. Cf. category 3a below.
11. 20   Th 2Gr(565,700) 1Cop
11. 31   N Si
11. 33   1Gr 1It 1Geo
12. 3   A C N W X Ga Th Pi Si Ph Ko Famm 1 & 13
12. 3 cont.   7+Gr 2Sy 1Cop Geo
12. 4   text: κακεινον; 2Gr: οι δε κακεινον.
12. 5   text: κακεινον; 1Gr: οι δε κακεινον.
12. 14   A N W X Ga Th Pi Si Ph Ko Famm 1 & 13 6+Gr 2Sy Geo
13. 3   W 1Gr (*de*)/1Gr (*oun*). Cf. category 3a below.
13. 11   A W X Y Ga De Th Pi Si Ph Ko Famm 1 & 13 7+Gr 3It 3Sy
         1Cop Arm
13. 12   A W X Y Ga De Th Pi Si Ph Ko Most minusc. 7It Vg 2Sy 1Cop
         1Geo Aeth Or. Cf. category 3a below.
14. 17   D Th Si 7It Vg 1Cop

[1] The change is from *kai* to *de* unless otherwise noted.

14. 48 D 2Gr(565,700) 6It 1Sy
14. 51 D It(−1) Vg
14. 51 W Th Famm 1 & 13 3Gr(incl. 565,700)
14. 54 2Gr 4It Vg 1Cop 1Geo
14. 57 Th Fam 13 3Gr(incl. 565,700) 2It Or
15. 33 A C E F H K P U V X Y Ga Th Pi Si 7+Gr 1Cop Aeth Eus. Cf.
        category 3a below.
15. 46 D Th Si 4Gr It(−1) Vg 1Sy Aug

THE APOCRYPHAL AND PATRISTIC TRADITIONS

Pseud. Thom. 19. 5; cf. Lk. 2. 51.
Pseud. Thom. 19. 5; cf. Lk. 2. 52.
Act. Pil. 3. 2; cf. Jn. 18. 33. Has *oun* for Jn.'s *kai*.
Act. Pil. 10. 2; cf. Lk. 23. 43.
Act. Pil. 11. 1; cf. Lk. 23. 44.
Act. Pil. 11. 3; cf. Lk. 23. 50. Has *de* for Lk.'s *kai idou*.
Jos. Arim. 2. 4; cf. Mt. 26. 48 par. Has *oun* for the *kai* of Mt. and Mk.
Just. Apol. 1. 15. 4; cf. Mt. 19. 12. Justin twice has *de* for *kai*.

2a The creation of parataxis by changing a participle to a finite verb and adding *kai*

THE TEXTUAL TRADITION

Matthew

13. 1 reads: ἐξελθὼν ὁ Ἰησοῦς...ἐκάθητο. D It(−3) 3Sy Geo Or read:
        ἐξῆλθεν ὁ Ἰησοῦς...καὶ ἐκάθητο. This is abbreviated as follows:
13. 1 D It(−3) 3Sy Geo Or
14. 12 9It 4Sy 2Cop Geo (note: no Greek support)

Mark

14. 1 1Gr 8It Vg 2Sy
14. 22 D 1Gr have 'he blessed and broke' for 'blessing he broke'.
14. 40 2It 1Sy (note: no Greek support)
15. 30 A C P X Y Ga Pi Si Ko Fam 13 9+Gr 3It 3Sy Geo Aeth Arm Eus
        (imperative)
16. 4 For και αναβλεψασαι θεωρουσιν D Th 1Gr(565) 2It Eus have και
       ερχονται και ευρισκουσι. Also having parataxis, but with varying
       verbs, are 2It 2Sy Geo.
Cf. also Matthew 11. 10. P 1Gr 4It have 'and (*kai*) he shall prepare' for 'who
       (*hos*) shall prepare'. The LXX has και επιβλεψεται (Mal. 3. 1).

THE APOCRYPHAL AND PATRISTIC TRADITIONS

Protev. Jms. 21. 2; cf. Mt. 2. 8. Has υπαγετε και 3ητησατε for Mt.'s
       πορευθεντες εξετασατε.

Act. Pil. 13. 3; cf. Mt. 28. 13. Has ηλθον...και εκλεψαν for Mt.'s ελθοντες εκλεψαν.

Just. Apol. I. 35. 8; cf. Mt. 27. 35 parr. Cf. Ps. 21. 19. Just. has parataxis where Mt., Mk., and Lk. have subordination with a participle. The Psalm also has parataxis, but Justin seems to be drawing on the Synoptics.

2b The avoidance of parataxis by changing a finite verb with *kai* into a participle

THE TEXTUAL TRADITION

Mark

9. 33   1Gr
11. 2   A D W X Y Ga Th Pi Si Ph Ko Famm 1 & 13 7+Gr (The text has two imperatives.)
11. 4   D Th 2Gr(565,700) 8It Vg 1Geo Or. Cf. category 1b above.
11. 17 A D N W X Y Ga Th Pi Si Ph Ko Fam 1 9+Gr It(−1) Vg 1Sy 1Cop Geo
11. 24 A N W X Y Ga Th Pi Si Ph Ko Famm 1 & 13 7+Gr 1Sy Arm
12. 4   W Fam 1 3Gr (incl. 565,700)
14. 13 text: 'he sends and says'; D Th 3Gr (incl. 565,700) 4It 1Cop Or: 'he sends saying'/W: 'sending he says'.
14. 61 text: 'asked...and says'; Th Ph Fam 1 5Gr (incl. 565,700) 1It 1Cop Or: 'asked...saying'. Cf. avoidance of Hist. Pres.
15. 24 1Gr

THE PATRISTIC TRADITION

Just. Apol. I. 16. 2. Mt. 5. 16. Has βλεποντες θαυμαζωσι for ιδωσιν... και δοξασωσιν.

Addendum to Categories 1 and 2: other instances of parataxis

Gosp. Pet. has a string of *kai*'s at the end of chp. 5 and the beginning of chp. 6: constant parataxis.

Protev. Jms., in the first seven chps., has, after full stops: *kai* 45 times, *de* 12 times (according to de Strycker's text). There are series of *kai*'s that could be translations of *waw*'s consecutive in 1. 2*b*–4*a*; 2. 3–4; 19. 1*b*–3*a*.

Act. Pil., although using asyndeton heavily, sometimes employs *kai* parataxis. See, for example, 15. 4. There are seven sentences. The first six begin *kai*-verb (the first has *kai*-ὀρθίσαντες -verb). In addition, the first sentence contains three instances of *kai*-verb besides the opening instance, the fifth sentence has two other such instances, and the other sentences have one other such instance each. The last sentence is introduced by *de*. Altogether, in 10½ lines of text, there are 15 instances of *kai*-verb, two of which have intervening participles. The only other conjunction is one *de*.

3a   The omission of the conjunction: creation of asyndeton

THE TEXTUAL TRADITION

Matthew

3. 1   reads: Ἐν δὲ ταῖς ἡμέραις ἐκείναις. D L N De Pi Si Ko(− 1) 5 + Gr 1Sy 1Cop Arm Geo read: Ἐν ταῖς ἡμέραις ἐκείναις. This is abbreviated as follows:

3. 1   D L N De Pi Si Ko(− 1) 5 + Gr 1Sy 1Cop Arm Geo

3. 2   5Gr 2Sy (in saying).

3. 3   3Gr

* 4. 6   3Gr (but conforms to Ps. 90. 12).

4. 10   1Gr 4It Vg Tert (in saying).

* 4. 13   1Gr

4. 18   E* 6Gr Aeth Arm

5. 13   2Gr 1Sy Arm Geo (in saying).

5. 18   8Gr 8It 1Cop Aeth Arm 1Geo (in saying).

5. 19   L 8Gr 1Cop Arm Geo Lucif Cyp (in saying).

5. 29   2Gr Aeth Arm Geo Theod Adam (in saying).

5. 29   1Gr (in saying).

5. 31   Al* K Pi 9 + Gr 3Sy 1Cop Geo (in saying).

5. 33   W (in saying).

* 5. 44   W (omits *kai* between imperatives in saying).

5. 46   4Gr Geo (in saying).

6. 2   3Gr Geo Cyp Or (in saying).

6. 14   D* L 7Gr 1Sy Geo (in saying).

6. 20   Ga 1Gr 1It 1Cop (in saying).

6. 22   Al 3Gr 4It Vg 1Sy Aeth Arm Geo (in saying).

6. 31   1Gr 2Cop 1Geo Cyp (in saying).

7. 12   Al* L 8Gr 1Vg 1Sy Arm Geo Aug (in saying).

* 7. 23   2Gr 1It 1Sy 1Cop Geo (in saying).

7. 24   K X 6Gr 2It 1Sy 1Cop Arm Geo Or Euch Lucif (in saying).

8. 5   V X 1Gr C³

* 8. 20   4Gr 4It 3Sy 1Cop 1Geo

* 8. 26   2Gr 3It 1Sy 1Cop

8. 30   2Gr

* 8. 32   1Gr 2Sy 1Cop

* An asterisk indicates that the conjunction omitted is *kai*: possibly parataxis is avoided.

9. 5   K M U Pi 13Gr 6It Vg 1Sy Aeth Arm Geo Cass (in saying).

9. 6   1Gr (in saying).

* 9. 9   Al*

9. 13   1Gr

9. 16   V 4Gr 3Sy 1Cop Arm Adam (in saying).

* 9. 20   1Gr 1Vg 1Cop

10. 2   D* Th 5Gr

10. 10   U 1Gr (in saying).

10. 17   D 2Gr 5It 2Sy Arm 1Geo Or (in saying).

10. 23   1Gr 1Sy 1Geo Clem Or Aug Hier (in saying).

10. 23   D M 10+Gr It(−1) (in saying).

10. 32   X 5Gr 1Sy 1Cop Geo Cyp Hil Tert (in saying).

10. 35   1Gr (in saying).

*11. 1   1Gr

11. 16   1Gr 1Cop Aeth Arm 1Geo (in saying).

11. 18   L 1It 1Vg Arm (in saying).

12. 6   2Gr 2Cop Aeth (in saying).

*12. 9   1Gr

12. 40   2Gr (in saying).

12. 43   L 1Gr 1Cop (in saying).

12. 50   1Gr (in saying).

13. 15   1Gr 1It Vg (in saying; quotation of Is. 6. 10).

13. 17   Al X Ph 4Gr 12It 4Vg Cop Aeth Arm Geo Hil (in saying).

13. 21   F L 3Gr 1It 1Vg 1Cop (in saying).

13. 27   1Gr 1Geo. Cf. category 1a above.

13. 28   D 1Gr Vss(−2It 1Cop) (in saying).

13. 29   D

13. 40   1Gr Arm Geo (in saying).

13. 52   D 3Gr 6It 4Sy

13. 56   M 3Sy 1Cop Geo (in saying).

*14. 14   G 1Cop

*14. 19   1Gr

14. 31   1Gr 1Sy 1Geo. Cf. category 1a above.

*15. 34   2Gr 1It 3Sy 1Cop

Mark

* 9. 5   X 2Gr 1It (in saying).

* 9. 20   W Arm

* 9. 35   W

9. 40   2Gr (in saying).

9. 50   V (in saying).

* An asterisk indicates that the conjunction omitted is *kai*: possibly parataxis is avoided.

10. 6	1Gr 1Cop (in saying).
10. 9	D 1It(*k**) 1Sy Or (in saying).
10. 21	W
10. 31	1Gr (in saying).
10. 39	1Gr 3Sy
*10. 41	D^{vid} 1Gr 1Cop 5It
10. 43	D W Th 3Gr 8It 1Vg 1Sy 2Cop Arm (in saying).
*11. 4	2Gr
11. 8	P* Fam 1(−1) 9+Gr 1It 1Sy
*11. 12	1Gr
*11. 14	D 1Gr(565) 2It Or
*11. 22	1Gr
11. 32	D 6+Gr 2It Vg 1Geo (in saying).
*12. 4	2Gr 2It 1Cop 1Geo (in narrative portion of parable).
12. 12	1Gr 1It
12. 16	A 2Gr 7It Vg 1Sy Aeth Arm. Cf. also category 4a below.
12. 17	1Gr 1Sy Arm
*12. 21	W⎫
*12. 21	W⎬ To avoid parataxis; in narrative portion of saying.
*12. 22	W⎭
*12. 30	De 2Gr (in saying).
*13. 3	L. Cf. category 1b above.
13. 7	1Gr 1Cop (in saying).
13. 8	W 3Gr 1Cop 1Geo (in saying).
*13. 12	V* 3Gr (in saying). Cf. category 1b above.
*13. 16	1Gr 1Geo (in saying).
13. 17	D 1Cop (in saying).
13. 18	Ps 2Gr 1Cop Arm Aug (in saying).
*13. 21	U Th Si Fam 1 13Gr 1It 1Sy 1Geo Arm (in saying).
*13. 22	D 1Gr 2It(*i, k*) (in saying).
13. 33	3Gr 1It (in saying).
13. 35	3Gr 2Vg 1Cop (in saying).
14. 1	1Gr (changes ptcple. to vb., adds no *kai*. Cf. category 2a above).
14. 5	D 1It(*k*) 1Geo Aeth Arm (in saying).
14. 7	E 1Gr (in saying).
14. 9	A C F H M U W X Th Si Ps Famm 1 & 13 6+Gr It(−1) Vg 2Sy 2Cop 1Geo Aeth Arm
*14. 14	W 1Gr 3It 1Sy Aeth. Probably to avoid parataxis.
*14. 15	A P W X Y Ga De Pi Si Ph 0116 Ko Famm 1 & 13(−1) 6+Gr 7It 3Sy 1Cop 1Geo Arm (in saying).
*14. 18	1Gr

* An asterisk indicates that the conjunction omitted is *kai*: possibly parataxis is avoided.

*14. 30 4Gr 1It 2Sy 1Cop 1Geo

 14. 31 B Fam 1 4Gr 4It 2Cop 1Geo Arm

*14. 37 A 1Cop. To avoid parataxis.

*14. 43 Th

*14. 61 1Gr 1Cop. Does not avoid parataxis.

*14. 65 1Gr

*14. 66 L

*14. 68 D

 15. 2 1Gr. Cf. category 1a above.

 15. 7 1Gr

 15. 11 1Gr (also omits the subject, perhaps by homoeoteleuton).

*15. 20 1Gr. Avoids parataxis.

*15. 24 L. To avoid parataxis.

 15. 25 F 1Gr 1Cop

*15. 33 0 59 0192 1Sy. Cf. category 1b above.

*15. 35 De (omits subj. and *kai*).

*16. 1 D 2It (large omission)

*16. 2 W. To avoid parataxis.

THE APOCRYPHAL AND PATRISTIC TRADITIONS

*Egerton Pap. 2 Fragm. 1, line 10 (de Santos, 97); cf. John 5. 39. Omits *kai*.

Protev. Jms. 11. 3; cf. Mt. 1. 21. Omits *gar*.

Protev. Jms. 21. 2; cf. Mt. 2. 5. Omits *de*.

Act. Pil. 3. 2; cf. Jn. 18. 36. Omits *de*.

Act. Pil. 3. 2; cf. Jn. 18. 37. Omits *oun*.

*Act. Pil. 4. 1; cf. Mt. 27. 25. Omits *kai*. But also changes wording. Mt.: 'And answering all the people said.' Pil.: 'The Jews say.'

*Act. Pil. 9. 4; cf. Mt. 27. 25. Omits *kai*. But also changes wording. Mt.: see above. Pil.: 'Again the Jews cry out that.'

*Act. Pil. 11. 1; cf. Lk. 23. 46. Omits *kai*.

Act. Pil. 13. 1; cf. Mt. 18. 6. Omits *gar*.

3b The addition of a conjunction: avoidance of asyndeton

THE TEXTUAL TRADITION

Matthew

**   5. 13 1Gr Or Clem

**   5. 14 De(+*de*)/Or(+*gar*)

**   6. 2 3Gr

---

* An asterisk indicates that the conjunction omitted is *kai*: possibly parataxis is avoided.

** A double asterisk designates sayings material.

**	6. 16	Al*
**	6. 34	Om 6Gr
**	7. 7	1Gr Geo
**	7. 14	B 2Gr 1Cop (after *hoti*)
**	7. 15	All uncs. but Al B Om Most minusc. 2It 1Sy 1Cop 1Geo Got (imperative + *de*)
**	7. 19	C** L Z Ph 10+Gr 4It 1Vg 1Sy 2Cop
*	8. 7	All uncs. but B Minusc.(−1) 6It Vg 2Sy 1Cop Aeth 1Geo (reading seems in doubt to me).
**	9. 6	Text: εγειρε αρον; D 6It 1Cop Aeth Hil: εγειρε και αρον; All uncs. but B D Most minusc. 1It Got: εγερθεις αρον.[1]
	9. 18	L 2Gr 2Sy 2Cop Aeth
	10. 5	Om
**	10. 15	L 7Gr
**	10. 25	1Gr(+*gar*)/Clem(+*de*)
**	10. 34	𝔓[19] 1Vg
**	10. 37	Clem
**	11. 10	All uncs. but Al B D Z Most minusc. 9It Vg 3Sy 2Cop Arm Geo Got
**	11. 11	3Gr 1Sy
**	11. 19	2Gr 1Sy
**	12. 30	8Gr 2It Vg
**	12. 35	1Gr 1It 3Vg
	12. 46	C W X Y Ga De Th Pi Si Ph Ko Famm 1 & 13 6+Gr 1It 1Sy (+*de*)/D L Z 1Gr 1It Or (+*de*, but different order)
	13. 1	C D L W X Y Ga De Th Pi Si Ph Ko Most minusc. 4It 2Sy 1Cop
**	13. 30	L U 11Gr 1It 1Sy
**	13. 44	Al[b]
	13. 48	D Th 3Gr 10It 3Sy (οτε δε for ἠν οτε).
*	14. 1	1Gr Aeth (+*kai*)/D 3Gr 1It 2Sy 1Cop (+*de*)
**	14. 15	Al C Z 5Gr 1Sy 2Cop Or
**	15. 7	1Gr
*	15. 28	Ga 1Vg Aeth
**	15. 33	D Th Fam 1 2Gr 10It Vg Aeth Arm (+*oun*)/1Gr (+*kai*)

Mark

*	9. 38	A C N X Ga Si Pi Ph Ko Fam 1 4+Gr 5It (+*de*)/W (+*kai*)
**	9. 45	A K Pi 11Gr 1Sy 2Cop
**	9. 50	Fam 13 1Gr

* An asterisk indicates that the conjunction added is *kai*: parataxis may be created.
** A double asterisk designates sayings material.
[1] The U.B.S. text accepts ἐγερθεὶς.

**	9. 50	W Fam 13(−1) 3Gr 1Cop 1Arm
**	10. 15	1Gr
** *	10. 21	1Gr 2It 1Vg (*kai* inserted between imprtvs.)
**	10. 25	A 1It (+*de*)/8+Gr 1Vg 1Sy 1Cop (+*gar*)
	10. 27	A C² D N W X Y Ga Th Pi Si Ph Ko Fam 13 8+Gr 2It 2Sy 1Cop Aeth
	10. 28	K N Pi Si 9+Gr 1It 2Cop (+*de*)/2Gr (+*oun*)
** *	11. 10	A D* K M Pi 7+Gr 1It(*d*) 1Sy
**	11. 23	A C L W X Y Ga De Si Ph Ko Fam 13(−1) 5+Gr 1It 2Sy 1Cop
** *	11. 24	Ph 1Cop Aeth
	12. 6	A C D N X Ga Pi Si Ph Ko 4+Gr 2It Vg 1Sy (+*oun*)/W Th Fam 13 5Gr 1Sy 1Cop (+*de*) (Narrative portion of parable)
**	12. 9	All uncs. but B L Minusc. (−2) It(−2) Vg 2Sy Geo Aeth Arm[1]
**	12. 20	3Gr 1Sy 2Cop (+*de*)/C² M Si 13Gr 3It Vg Aeth Arm (+*oun*)
	12. 22	G M U Th Si Fam 1(−1) Fam 13(−1) 11Gr 1It 3Vg (+*de*)/ De (+*gar*) (Narrative portion of speech)
**	12. 23	A C² K M Pi D G W Th Si Fam 1 12+Gr 8It Vg 3Sy 1Cop Arm
*	12. 24	A X Ga Pi Si Ph Ko 7+Gr 2It Vg 1Sy (+*kai*)/D W Th Famm 1(−1) & 13 5Gr 5It (+*de*)
**	12. 27	G Fam 1 4Gr 4It 1Sy 1Geo Aeth (+*de*)/A D X Ga Th Pi Si Ph Ko(−1) Fam 13 5+Gr 5It Vg 2Sy 1Geo Arm (+*oun*)
	12. 29	A C X Ga Pi Si Ph Ko W Th D Fam 13(−1) 12+Gr 9It Vg 1Sy Aug
** *	12. 31	A W X Pi Si Ph Ko Famm 1 & 13 5+Gr 2It 4Sy Geo Aeth Arm Cyp Eus (+*kai*)/D Th 6Gr 5It Vg 2Cop Aug (+*de*)/Ga 1Gr (+*kai...de*)
**	12. 31	Al L 1Gr 2It Hil
** *	12. 36	A X Ga Th Pi Si Ph 092 Ko Fam 1 8+Gr 6It Vg(−1) 3Sy 1Geo Hil (+*gar*)/D 1Gr 1It(*d*) 1Sy Arm (+*kai*)
**	12. 37	A X Pi Ph 092 Ko Famm 1 & 13 9+Gr 2It Vg 2Sy 1Cop Aeth
** *	12. 40	1Gr Arm (+*gar*)/1Gr 1Sy (+*kai*)
**	13. 6	A D X Y Ga De Th Pi Si Ph Ko Minusc. Vss.
**	13. 7	Alª A D L X Y Ga De Th Pi Si Ph Ko Minusc. It Vg 3Sy Geo Aeth Arm
** *	13. 8	A X Y Ga De Pi Si Ph Ko Most minusc. 1It 2Sy 2Geo Aeth Arm
**	13. 9	Th Fam 13 5Gr

* An asterisk indicates that the conjunction added is *kai*: parataxis may be created.
** A double asterisk designates sayings material.
[1] *Oun* is placed in brackets in the U.B.S. text.

** 13. 9 Al A X Y Ga De Pi Si Ph Ko Fam 13(−1) 9+Gr 5It Vg 2Sy
* (+*gar*)/3Gr 1Sy Geo Aeth (+*kai*)/1Gr (+*de*)
** *13. 15 D Th 2Gr 10It Vg 2Sy 1Geo Aeth Arm Aug (+*kai*)/Al A L W
X Y Ga De Pi Si Ps Ko(−2) Famm 1 & 13 7+Gr 1Sy (+*de*)
** 13. 21 Between ιδε and ιδε, A C K X Y Ga De Th Pi Si Ph Ko(−1)
Fam 1 4+Gr It(−6) 1Vg 1Sy 1Cop Geo Aeth Arm Cat insert
* ἥ (*or*)/B 1It 1Vg 1Sy 1Cop insert *kai*.
** 13. 30 L W 1Gr
** 13. 33 W Th Si Fam 13 5Gr 1Geo Aeth (+*de*)/D 5It (+*oun*)
* 14. 3 A C D W X Y Ga De Th Pi Si Ph 0116 Ko Most minusc.
It(−1) Vg 2Sy 1Geo
** 14. 6 Al G W Fam 13 7Gr 1It 3Sy 1Cop
** *14. 13 Fam 13 2Gr Aeth (was asyndeton command)
* 14. 19 C 3Gr Aeth Arm (+*kai*)/A D P W X Y Ga De Th Pi Si Ph
0116 Ko Most minusc. 4It 3Sy 2Cop Geo (+*de*)
** 14. 25 F S V Ga De Pi² Om 10+Gr (+*de*)/2Gr (+*gar*)
* 14. 61 067 1Gr 1It (+*oun*)/W Th Famm 1 & 13 2Gr 2Sy 1Geo (+*kai*)
15. 31 C² M² Si Om 5+Gr

THE APOCRYPHAL AND PATRISTIC TRADITIONS

Act. Pil. 3. 2; cf. Jn. 18. 36. Adds *gar* after *ei*.
Act. Pil. 3. 2; cf. Jn. 18. 37. Adds *gar* after 'unto this'.
Just. Apol. 1. 16. 11; cf. Mt. 7. 22. Adds *de* after 'many' (in saying).
Just. Apol. 1. 16. 13; cf. Mt. 7. 19. Adds *de* (in saying).

Addendum to Category 3: other instances of asyndeton

Oxy. Pap. 840. See Appendix v. 11. There are at least two instances of asyndeton, in lines 24 and 30.
Pap. 11710. See new creation. The story is asyndetic throughout.
Oxy. Pap. 1 (de Santos, p. 89). There are new sayings which open with the historic present without a conjunction. See lines 4 and 11.
Fragm. P. Ryl. III. 463. See new creation. In a few lines there are five cases of asyndeton. In at least one instance, the parallel Coptic text (P. Berol.) has a *de* where the Greek has asyndeton. The date of the papyrus is probably in the early part of the third century.
Act. Pil. 3. 2; cf. Jn. 18. 37. A new conversation is added (see dialogue) which is completely asyndetic.
Act. Pil. 4. 1. A new conversation (*q.v.*) is added, which is asyndetic.
Act. Pil. 5. 2 has six full sentences, only one of which has a conjunction introducing it. Three sentences at the end of 6. 1 lack introductory conjunctions. Of the first six sentences in 14. 2, five have no introductory conjunction.

* An asterisk indicates that the conjunction added is *kai*: parataxis may be created.
** A double asterisk designates sayings material.

4a Verbs changed to the historic present[1]

Matthew

4. 9	reads: καὶ εἶπεν αὐτῷ. L P W Ga De Th Si Ko Fam 1 8+Gr 1Sy read: καὶ λέγει αὐτῷ. This is abbreviated as follows:
4. 9	L P W Ga De Th Si Ko Fam 1 8+Gr 1Sy
8. 10	1Gr
9. 23	C L N W Y Ga De Th Pi Ph Ko 5+Gr Aeth Arm
13. 11	1Gr 10It Vg
13. 29	D 4Gr (This is a change from one hist. pres. (φησιν) to another (λεγει). Cf. also 4b below.)
13. 51	All uncs. but Al B D Most minusc. 2It 1Vg 2Sy Arm (This is the addition of a gloss which contains a hist. pres.)
13. 52	B² D 4Gr 6It 4Sy
13. 57	Z
15. 32	C

Mark

9. 24	D Th 2Gr 4It
9. 31	W
9. 36	Fam 1 It(−2) Vg Aeth Arm
9. 38	Fam 1(−1) 3Gr 3It (hist. pres. in gloss)
10. 20	Clem It(−3) Vg
10. 21	Fam 13 6Gr 1It
10. 29	Clem
10. 36	D Th 1Gr 5Vg 2Sy Aeth Arm
10. 39	Ps 1Gr 4Sy
10. 49	D (This is a change from φωνουσι to λεγουσι.)
10. 51	A W X Ga Th Pi^mg Si Ph 069 Ko(−1) Famm 1 & 13 4+Gr 2It also K Pi* Y 6+Gr 1Sy
10. 52	K Pi 4Gr 7It Vg
11. 7	D W Fam 1(−1) 6Gr 'sits' for 'sat'. The tense thus agrees with 'throw'. Cf. category 4b.
11. 23	A C W X Y Ga Pi Ph Ko Famm 1 & 13 6+Gr (Change λαλει to λεγει. Cf. category 4b).
11. 28	A D N X Y Ga Th Pi Si Ph Ko Fam 13 10+Gr It Vg 3Sy Aeth Arm
12. 2	1Gr 'he sends' for 'he sent'.
12. 10	1Gr (This is a gloss containing a hist. pres.)
12. 16	A 2Gr 7It Vg 1Sy Aeth Arm
12. 17	1Gr 3It
12. 26	1Gr

[1] The change involves a verb of saying unless otherwise noted.

12. 35   W 2It 1Sy
12. 36   X 092 7Gr 9It Vg 2Cop 1Geo
12. 36   A D Y Pi Ph Ko(−2) 9+Gr 5It Aeth ('The Lord says': perhaps not true hist. pres.).
12. 43   W X Ga Ph Ko(−2) Famm 1 & 13 8+Gr It(−2) Vg Aeth Arm
14. 18   D Th 2Gr 5It Vg
14. 19   3Gr 1It (changed to hist. pres. from infinitive)
14. 20   D Th Ps 3Gr It Vg
14. 29   D Ps It(−2) Vg 1Sy also W Th Famm 1 & 13 3Gr
14. 31   1Gr
14. 36   1Gr Arm
14. 62   D Th 1Gr 3It Aeth Or
15. 9   D 1Gr (changed to hist. pres. from ptcple.)
15. 12   Ga
15. 14   N 2Gr Arm

THE APOCRYPHAL TRADITION

Egerton Pap. 2, Fragm. 1, line 33 (de Santos, p. 98); cf. Mt. 8. 2 *legei* for *legōn*.

Protev. Jms. 14. 2; cf. Mt. 1. 20. Has *phainetai* for *ephanē*.

Protev. Jms. 21. 2; cf. Mt. 2. 5. Has *legousin* for *hoi de eipan*.

Act. Pil. 4. 1; cf. Mt. 27. 25. 'say' for 'said'. Also asyndeton.

Act. Pil. 9. 1; cf. Mt. 27. 21. 'cry out' for 'said'.

Act. Pil. 9. 4; cf. Mt. 27. 25. 'cry out' for 'said'. Also asyndeton.

Jos. Arim. 2. 3; cf. Mt. 26. 14 f. 'says' for 'said'.

Jos. Arim. 2. 4; cf. Mt. 26. 48. 'says' for 'saying'.

4b   Verbs changed from the historic present[1]

THE TEXTUAL TRADITION

Matthew

4. 6   Al^b W Z 2Gr It Vg 2Sy 2Cop Aeth Geo Aug
8. 4   Al* 1It 3Sy 2Cop Geo
8. 22   All uncs. but Al B C Minusc.(−Fam 1 8Gr) 2Sy 2Cop Aeth Arm Geo
13. 28   L N O W X Y Ga De Th Pi Si Ph Ko Most minusc. 6It Vg Geo
13. 29   All uncs. but Al B C D Many minusc. 2Sy 2Cop Geo. Cf. category 4a.
15. 12   All uncs. but B D Th 6+Gr It Vg 1Sy 1Cop

Mark

9. 5   D W Th 𝔓⁴⁵ 3Gr 3It 1Vg 3Sy 1Cop 1Geo (aorist)/Fam 1(−1) Fam 13 2Gr (imperf.)

---

[1] The change involves a verb of saying unless otherwise noted.

9. 19   Th 𝔓⁴⁵ 4Gr It 1Vg
10. 23   Al* C 1Gr (imperf.)/De 4Gr 2It 3Sy 1Cop Geo (aorist)
10. 24   De Th Ps 7Gr 2It
10. 27   Al* Ga 1Gr (ειπεν)/3Gr (εφη)
10. 42   1Gr 1It
11. 1   Si (ηγγιζον)/M Fam 13(−1) 3Gr (ηγγισαν)/D 8Gr (ηγγιζ(σ)εν).
11. 1   F H 5Gr 7It 2Sy 2Cop (απεστειλεν)/C (επεμψεν)
11. 2   D 2Sy Geo (aorist)/W Th Fam 1(−1) Fam 13(−1) 4Gr 1It 1Cop
         (ptcple.)
11. 7   A D X Y Ga Pi Si Ph Ko 6+Gr 5It Vg 3Sy 2Cop Geo Aeth Arm
         'they brought' for 'they bring'.
11. 7   A X Y Ga Pi Si Ph Ko Fam 13 4+Gr 4It 3Vg 3Sy 1Cop Geo Aeth
         Arm/6Gr/1Gr 'threw' and 'placed' for 'throw'. Cf. Mk. 11. 7,
         category 4a.
11. 21   Th Ps 2Gr 1It 3Vg 2Sy 2Cop Geo
11. 22   Th 5Gr 1It 3Vg 3Sy 1Cop Geo
11. 23   1Gr. Cf. 4a above.
11. 33   1Gr 2It 1Sy 1Cop Geo
12. 16   1Gr
13. 1   1Gr
14. 17   Text: ερχεται/1Gr ανεκειτο/1Gr 2Sy 2Cop ηλθε.
14. 30   1Gr 5It 2Cop Geo
14. 34   E G H De Ps 5+Gr (changed to inf.)
14. 37   1Gr 1It 2Sy 2Cop Geo
14. 61   Th Ph Fam 1 5Gr 1It 1Cop Or (changed to ptcple.)
14. 63   1Gr 1It 2Sy Geo Arm (aorist)/2Gr 1It 1Cop (ptcple.)
14. 67   1Gr
15. 2   A N X Y Ga De Pi Si Ko(−1) Fam 13 8+Gr 1It 3Sy 1Cop Geo
         Aeth also W 2Gr 1It

THE APOCRYPHAL TRADITION

Pseud. Thom. 19. 3. Lk. 2. 48. εζητουμεν σε for Lk.'s ζητουμεν σε. So also
C Ko D Th Many minusc.

Addendum to Category 4: other instances of the historic present

Oxy. Pap. 840 (de Santos, p. 80). See new creation and asyndeton. Line 24
begins *legei*.

Oxy. Pap. 1 (de Santos, p. 89). Two sayings, lines 4 and 11, begin with *legei*
asyndeton.

Fragm. P. Ryl. III. 463 (de Santos, pp. 100 f.). There are at least two historic
presents, in lines 5 and 18. Both *legei*.

Act. Pil. 3. 2. A new conversation (*q.v.*) is added with three instances of the
historic present *legei*.

Act. Pil. 4. 1. A new conversation (*q.v.*) is added with two instances of the historic present *legei*.

The historic present with *legō* is usual in Act. Pil. It occurs occasionally with other verbs. In the first two chapters, for example, there are forty-six historic presents, including *krazousin* (1. 4) and *keleuei* (2. 6). Rarely a preterite of a verb indicating speech is used; see *ephē* (2. 2). The aorist is used in most of chp. 3, except for one historic present at the first and four at the end of the chapter. The historic present then becomes regular again.

5a The use of *heis* for *tis*; the addition of *heis* to mean *tis*

THE TEXTUAL TRADITION

Mark

9. 36   2Sy '(+one) child'. (Perhaps used as indefinite article.)

11. 13   Al K M Y Pi 8+Gr 1Sy Arm συκην+μιαν.

14. 47   Text: εἰς δε τις/Al A L M Ps 13Gr 1It 1Sy 2Cop Aeth omit *tis*[1]/D 5It 1Sy read *kai heis*.

14. 51   Text: *tis*/A N P W X T Ga De Th Pi Si Ph o116 Ko Famm 1 & 13 8+Gr 1Sy Geo have *heis tis* (perhaps in imitation of 14. 47)/1Gr has only *heis*.

15. 36   Text: *tis*/A C D N P Y Ga Th Pi Si Ko Fam 1 7+Gr It Vg 3Sy 2Cop Aeth Aug: *heis*/1Gr 1Vg: εἰς εξ αυτων.

THE APOCRYPHAL TRADITION

Cf. Pap. Oxy. 1. 5, line 25 (de Santos, p. 90). Not Synoptic material, but εἰς is used to mean τις.

5b The change of *heis* to *tis*; the omission of *heis* with the meaning of *tis*

THE TEXTUAL TRADITION

Matthew

9. 18   Text: αρχων εἰς/A*ᶜ C* D E M N W X De Th Si Ph Fam 1 10+Gr 1It 1Vg 2Cop omit *heis*/C³ F G L U Ga Fam 13(−1) 7+Gr 3It Geo have *tis* for *heis*.

Mark

10. 17   A K M W Th Pi Fam 13 19+Gr have *tis* for *heis*.

12. 28   6Gr have *tis* for *heis*.

12. 42   Al 2Gr 1It 2Cop (−μια) χηρα.

---

[1] *Tis* is bracketed in the U.B.S. text.

Just. Apol. 1. 16. 7; cf. Mk. 10. 17 parr. Justin has *tis* with Lk., against *heis* in Mt. and Mk.

6a Wording made more Semitic

THE TEXTUAL TRADITION

Matthew

3. 5   2Sy have 'sons of Jerusalem' for 'Jerusalem'.

3. 11   1Gr 'of whom I am not worthy to take off (+his) shoes'.

5. 16   1Sy has 'sons of men' for 'men'.

6. 4   D E M S W X De Pi Si Ph 6Gr 2It 3Sy 'the father... (+he) will reward you'.

6. 18   W 1Sy 1Geo as 6. 4

7. 21   C² W Th Ph 4Gr 10It Vg 1Sy Aug Cyp Hil 'but the one doing... +this one (or, *he*) will enter the kingdom of the heavens'.

10. 11 D (1Gr) 1It(*d*) have 'the city into whichever you enter into it' for 'into whichever city or village you enter'.

12. 11 D 3+Gr 'and (−if) it falls'.

12. 15f. Text: 'and he healed them all, and he rebuked them...' D W 2Gr 6It: 'and he healed them. And all whom he healed he reproved them...'

13. 4   1Gr και (+εγενετο) εν τω σπειρειν.

13. 44 2It 4Sy 'which finding, a man hid+it'.

Mark

9. 2   1Gr και+εγενετο εν τω προσευχεσθαι αυτον.

9. 3   1Sy has 'sons of men' for 'fuller'.

10. 12 D Th Fam 13 4Gr 4It Arm have 'If a woman departs from the husband' for 'If she divorces her husband'. (The alternate reading is favored by Taylor, *Commentary on Mark, ad loc.*)

10. 12 A N X Y Ga Pi Si Ph Ko 6+Gr have 'is married to another' for 'marries another'.

13. 20 1Gr 1Sy have 'if the days had not been shortened' for 'if the Lord had not shortened the days'.

13. 32 4Vg Hil have 'the son of man' for 'the son' (in a saying of Jesus).

14. 20 At end, 5Gr 1It add 'he will betray me'.

14. 25 D Th 1Gr 2It Arm have ου προσθω(-θωμεν, Θ) πιειν (πειν, D) for ου μη πιω.

THE APOCRYPHAL AND PATRISTIC TRADITIONS

Oxy. Pap. 1. 6, lines 30–5. This basically depends upon Lk. 4. 24. The parallels in Mt. 13. 57 and Mk. 6. 4 have the more Semitic *ouk estin*, while Lk. has *oudeis*. The papyrus agrees with Mt. and Mk. See Beyer, *op. cit.*, pp. 111 fn., 131.

Protev. Jms. 11. 2 has ενωπιον του παντων δεσποτου for Lk. 1. 30's παρα τω θεω. Both the preposition and the circumlocution in James are more Semitic.

Act. Pil. 10. 1; ctr. Lk. 23. 37. '(−if) you are the king of the Jews, save yourself'.

Jos. Arim. 2. 4; ctr. Mt. 26. 48 par. 'whomever I kiss (−is he); seize him'.

Just. Apol. 1. 15. 10; ctr. Mt. 5. 42//Lk. 6. 30. Justin has *panti* as does Lk. This is the more Semitic of the two readings.

Just. Apol. 1. 16. 2; cf. Mt. 5. 41. Justin has *panti* for *hostis*.

6b Wording made less Semitic

Matthew

5. 40   Or omits 'to him'. (N.B.: no MSS support.)
5. 47   L W De Th Pi Si Ko Fam 13 4+Gr have τελωναι for εθνικοι.
6. 1   L W Z De Th Pi Si Ko Fam 13 8+Gr 2It 2Sy Aeth Arm Geo Got have 'charity' (ελεημοσυνη) for 'righteousness'.
6. 7   B 1Gr 1Sy 1Geo have υποκριται for εθνικοι.
7. 9   Al[b] E G K[2] N O S U V W X Pi Si Ph Most minusc. 7It Vg Cyp Aug 'whom (+if) his son asks'.
10. 32 D 2Gr 1It(*d*) 'I shall also confess (−him)'.
12. 36 C N W X Y Ga De Th Pi Si Ph Ko Famm 1 & 13 7+Gr 'which (+if) men speak'.
13. 20 U omits 'this is'.
13. 38 1Gr omits 'these'.
15. 11 3Gr 4It 1Geo omit 'this'.

Mark

10. 43 Al C X De 6+Gr 1Geo have 'let him be (εστω) your servant' for 'will be (εσται) your servant'.
10. 44 2Gr 1Geo Bas make the same change.
11. 29 D W Th 2Gr It(−1) 'I will ask you one thing, (−and) answer me, and I will tell you'./1Gr changes the 'and' before 'answer' to 'if', and omits the one after 'me': 'I will ask you one thing. If you answer me, I will tell you.'
12. 2   Th 1Gr have λαβη τους καρπους for λαβη απο των καρπων/Ga omits των καρπων. The resultant reading is απο του αμπελωνος. (Both avoid the partitive *apo*.)
13. 13 W Si 1Vg omit 'this one'/X 2Gr change ουτος to ουτως.
15. 32 A C P X Y Ga Th Si 0192 Ko(−1) 10+Gr 2Cop Eus ο βασιλευς (+του) Ισραηλ.

THE APOCRYPHAL AND PATRISTIC TRADITIONS

Protev. Jms. 11. 3; cf. Lk. 1. 35. Jms. has 'Lord' for 'highest'.

Ps. Thom. 19. 2; cf. Lk. 2. 46. και (– εγενετο)...ευρον.

Act. Pil. 18. 2 has 'the voice of the God and Father' where Mt. 3. 17 has 'the voice out of heaven'.

Just. Apol. I. 15. 1; cf. Mt. 5. 28. ος αν εμβλεψη for πας ο βλεπων.

Just. Apol. I. 15. 16; cf. Mt. 6. 21. 'there also (is) the mind of man' for 'there will be your heart also'.

Just. Apol. I. 16. 2; cf. Mt. 5. 22. ος δ'αν for πας ο.

Just. Apol. I. 16. 2; cf. Mt. 5. 41 'follow' for 'go with him'. The omission of 'with him' avoids casus pendens.

Just. Apol. I. 17. 4; cf. Lk. 12. 48. 'God gave' for 'was given' (but the verbatim agreement is not too close).

Athen. I. 1; ctr. Mt. 5. 40 par. Athenagoras avoids Mt.'s casus pendens. There is no casus pendens in the Lukan parallel.

Athen. 32. 1; cf. Mt. 5. 28 'the one seeing' for 'everyone (pas) who sees'.

Theo. III. 13 has hos as Mt. 19. 9//Mk. 10. 11. This is less Semitic than the parallel at Mt. 5. 32//Lk. 16. 18 (pas ho).

II Clem. 3. 2; cf. Mt. 10. 32 par. Clem. has 'the one confessing' for 'everyone who confesses'.

Addendum to Category 6: Semitisms in material not strictly paralleled in the Synoptics

Gosp. Phil. Epiph. Haer. 26. 13. 2–3 (de Santos, 63 f.). Has this hyperbaton: και οιδα σε τις ει.

Oxy. Pap. 1. 3, lines 11–22 (de Santos, pp. 89–90). Jeremias (Unknown Sayings, pp. 69–71) finds these Semitisms: (1) Two instances of synonomous parallelism. (2) Constant parataxis. (3) 'ἐν μέσῳ without any stress on the idea of location in the middle.' (4) ὤφθην, 'a Semitism which arises from the double meaning of 'ithchami in Aramaic, (a) "he was seen"; (b) "he appeared"'. (5) ἐν αὐτοῖς instead of αὐτῶν. (6) πονεῖν with ἐπί. (7) 'My soul' for 'I'. (8) The 'sons of men'. (9) The singular τῇ καρδίᾳ.

Act. Pil. 4. 2, end. Attributes a new argument qal wahomer to some Jews.

Act. Pil. 12. 1. μεχρι της μιας του σαββατου.

Act. Pil. 15. 5. τη μια του σαββατου.

Act. Pil. 9. 1. ...τον Ιησουν, εις ον ουδεμιαν αιτιαν ευρισκω εν αυτω.

Act. Pil. 12. 2; 15. 4; 15. 5, etc. The use of ορθισαντες is a Septuagintalism. This word regularly translates הִשְׁכִּים in the LXX, and the form appears to occur nowhere outside of biblical literature. It is found 57 times in the LXX and once in the N.T. The introductory ανεστη in 15. 1 may also be a Septuagintalism.

15-2

Act. Pil. 15. 6. A phantom 'really flees', φυγῃ φευγει.

Act. Pil. 16. 7. 'You shall surely know, O house of Jacob', γινωσκοντες γνωσεσθε, οικος Ιακωβ.

The omission of the article in the Act. Pil. in a way to indicate Semitic influence is frequent. For example, 15. 1 λαος κυριου and εν παντι οριω Ισραηλ. The usage is not perfectly regular, however. See 16. 8: The people praised *the* Lord and said: 'Blessed be (the) Lord who has given rest to *the* people (of) Israel.'

Gosp. Pet. 9. 'as the soldiers kept watch 2 by 2', ανα δυο δυο. Cf. Lk. 10. 1.

Gosp. Pet. 2, end. μιας των αζυμων.

Protev. Jms. 1. 3. Hyperbaton: 'I found all the righteous that they had raised up offspring in Israel.'

Protev. Jms. In the first seven chapters, the verb precedes the subject 66 times, the subject precedes the verb 23 times.

Protev. Jms. The article is sometimes omitted in such a way as to suggest Semitic influence: 6. 3 ο θεος Ισραηλ (cf. ο θεος του Ισραηλ, 16. 3); '*the* virgin of (the) Lord', 9. 1, 10. 1 *bis* (cf. '*the* virgin of *the* Lord', 11. 1) 'sons of Israel', 17. 1; 'region of Bethlehem', 18. 1; 'seed of Abraham, Isaac, and Jacob', 20. 2.

Protev. Jms. 10. 1. Hyperbaton: 'And remembered the priest the child Mary, that she was of the Tribe (of) David.'

The results of a study of these lists may be summarized as follows:

1. There is a tendency in both the manuscripts and the Apocryphal Gospels to increase the use of *kai* when Matthew is being used. When Mark is being copied, the use of *kai* is decreased.

2. Both the manuscripts and the Apocryphal Gospels, when using Matthew, show a slight tendency to create parataxis by changing a participle to a finite verb with *kai*, rather than to avoid parataxis by making the reverse change. The manuscripts of Mark, however, have the reverse tendency, avoiding parataxis more often than they create it.

The addendum on parataxis in material not strictly paralleled in the Synoptics shows that there was, by and large, no hesitancy in later Christian literature about the use of parataxis. The Semitic style seems especially to be cultivated in the Protev. Jms., but there are other documents which also, at least in certain portions, have a higher degree of parataxis than is to be found anywhere in the New Testament.

3. On the whole, asyndeton is avoided more than created in

228

the manuscripts. Justin avoids asyndeton. But the reverse tendency is observable in the Apocryphal Gospels. It may be that some of the instances in which certain of the manuscripts create asyndeton in Mark by dropping a *kai* are really to be attributed to a desire to avoid parataxis. Thus in Mk. 11. 12–14 *kai* appears five times. The *kai* in vs. 12 is omitted by 506; the second *kai* in vs. 13 is changed to *de* by 0188 and 565; the first *kai* in vs. 14 is omitted by D and 565. The omissions of *kai* are listed as creations of asyndeton, but they could have been occasioned by the desire to avoid parataxis. This desire is noticeable in the minuscule 565, in which *kai* is avoided twice in these verses— once by being changed to *de* and once by being omitted.

Later Christian works, especially the Act. Pil., do not avoid asyndeton. On the contrary, asyndeton is far more common in the Act. Pil. than in any of our Synoptics. Matthew Black has also noted that asyndeton is frequently used in the Shepherd of Hermas.[1]

4. Surprisingly enough, the use of the historic present is increased rather than decreased in the manuscripts and the Apocryphal Gospels. This is especially the case with regard to verbs of saying. In material which does not directly parallel the Synoptics, the Apocryphal Gospels show a considerable tendency to use the historic present, more often with verbs of saying than not.

5. There is a slight tendency to use *heis* for *tis* rather than to correct *heis* to *tis*.

6. The evidence in the miscellaneous category is evenly balanced. Semitisms of various kinds, especially such syntactical constructions as casus pendens, are added as often as they are omitted.

There is also no shortage of Semitic-like constructions in the Apocryphal Gospels in material which is not taken from the Synoptics. The addendum to Category 6 is by no means a complete listing of such Semitisms, but gives some interesting examples. Especially striking is Act. Pil. 9. 1: ...τὸν Ἰησοῦν, εἰς ὃν οὐδεμίαν αἰτίαν εὑρίσκω ἐν αὐτῷ. The repetition of a preposition (εἰς and ἐν could both translate *beth* in Hebrew or Aramaic) with a relative pronoun and then at the end of the sentence with a personal pronoun is usually regarded as being

---

[1] *An Aramaic approach*², p. 42 (3rd ed. p. 60).

a strong indication of a Semitic source.[1] The construction is almost as awkward in Greek as in English. Yet one could hardly argue that the quotation from Pilate in the Act. Pil. actually goes back to a primitive Aramaic source. Whether the Semitism was created through imitation (although why anyone would attribute a Semitism to *Pilate* is hard to imagine) or occurs because some of the material in the Act. Pil. at some time passed through a Semitic community cannot be said. ⌈This is clear evidence that even relatively strong Semitisms could be created at a later stage of the tradition, however.⌋

⌈We must conclude, then, that no tendency to do away with Semitisms can be proved on the basis of this evidence.⌋ It is true that not every Semitism which has been used by such scholars as Black has been discussed, but that is because there was not enough evidence to make the discussion of some possible Semitisms profitable. Our information covers the supposedly Semitic characteristics which are most common and which have been most discussed. Although some of them are frequently avoided in the post-canonical tradition, they are also fairly frequently added. The manuscripts show a leveling tendency. Thus the copyists of Mark, where *kai* is used a great deal, tended to substitute other conjunctions. The copyists of Matthew, where *kai* is not used so much, tended somewhat to replace other conjunctions with *kai*. One can hardly use this kind of evidence to prove antiquity, relative or otherwise, but it may prove enlightening for the study of redactional method. It is noteworthy that two Greek minuscules (565 and 700) avoid parataxis with a fair degree of consistency. Such redactional observations could be important for the study of the Synoptic Gospels. Thus the observation that a certain author did not often employ parataxis might facilitate the separation of his own work from his sources.[2]

---

[1] See Black, *An Aramaic approach*[2], p. 75 (3rd ed. p. 100). He also cites C. F. Burney, *The Aramaic origin of the Fourth Gospel* (Oxford, 1922), pp. 84 f. See also Howard, *op. cit.* p. 434.

[2] A great deal of work has yet to be done on the relationship between observations about literary characteristics (such as the use of Semitisms) and source criticism. A beginning was made in Mark by Vincent Taylor, *The Gospel according to St Mark*, pp. 56, 65 f., and especially 653–64. Bultmann attempted to relate stylistic observations to source criticism in his commentary on John (*Das Evangelium des Johannes*[17], Göttingen, 1962). See on this D. M. Smith Jr., *The composition and order of the Fourth Gospel* (New Haven, 1965), pp. 9–11. To use

We cannot rule out the possibility that Semitisms other than the grammatical and syntactical ones which we have considered would yield more positive results. We may refer here, for example, to Semitic poetic forms which have been detected in the sayings of Jesus. One might wish to argue that later users of Jesus' sayings would not understand their poetic form and thus destroy it.[1] Evidence for this is hard to gather, since the early Fathers and the Apocryphal Gospels rarely quote the poetic sayings of Jesus at sufficient length or sufficiently accurately to enable any judgements to be made. It is nevertheless not inconceivable that a case could be made out that the poetic form of sayings tends to be destroyed rather than that poetic form tends to be given to sayings which originally lacked it. Even here, however, there are differences of opinion. Dibelius, in discussing Burney's effort to test the authenticity of sayings of Jesus by poetic consideration, warns that the smoothest and most poetic form is not necessarily the earliest. The more rhythmic form of the Lord's prayer in Matthew, for example, could stem from cultic use.[2]

It is also possible that further historical work will make what we have called 'Semitisms of content' usable in discussions of antiquity. Thus if a tradition in one of its forms presupposes Jewish customs, while in another it presupposes Hellenistic customs, it might be argued that the former is earlier.[3] When

stylistic characteristics to distinguish sources is very difficult in John, because of the thorough editorial work of the final evangelist. See Smith, *op. cit.* pp. 57 f., and R. T. Fortna, *The Gospel of signs* (unpublished Th.D. dissertation, Union Theological Seminary, New York, 1965), especially pp. 59–66.

[1] Note the following statement by C. F. Burney, *The poetry of Our Lord* (Oxford, 1925), p. 7: 'The present writer confidently states that the criterion of poetical form which he puts forward may be of service in determining which version of Q has the better claim to be considered a literally faithful record. If his deductions are correct, it appears that in most cases, though not in all, the verdict should go to the First Gospel.'

[2] 'Zur Formgeschichte', p. 212.

[3] This was the view of Schniewind. He thought that one could follow 'the experts in Rabbinic Judaism when they, in spite of the two source hypothesis, grant to a passage in Matthew the better tradition over against Mark'. The best-known examples, he says, are the pericopes about the Syro-Phoenician woman and divorce. In regard to the latter, he points out that 'in unserem Mk. ist der Aufbau des Gesprächs zerstört, weil die dem Gespräch zugrunde liegende Debatte Hillel-Schammaj nicht mehr verstanden wird'. He concludes, significantly enough, 'So zu konstruieren ist in der Tat berechtigt, sobald die *Starrheit* der Zwei-Quellen-Theorie in Flüssigkeit aufgelöst wird...' See 'Zur Synoptiker-Exegese', *Theologische Rundschau*, N.F. 2 (1930), 149 f.

we consider, however, that certain segments of the Church, up until about the year 135, were in as close contact with Jewish communities as other segments were with Hellenistic communities, we might be more inclined to think that 'Semitisms of content' tell us more about environment than date.[1]

The study which we have undertaken here, however, deals only with the more frequent grammatical and syntactical Semitisms.[2] The results of this study, while not positive in one sense, are quite positive in another. Consideration of them should spell an end to the abuse of supposed Semitisms in efforts to prove either antiquity or authenticity. The tendency which exists today to attribute any passage which contains a few grammatical or syntactical Semitisms to Jesus or even to the most primitive Palestinian Church is clearly misguided. Such Semitisms may be characteristic of primitive tradition, but they are also common enough in traditions which are quite late. They thus lose their character as proofs of antiquity.

The use or non-use of Semitisms may, however, throw light on the redactional tendencies of certain writers as well as upon the environment in which they wrote, so that it is still profitable to study Semitisms in the Synoptic Gospels.

THE EVIDENCE FROM THE SYNOPTIC GOSPELS

Semitisms in the Synoptic Gospels have been used not only to decide what passages have the best claims to antiquity, but also to prove the priority of Mark to Matthew and Luke. C. H. Weisse argued over a century ago that Mark's style is the most Hebraic of any of the Gospels and that the Hebraic style points to his independence and originality.[3] This argument has been repeated so often that it need hardly be documented, but we may note that in the most recent edition of a standard German introduction to the New Testament it keeps its place: 'Matthew and Luke have frequently altered the popular and semitically

---

[1] On Semitisms and provenance, see Appendix IV.

[2] It might be argued that the Semitisms with which we have dealt are vernacularisms rather than true Semitisms. I would not be necessarily opposed to a reclassification of these constructions, but do not wish to undertake one here. I am content to call them Semitisms but to insist that they could have entered the tradition, from some source or other, at any stage in its transmission.

[3] C. H. Weisse, *Die evangelische Geschichte*, I, p. 67.

colored text of Mark to better Greek in the same or in different ways.'[1] This is considered one of the decisive proofs for Mark's priority.[2] This argument presumes either that the tendency of the tradition was to become less Semitic and to be written in better Greek, which we have shown not always to have been the case, or that Matthew and Luke had the redactional tendency to avoid Semitisms while Mark had no redactional tendency to add them.

The second alternative is an interesting one, and deserves further exploration. It will be best to present what evidence we have collected on Semitisms in the Synoptics and then to discuss the significance of it.

1′ The use of *kai* in one Gospel but not in another[3]

Matthew

8. 14 reads: καὶ ἐλθὼν ὁ 'Ιησοῦς, and Mk. 1. 29 reads: καὶ εὐθὺς... ἐξελθών; but Lk. 4. 38 reads: ἀναστὰς δὲ...εἰσῆλθεν. This is abbreviated as follows:

8. 14 and Mk. 1. 29; ctr. Lk. 4. 38.
7. 26; ctr. Lk. 6. 49.
8. 25 and Mk. 4. 38*b*; ctr. Lk. 8. 24.
8. 26 and Mk. 4. 40; ctr. Lk. 8. 25.
9. 3 and Lk. 5. 21; ctr. Mk. 2. 6.
9. 4 and Mk. 2. 8; ctr. Lk. 5. 22.
9. 15 and Mk. 2. 19; ctr. Lk. 5. 34.
9. 23 and Mk. 5. 38; ctr. Lk. 8. 51.
10. 1 and Mk. 6. 7; ctr. Lk. 9. 1.
*10. 38; ctr. Lk. 14. 27.
12. 10 and Mk. 3. 2; ctr. Lk. 6. 7.
12. 26 and Mk. 3. 26; ctr. Lk. 11. 18.
12. 27; ctr. Lk. 11. 19.
13. 34; ctr. Mk. 4. 34.
15. 21; ctr. Mk. 7. 24.
15. 22; ctr. Mk. 7. 25 (*alla*).
17. 18; ctr. Lk. 9. 42 (cf. Mk. 9. 25).
20. 32 and Mk. 10. 49; ctr. Lk. 18. 40.
24. 4; ctr. Mk. 13. 5 and Lk. 21. 8.

[1] W. G. Kümmel, *Einleitung in das neue Testament*[13], p. 30.
[2] *Ibid.* p. 29. Cadbury (*The making of Luke-Acts*, pp. 84 f.), however, does not think that 'primitiveness of origin' is a 'necessary corollary' of Mark's having a Semitic background.
[3] Unless otherwise noted, the passage cited after *ctr.* has *de*.
* An asterisk indicates that the passage cited after *ctr.* has no conjunction.

*24. 7*b*; ctr. Mk. 13. 8*b* (asyndeton) and Lk. 21. 11 (*te*).

26. 19 and Mk. 14. 16; ctr. Lk. 22. 13.

*26. 22; ctr. Mk. 14. 19.

*26. 47 and Mk. 14. 43; ctr. Lk. 22. 47 (*eti*).

26. 51 (cf. Lk. 22. 50); ctr. Mk. 14. 47.

*26. 63; ctr. Mk. 14. 61 (*palin*).[1]

26. 72; ctr. Mk. 14. 70 (cf. Lk. 22. 58).

27. 11 and Mk. 15. 2; ctr. Lk. 23. 3.

27. 48; ctr. Mk. 15. 36.

Mark

1. 16; ctr. Mt. 4. 18.

1. 18; ctr. Mt. 4. 20.

1. 20; ctr. Mt. 4. 22.

1. 35; ctr. Lk. 4. 42.

1. 38; ctr. Lk. 4. 43.

2. 17 and Lk. 5. 31; ctr. Mt. 9. 12.

* 2. 23; ctr. Mt. 12. 1 ('in that hour', no conj.) and Lk. 6. 1 (*de*).

2. 23*b* and Lk. 6. 1*b*; ctr. Mt. 12. 1*b*.

2. 24; ctr. Mt. 12. 2 and Lk. 6. 2.

2. 25 and Lk. 6. 3; ctr. Mt. 12. 3.

3. 3; ctr. Lk. 6. 8.

3. 4; ctr. Lk. 6. 9.

3. 7 and Lk. 6. 17; ctr. Mt. 12. 15. (But there is no verbatim agreement between Luke and Matthew.)

3. 32; ctr. Mt. 12. 47 and Lk. 8. 20. (But this verse in Mt. may not be original.)

3. 33; ctr. Mt. 12. 48.

4. 6; ctr. Mt. 13. 6.

4. 11; ctr. Mt. 13. 11 and Lk. 8. 10.

4. 16; ctr. Mt. 13. 20 and Lk. 8. 13.

4. 17 and Lk. 8. 13; ctr. Mt. 13. 21.

4. 18; ctr. Mt. 13. 22 and Lk. 8. 14.

4. 20; ctr. Mt. 13. 23 and Lk. 8. 15.

* 4. 33; ctr. Mt. 13. 34 (*tauta panta*).

4. 38; ctr. Mt. 8. 24.

* 4. 39; ctr. Lk. 8. 24 (*de*) and Mt. 8. 26*b* (*tote*).

4. 41; ctr. Mt. 8. 27 and Lk. 8. 25.

5. 2; ctr. Lk. 8. 27.

5. 6; ctr. Lk. 8. 28.

* An asterisk indicates that the passage cited after *ctr.* has no conjunction.

[1] Instances such as this use of *palin* in Mark and the frequent use of *tote* in Matthew in place of a conjunction, while marked with an asterisk in this category, are not true cases of asyndeton, and so are not listed in category 3′ below.

5. 9; ctr. Lk. 8. 30.

5. 9*b*; ctr. Lk. 8. 30*b*.

5. 12 and Lk. 8. 32; ctr. Mt. 8. 31.

5. 13; ctr. Mt. 8. 32 and Lk. 8. 33.

5. 14; ctr. Mt. 8. 33 and Lk. 8. 34.

5. 14*b*; ctr. Lk. 8. 35.

5. 18; ctr. Lk. 8. 37.

5. 41; ctr. Lk. 8. 54.

6. 4; ctr. Mt. 13. 57 and Lk. 4. 24.

6. 12; ctr. Lk. 9. 6.

* 6. 14; ctr. Mt. 14. 1 ('in that time', no conj.) and Lk. 9. 7 (*de*).

6. 35; ctr. Mt. 14. 15 and Lk. 9. 13.

6. 37; ctr. Mt. 14. 17 and Lk. 9. 13.

6. 41; ctr. Lk. 9. 16.

6. 47; ctr. Mt. 14. 23.

* 7. 1; ctr. Mt. 15. 1 (*tote*).

7. 18; ctr. Mt. 15. 16.

* 7. 29; ctr. Mt. 15. 28 (*tote*).

8. 15; ctr. Mt. 16. 6.

8. 17; ctr. Mt. 16. 8.

8. 27 (cf. Lk. 9. 18); ctr. Mt. 16. 13.

8. 28*b*; ctr. Mt. 16. 14*b* and Lk. 9. 19*b*.

* 8. 29; ctr. Mt. 16. 15 (asyndeton) and Lk. 9. 20 (*de*).

* 8. 30; ctr. Mt. 16. 20 (*tote*) and Lk. 9. 21 (*de*).

* 8. 31; ctr. Mt. 16. 21 (*apo tote*).

8. 36; ctr. Mt. 16. 26 and Lk. 9. 25.

9. 5; ctr. Mt. 17. 4.

* 9. 7; ctr. Mt. 17. 5 (*eti*) and Lk. 9. 34 (*de*).

9. 42; ctr. Mt. 18. 6.

9. 43; ctr. Mt. 18. 8.

*10. 13; ctr. Mt. 19. 13 (*tote*) and Lk. 18. 15 (*de*).

10. 23; ctr. Mt. 19. 23 and Lk. 18. 24.

*10. 35; ctr. Mt. 20. 20 (*tote*).

10. 42; ctr. Mt. 20. 25 and Lk. 22. 25.

10. 47; ctr. Lk. 18. 36.

10. 48 and Lk. 18. 39; ctr. Mt. 20. 31.

10. 52 and Lk. 18. 42; ctr. Mt. 20. 34. (But Matthew does not agree closely with Mark and Luke.)

11. 3; ctr. Mt. 21. 3.

11. 4; ctr. Lk. 19. 32 (cf. Mt. 21. 6).

11. 8; ctr. Mt. 21. 8 and Lk. 19. 36.

11. 9; ctr. Mt. 21. 9.

* An asterisk indicates that the passage cited after *ctr.* has no conjunction.

11. 18; ctr. Lk. 19. 47.

11. 22; ctr. Mt. 21. 21.

11. 31; ctr. Mt. 21. 25 and Lk. 20. 5.

*11. 33 and Lk. 20. 8; ctr. Mt. 21. 27.

12. 1; ctr. Lk. 20. 9.

12. 2 and Lk. 20. 10; ctr. Mt. 21. 34.

*12. 18; ctr. Mt. 22. 23 ('in that day', no conj.) and Lk. 20. 27 (*de*).

13. 2; ctr. Mt. 24. 2.

13. 3; ctr. Mt. 24. 3.

13. 11; ctr. Mt. 10. 19.

14. 3; ctr. Mt. 26. 6.

*14. 10; ctr. Mt. 26. 14 (*tote*) (cf. Lk. 22. 3).

14. 12; ctr. Mt. 26. 17 and Lk. 22. 7.

14. 17 and Lk. 22. 14; ctr. Mt. 26. 20.

14. 22 and Lk. 22. 19; ctr. Mt. 26. 26.

*14. 27; ctr. Mt. 26. 31 (*tote*).

*14. 30; ctr. Mt. 26. 34 (asyndeton) and Lk. 22. 34 (*de*).

*14. 32; ctr. Mt. 26. 36 (*tote*).

*14. 34; ctr. Mt. 26. 38 (*tote*).

*14. 39; ctr. Mt. 26. 42 (asyndeton).

*14. 41; ctr. Mt. 26. 45 (*tote*).

*14. 48; ctr. Mt. 26. 55 ('in that hour', no conj.) and Lk. 22. 52 (*de*).

*14. 50; ctr. Mt. 26. 56 (*tote*).

14. 53; ctr. Mt. 26. 57 (cf. Lk. 22. 54).

14. 54; ctr. Mt. 26. 58 and Lk. 22. 54*b*.

14. 66; ctr. Mt. 26. 69.

14. 70; ctr. Mt. 26. 73.

15. 1 and Lk. 22. 66; ctr. Mt. 27. 1.

15. 15; ctr. Mt. 27. 26 and Lk. 23. 25.

15. 21 and Lk. 23. 26; ctr. Mt. 27. 32.

15. 24; ctr. Mt. 27. 35.

*15. 27; ctr. Mt. 27. 38 (*tote*).

15. 29; ctr. Mt. 27. 39.

15. 33 and Lk. 23. 44; ctr. Mt. 27. 45.

15. 34; ctr. Mt. 27. 46.

15. 35; ctr. Mt. 27. 47.

15. 42 and Lk. 23. 50; ctr. Mt. 27. 57.

16. 1; ctr. Mt. 28. 1 and Lk. 24. 1.

16. 5; ctr. Lk. 24. 3.

Luke

* 4. 5; ctr. Mt. 4. 8 (*palin*).

* 4. 8; ctr. Mt. 4. 10 (*tote*).

* An asterisk indicates that the passage cited after *ctr.* has no conjunction.

* 4. 12; ctr. Mt. 4. 7.
  6. 31; ctr. Mt. 7. 12 (*oun*).
  13. 25; ctr. Mt. 25. 12.
*20. 34; ctr. Mt. 22. 29 (*de*) and Mk. 12. 24 (asyndeton).
  23. 24 (cf. Mk. 15. 15).

Summary

Mt. *kai* Mk. not 11 times.	Mt:Mk::11:89
Mt. *kai* Lk. not 19 times.	Mt:Lk::19:22
Mk. *kai* Mt. not 89 times.	Mk:Lk::63:3
Mk. *kai* Lk. not 63 times.	
Lk. *kai* Mt. not 22 times.	
Lk. *kai* Mk. not 3 times.	

Omitting asterisked instances

Mt. *kai* Mk. not 8 times.	Mt:Mk::8:65
Mt. *kai* Lk. not 17 times.	Mt:Lk::17:18
Mk. *kai* Mt. not 65 times.	Mk:Lk::62:2
Mk. *kai* Lk. not 62 times.	
Lk. *kai* Mt. not 18 times.	
Lk. *kai* Mk. not 2 times.	

2' The use of a finite verb with *kai* in one Gospel where another Gospel has a participle

Matthew

5. 15 ('they light and place'); ctr. Lk. 11. 33 ('lighting, he placed').
8. 21 ('to go away and bury' [infinitives]); ctr. Lk. 9. 59 ('going away, to bury').
13. 7 and Mk. 4. 7 ('and the thorns came up and choked'); ctr. Lk. 8. 7 ('and growing up with it, the thorns choked').
13. 23 ('hearing and understanding' [participles]) and Mk. 4. 20 ('they hear and accept'); ctr. Lk. 8. 15 ('hearing they held fast').
13. 54 ('they were astonished and said' [infinitives]); ctr. Mk. 6. 2 ('they were astonished, saying').
14. 6 ('she danced and pleased'); ctr. Mk. 6. 22 ('coming in and dancing, she pleased').
15. 39 ('and dismissing he embarked and went'); ctr. Mk. 8. 9f. ('and he dismissed and embarking went').
17. 1 and Mk. 9. 2 ('and Jesus takes and leads up'); ctr. Lk. 9. 28 ('and taking he went up').
17. 11 ('Elijah comes and will restore'); ctr. Mk. 9. 12 ('Elijah coming restores').

* An asterisk indicates that the passage cited after *ctr.* has no conjunction.

237

20. 19 ('to mock and to scourge and to crucify' [infinitives]) and Mk. 10. 34 ('they will mock and spit and scourge and kill'); ctr. Lk. 18. 32 f. ('he will be mocked and shamefully treated and spit upon, and having scourged, they will kill').

21. 7 ('they led and placed and he sat') and Mk. 11. 7 ('they bring and throw and he sat'); ctr. Lk. 19. 35 ('they led and casting, they set Jesus').

21. 12 ('he entered and cast out'); ctr. Mk. 11. 15 and Lk. 19. 45 ('entering he cast out').

21. 39 ('and taking they cast out and killed') and Mk. 12. 8 ('and taking they killed and cast out'); ctr. Lk. 20. 15 ('and casting out they killed').

22. 23 and Mk. 12. 18 ('they came and asked'); ctr. Lk. 20. 27 ('coming they asked').

22. 25 ('and the first made an end and left') and Mk. 12. 20 ('and the first took, and dying did not leave'); ctr. Lk. 20. 29 ('and the first taking died').

26. 40 and Mk. 14. 37 ('and he comes and finds'); ctr. Lk. 22. 45 ('coming he found').

26. 69 ('Peter sat outside and she came up'); ctr. Mk. 14. 66 ('while Peter was below, she comes').

Mark

1. 35 ('rising up, he went out and went away'); ctr. Lk. 4. 42 ('going out he went').

1. 41 ('he touched and says'); ctr. Mt. 8. 3 and Lk. 5. 13 ('he touched, saying').

2. 12 ('and he rose and taking, went out'); ctr. Mt. 9. 7 ('and rising he departed') and Lk. 5. 25 ('and rising, taking, he departed').

2. 18 ('they come and they say'); ctr. Mt. 9. 14 ('they come saying') and cf. also Lk. 5. 33 ('they said').

4. 4 ('and they came and ate'); ctr. Mt. 13. 4 ('and coming they ate').

4. 38 ('they wake and say'); ctr. Mt. 8. 25 and Lk. 8. 24 ('coming up they woke saying').

4. 41 ('and they feared and said'); ctr. Mt. 8. 27 ('now the men marveled saying') and Lk. 8. 25 ('now fearing they marveled, saying').

5. 20 ('and he departed and began to preach'); ctr. Lk. 8. 39 ('and he departed preaching').

5. 22 f. ('he comes and seeing he falls and beseeches'); ctr. Mt. 9. 18 ('coming he worshipped') and Lk. 8. 41 ('falling he besought').

5. 33 ('she came and fell and said'); ctr. Lk. 8. 47 ('she came and falling announced').

5. 37 f. ('and he did not permit, and they come'); ctr. Lk. 8. 51 ('coming, he did not permit').

6. 1 f. ('he comes and they followed and on the sabbath he began to teach'); ctr. Mt. 13. 54 ('coming he taught').

6. 7 ('and he calls and he began to send, and he gave'); ctr. Mt. 10. 1 and Lk. 9. 1 ('calling he gave').

6. 29 ('hearing they came and took'); ctr. Mt. 14. 12 ('coming they took').

6. 30 ('they gather and announced'); ctr. Lk. 9. 10 ('returning they related').

6. 50 ('he spoke and says'); ctr. Mt. 14. 27 ('he spoke, saying').

8. 30 f. ('and he charged them and began to teach'); ctr. Lk. 9. 21 f. ('now having charged them, he announced, saying').

10. 14 ('Jesus was indignant and said'); ctr. Lk. 18. 16 ('Jesus called them saying'). (Mt. 19. 14: 'Jesus said'.)

10. 28 and Mt. 19. 27 ('we left and followed'); ctr. Lk. 18. 28 ('leaving we followed').

11. 1 f. ('he sends and says'); ctr. Mt. 21. 1 f. and Lk. 19. 29 f. ('he sent saying').

11. 2 ('loose and bring'); ctr. Mt. 21. 2 and Lk. 19. 30 ('loosing lead').

11. 4 ('and they departed and found'); ctr. Lk. 19. 32 ('now departing they found').

12. 3 ('they beat and sent away'); ctr. Lk. 20. 12 ('they sent away, having beaten').

14. 13 ('and he sends and says'); ctr. Lk. 22. 8 ('and he sent saying').

14. 16 ('they went out and came and found'); ctr. Lk. 22. 13 ('going away they found').

14. 22 ('having blessed, he broke and gave and said'); ctr. Mt. 26. 26 ('having blessed, he broke and giving said') and Lk. 22. 19 ('having given thanks, he broke and gave saying').

14. 33 ('and he takes and began'); ctr. Mt. 26. 37 ('and taking he began').

14. 35 ('he fell and prayed'); ctr. Mt. 26. 39 ('he fell praying').

15. 16 ('they led and called together'); ctr. Mt. 27. 27 ('taking, they gathered').

15. 17 (ἐνδιδύσκουσιν...καὶ περιτιθέασιν); ctr. Mt. 27. 28 (ἐκδύσαντες... περιέθηκαν).

15. 22 f. ('and they bring and they gave'); ctr. Mt. 27. 33 f. ('and coming they gave').

15. 24 ('and they crucify and they divide'); ctr. Mt. 27. 35 ('then crucifying they divide'). Cf. Lk. 23. 33 f. ('There they crucify him...and (de) dividing...').

15. 43 ('taking courage he went in and requested'); ctr. Mt. 27. 58 and Lk. 23. 52 ('going up he requested').

Luke

9. 34 (ἐγένετο...καὶ ἐπεσκίαζεν); ctr. Mk. 9. 7 (ἐγένετο...ἐπισκιάζουσα).

Summary

Mt. parataxis Mk. participle 6 times.   Mt:Mk::6:22

Mt. parataxis Lk. participle 13 times.   Mt:Lk::13:0

Mk. parataxis Mt. participle 22 times.   Mk:Lk::33:1

Mk. parataxis Lk. participle 33 times.

Lk. parataxis Mk. participle 1 time.

3′   The use of asyndeton in one Gospel where another Gospel has a conjunction[1]

Matthew

4. 7 reads: ἔφη αὐτῷ ὁ Ἰησοῦς. Lk. 4. 12 reads: καὶ ἀποκριθεὶς εἶπεν αὐτῷ ὁ Ἰησοῦς. This is abbreviated as follows:

*   4. 7; ctr. Lk. 4. 12.

**   12. 3 (*ouk*); ctr. Mk. 2. 25 (*oudepote*) and Lk. 6. 3 (*oude*).

**   13. 13 (*dia touto*); ctr. Mk. 4. 11 and Lk. 8. 10.

*   13. 34; ctr. Mk. 4. 33.

*   16. 15; ctr. Mk. 8. 29 (*kai*) and Lk. 9. 20 (*de*).

      19. 7; ctr. Mk. 10. 3.

      19. 8; ctr. Mk. 10. 5.

      19. 20; ctr. Mk. 10. 20 and Lk. 18. 21.

      19. 21; ctr. Mk. 10. 21 and Lk. 18. 22.

      20. 21; ctr. Mk. 10. 37.

      20. 22; ctr. Mk. 10. 39.

      20. 23; ctr. Mk. 10. 39 *b*.

**   20. 26; ctr. Mk. 10. 43 and Lk. 22. 26.

      20. 33; ctr. Mk. 10. 51 and Lk. 18. 41.

*   21. 27; ctr. Mk. 11. 33 and Lk. 20. 8.

      22. 21; ctr. Mk. 12. 16 and Lk. 20. 24.

**   22. 32 and Mk. 12. 27; ctr. Lk. 20. 38.

*   26. 34; ctr. Mk. 14. 30 (*kai*) and Lk. 22. 34 (*de*).

      26. 35; ctr. Mk. 14. 31.

*   26. 42 (*palin*); ctr. Mk. 14. 39 (*kai palin*).

      26. 64; ctr. Mk. 14. 62.

      27. 22; ctr. Mk. 15. 13 and Lk. 23. 21.

Mark

**   1. 8; ctr. Mt. 3. 11 and Lk. 3. 16 (*men*).

**   2. 9 and Lk. 5. 23; ctr. Mt. 9. 5 (*gar*).

**   2. 17 and Lk. 5. 32; ctr. Mt. 9. 13 (*gar*).

---

[1] Unless otherwise noted, the passage cited after *ctr.* has *de*.

* An asterisk indicates that the passage cited after *ctr.* has *kai*.

** A double asterisk indicates sayings material.

**   2. 21; ctr. Mt. 9. 16 (cf. also Lk. 5. 36).

**   3. 35; ctr. Mt. 12. 50 (*gar*).

**   4. 24*a*; ctr. Lk. 8. 18 (*oun*).

**   4. 24*b*; ctr. Lk. 6. 38 (*gar*). Cf. Mt. 7. 2.

**   5. 39 and Lk. 8. 52; ctr. Mt. 9. 24 (*gar*).

**   6. 36 and Lk. 9. 12; ctr. Mt. 14. 15 (*oun*). (But in command.)

** * 8. 15; ctr. Mt. 16. 6 (cf. Lk. 12. 1). In double imperative.

     8. 29*b*; ctr. Mt. 16. 16 and Lk. 9. 20*b*.

     9. 38; ctr. Lk. 9. 49.

** *10. 14; ctr. Mt. 19. 14 and Lk. 18. 16. In double imperative.

** 10. 25 (cf. Mt. 19. 24); ctr. Lk. 18. 25 (*gar*).

     10. 27; ctr. Mt. 19. 26 and Lk. 18. 27.

     10. 28; ctr. Mt. 19. 27 (*tote*) and Lk. 18. 28 (*de*).

     10. 29; ctr. Mt. 19. 28 and Lk. 18. 29.

** 12. 9; ctr. Lk. 20. 15 (*oun*) (cf. Mt. 21. 40) (interrogative).

** 12. 17; ctr. Mt. 22. 21 (*oun*) and Lk. 20. 25 (*toinun*). In command.

** 12. 20; ctr. Mt. 22. 25 (*de*) and Lk. 20. 29 (*oun*). But D has no conj. in
     Mt. and Lk.

** 12. 22 and Lk. 20. 32; ctr. Mt. 22. 27.

** 12. 23; ctr. Mt. 22. 28 and Lk. 20. 33 (*oun*).

*   12. 24; ctr. Mt. 22. 29 (*de*) and Lk. 20. 34 (*kai*).

** 12. 36; ctr. Mt. 22. 43 (*oun*) and Lk. 20. 42 (*gar*).

** 12. 37; ctr. Mt. 22. 45 (*ei oun*) and Lk. 20. 44 (*oun*).

** 13. 6; ctr. Mt. 24. 5 and Lk. 21. 8 (*gar*).

** 13. 7; ctr. Mt. 24. 6 and Lk. 21. 9 (*gar*).

** *13. 8*b*; ctr. Mt. 24. 7*b* (*kai*) and Lk. 21. 11 (*te*).

** 13. 8*d*; ctr. Mt. 24. 8 (*de*).

** 13. 9; ctr. Mt. 10. 17 (*gar*).

** 13. 34; ctr. Mt. 25. 14 (*gar*).

** 14. 6; ctr. Mt. 26. 10 (*gar*).

*   14. 19; ctr. Mt. 26. 22.

** 14. 64; ctr. Lk. 22. 71 (*gar*; but Lk.'s parallel is not too close). Cf. also
     Mt. 26. 65, *ide nun*.

** 16. 6; ctr. Lk. 24. 6 (*alla*) and cf. Mt. 28. 6 ('*for* he is risen *as he said*').

Luke

**   4. 8*b*; ctr. Mt. 4. 10*b* (*gar*).

**   6. 42; ctr. Mt. 7. 4 (ἤ).

** 11. 24; ctr. Mt. 12. 43.

** 11. 52; ctr. Mt. 23. 13.

** 12. 7; ctr. Mt. 10. 31 (*oun*).

** *14. 27; ctr. Mt. 10. 38.

       * An asterisk indicates that the passage cited after *ctr.* has *kai*.

      ** A double asterisk indicates sayings material.

** 21. 23; ctr. Mt. 24. 19 and Mk. 13. 17.
* 22. 47; ctr. Mt. 26. 47 and Mk. 14. 43.

Summary

Mt. asyndeton Mk. not 20 times.	Mt:Mk::20:29
Mt. asyndeton Lk. not 13 times.	Mt:Lk::13:13
Mk. asyndeton Mt. not 29 times.	Mk:Lk::22:2
Mk. asyndeton Lk. not 22 times.	
Lk. asyndeton Mt. not 13 times.	
Lk. asyndeton Mk. not 2 times.	

Omitting items marked with a single asterisk

Mt. asyndeton Mk. not 15 times.	Mt:Mk::15:25
Mt. asyndeton Lk. not 11 times.	Mt:Lk::11:11
Mk. asyndeton Mt. not 25 times.	Mk:Lk::20:1
Mk. asyndeton Lk. not 20 times.	
Lk. asyndeton Mt. not 11 times.	
Lk. asyndeton Mk. not 1 time.	

4′ The use of the historic present in one Gospel but not in another[1]

Matthew

3. 13 (παραγίνεται); ctr. Mk. 1. 9 (ἐγένετο...ἦλθεν).
4. 5 ('takes'); ctr. Lk. 4. 9 ('led').
4. 6; ctr. Lk. 4. 9.
4. 8 ('takes'); ctr. Lk. 4. 5 ('leading').
4. 8 ('he shows'); ctr. Lk. 4. 5 ('he showed').
4. 10; ctr. Lk. 4. 8.
4. 11 (ἀφίησιν); ctr. Lk. 4. 13 (ἀπέστη).
4. 19; ctr. Mk. 1. 17.
8. 4 and Mk. 1. 44 ('says'); ctr. Lk. 5. 14 ('announced').
8. 20; ctr. Lk. 9. 58.
8. 22; ctr. Lk. 9. 60.
8. 26; ctr. Mk. 4. 40 and Lk. 8. 25.
9. 6 and Mk. 2. 10; ctr. Lk. 5. 24.
9. 9 and Mk. 2. 14; ctr. Lk. 5. 27.
9. 37; ctr. Lk. 10. 2.
12. 13 and Mk. 3. 5; ctr. Lk. 6. 10.
14. 8 ('she says'); ctr. Mk. 6. 25 ('she asked, saying').
14. 17 and Mk. 6. 37; ctr. Lk. 9. 13.

* An asterisk indicates that the passage cited after *ctr.* has *kai*.
** A double asterisk indicates sayings material.
[1] Unless otherwise noted, the verb involved is a verb of saying.

15. 33 ('they say'); ctr. Mk. 8. 4 ('they answered').

15. 34 ('he says'); ctr. Mk. 8. 5 ('he asked').

16. 15 ('he says'); ctr. Mk. 8. 29 ('he asked') and Lk. 9. 20 ('he said').

17. 1 and Mk. 9. 2 ('takes'); ctr. Lk. 9. 28 ('taking').

17. 1 and Mk. 9. 2 ('leads up'); ctr. Lk. 9. 28 ('went up').

17. 20; ctr. Lk. 17. 6.

19. 7; ctr. Mk. 10. 3.

19. 8; ctr. Mk. 10. 5.

19. 20; ctr. Mk. 10. 20 and Lk. 18. 21.

20. 21; ctr. Mk. 10. 37.

20. 22; ctr. Mk. 10. 39.

20. 23; ctr. Mk. 10. 39b.

20. 33; ctr. Mk. 10. 51 and Lk. 18. 41.

21. 13; ctr. Mk. 11. 17 and Lk. 19. 46 (Luke has a participle).

21. 19; ctr. Mk. 11. 14.

22. 16 and Mk. 12. 13 ('they send'); ctr. Lk. 20. 20 ('they sent').

22. 21; ctr. Mk. 12. 16 and Lk. 20. 24.

22. 21b; ctr. Mk. 12. 17 and Lk. 20. 25.

26. 35; ctr. Mk. 14. 31.

26. 40 and Mk. 14. 37 ('he comes'); ctr. Lk. 22. 45 ('coming').

26. 40b and Mk. 14. 37b ('he finds'); ctr. Lk. 22. 45 ('he found').

26. 40c and Mk. 14. 37c; ctr. Lk. 22. 46.

26. 64; ctr. Mk. 14. 62.

26. 71 ('says'); ctr. Mk. 14. 69 ('began to say').

27. 13 ('says'); ctr. Mk. 15. 4 ('asked').

27. 22 ('they say'); ctr. Mk. 15. 13 ('they cried out') and Lk. 23. 21 ('they shouted, saying').

Mark

1. 12 ('casts out'); ctr. Mt. 4. 1 ('was led up') and Lk. 4. 1 ('was led').

1. 21 ('they enter'); ctr. Lk. 4. 31 ('he went down').

1. 30 ('they say'); ctr. Lk. 4. 38 ('they asked').

1. 38; ctr. Lk. 4. 43.

1. 41; ctr. Mt. 8. 3 and Lk. 5. 13 (participle).

2. 3 ('they come bearing'); ctr. Mt. 9. 2 ('they bore') and Lk. 5. 18 ('bearing').

2. 5; ctr. Mt. 9. 2 and Lk. 5. 20.

2. 8; ctr. Mt. 9. 4 and Lk. 5. 22.

2. 15 ('it happens'); ctr. Mt. 9. 10 ('it happened').

2. 17; ctr. Mt. 9. 12 and Lk. 5. 31.

2. 18 ('they come and they say'); ctr. Mt. 9. 14 ('they come saying') and Lk. 5. 33 ('they said').

2. 25; ctr. Mt. 12. 3 and Lk. 6. 3.

3. 3; ctr. Lk. 6. 8.

3. 4; ctr. Lk. 6. 9.

3. 13 ('he goes up'); ctr. Lk. 6. 12 ('it happened that he went out').

3. 13 ('he calls'); ctr. Lk. 6. 13 ('he called').

3. 31 ('they come'); ctr. Lk. 8. 19 ('they came up').

3. 32 ('they say'); ctr. Mt. 12. 47 ('he said') [if genuine] and Lk. 8. 20 ('it was announced').

3. 33; ctr. Mt. 12. 48 and Lk. 8. 21.

3. 34; ctr. Mt. 12. 49.

4. 1 ('gathers together'); ctr. Mt. 13. 2 ('gathered together') and cf. also Lk. 8. 4 ('being together').

4. 35 ('he says'); ctr. Mt. 8. 18 ('he commanded') and Lk. 8. 22 ('he said').

4. 37 ('it happens'); ctr. Mt. 8. 24 ('it happened') and Lk. 8. 23 ('it came down').

4. 38; ctr. Mt. 8. 25 and Lk. 8. 24 (participle).

4. 38 ('they wake'); ctr. Mt. 8. 25 and Lk. 8. 24 ('they waked').

5. 7 ('crying out he says'); ctr. Mt. 8. 29 ('they cried out saying') and Lk. 8. 28 ('he said').

5. 9; ctr. Lk. 8. 30.

5. 15 ('come'); ctr. Mt. 8. 34 and Lk. 8. 35 ('came').

5. 15b ('they behold'); ctr. Lk. 8. 35 ('they found').

5. 19; ctr. Lk. 8. 38 (participle).

5. 22 ('he comes and falls'); ctr. Mt. 9. 19 ('coming up he worshipped') and Lk. 8. 41 ('he came falling').

5. 36 ('says'); ctr. Lk. 8. 50 ('answered').

5. 38 ('they come'); ctr. Mt. 9. 23 and Lk. 8. 51 ('coming').

5. 38 ('he beholds'); ctr. Mt. 9. 23 ('seeing').

5. 39; ctr. Mt. 9. 23 and Lk. 8. 52.

5. 41; ctr. Lk. 8. 54 (participle).

6. 1 ('comes'); ctr. Mt. 13. 54 ('coming').

6. 7 ('he calls'); ctr. Mt. 10. 1 and Lk. 9. 1 ('calling').

6. 30 ('they gather together'); ctr. Lk. 9. 10 ('returning').

6. 48 ('comes'); ctr. Mt. 14. 25 ('came').

6. 50; ctr. Mt. 14. 27 (participle).

7. 18; ctr. Mt. 15. 16.

7. 28; ctr. Mt. 15. 27.

8. 1; ctr. Mt. 15. 32.

8. 6 ('he announces'); ctr. Mt. 15. 35 ('announcing').

8. 12; ctr. Mt. 16. 2.

8. 17; ctr. Mt. 16. 8.

8. 29; ctr. Mt. 16. 16 and Lk. 9. 20.

8. 33; ctr. Mt. 16. 23.

9. 5; ctr. Mt. 17. 4 and Lk. 9. 33.

9. 19; ctr. Mt. 17. 17 and Lk. 9. 41.

10. 1 ('comes'); ctr. Mt. 19. 1 ('came').

10. 1 ('they go along'); ctr. Mt. 19. 2 ('they followed').

10. 23; ctr. Mt. 19. 23 and Lk. 18. 24.

10. 27; ctr. Mt. 19. 26 and Lk. 18. 27.

10. 35 ('they come up'); ctr. Mt. 20. 20 ('they came up').

10. 42; ctr. Mt. 20. 25 and Lk. 22. 25.

10. 46 ('they come'); ctr. Lk. 18. 35 ('it happened when he drew near').

11. 1 ('they draw near'); ctr. Mt. 21. 1 ('they drew near') and Lk. 19. 29 ('he drew near').

11. 1 ('sends'); ctr. Mt. 21. 1 and Lk. 19. 29 ('sent').

11. 2; ctr. Mt. 21. 2 and Lk. 19. 30 (participle).

11. 4 ('they loose'); ctr. Lk. 19. 33 ('loosing').

11. 7 ('they bring'); ctr. Mt. 21. 7 and Lk. 19. 35 ('they brought').

11. 7 ('they throw upon'); ctr. Mt. 21. 7 ('they placed upon') and Lk. 19. 35 ('casting upon').

11. 21 ('remembering he says'); ctr. Mt. 21. 20 ('they marveled saying').

11. 22; ctr. Mt. 21. 21.

11. 27 ('they come'); ctr. Mt. 21. 23 ('coming').

11. 27 (ἔρχονται); ctr. Mt. 21. 23 (προσῆλθον) and Lk. 20. 1 (ἐπέστησαν).

11. 33 ('answering they say'); ctr. Mt. 21. 27 ('answering they said') and Lk. 20. 7 ('they answered').

11. 33; ctr. Mt. 21. 27 and Lk. 20. 8.

12. 14; ctr. Mt. 22. 16 and Lk. 20. 21 (participle).

12. 18 ('they come'); ctr. Mt. 22. 23 ('they came up') and Lk. 20. 27 ('coming up').

14. 12; ctr. Mt. 26. 17 (participle) and Lk. 22. 9.

14. 13; ctr. Mt. 26. 18 and Lk. 22. 10.

14. 13 ('he sends'); ctr. Lk. 22. 8 ('he sent').

14. 30; ctr. Mt. 26. 34 and Lk. 22. 34.

14. 33 ('he takes'); ctr. Mt. 26. 37 ('taking').

14. 43 ('he appears'); ctr. Mt. 26. 47 ('he came') and cf. also Lk. 22. 47 ('he went before them and drew near').

14. 45; ctr. Mt. 26. 49.

14. 53 ('they come together'); ctr. Mt. 26. 57 ('they gathered together').

14. 61 ('asked and says'); ctr. Mt. 26. 63 ('said') and Lk. 22. 67 ('saying').

14. 63; ctr. Mt. 26. 65 (participle) and Lk. 22. 71.

14. 66 ('she comes'); ctr. Mt. 26. 69 ('she came up').

14. 67; ctr. Mt. 26. 69 (participle) and Lk. 22. 56.

15. 2; ctr. Mt. 27. 11 and Lk. 23. 3.

15. 16 ('they call together'); ctr. Mt. 27. 27 ('they gathered together').

15. 17 ('they clothe'); ctr. Mt. 27. 28 ('they did put on').

15. 17 ('they place around'); ctr. Mt. 27. 29 ('they placed upon').

15. 20 ('they lead out'); ctr. Mt. 27. 31 ('they led away').

15. 21 ('they impress'); ctr. Mt. 27. 32 ('they impressed') and cf. also Lk. 23. 26 ('they placed upon').

15. 22 ('they lead him'); ctr. Mt. 27. 33 ('coming') and Lk. 23. 33 ('they came').

15. 24 ('they crucify him'); ctr. Mt. 27. 35 ('crucifying') and Lk. 23. 33 ('they crucified').

15. 24 ('they divide'); ctr. Mt. 27. 35 ('they divided') and Lk. 23. 34 ('dividing').

16. 2 ('they come'); ctr. Mt. 28. 1 ('she came') and Lk. 24. 1 ('they came').

16. 4 ('they behold'); ctr. Lk. 24. 3 ('they found').

16. 6; ctr. Mt. 28. 5 and Lk. 24. 5.

Summary

Mt. historic present Mk. not 23 times.	Mt:Mk::23:78
Mt. historic present Lk. not 29 times.	Mt:Lk::29:0
Mk. historic present Mt. not 78 times.	Mk:Lk::80:0
Mk. historic present Lk. not 80 times.	

5′ The use of *heis* in one Gospel where another has *tis*

Matthew

8. 19 ('one scribe'); ctr. Lk. 9. 57 ('a certain one').

19. 16 and Mk. 10. 17; ctr. Lk. 18. 18.

22. 35 ('One of them, a lawyer') and Mk. 12. 28 ('one of the scribes'); ctr. Lk. 10. 25 ('a certain lawyer').

26. 51 (*heis*); ctr. Mk. 14. 47 and Lk. 22. 50 (*heis tis*).

27. 48; ctr. Mk. 15. 36.

Mark

12. 42 ('one widow'); ctr. Lk. 21. 2 ('a certain widow').

Summary

Mt. *heis* Mk. *tis* 2.
Mt. *heis* Lk. *tis* 4.
Mk. *heis* Lk. *tis* 3.

6′ More Semitic wording in one Gospel than in another

Matthew

5. 39 ('whoever strikes you on the right cheek, turn to him also the other'); cf. Lk. 6. 29 ('to the one striking you on the cheek, offer the other also'). See Beyer, pp. 210 and fn. 1, 214, 217, 176.

6. 32 (τὰ ἔθνη = Gentiles); ctr. Lk. 12. 30 (τὰ ἔθνη τοῦ κόσμου = nations).

7. 12 ('all things whatever you want...thus also'); ctr. Lk. 6. 31 ('just as you want'). See Beyer, p. 178.

7. 26 ('everyone who hears'); ctr. Lk. 6. 49 ('he who hears'). See Beyer, p. 212.

10. 33 ('whoever denies me..., also I will deny him'); ctr. Lk. 12. 9 ('the one denying me shall be denied'). See Beyer, p. 176.

10. 37 ('the one loving'); ctr. Lk. 14. 26 ('if anyone does not hate'). But the agreement here is slight. See Beyer, p. 227.

12. 24 ('this one does not cast out demons except by Beezebul'); ctr. Mk. 3. 22 and Lk. 11. 15 ('he casts out demons by Beezebul', and the like). Mt. 9. 34 also has the less Semitic form. See Beyer, p. 131.

12. 25 and Lk. 11. 17 ('every kingdom divided'); ctr. Mk. 3. 24 ('if a kingdom is divided'). See Beyer, p. 227.

12. 25 ('every city or house'); ctr. Mk. 3. 25 ('if a house'). See Beyer, p. 227.

12. 32b ('whoever says..., it will not be forgiven to him'); ctr. Lk. 12. 10b ('it will not be forgiven to the one blaspheming'). See Beyer, pp. 210 fn. 1, 218.

13. 19 ('everyone hearing'); ctr. Mk. 4. 15 ('and when they hear'). See Beyer, p. 227.

13. 20 ('that which was sown on rocky ground, this is'); ctr. Mk. 4. 16 ('these are like the ones sown..., which, when they hear...') and Lk. 8. 13 ('those upon the rocky ground are those [which], when they hear...').

13. 22 and Lk. 8. 14; ctr. Mk. 4. 18. This is similar to the instance immediately above.

13. 23 and Lk. 8. 15; ctr. Mk. 4. 20. This is similar to the two instances immediately above.

13. 57 and Mk. 6. 4 (οὐκ ἔστιν προφήτης); ctr. Lk. 4. 24 (οὐδεὶς προφήτης). See Beyer, pp. 111 fn., 131.

15. 5 ('whoever should say to his father'); ctr. Mk. 7. 11 ('if a man should say').

15. 11 ('what comes out..., this defiles'); ctr. Mk. 7. 15 ('the things which come out are the things which defile').

18. 8, 9 (καλόν σοί ἐστιν εἰσελθεῖν); ctr. Mk. 9. 43, 47 (καλόν σέ ἐστιν εἰσελθεῖν). See Beyer, p. 28 fn.

20. 23; ctr. Mk. 10. 40 'to sit...(+this) is not mine to give'.

21. 2 and Mk. 11. 2 ('go...and you will find'); ctr. Lk. 19. 30 ('go...in which you will find'). See Beyer, p. 254.

24. 22 ('except those days were shortened'); ctr. Mk. 13. 20 ('except the Lord shortened the days').

24. 26 ('If therefore they say to you, "Behold, he is in the desert", do not go out. "Behold in the private rooms", do not believe'); ctr. Lk. 17. 23 ('And they will say to you, "Behold here! behold there!" Do not go out nor follow'). See Beyer, p. 97.

25. 29*b* ('but of the one not having, also what he has will be taken away from him'); ctr. Lk. 19. 26 ('from the one not having, also that which he has will be taken away'). See Beyer, p. 210 fn. 1.
26. 23; ctr. Mk. 14. 20 'the one dipping + this one will betray me'.
26. 55 and Mk. 14. 49 ('I sat (Mk.: I was) in the temple teaching, and you did not seize me'); ctr. Lk. 22. 53 ('while I was in the temple, you did not stretch forth your hands against me'). See Beyer, p. 279.
27. 42 ('let him come down and we will believe'); ctr. Mk. 15. 32 ('let him come down in order that we may see and believe'). See Beyer, p. 253.

Mark

2. 7 ('except one, God'); ctr. Lk. 5. 21 ('except God alone').
4. 12 ('seeing they may see and not see', etc.); ctr. Mt. 13. 13 and Lk. 8. 10 ('seeing they do not see'). See Beyer, p. 266.
4. 22 ('for nothing is hid, except that it may be made manifest', etc.); ctr. Mt. 10. 26 and Lk. 8. 17 ('for nothing is hid which shall not be made manifest', etc.). See Beyer, p. 131.
5. 28 ('if I might touch'); ctr. Mt. 9. 21 ('if only I might touch'). See Beyer, p. 126 fn. 4.
7. 20 ('that which comes out...that defiles'); ctr. Mt. 15. 18 ('the things coming out of the stomach come out of the heart, and these defile').
8. 36 ('to gain the whole world and forfeit'); ctr. Mt. 16. 26 ('gain but forfeit') and Lk. 9. 25 ('gain but lose or forfeit'). See Beyer, pp. 270f.
8. 38 ('the Son of man will be ashamed of him'); ctr. Lk. 9. 26 ('this one the Son of man will be ashamed of'). See Beyer, pp. 170, 176.
9. 9 ('except when the Son of man rises'); ctr. Mt. 17. 9 ('until the Son of man rises'). See Beyer, pp. 133 f.
11. 13 ('except leaves'); ctr. Mt. 21. 19 ('except leaves alone').
11. 23 (ὃς ἂν εἴπῃ); ctr. Mt. 21. 21 (κἂν...εἴπητε). See Beyer, pp. 227, 267.
11. 23 (ἔσται αὐτῷ); ctr. Mt. 21. 21 (γενήσεται). See Beyer, p. 176.
11. 24 ('and it will be to you'); ctr. Mt. 21. 22 ('you shall receive'). See Beyer, p. 254.
11. 29 ('answer me, and I shall tell you'); ctr. Mt. 21. 24 ('if you tell me, I shall tell you') and Lk. 20. 3 ('tell me'). See Beyer, p. 254.
11. 32 ('but we say'); ctr. Mt. 21. 26 and Lk. 20. 6 ('if we say').
12. 2 and Lk. 20. 10 (λάβη ἀπὸ τῶν καρπῶν); ctr. Mt. 21. 34 (λαβεῖν τοὺς καρπούς).
12. 7 ('and ours will be the inheritance'); ctr. Mt. 21. 38 ('and we shall have his inheritance') and Lk. 20. 14 ('in order that ours may be the inheritance').
12. 19 ('if the brother of anyone should die and leave a wife and not leave a child'); ctr. Mt. 22. 24 ('if anyone should die not having children') and Lk. 20. 28 ('if the brother of anyone should die having a wife'). See Beyer, p. 267.

13. 11 ('whatever is given to you, this say'); ctr. Mt. 10. 19 ('what you shall say will be given to you').

13. 32 ('except the Father'); ctr. Mt. 24. 36 ('except the Father alone'). See Beyer, p. 126.

14. 13 ('go into the city and a man will meet you'); ctr. Mt. 26. 18 ('go into the city') and Lk. 22. 10 ('while you are going into the city, a man will meet you'). See Beyer, p. 254.

Luke

6. 30 ('to everyone asking'); ctr. Mt. 5. 42 ('to the one asking'). See Beyer, p. 212.

6. 37 ('and you will not be judged'); ctr. Mt. 7. 1 ('in order that you may not be judged'). See Beyer, p. 254.

7. 7*b* ('but say the word'); ctr. Mt. 8. 8 ('but only say the word'). See Beyer, p. 126 fn. 4.

9. 13 ('there are not to us here'); ctr. Mt. 14. 17 ('we do not have here').

9. 24; ctr. Mt. 16. 25 and Mk. 8. 35 '(+this one) will save it'. See Beyer, pp. 172 f., who thinks the casus pendens probably is not Semitic.

14. 5 ('it falls'); ctr. Mt. 12. 11 ('if it falls'). See Beyer, p. 281.

15. 4 ('which man from among you'); ctr. Mt. 18. 12 ('if it happened to which man'). See Beyer, p. 287.

19. 29 ('and it happened as he drew near'); ctr. Mt. 21. 1 and Mk. 11. 1 ('and when they drew near'). See Beyer, p. 260.

20. 11 (καὶ προσέθετο ἕτερον πέμψαι); ctr. Mt. 21. 36 and Mk. 12. 4 ((καὶ) πάλιν ἀπέστειλεν).

20. 12 ('and he added a third time to send'); ctr. Mk. 12. 4 ('and he sent another').

21. 6 ('these things which you see..., stone shall not be left'); ctr. Mt. 24. 2 ('do you not see all these things? Stone shall not be left') and similarly Mk. 13. 2.

Summary

Mt. more Semitic than Mk. 14 times.	Mt:Mk::14:18
Mt. more Semitic than Lk. 14 times.	Mt:Lk::14:11
Mk. more Semitic than Mt. 18 times.	Mk:Lk::13:8
Mk. more Semitic than Lk. 13 times.	
Lk. more Semitic than Mt. 11 times.	
Lk. more Semitic than Mk. 8 times.	

We may summarize these lists as follows:

1 and 2. It comes as no surprise to see that Mark is a great deal more paratactic than Matthew and Luke. The only question is what significance this fact has. Black would argue that it

at least indicates proximity to a Semitic source. While granting that parataxis is characteristic of non-literary Greek, he argues that 'the high proportion, nevertheless, of instances of parataxis in the Gospels and Acts cannot be set down as unliterary Greek only; Aramaic influence must have been a contributory factor'.[1]

This argument presumably would apply most persuasively of all to Mark, since there the degree of parataxis is at its height. We should recall, however, that the Protev. Jms. has a high degree of parataxis. De Strycker points out that in the narrative sections of Protev. Jms. there is an 'extreme poverty of choice of particles'. Altogether there are only four, of which two are barely represented. Besides a great number of instances of *kai* and fewer of *de*, there are only three instances of *gar* and three of *alla*. A slightly better choice appears in the discourse sections, but the improvement is not great.[2] De Strycker clearly does not regard the parataxis of the Protev. Jms. as indicating a Semitic source. 'Les sections narratives du *Protévangile* sont écrites dans un "style καί" populaire plus prononcé encore que celui des Évangiles, Marc y compris.'[3]

We can hardly think, then, that parataxis can really serve to prove what Black claims for it. But will the argument stand that Mark's parataxis proves or helps to prove that Gospel prior to Matthew and Luke? The argument would be that Matthew and Luke avoided parataxis in order to improve the Greek of the Gospel narrative. There can be little doubt that Matthew, and more especially Luke, did not favor the overuse of *kai*. But there can be just as little doubt that Mark did favor its use, though not so much as did the author of the Protev. Jms. The argument, in other words, cuts both ways. It could as well be argued that Mark changed Matthew to the *kai* style, in order to agree with his own proclivities, as that Matthew and Luke made the reverse change. We have already seen something of this in the manuscript tradition, where Matthew's Greek is actually made slightly more paratactic, while Mark's is made less paratactic. We seem to be dealing here with personal preferences rather than a decisive proof of relative antiquity. If we know on other grounds that Matthew and Luke used Mark,

[1] *An Aramaic approach*, p. 51.   [2] De Strycker, *op. cit.* pp. 293–5.
[3] *Ibid.* pp. 293 f.

we must conclude that they changed his Greek in order to avoid parataxis. But the mere fact of their being less paratactic than Mark does not prove that they are later.

3. Asyndeton, as our lists show, is more common in Mark than in Matthew and Luke. Asyndeton is typical of neither Greek nor Hebrew, but is, as Black says, 'highly characteristic of Aramaic'.[1] Asyndeton is also characteristic of Latin, although this is not noted by Aramaic scholars. According to Black, there are two possible explanations of asyndeton in the Gospels. Referring especially to Mark, he says that it could either be

that Mark wrote Jewish Greek as deeply influenced in this respect as the Greek of the *Shepherd of Hermas*, or else that he is translating Aramaic sources or employing such translations. It is probable that he did both: where Mark is reporting the Words of Jesus, not as single isolated sayings but in a group of collected sayings, he is most probably incorporating in his Gospel the translation Greek of a sayings-tradition: Mk. 13. 6–9, where asyndeton occurs no less than 4 times in 7 connected sentences, is an instance of translation Greek.[2]

But it is very doubtful that this amount of asyndeton is sufficient to prove what Professor Black claims for it. In the Act. Pil. 5. 2 and 14. 2, as may be seen in the addendum to category 3 above, a higher degree of asyndeton is to be found than occurs anywhere in Mark. Nevertheless, we surely cannot think that these verses in Act. Pil. are translated from a primitive Aramaic sayings source. If this 'Aramaism' can appear in such abundance in an apocryphal document of the fifth century, can it still be used to prove anything about the antiquity of tradition?

Actually, we are here forced back to the question of what an Aramaism is. The asyndeton in Act. Pil. may be caused by Latin influence. But Latin influence could also be responsible for the frequent asyndeton in the Shepherd of Hermas, which was most likely written in Rome.[3] And if this be so, can Latin

---

[1] *An Aramaic approach*[2], p. 38 (3rd ed. p. 56).

[2] *Ibid.* p. 42 (3rd ed. p. 60). Black also notes that the same choice applies to John, where asyndeton is also high.

[3] The primary evidence for the Roman origin of Hermas is the statement to that effect in the Muratorian fragment, lines 73 ff. The text is conveniently reprinted in A. Souter, *The Text and Canon of the New Testament*, revised by C. S. C. Williams (London, 1960), pp. 191 ff. R. M. Grant (*The Apostolic Fathers*, vol. 1, New York, 1964, p. 85) states that 'there is no question about the Roman origin of Hermas'.

influence on Mark be altogether ruled out, especially when other Latinisms appear in that Gospel?[1]

Couchoud has argued that Mark was written in Latin.[2] Not all of his evidence is of equal relevance, however. The first portion of his study[3] is devoted to showing that the earliest Latin MSS (*k* and *e*) make better sense at certain points than do the earlier Greek MSS (he uses B, D, and W). This is interesting, but does not bear on the original language of the Gospel. He has better evidence, however. On pp. 177–83 he shows that many variants in the Greek manuscripts could be understood as divergent translations of the same Latin. Aramaic scholars use this same type of evidence for proving the Aramaic background of the Gospels, but their evidence seems no more striking than Couchoud's. Especially strong is the section on 'literalisms' (pp. 182 f.). Some Greek manuscripts avoid the literalism which others accept. More evidence for variant Greek translations from Latin is given on pp. 186–90. Couchoud does not deal, unfortunately, with syntax, and his evidence cannot be considered conclusive; nevertheless, it should not be overlooked. It may be taken as a methodological warning: if the same methodology yields evidence both for an Aramaic and a Latin background, the method itself may be at fault.

It is not our purpose here to prove Latin influence on Mark's grammar, but only to show that proofs for antiquity which are based on grammatical and syntactical considerations are often problematical. Those who would argue that, while 'Aramaisms' in the Act. Pil. do not indicate antiquity, they do so in Mark because of the other evidence of primitiveness in Mark are engaging in the very circular argument which we are trying to avoid. The point of this study is to ascertain what elements, if any, of themselves indicate antiquity. So far, it appears that asyndeton is not one of them.

Before leaving asyndeton, however, we may observe that most of the asyndeton in Mark is in sayings material, while most of the asyndeton in Matthew is in narrative material. The few cases in which Luke alone has asyndeton are almost altogether in sayings material.[4] The significance of this is somewhat

---

[1] See V. Taylor, *The Gospel according to St Mark*, p. 45.
[2] P. L. Couchoud, 'L'Évangile de Marc a-t-il été écrit en Latin?' *Revue de l'Histoire des Religions*, XCIV (1926), 161–92.
[3] Pp. 161–73.
[4] De Strycker (*op. cit.* pp. 295 f.) notes that in the Protev. Jms. asyndeton is rare in narrative but more frequent in discourse.

difficult to assess. Hawkins was of the view that the type of asyndeton which appears in Matthew does not 'convey the impression of abruptness' which the asyndeton in Mark does.[1] Black, on the other hand, identified Matthew's use of asyndeton with a verb of saying in the present tense as a genuine Aramaism.[2] It is doubtful if much can be made of the distinction between asyndeton in narrative and in sayings material. Matthew, after all, has several instances of asyndeton in sayings material which he does not share with Mark or Luke.[3]

4. Although the use of the historic present in narrative has been taken as reflecting the Aramaic participle,[4] modern Aramaic scholars seem not to consider it an Aramaism, and it is not included in their discussions. Even so, however, the preponderance of the historic present in Mark is still held to prove the priority of that Gospel to Matthew and Luke. Thus Howard writes that 'it is evident that both Matthew and Luke regarded [the historic present] as a vulgarism to be removed when possible'.[5] Howard continues by noting that in the classical age the historic present 'was common to the literary style and to vernacular, whereas in Hellenistic it was increasingly regarded as vernacular'.[6] The argument here is that Mark wrote in the vernacular, but Matthew and Luke wished to achieve a more elevated style. This is perhaps the conclusion that should be drawn if it were already established on some other ground that Matthew and Luke used Mark, but the above argument does not serve to prove that that was the case. It is not intrinsically more likely that Matthew and Luke avoided the vernacular than that Mark courted it. Cadbury has noted that Josephus frequently changed a past tense in I Macc. to a historic present.[7] The usage seems to be entirely one of personal preference. That

[1] Hawkins, *op. cit.* p. 138. [2] *An Aramaic approach*[2], p. 39 (3rd ed. p. 57).
[3] For example, Mt. 5. 13, 14; 6. 34c.
[4] W. C. Allen, 'The original language of the Gospel according to St Mark', *The Expositor*, 6th Series, I (1900), 436 ff.; 'The Aramaic element in St Mark', *Exp. Times*, XII (1901), 328–30; C. F. Burney, *The Aramaic origin of the Fourth Gospel*, pp. 87 ff. See also the discussion in Howard, *op. cit.* pp. 456 f.
[5] Howard, *op. cit.* p. 456. In the opinion of Hawkins (*op. cit.* p. 143), Matthew and Luke, in changing the historic present to another tense, 'were only preferring a more usual to a less usual mode of expression'. G. D. Kilpatrick, 'The Greek New Testament text of today', p. 198, is of a similar opinion.
[6] Howard, *op. cit.* p. 456.
[7] *The making of Luke-Acts*, p. 174.

this is the case is indicated by Dalman. In discussing whether the historic present is a Semitism, he comments that

the secular Greek also allows the use of a present in historical narrative, and that not only in more extended passages for the sake of vivid presentation, but also in detached instances throughout the context of a narrative. Mark's fondness for the present tense is an individual trait, like his constant use of εὐθέως.[1]

Dalman's view seems the safest one to take.

5. There is little to be said about the use of *heis* for *tis*. This usage may perhaps stand as representative of other instances of Semitisms of vocabulary usage which have not been included in this study because of a lack of evidence. The manuscript evidence shows that this kind of Semitism was not offensive to Greek writers, and there is no reason to think that its use or disuse in the Synoptics indicates anything about either the antiquity of tradition or the relative order of our Gospels.

6. In the category of miscellaneous Semitic constructions Mark comes out slightly ahead of Matthew and Luke, while Matthew is somewhat more Semitic than Luke. It should be remembered that the figures at the end of category 6' do not show the total number of Semitisms in each of the Gospels, but the number of times that one Gospel has a Semitism not in each of the others, when the material in the two is in basic agreement. In parallel material, Mark has more Semitisms than do Matthew and Luke. It thus might be argued that Matthew and Luke wished to improve Mark's Semitic style. The recent study by Klaus Beyer makes this conclusion unlikely, however. Beyer has traced certain constructions throughout the Gospels, distinguishing between relatively more Semitic and relatively more Greek ways of saying the same thing. He summarizes his results in a table showing the percentage of the incidence of Semitic constructions relative to Greek constructions in each book of the New Testament.[2] The larger the figure is, the greater is the incidence of Semitic constructions relative to Greek. In Matthew as a whole, the percentage is 329·0, the highest of all the books in the New Testament; in Luke the percentage is 308·0; in Mark it is 185·2. It is thus very difficult to argue that Matthew and Luke had the redactional tendency of avoiding

---

[1] *The words of Jesus*, p. 36.　　　[2] Beyer, *op. cit.* p. 298.

Semitisms. One would have to argue that they had the redactional tendency of avoiding Semitisms in Mark, while freely accepting them from other sources and perhaps even creating several of their own in material which they composed. Such a view is unacceptable. If Matthew and Luke in their entirety are more Semitic than Mark, we cannot think that they can be shown to be later than Mark because they are somewhat less Semitic in those sections where their material parallels his.

Although the conclusion that Semitic syntax and grammar do not necesarily prove a tradition to be either relatively or absolutely early doubtless goes against the current of a great deal of modern scholarship, this chapter offers no other surprises. As everyone has always known, Mark is richer in parataxis, asyndeton, and the use of the historic present than Matthew and Luke. On the whole, in the material common to two or more of our Gospels, other Semitic constructions are also somewhat more common in Mark than in Matthew and Luke. It certainly suited Mark's redactional style to write vernacular Greek more than it did the style of Matthew and Luke, but we cannot thereby prove Mark to be the earliest of the Gospels.[1]

---

[1] On Mark's Greek as representative of the spoken Greek of the lower classes, see Black, 'Second Thoughts', p. 23.

CHAPTER V

DIRECT DISCOURSE AND CONFLATION

This chapter will deal with two somewhat different categories which may be used in ascertaining the relative antiquity of tradition. Doubtless many other items could have been included in a chapter devoted to miscellany. One might think, for example, of the supposed tendency of the tradition to become more miraculous or more 'pious', or perhaps to develop a 'higher' Christology. As a matter of fact, material was collected on these and some ten other possible criteria. Since most of these proved indecisive, however, it was decided, in the interest of reasonable brevity, to eliminate all but two from discussion. Thus this chapter deals only with two items selected from a total of fifteen. One item is selected because it appears usable for establishing relative antiquity, the other because— contrary to expectations—it does not.

THE USE OF DIRECT DISCOURSE

Introduction

It was the opinion of Bultmann that speeches which had been indirectly reported came to be reported directly.[1]

There appears in the Tradition a further tendency to produce new sayings of the person engaged, in part as a continuation and expansion of sayings already there, in part as a transposition of an earlier report into direct speech. Of course it is not possible to speak of a natural law here; it also happens that a saying in direct speech is put into indirect, but the opposite tendency is remarkable everywhere.[2]

After considering examples from the Synoptics (which are included in the lists which follow), he is able to reach a stronger conclusion: 'So it is in fact possible to speak of a certain regularity and accordingly to judge critical cases in terms of

[1] See *Die Erforschung*, p. 23 (E.T. p. 34).
[2] *Die Geschichte*, p. 340 (E.T. p. 312).

it.'[1] The general tendency is for indirect speech to be made into direct speech.

Vincent Taylor, on the basis of his experiments with oral narration, came to the opposite conclusion. 'Direct speech is replaced by indirect, though not entirely.'[2] As we shall see, this is one instance in which Bultmann's view, rather than Taylor's, is consistent with the two-document hypothesis.

Before presenting our evidence on this matter, we may briefly point out that direct speech was widely employed in koine Greek. Thus Nigel Turner observes that

the Koine found it much more difficult than the classical Greek and Latin languages to sustain indirect speech for very long, and in the New Testament direct speech is preferred in narrative wherever possible, especially in Mark and John (but not so much in Luke, and even less in Matthew).[3]

Blass and Debrunner concur that the New Testament writers could not maintain indirect discourse and note that the frequency of direct discourse introduced by *hoti* in Mark is 'due to the fact that it is non-literary'.[4] Although it has not, to my knowledge, been done, one could conceivably attribute frequency of direct discourse to Semitic influence, since Hebrew and Aramaic avoided indirect speech. It is doubtless better, however, with the grammarians above, to think only of unsophisticated Greek. Indirect discourse is nearly always uncommon in simple writing.

We may now examine the post-canonical tradition to see where the balance of probability lies in this regard.

[1] *Ibid.* p. 342 (E.T. p. 313). [2] *Formation*, p. 208.

[3] *Grammar of New Testament Greek*, III, pp. 325–6. Abbreviations are removed. For the statement that Matthew and Luke use indirect speech more than Mark and John, Turner refers to C. H. Turner, 'Marcan usage', *J.T.S.* XXVIII (1927), 9–30. C. H. Turner dealt, however, only with the use of *hoti recitativum*, not with direct and indirect discourse as such.

[4] F. Blass and A. Debrunner, *A Greek grammar of the New Testament and other early Christian literature*, translated and edited by R. W. Funk (Cambridge, 1961), p. 247, section 470 (1).

THE EVIDENCE FROM THE POST-CANONICAL TRADITION

The use of direct discourse; changes to first person from second or third

THE TEXTUAL TRADITION

Matthew

9. 21   1It(*c*) adds Mark 5. 29–33 to Mt. 9. 21. Instead of Mark's 'knowing power had gone out of him', however, *c* has Luke's 'for I knew
power had gone out of me' (Lk. 8. 46).

Mark

14. 35   1Gr 1Cop have 'from me' for 'from him'.
16. 7   D W 1Sy 1It have 'I go before' for 'he goes before'.
16. 7   D 1It Eugip have 'you will see me' for 'you will see him'.
16. 7   D 2Gr 3It have 'just as I said' for 'just as he said'.

THE APOCRYPHAL AND PATRISTIC TRADITIONS

Gosp. Heb. Origen *In Io.* 2. 6 (see Appendix v. 5). The story of the carrying
away to the Mount (cf. Mt. 4. 1, 8) is told in the first person.

Gosp. Ebion. Epiph. Haer. 30. 13. 2f. (de Santos, p. 50; H.-S. p. 156). The
call of the Twelve is narrated in the first person by Jesus, and the
introduction is told in the first person, as if by a disciple.

Protev. Jms. 14. 1; cf. Mt. 1. 19. Jms.: 'I will put her away secretly from
me.'

Arundel Latin Inf. Gosp. 90. The magi tell their story in the first person,
considerably expanded.

Act. Pil. Several of Jesus' miracles are briefly narrated in the first person
by the object of his mercy, *viz*: (1) 6. 1 = Mk. 2. 1 ff., cf. Jn. 5. 1 ff.;
(2) 6. 2 = Mk. 10. 46 ff.; (3) 6. 2 includes two other miracles, the
Synoptic reference of which is not clear; (4) 7. 1 = Mk. 5. 25 ff. In all
cases, verbatim agreement is scant.

Act. Pil. 9. 1; cf. Mt. 27. 15 par. The custom of releasing a prisoner is told
by Pilate in the first person.

Act. Pil. 13. 1. The events of Mt. 28. 2–4 are told in the first person by some
of the guard.

Act. Pil. 14. 1. Jesus' speech in Mark 16. 15–18 is told in the first person by
three named men.

Act. Pil. 18. 2. John the Baptist narrates his baptism of Christ in the first
person.

Act. Pil. 26. One of the thieves crucified with Christ tells the story in the first
person. There is only a little verbatim agreement with Lk. 23. 43.

Jos. Arim. 2. 3; cf. Mt. 26. 15 parr. The promise to give Judas money is given in the first person.

Protev. Jms. 21. 2 has 'saying, "where is it written concerning the Christ, where he shall be born?"' for Mt. 2. 4, 'he inquired from them where the Christ would be born'.

Protev. Jms. 22. 1; cf. Mt. 2. 16. The order to kill children is given as a direct command. (So Tischendorf, following A E. The other MSS of the Protev. are conformed in various ways to Mt.)

Pseud. Matt. Lat. 15. 3 has 'and coming up she adored the child, saying, "In Him is the redemption of the world"' for Lk. 2. 38, 'and coming up at that very hour, she gave thanks to God and spoke of him to all who were looking for the redemption of Jerusalem'.

This category is remarkable in that it is the only one we study in which all the evidence collected points in one direction. I have not found a single instance in the post-canonical tradition in which a saying in direct discourse was changed to indirect discourse, but several in which the reverse change took place. The tendency to use direct speech is especially strong in the Apocryphal Gospels, as the lists show. It will be a matter of considerable interest to see how the balance between direct and indirect speech lies in the Synoptic Gospels.

THE EVIDENCE FROM THE SYNOPTIC GOSPELS

Before presenting the material, we may first note that the antecedent expectation would be that Mark would have more direct speech than Matthew and Luke. We have already seen that Mark's frequent use of direct speech is remarked by Nigel Turner and Blass-Debrunner. They refer especially, however, to the use of *hoti recitativum*, rather than to direct speech in general. The use of *hoti* to introduce direct speech is doubtless most frequent in Mark among the Synoptics, but the question remains, whether Mark has direct speech where Matthew and Luke do not.[1]

---

[1] Bultmann, *Die Geschichte*, pp. 340–1 (E.T. pp. 312–13), gives a list of most of the examples in which Matthew and Luke have direct discourse where Mark has indirect discourse, but only three instances of Mark's use of direct discourse where Matthew or Luke has indirect. We may once again note that such selective listing is misleading. Jeremias, *The eucharistic words of Jesus* (Oxford, 1955), p. 113, lists eleven passages in which Matthew has direct discourse in contrast to Mark, and three in which Mark has direct discourse in contrast to Matthew. In the revised edition (London, 1966), p. 171 n. 2, a slightly different list is given. The figures are now 12 and 3.

The use of direct discourse and the first person in one Gospel where they do not appear in another

Matthew

3. 2; ctr. Mk. 1. 4 and Lk. 3. 3. John's preaching is given in direct discourse in Matthew.

6. 31 ('what shall we eat' etc.); ctr. Lk. 12. 29 ('what you shall eat' etc.).

8. 6; ctr. Lk. 7. 2. The report about the centurion's servant is given in direct speech in Mt., but there is no verbatim agreement with the report in Luke.

8. 31 and Mk. 5. 12; ctr. Lk. 8. 32. The plea of the demons is in direct speech in Mt. and Mk.

8. 32 ('and he said to them, "Go"'); ctr. Mk. 5. 13 and Lk. 8. 32 ('and he permitted them').

9. 18 and Mk. 5. 23; ctr. Lk. 8. 42 'My daughter has died' etc.

10. 9 f. and Lk. 9. 3; ctr. Mk. 6. 8. The instructions on what the disciples should take on their journey are in direct discourse in Mt. and Lk., but Mk. also has direct discourse beginning in 6. 9*b*.

12. 10; ctr. Mk. 3. 2 and Lk. 6. 7 'Is it lawful to heal on the Sabbath?'

13. 10; ctr. Mk. 4. 10 and Lk. 8. 9 'Why do you speak to them in parables?'

14. 2 and Mk. 6. 14; ctr. Lk. 9. 7 'John the Baptist has been raised' etc.

15. 15; ctr. Mk. 7. 17 'Explain the parable to us'.

15. 22; ctr. Mk. 7. 25 'Have mercy on me...my daughter is possessed by a demon'. But the verbatim agreement is slight.

15. 25 ('saying, "Lord, help me"'); ctr. Mk. 7. 26 ('she asked him that he would cast out' etc.). There is no verbatim agreement.

17. 9; ctr. Mk. 9. 9 'Tell no one' etc.

18. 1 (the disciples say, 'Who is greatest in the kingdom of heaven') and Mk. 9. 33 (Jesus asks 'What were you discussing in the road'); ctr. Lk. 9. 46 ('now an argument arose among them, which was the greatest of them').

21. 27 and Mk. 11. 33; ctr. Lk. 20. 7 'We do not know'.

21. 33 ('hear another parable'); ctr. Mk. 12. 1 ('he began to speak in parables') and Lk. 20. 9, similarly.

26. 2; ctr. Mk. 14. 1 and Lk. 22. 1 'You know that after two days is the Passover'.

26. 15; ctr. Mk. 14. 10 and Lk. 22. 4 'What do you want to give me, and I shall hand him over to you'. Perhaps Semitic *kai*.

26. 27 ('all of you drink of it'); ctr. Mk. 14. 23 ('they all drank of it'). Mk. begins direct discourse in vs. 24.

26. 66; ctr. Mk. 14. 64 'He is guilty of death'.

27. 23 ('let him be crucified') and Mk. 15. 14 ('crucify him'); ctr. Lk. 23. 23 ('that he should be crucified').

Mark

4. 35 and Lk. 8. 22; ctr. Mt. 8. 18 'Let us go across to the other side'.

4. 39 ('"Peace! be still"'); ctr. Mt. 8. 26 and Lk. 8. 24 ('he rebuked the wind', etc.).

5. 8; ctr. Lk. 8. 29 'Unclean spirit, depart' etc.

6. 15; ctr. Lk. 9. 8 'It is Elijah', 'it is a prophet'.

6. 23; ctr. Mt. 14. 7 'whatever you ask me' etc.

10. 35 ('Teacher, we want you to do for us whatever we ask you'); ctr. Mt. 20. 20 ('She asked something from him').

10. 49 ('Jesus said, "Call him"'); ctr. Mt. 20. 32 ('Jesus called them') and Lk. 18. 40 ('Jesus commanded him').

11. 3 ('If anyone should ask you, "Why are you doing this?", say, "The Lord has need"', etc.) and similarly Lk. 19. 31; ctr. Mt. 21. 3 ('If anyone says anything to you, you shall say, "The Lord has need"', etc.).

13. 1; ctr. Mt. 24. 1 and Lk. 21. 5 'Teacher, see what stones and what buildings'.

Luke

8. 46; ctr. Mk. 5. 30 'I know power has gone out from me'.

9. 14; ctr. Mt. 14. 19 and Mk. 6. 39 'Make them sit down in companies', etc.

15. 6; ctr. Mt. 18. 13 'Rejoice with me, for I have found my sheep which was lost'.

19. 34; ctr. Mk. 11. 6 (cf. Mt. 21. 6) 'The Lord has need of it'.

20. 13; ctr. Mt. 21. 37 and Mk. 12. 6 'What shall I do? I will send my beloved son'.

22. 58 ('"Man, I am not"'); ctr. Mk. 14. 70 ('he again denied'). See also Mt. 26. 71, Speech Added.

Summary

Matthew has direct speech, Mark indirect 15 times.	Mt:Mk::14:7
Matthew has direct speech, Luke indirect 14 times.	Mt:Lk::15:5
Mark has direct speech, Matthew indirect 7 times.	Mk:Lk::11:6
Mark has direct speech, Luke indirect 11 times.	
Luke has direct speech, Matthew indirect 5 times.	
Luke has direct speech, Mark indirect 6 times.	

If the tendency of the tradition was to substitute direct speech for indirect, then it appears that the order of the Gospels was Luke, Mark, Matthew. Cadbury, however, suggests that Luke had the editorial tendency of turning direct discourse into indirect. He finds the same tendency in Josephus' use of I Macc.[1] In this case it would have to be argued that Luke's

[1] *The making of Luke-Acts*, p. 171.

lack of direct discourse is only one more example of his avoidance of the vernacular. It is, then, somewhat surprising that Matthew and Luke stand at opposite poles on this matter, since ordinarily it is said that Matthew shares the tendency to avoid Mark's vernacularisms.[1] In this instance the First Gospel is closer to popular speech than the Second. We have earlier seen reason to question whether Matthew and Luke followed the same editorial policy, and this is further evidence that they did not. Whatever one may conclude about the relation of Matthew and Luke to Mark, it is clear that in at least one respect Matthew's Gospel stood nearer to popular speech than Luke's, whose literary abilities here come to light.

CONFLATION

Introduction

The category of conflation differs from the other categories with which we have dealt in that it cannot be taken to be a growing tendency. Thus one cannot look here, as we have elsewhere, for the balance of probability. Conflation may be defined as the weaving together of two or more separate items into one item containing parts of each. If *one* instance of conflation can be *proved*, then there is no longer any doubt about the place of the conflator: his work must be later than the works he conflates. Conflation was a common practice in the ancient world, and there is no shortage of examples of it in the Christian tradition.[2] A study of these allows us to differentiate various kinds of conflation, the most important of which may be briefly described.

1. If a conflator has two or more accounts which basically agree with each other, but which exhibit some differences, he may use what is common to his sources as well as some of the matter peculiar to each. His account will thus show some agreement with both of his sources together and some with each of them separately. An example of this type of conflation may be seen in such passages as Protev. Jms. 11. 3 and Just. Apol. 1. 19. 7.

---

[1] So, for example, Streeter, *op. cit.* p. 162.
[2] For some examples, see Protev. Jms. 11. 3; Theoph. III. 14; II Clem. 5. 4; Athen. 11. 1, 12. 3; Justin, Apol. 1. 33. 5, 1. 19. 7, 1. 15. 9; Dial. 133. 6.

2. If a conflator has two or more alternative accounts which do not agree with each other, he may simply quote one and then the other. Thus the Gospel of the Ebionites has the voice at Jesus' baptism speak three times. Once it says 'you are my beloved son, in you I am well pleased' (Mk. 1. 11), and then 'I have begotten you today' (Lk. 3. 22, according to D It Ju (Cl) Or), and finally 'this is my beloved son in whom I am well pleased' (Mt. 3. 17).[1] The conflator could, of course, simply choose one or the other alternative, but in this case he would no longer be conflating.

3. A conflator may construct a new narrative or speech by plucking phrases from here and there in his sources. In this case he can 'conflate' with only one source before him. An example of this type of conflation may be seen in Just. Dial. 17. 3–4; see Appendix v. 23.[2]

4. A conflator faced by synonyms in his sources may utilize them both. This is the same type of conflation as that described in number 2, but is limited to words and phrases. An example may be found in the textual apparatus to Mt. 5. 44. Matthew reads: 'pray for those who persecute you'; the Lukan parallel (6. 28) reads: 'pray for those who abuse you.' (D) L W De Th Pi Si Ko and other manuscripts read: 'pray for those who abuse (you) and persecute you.' Several Latin manuscripts read: 'pray for those who persecute and abuse you.'

It can be shown that writers did conflate in these and other ways. The proof is especially easy if one already knows that a certain writer had access to certain sources and if the modern student has access to both the conflator's work and his sources. If it be in doubt, however, whether a writer actually did have access to certain other documents, or if one of the documents he used is no longer available, the hypothesis that conflation has taken place may be made, but it is difficult to prove. Thus it has been argued that Matthew conflated Q and Mark.[3] This is conceivable, but difficult to prove, since Q is not available for comparison. It has also been suggested that Mark conflated

---

[1] See de Santos, *op. cit.* p. 51, and Hennecke-Schneemelcher, *op. cit.* p. 157.

[2] For further discussion and some bibliography, see my 'Literary dependence in Colossians', *J.B.L.* LXXXV (1966), 28 ff.

[3] See Streeter, *op. cit.* pp. 246 ff.

Luke and Matthew.[1] This is also conceivable, but those who think Mark preceded Matthew and Luke can explain the apparent instances of conflation in another way. The difficulty may be easily illustrated. If one document has 'A', another 'B', and another 'AB', the explanation comes readily to mind that the third conflated the first two. But it is also conceivable that the first and second used the third, each one copying a portion. The difficulty, then, is how to distinguish between apparent conflation and true conflation. There are no certain tests to distinguish true from apparent conflation, and frequently the decision as to whether one is dealing with true or apparent conflation is made on the basis of a prior view of the relationship among several documents. It may be argued in particular circumstances, however, that conflation is more or less likely in certain passages in which the question arises. At certain points, for example, it may be thought that an apparent conflation would really have been too difficult for an author to make,[2] so that some other explanation becomes more likely. Conversely, it could be argued that the alternative to conflation (independent use of one document by two or more documents, each of which uses a portion) requires too great a stretch of the imagination. An example may make this clear. If one document has 'ABCDE', another 'ACE', and another 'BD', it may be argued that conflation is the more likely explanation, since two writers probably would not independently have decided to choose alternating phrases from their source. It is more likely that the first document used the other two, choosing a phrase from one, then from the other, and so forth. The total number of apparent conflations in a document must also be considered, to see if the hypothesis of conflation consistently explains the phenomena.

It will now be helpful to look at instances of conflation and apparent conflation which we have collected from the post-canonical tradition. These lists are not necessarily complete, but represent a fairly full collection of instances of possible conflation in the post-canonical tradition. Many of the instances

[1] W. R. Farmer, op. cit., calls this the 'Griesbach hypothesis' after J. J. Griesbach, and gives the history of the theory. Other early scholars who advanced this view were W. M. L. DeWette and F. Bleek. Farmer himself believes this view to be correct. See pp. 7 ff., 233 ff. and frequently.
[2] See the quotation from Abbott, below, pp. 269 f.

are genuine examples of conflation. Others, however, are obviously only apparent conflation. These are instances in which the original text has the longer reading, while various manuscripts have portions of it. Such cases are marked with an asterisk. Other instances are in doubt. Without knowing more about the interrelationships of manuscripts, we cannot say whether what appears to be conflation is actually conflation or only happenstance.

THE EVIDENCE FROM THE POST-CANONICAL TRADITION

THE TEXTUAL TRADITION

Matthew

2. 14   To 'rising up', *a* adds 'from sleep'; *q* Prisc add 'Joseph'; *c* adds 'Joseph from sleep'.

5. 44   2Gr Clem Lucif add 'Bless the ones cursing you'; 7It 1Vg Cass add 'do good to those who hate you'; D L W De Th Pi Si Ko Fam 13 7+Gr 4It Vg 3Sy 1Cop Aeth Arm Tat add both phrases. (But they are from Luke 6. 27, 28.)

* 8. 17   1Sy has only 'Isaiah'; 1Gr only 'the Prophet'; the text reads both.

8. 20   The text has 'The birds...(have) nests'; 1It has 'The birds... (have) where they rest'; 7It Vg Hil have '...nests where they rest'.

9. 21   The text has 'his garment'; Fam 13 1Gr have 'his hem'; 7Gr 1It have 'The hem of his garment'.

9. 32   The text has 'dumb'; 1It has 'deaf'; 7It Vg have 'dumb and deaf'.

*10. 1   1Sy has 'the twelve'; 1Gr has 'the disciples'; the text has 'the twelve disciples'.

*11. 25   1Vg has 'Lord'; 1Gr has 'Father'; the text has 'Father, Lord'.

13. 55   The text has 'Joseph'; Al* D E F G M S* U N X Ga 17Gr 2It 1Vg Or have 'John'; 3Vg have 'John and Joseph'.

15. 19   The text has 'murders'; 1Gr has 'envies'; 1Gr has 'murders and envies'. ('Envies' is also added after 'fornications' by 2Gr.)

15. 31   The text has 'the dumb speaking'; B Ph 4Gr 1It have 'the dumb hearing'; N O Si have 'The dumb hearing and speaking'. (2Gr have 'the dumb hearing and the speechless speaking'.)

* An asterisk indicates original double terms, each of which is omitted by various MSS.

Mark

* 9. 2   7Gr 2Geo have 'by themselves'; 4Gr 1It 2Sy 1Cop Aeth have 'alone'; the text has 'by themselves alone'.

* 9. 25   1Gr has 'the unclean'; W 𝔓⁴⁵ Fam 1 1Sy Geo have 'the spirit'; the text has 'the unclean spirit'.

* 9. 43   Al^c L De Ps 5Gr 1Sy Aeth have 'into Gehenna'; W Fam 1 2Gr 1Sy have 'into the unquenchable fire'; the text has 'into Gehenna, into the unquenchable fire'. (D 5It avoid the duplication by changing the second phrase to 'where the fire is unquenchable'.)

  9. 49   The text has 'everyone will be salted with fire'; D 5It have 'every sacrifice will be salted' (and the like); A C N X Ga Th Pi Si Ph Ps Ko Fam 13 7+Gr 4It Vg 2Sy 1Cop Aeth have both.

  10. 4   Text 'to write'; 1Gr 2It 1Geo 'to give'; D 'to give to write'.

  10. 29   Text 'or children'; Ga 'or wife'; A C N X Y P Si Ph Ps Ko Fam 13 7+Gr 2It 2Sy 1Geo Aeth have both.

  10. 30   Al^a A C D W Th 10+Gr It(−1) 2Sy 2Geo 'and mother'; 1Gr 'and Father'; Al^c K M X Pi Fam 1 9+Gr Aeth 'And Father and Mother'.

*10. 34   D 5Gr 3It 'and they spat on him'; 12Gr 'and they flogged him'; text has both.

  10. 44   Text 'slave of all'; D 4Gr 2It Aeth 'slave of you'; W 1Gr 2Sy 2Cop Arm 'slave of you all'.

  10. 46   Text 'from Jericho'; D 7It 'from there'; Th 2Gr have both.

  10. 50   Text 'Jesus'; D Th 3Gr It(−2) Vg 'him'; 1Gr has both.

  11. 18   Text 'The chief priests and the scribes'; M^{mg} 5Gr 'the scribes and the Pharisees'; 9Gr 'The scribes and the Pharisees and the chief priests'.

*11. 27   Fam 1(−1) 1Gr 'Chief priests and scribes'; 1Gr 'elders and scribes'; text has all three.

*12. 14   D 1Gr It(−2) 2Vg 'To Caesar or not?'; Si 1Geo 'to Caesar? Shall we give or not give?'; text has 'To Caesar or not? Shall we give or not give?'

  13. 7   Text 'rumours of wars'; 4Gr 'insurrections'; 2Gr 'insurrections and rumours of wars'.

*13. 30   3Gr 4It 'all things'; 1Gr 1Sy 'these things'; text 'all these things'.

*14. 3   1It(*d*) 'of pure nard'; D 1Gr 1Sy 'of myrrh'; text 'of myrrh of pure nard'. (D also omits 'very costly'.)

  14. 22   Text 'blessing'; U 1Gr 'giving thanks'; 1Gr has both.

  14. 27   G 2Gr 6It 2Vg 1Sy 1Cop 'all will be scandalized + in me'; 5Gr Vg 1Cop + 'in this night'; A C² E F K M N U X Y Th Pi* Si Ph

---

* An asterisk indicates original double terms, each of which is omitted by various MSS.

Famm 1 & 13 5+Gr 2It 5Vg 2Sy 1Cop Geo Aeth Arm+'in me in this night'.

14. 51 Text τις; 1Gr εἰς/A N P W X Y Ga De Th Pi Si Ph 0116 Ko Famm 1 & 13 8+Gr 1Sy Geo εἰς τις.

14. 65 Text 'spit upon'; 1Gr 1It 'mock'; 1Vg has both.

15. 17 Text 'Purple robe'; 3Gr 2Cop 'crimson cloak'; Th Fam 13 6Gr 1Sy Arm have both. (N.B. 'crimson cloak' is in Mt. 27. 18. Th etc. actually conflate the two gospels.)

15. 20 There is similar conflation as in 15. 17, with similar support. 'Cloak' is from Mt. 27. 31.

15. 47 Text 'of Joses'; D 2Gr 3It 2Vg 1Sy Arm 'of James'; Th 'of James and Joses'; 1It 'of James and Joseph (sic)'. (A Si 1Gr 2It Vg Aug also have Joseph for Joses.)

THE APOCRYPHAL TRADITION

Gosp. Heb. Jerome, Contra Pelag. III. 2. A new saying is created by conflating sentences from the Gospels. See Appendix v. 6.

Gosp. Ebion. Epiph. Haer. 30. 13. 4 f. echoes bits of Mt. 3. 5, 7; Mk. 1. 5: 'Pharisees and all Jerusalem went out to him and were baptized.'

Gosp. Ebion. Epiph. Haer. 30. 13. 6 conflates pieces of Mt., Mk., Lk. See Appendix v. 9.

Gosp. Ebion. Epiph. Haer. 30. 13. 7 same. See Appendix v. 8.

Fayum Fragm.; cf. Mt. 26. 31–4 parr. Fayum abbreviates and conflates Mt. and Mk. See Appendix v. 27.

Pap. Oxy. 1. 6, lines 30–5. Conflates Mt. 13. 57, Mk. 6. 4, and Lk. 4. 24. See Appendix v. 28.

Egerton Pap. 2, Fragm. I, lines 1–20 (de Santos, pp. 97 f.; H.-S. p. 96). Serial quotation of Jn. 5. 39; 5. 45; 9. 29.

Egerton Pap. 2, Fragm. II, lines 43–59 (de Santos, p. 99; H.-S. p. 97). Serial quotation of Jn. 3. 2; 10. 25; Mt. 12. 17 f. parr. (conflating also Mk. 1. 43); Lk. 6. 46; Mt. 15. 7.

Protev. Jms. 11. 1; cf. Lk. 1. 28. 'The Lord is with you+blessed are you among women' (from 1. 42). So also C Ko D Th Many minusc. It Sy.

Protev. Jms. 11. 3. Conflates Lk. 1. 31, 32; Mt. 1. 21, reversing Lk.'s order to do so, and omitting Lk. 1. 32 b, 33. This same conflation, beginning with huios, may be found in Justin, Apol. 1. 33. 5. Note also that both Justin and Protev. Jms. add different ek phrases.

Act. Pil. 10. 1. After Lk. 23. 35, adds 'Let him come down from the cross' (conflated from Mt. 27. 42 par.).

Gosp. Ebion. Epiph. Haer. 30. 14. Conflates Lk. 8. 21; Mt. 12. 50. So also II Clem. See Köster, op. cit. p. 77.

A study of these lists and the items in the appendix to which reference is made will readily show (1) that later documents did conflate earlier ones, as well as how they did it, and (2) that everything that looks like conflation is not necessarily conflation. Without further discussion, we may now present the evidence from the Synoptics themselves.

THE EVIDENCE FROM THE SYNOPTICS GOSPELS

Matthew

3. 5: 'Jerusalem and all Judea (cf. Mk. 1. 5) and all the region of the Jordan' (Lk. 3. 3).

4. 11: 'Then the devil left him (cf. Lk. 4. 13) and angels...ministered to him' (Mk. 1. 13).

10. 2: 'Peter and Andrew his brother (cf. Lk. 6. 14) and James the son of Zebedee and John his brother' (cf. Mk. 3. 17).

13. 32: 'It is the greatest of shrubs (Mk. 4. 32) and becomes a tree' (Lk. 13. 19).

14. 13: 'The crowds followed him (Lk. 9. 11) on foot from the cities' (Mk. 6. 33).

17. 2: 'He was transfigured before them (Mk. 9. 2) and his face shone as the sun' (cf. Lk. 9. 29: 'the appearance of his face became other').

19. 24: τρήματος (Lk. 18. 25) ῥαφίδος (Mk. 10. 25).

22. 35–7: 'One from among them (cf. Mk. 12. 28: "one of the scribes"), a lawyer, tempting him, (Lk. 10. 25) asked, (Mk. 12. 28) "Teacher, (Lk. 10. 25) which is the great commandment (cf. Mk. 12. 28) in the law?" (Lk. 10. 26). And he said to him' (cf. Lk. 10. 26, 27).

23. 1: 'Jesus spoke to the crowds (cf. Mk. 12. 37b) and to his disciples' (cf. Lk. 20. 45).

Mark

1. 32: 'When evening came (Mt. 8. 16), when the sun set' (cf. Lk. 4. 40).

1. 42: 'The leprosy left him (Lk. 5. 13) and he was cleansed' (cf. Mt. 8. 3).

3. 8: 'Beyond the Jordan (Mt. 4. 25) and around Tyre and Sidon' (cf. Lk. 6. 17).

4. 37: γίνεται (Mt. 8. 24: ἐγένετο) λαῖλαψ (Lk. 8. 23) μεγάλη (Mt. 8. 24: μέγας) ἀνέμου (Lk. 8. 23).

5. 2, 3: 'out of the tombs (Mt. 8. 28)...in the tombs' (Lk. 8. 27).

5. 38: 'He beholds a tumult (cf. Mt. 9. 23) and [people] weeping (cf. Lk. 8. 52) and wailing loudly.'

10. 46: 'Into Jericho (Lk. 18. 35) and coming out from Jericho' (Mt. 20. 29).

11. 2: 'And immediately (Mt. 21. 2) entering' (Lk. 19. 30).

14. 1–2: '...the unleavened bread (cf. Lk. 22. 1) after two days (Mt. 26. 2) and the chief priests (both Mt. and Lk.) and the scribes sought how (Lk. 22. 2), with guile taking, they might kill (Mt. 26. 4) him' (Lk. 22. 2; Mt. has 'Jesus').

268

14. 12: 'On the first (Mt. 26. 17) day' (Lk. 22. 7).

14. 30: 'Today (Lk. 22. 34) in this night' (Mt. 26. 34).

14. 37: 'Are you asleep? (cf. Lk. 22. 46) Are you not able to watch one hour?' (Mt. 26. 40).

15. 26: 'The superscription (Lk. 23. 38) of the charge against him' (Mt. 27. 37).

15. 32: 'the Christ (Lk. 23. 35) the king of Israel' (Mt. 27. 42).

15. 42: 'When evening had come (Mt. 27. 57), since it was the day of preparation' (cf. Lk. 23. 54).

Luke

3. 3: 'All the region of the Jordan (Mt. 3. 5) preaching a baptism of repentance unto forgiveness of sins' (Mk. 1. 4). Cf. Mt. 3. 5, same category.

5. 26: 'Amazement seized [them] all (cf. Mk. 2. 12) and they glorified God (both Mk. and Mt.), and were filled with fear (cf. Mt. 9. 8), saying, "We have seen strange things today"' (cf. Mk. 2. 12).

5. 30: 'The Pharisees (Mt. 9. 11) and the scribes' (Mk. 2. 16).

8. 17: 'Which shall not be made known (Mt. 10. 26) and come into the open' (Mk. 4. 22).

8. 25: 'Fearing (cf. Mk. 4. 41) they marveled' (Mt. 8. 27).

As we have observed before, the number of instances of possible conflation is not necessarily significant. The question is whether any instance of actual conflation can be proved. We may first note that the suggestion that Mark conflated Matthew and Luke was put forward long ago, and, after having fallen into disrepute, has now been revived.[1] There are basically two arguments against this hypothesis. In the first place, it was argued by Abbott that it would have been too difficult for Mark to have composed his account by conflating Matthew and Luke.

For suppose that he did so copy; it follows that he must not only have constructed a narrative based upon two others, borrowing here a piece from St Matthew and here a piece from St Luke, but that he must have deliberately determined to insert, and must have adapted his narrative so as to insert, every word that was common to St Matthew and St Luke. The difficulty of doing this is enormous, and will be patent to any one who will try to perform a similar literary feat himself. To embody the whole of even one document in a narrative of one's own, without copying it *verbatim*, and to do this in a free and natural manner, requires no little care. But to take

[1] See p. 264 n. 1 above.

two documents, to put them side by side and analyse their common matter, and then to write a narrative, graphic, abrupt, and in all respects the opposite of artificial, which shall contain every phrase and word that is common to both—this would be a *tour de force* even for a skilful literary forger of these days, and may be dismissed as an impossibility for the writer of the Second Gospel.[1]

A similar argument has been made by Butler against Matthew's having conflated Q and Mark in the passage concerning the Beelzebul controversy.[2] It must be pointed out, however, that Abbott's statement of the case is not quite accurate. If Mark had conflated Matthew and Luke, he would not have had to analyze their common matter and labor to include it. He could simply have copied first one then the other, thereby automatically including what was common to them, excluding any chance that they would agree together against him, and also creating agreements with each of them against the other. Whether one attributes conflation to Matthew or to Mark, the matter will be difficult, but not so nearly impossible as Abbott thought.

A second objection to the hypothesis that Mark conflated Matthew and Luke was put forward by Hawkins. He observed that places in Mark where the question of conflation arises are frequently places which contain a double or redundant phrase. He argued as follows:

It used to be thought that in such passages as 1. 32, 42; 14. 30...Mark had put together phrases from Matthew and Luke. But after looking through all these instances of Mark's habitual manner of duplicate expression, it will appear far more probable that he had here used two phrases in his customary way, and that in these cases Matthew happened to adopt one of them and Luke the other, whereas in some cases, e.g. Mk. 2. 25; 14. 43..., they both happened to adopt the same one.[3]

[1] E. A. Abbott, *Encyclopaedia Britannica*, vol. 10, p. 791, *s.v.* Gospels. This passage also appears in W. G. Rushbrooke, *Synopticon* (London, 1880), p. ix. Farmer, *op. cit.* pp. 75 ff., also cites and discusses this passage.
[2] B. C. Butler, *The Originality of St Matthew*, pp. 11 f. Butler argues that Matthew's version (12. 25–32) is 'a passage of harmonious literary and logical architecture, superior in both respects to Mark's and Luke's versions'. He doubts that such a passage could have been derived by conflating Mark and Q. If that were the case, 'we can only say that his two sources complemented each other, with a preordained harmony, like the two pieces of a wishbone. The alternative is to say that these harmonies existed ready-made in Q; in other words that Q in this passage is indistinguishable from Matthew. In fact, Q *is* Matthew.'
[3] Hawkins, *op. cit.* p. 142.

That what Hawkins suggested to have happened in Matthew's and Luke's use of Mark actually did happen in the use of Mark in the post-canonical tradition cannot be denied. As we may see in the list above, for example, where Mark wrote one of his characteristic double phrases, 'by themselves alone' (9. 2), some manuscripts wrote only 'by themselves' and others only 'alone'. Thus the apparent conflation is not conflation at all, but the original reading, portions of which are copied by various scribes. This is, then, possible, and can be seen frequently to have happened in the manuscript tradition where there are hundreds of scribes and thus hundreds of possibilities. If we selected, however, any two manuscripts of Mark, I doubt if we would find a single instance in which, *on more than one occasion,* one copied one half of a double Markan phrase and the other the other half. The difficulty with Hawkins's explanation is the frequency with which Matthew and Luke independently would have had to decide to select one half of a Markan double phrase and would have, by happenstance, selected different halves. Furthermore, Hawkins's explanation does not account for the kind of apparent conflation which is seen in Mk. 14. 1–2. These verses, to me at least, look like an instance of genuine conflation.

But if Mk. 14. 1–2 appears to be a case of genuine conflation, so do Mt. 22. 35–7 and Lk. 5. 26. If any one of these three cases appeared in one of the Apocryphal Gospels, we should put it down as a certain case of conflation. We must conclude, then, that the arguments for conflation in one Gospel are not appreciably stronger than they are in another Gospel. The evidence for conflation in each of the Synoptics is more or less even. It thus follows that the Synoptic problem cannot be solved by appeal to conflation.

CHAPTER VI

CONCLUSIONS

SUMMARY OF RESULTS

Since the individual results of this study have been summarized throughout the body of the work, it will not be necessary to offer a lengthy conclusion here. We may briefly indicate the principal results of the study, and then discuss the significance of this study for the Synoptic problem and the study of the pre-canonical Synoptic tradition. The principal conclusions, then, are as follows:

There are no hard and fast laws of the development of the Synoptic tradition. On all counts the tradition developed in opposite directions. It became both longer and shorter, both more and less detailed, and both more and less Semitic. Even the tendency to use direct discourse for indirect, which was uniform in the post-canonical material which we studied, was not uniform in the Synoptics themselves. For this reason, *dogmatic statements that a certain characteristic proves a certain passage to be earlier than another are never justified.*

On all points it was necessary to consider the question of editorial tendencies. Some particular writers would have an editorial custom contrary to the general course of development. For the sake of convenience, the tradition is often personified; that is, it is given characteristics of its own. We have spoken in this manner in this work. At each point, however, we were reminded that the tradition has no tendencies apart from the sum of the tendencies of the individuals who transmit it. To say that the tradition tends to become more specific is actually to say that, more often than not, the transmitters tend to make it more specific. For this reason, we must always give room for human differences and be alert to the editorial tendencies of each particular writer.

A brief digression to consider a modern parallel may make this point clearer. The stock market resembles the Christian tradition in many respects. Both are personified. Just as it is said that 'the tradition tended to become more specific', it is also said that 'the stock market did so and so'. The market is said not only to go up or down, but to hesitate, waver, and even spit.[1] After a period of hesitation, it 'decides' to move in one way or another. Further, the market, like the tradition, is said to operate according to certain laws. Thus, to take one of the simplest of the stock market 'laws' as an example, it is said that a sharp increase of odd lot purchases over odd lot sales indicates the approaching end of a bull (rising) market. The reasoning behind the 'law' is that those who buy odd lots (usually fewer than one hundred shares), the small investors, are always on the wrong side. Small investors are thought to buy at the top and sell at the bottom.[2] It is clear that this 'law', like all other 'laws' of the stock market, is only a law in the sense that it is an observation based on the behavior of most of the individuals who buy and sell stocks. It is thus possible not only that an individual small investor could break the 'law' and be on the right side of the market, but even that, through better public advice, a majority of small investors could be on the right side, thus reversing the 'law'. Although it is convenient in discussing the Christian tradition, as in discussing the stock market, to personify it and attribute to it a regular form of behavior which can be characterized by laws, it must never be forgotten that this is only a convenience of speech, and that the 'laws' do not necessarily control the behavior of individuals. This consideration does not prevent us from identifying general tendencies of the transmitters of early Christian tradition, but it cautions us against too easily supposing that each individual transmitter conforms to the general pattern.[3]

Some tendencies which have been thought to have been generally operative among the transmitters of the early Chris-

---

[1] See *The New York Times*, Sunday, 27 Feb. 1966, section 3, p. 1, col. 3: 'The stock market, which has been trying to say something for more than a month, spit it out last week.'

[2] It is perhaps worth noting that this law of the market, like the form-critical laws of the Christian tradition, is oversimplified and applied too inflexibly when used by those who are dependent on the experts. The statement of the odd lot law just presented is derived from newspaper accounts. A much more sophisticated, complex, and flexible version is presented by professional stock market technicians.

[3] A similar problem is the application of 'national characteristics' to individual citizens of the nation. It may be more or less valid to characterize national groups in certain terms, but to suppose that any individual from that group must fit the stereotype is often misleading and unfair.

tian tradition have been shown not to have been so common. Thus we have seen that the material did not necessarily grow in overall length[1] and did not necessarily become less Semitic.[2] Some tendencies, however, appear to have been fairly common. On the whole, there was a tendency to make the material more detailed[3] and a considerable tendency to change indirect to direct discourse.[4] Speeches, conversations, and scenes were frequently added to material which was being used, but abbreviation was common enough to make the use of these categories dubious.[5] Unless there are offsetting considerations (for example, the redactional tendency of a certain editor), it may be held that material which is richer in detail and direct speech (and perhaps also in speeches, conversations, and scenes) is probably later than parallel material less rich in these items. Even here, however, certainty cannot be achieved. One may only say that the *balance of probability* is that material richer in detail and direct speech is later. Further, these criteria should be applied to an entire document, and not to any one pericope. The canons are not so certain that one may say that a detail in one of Matthew's pericopes proves it to be later than the parallel in Luke. Yet if the pericope in Matthew has several different aspects which are characteristic of later tradition, it may be justifiable to argue that Matthew's pericope is probably later than Luke's.

Since it may appear that the principal force of this section of the study is negative, I should emphasize its positive aspects. In arguing that the criteria which have claimed our attention cannot be simply applied to any one passage to test its antiquity, I have attempted to counteract certain abuses of these criteria. They have often been used as if they were all of equal weight and all universally applicable, as if the tradition uniformly moved in one direction or other. It has become evident that some of the criteria which have been used ought not to be used at all. To this extent, the study is negative. But other criteria have been shown to be useful. Here I have tried to determine how strong each criterion is in order to establish relative degrees of confidence with which the criteria should be used. This is intended as a contribution on the positive side. As long as

[1] See above, p. 68.   [2] See above, p. 230.   [3] See above, p. 146.
[4] See above, p. 259.   [5] See especially pp. 64–6 above.

scholars had only a large number of possible criteria with no way of determining their relative reliability, and, indeed, with different scholars taking totally opposite positions on some of the criteria, these criteria were really useless, even though they were employed. Perhaps a step has been taken here toward improving this situation. In saying that certain criteria do not always hold true, but hold true more frequently than not, I have tried to show how they must be used and what degree of confidence should be attached to each of them. The degree of confidence which each criterion deserves cannot be stated statistically (e.g. this criterion holds true three times out of five), but rather in general terms of strength or weakness. Such assessments have been made throughout this study.

In some categories of the present study, we saw that the tradition followed no more or less regular tendency. No criteria can be derived from such categories. In other cases, however, a tendency to change in one way or other was more or less pronounced, and from these categories useful criteria may be derived. The strength of each criterion depends upon the degree of uniformity shown by the post-Synoptic tradition on each point. The relative strength of each of the useful criteria may now be indicated by way of summary. Numbers in parentheses refer to the chapters in which each item is discussed.

Not Very Strong: new speeches (ii); new scenes (ii); addition of adjectives (iii); addition of nouns to proper names (iii).

Fairly Strong: new dialogues (ii); addition of subjects (iii); genitive pronouns (iii); addition of proper names to nouns (iii); nouns substituted for pronouns (iii); nouns added to pronouns (iii); addition of circumstances (iii).

Strong: addition of proper names (iii); substitution of proper names for nouns and pronouns (iii); addition of miscellaneous small details (iii); addition of genitive nouns (iii).

Very Strong: direct discourse and first person (v).

18-2

CONCLUSION

THE SYNOPTIC PROBLEM

It has been seen that, while certain of the useful criteria support Mark's priority,[1] some do not.[2] Both Matthaean priorists and Lukan priorists can find some support in this study. There are several possible responses to this situation.

It could be argued that the conclusions we have reached about what categories are useful for assessing relative antiquity are simply wrong. That is a possibility which must remain open. Future research may alter some of our conclusions. I doubt, however, that future research will produce a situation in which all the useful categories point toward the same solution of the Synoptic problem. In the meantime, we must use what results we have. Far from there being a unanimity of witness by the useful categories to the priority of any one of the Gospels, there is not even a clear majority pointing in one direction. This ambiguity would probably not be changed by reaching different conclusions on one or two points.

It could also be argued that the method followed by Bultmann and Taylor with regard to internal criteria is the correct one.[3] The internal criteria should be determined by noting how the later Gospels used the earlier. On this view, the internal criteria would not be used to help in investigating the Synoptic problem, but rather a solution to the Synoptic problem would be the basis for determining the criteria. We have already indicated that this view is unsatisfactory.[4] It would be satisfactory only if the Synoptic problem could be decisively solved without appeal to the tendency of the tradition and to criteria which are derived from knowledge of it. This raises the question of the proofs of the two-document hypothesis.

It is not possible here to deal with the traditional proofs. One can only make two observations. In the first place, one of the principal arguments for the two-document hypothesis has

---

[1] Mark's priority is supported by the following categories: subjects (chap. III) and genitive nouns (chap. III).
[2] Matthew's priority is favored by the following categories: 'new scenes' (chap. II), proper names added to nouns and to other proper names (chap. III), circumstances (chap. III), and miscellaneous details (chap. III). Luke's priority is supported by the following categories: genitive pronouns (chap. III), nouns used for pronouns (chap. III), proper names (chap. III), and direct discourse (chap. v).
[3] See pp. 17–20 above.   [4] See pp. 23–5 above.

always been the phenomenon of order. As has been previously observed, this argument does not logically prove what it is thought to prove. Furthermore, the facts of order as they are usually stated are misleading; the phenomenon of order has yet to be stated and explained adequately. The argument from order is not adequate to prove the two-document hypothesis with the degree of certainty which would be necessary in order to justify the procedure followed by Bultmann and Taylor. The same thing could be said of other arguments for the two-document hypothesis which do not make use of internal criteria.[3]

One may observe, secondly, that the basis for deciding on a solution to the Synoptic problem is somewhat elusive. Thus Styler, in referring to an article by Farmer, grants that the arguments for Mark's priority which were used in the past are 'insecure'. He nevertheless remains convinced of Mark's priority.[4] To take another example, Streeter placed great reliance on Hawkins's minute and detailed studies in the Synoptics as proving Mark's priority.[5] Yet Hawkins did not regard his own work in this light. He thought Mark's priority was established by the argument from order, as set forth by

[1] See p. 7 above. Butler (*op. cit.* pp. 62 ff.) and Farmer (*op. cit.* pp. 63 ff.) argue that the attempt to prove our Mark's direct priority to Matthew and Luke on the basis of order involves a logical fallacy. The argument from order was designed to prove that our Mark has most closely followed the sequence of events in the Ur-Gospel, and cannot logically prove that our Mark is directly prior to the other Gospels. See also N. H. Palmer, 'Lachmann's argument', *N.T.S.* XIII (1967), 368 ff.

[2] The usual statement is that either Matthew or Luke supports Mark's order except where both omit the passage entirely (see Streeter, *op. cit.* p. 161). This statement is true, however, only if one limits one's view to *complete pericopes as they are set forth in Tischendorf's synopsis.* Such a limitation would be justifiable only if one wished to establish, by comparing our Gospels, the original order of *events* in the Ur-Gospel, and thus, it would be hoped, in Jesus' own life. This limitation is completely unwarranted if one wishes to investigate the literary relations among our Gospels. When smaller units are brought into view, it is readily seen that there are places in which neither Matthew nor Luke follows Mark's order (e.g. the saying about salt, Mk. 9. 50; Mt. 5. 13; Lk. 14. 34: in Huck's synopsis this is a separate pericope, in Tischendorf's synopsis it was only the conclusion of the pericope on offences, Mk. 9. 42–50; thus it was not observed to be an exception to the rule by the early researchers) as well as places in which Matthew and Luke agree against Mark in order (e.g. the phrase 'and these things will be added to you', Mt. 6. 33; Lk. 12. 31; Mk. 4. 24 c). I have spelled this out in a paper which I hope to publish in the near future.

[3] See those mentioned by Streeter, *op. cit.* pp. 159–62.

[4] Styler, *op. cit.* p. 232 n. 3.   [5] Streeter, *op. cit.* p. 164.

Woods.[1] But the argument from order, according to Woods, was designed to prove only that the source used by all three of our Gospels was most faithfully preserved by Mark with regard to order and length.[2] It is not capable of showing that our Mark is prior to our Matthew and our Luke.[3] It seems, then, unsatisfactory to argue that the two-document hypothesis (or any other hypothesis) can be established— apart from internal criteria—so firmly that it can be used as a basis for determining the tendency of the tradition.

The purpose of this study has been to determine the basis (or bases) for making judgements about the relative antiquity of parallel traditions. I have attempted to find some definite points which would decide such issues as those raised by the agreements and disagreements of the Synoptic Gospels, but they fail to yield a definite solution. To say that the particular items with which we deal can be decided by appeal to the relative order of the Synoptics and to suppose that the relative order of the Synoptics has been determined apart from internal criteria is only to push the problem back one step and ask what canons are to be used to solve the Synoptic problem. These canons themselves turn out to be indecisive and slippery.

In the third place, it might be argued that certain of the useful categories which we have found should be followed (for example, those which support Mark's priority), while the ones which point toward Matthew's or Luke's priority should be attributed to the editorial inclinations of the authors of those Gospels. This position would be admissible, however, only if we knew on some other basis that Mark indeed is first. We are thus led back to the problem discussed immediately above. This position, then, does not lead out of the dilemma.

The final possibility, and the one here recommended, is that we should take seriously the ambiguity of our results and regard the Synoptic problem with some uncertainty. *The evidence does not seem to warrant the degree of certainty with which many scholars hold the two-document hypothesis.* It would also seem to forbid that a similar degree of certainty should be accorded any other hypothesis.

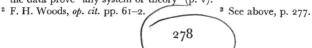

---

[1] Hawkins, *op. cit.* p. 114, n. 3. The preface to the work contains a disclaimer that the data prove 'any system or theory' (p. v).
[2] F. H. Woods, *op. cit.* pp. 61–2.   [3] See above, p. 277.

278

It is true that scholarship will regard such a situation as unsatisfactory, but this seems better than forcing the evidence to fit some one solution. Nor need it be thought that, were this position adopted, uncertainty would have to be our permanent stance toward the Synoptic problem. I only suggest that the time has come to look at the whole matter freshly. I believe our entire study of the Synoptic Gospels would profit from a period of withholding judgements on the Synoptic problem while the evidence is resifted.

The difficulty with the present situation is not that there is a dominant hypothesis, but that the dominant hypothesis is frequently held too rigidly.[1] As has been said before, it is accorded a degree of certainty which it does not merit. Very few scholars who have made a special and detailed study of the Synoptic Gospels have actually held a rigid view of the Synoptics. This may readily be seen in Appendix II, where a group of instances is collected in which some scholar believed Matthew or Luke to be earlier than Mark. Unfortunately, however, this broad view has not become widely spread, and rigidity seems to be the rule.[2]

I rather suspect that when and if a new view of the Synoptic problem becomes accepted, it will be more flexible and complicated than the tidy two-document hypothesis. With all due respect for scientific preference for the simpler view,[3] the evidence seems to require a more complicated one.

THE PRE-CANONICAL TRADITION

As was pointed out in the introductory chapter, the purpose of this work is to deal with a certain aspect of the tradition about Jesus. A comprehensive view of that tradition cannot be derived from this study, but some light should be shed by this study on related aspects of the larger question of the nature of the pre-

[1] See, for example, the statement by Willi Marxsen, *Einleitung in das neue Testament* (Gütersloh, 1963), p. 106: 'Diese Zweiquellentheorie hat sich in der Forschung so sehr bewährt, dass man geneigt ist, die Bezeichnung "Theorie" (im Sinne von "Hypothese") dafür aufzugeben.'

[2] A refreshing contrast is the view of W. D. Davies, *Invitation to the New Testament* (New York, 1966), p. 96.

[3] Farmer, *op. cit.* p. 209, writes: 'a critic should not posit the existence of hypothetical documents until he has made an attempt to solve the problem without appeal to hypothetical documents.'

canonical Synoptic tradition. The assumption of this study, or of any similar study, must be that the changes which occurred in the tradition during the pre-canonical period were similar to those which occurred during the post-canonical period. As we noted in the introductory chapter, this assumption cannot be proved, but it seems to be the best working hypothesis.

If this assumption is accepted, what conclusions may be drawn concerning the pre-canonical Synoptic tradition? They may be summarized as follows:

Broadly speaking, the tradition was readily subject to change. We have found that new material was added, old dropped, and that alterations of various kinds took place. No hesitation was felt toward expanding or abbreviating the material to make it clearer or more useful. We may here refer to the Synoptic material in the Apostolic Fathers, which frequently differs so widely from the canonical material that it appears that the two groups of material may have separate histories.[1] This shows that at some point or points changes were made in one or both of the traditions. Within this framework of verbal change, the meaning of the material frequently remained the same. Even here, however, changes did take place. Sometimes a portion of a pericope was so emphasized that the original meaning of the whole was lost. This happened, for example, in Justin's citations of the story of the rich young man.[2] He was interested only in Jesus' statement to the effect that only God is good. Justin quoted this to defend Christianity against the charge of polytheism. The wording was fairly accurately preserved, but the meaning was altered by quoting Jesus' reply out of the context of the entire story.

It has already been pointed out that this study would of necessity emphasize the changing character of the tradition rather than its rigidity. It has indeed done so, but not, I think, unfairly. The Synoptic tradition was earlier compared to the stock market, and may be once again. When J. P. Morgan was once asked what the stock market was going to do, he is said to have replied: 'The market will continue to fluctuate.'[3] The thing that may be said about the Christian tradition with

---

[1] See the section on the Apostolic Fathers above, pp. 35–7.
[2] Justin, Apology I. 16. 6–7; Dialogue 101. 2.
[3] This story is current in an oral tradition, and I cannot vouch for its accuracy.

the greatest degree of assurance is that it was subject to alteration.

How does this statement place us with regard to the present debate over the pre-canonical Synoptic tradition? If we may polarize the two extreme positions, we may characterize them in the following way. On the one extreme is to be found the view that the Christian tradition was largely created and shaped to fit the needs of the expanding Church. We have here and there the words of Jesus, or at least primitive Palestinian sayings, but even these few words have frequently been put into new contexts and given new meanings.[1] Rudolf Bultmann stands closest to this pole, although he sometimes grants more to the continuity of tradition than his critics realize.[2]

On the other extreme is to be found the view that the Synoptic tradition is comprised of material which has been carefully and literally handed down by trained transmitters. The tradition was originated by Jesus himself, who taught it to his disciples, who in turn supervised its transmission to insure the accuracy of the tradition.[3] Riesenfeld and Gerhardsson stand closest to this view, although they too grant a certain amount of flexibility to the tradition.[4]

Looked at from the standpoint of the *post-canonical tradition*, there is not a great deal of support to be seen for the view of the *pre-canonical tradition* which is represented by Riesenfeld and Gerhardsson. Their point of departure is the Rabbinic tradition rather than the post-canonical Christian tradition,[5] however, and it must be granted that from such a standpoint their position has much to recommend it. The question is, then, whether such a standpoint is an adequate one for viewing the early Christian tradition. It is inadequate to the degree that the Christian tradition differed in nature from the Rabbinic.[6] Thus it must be pointed out that the attempt to understand

[1] Cf. Bultmann, *Die Geschichte*, p. 49 (E.T. p. 47). In discussing apophthegms, Bultmann states that 'In any case— and this must be emphasized once more... —the sayings have commonly generated the situation, not vice-versa'.

[2] Thus in *Die Geschichte*, p. 57 (E.T. p. 55), he notes that the 'scholastic dialogues' 'could easily contain an historical reminiscence'. See also his remarks on the possible accuracy of geographical statements, *ibid.* p. 68 (E.T. p. 65).

[3] See, for example, Riesenfeld, *op. cit.* especially pp. 16–20.

[4] See pp. 1 f. above.

[5] See Gerhardsson, *Memory and manuscript*, pp. 201 f.; *Tradition and transmission*, p. 11; Riesenfeld, *op. cit.* pp. 16 ff.   [6] See the discussion on pp. 27 f. above.

the pre-canonical Synoptic tradition on the basis of a study of the Rabbinic tradition is not altogether adequate. An understanding of the Rabbinic tradition should prove of value for understanding the pre-canonical Christian tradition, however, and Riesenfeld and Gerhardsson have performed a real service in illuminating this area.

The pre-canonical Synoptic tradition cannot be studied directly. Light may be thrown on it, however, from four areas. One area, folk tradition, was studied by the German form critics. Another, the Rabbinic tradition, is being investigated by the Scandinavians. A third, the early Christian church as it is revealed by a study of the epistles, has been widely employed.[1] The fourth, the post-canonical Synoptic tradition, is the object of this study. A person who studies one of these four areas may be said to have a certain standpoint from which to view the unknown area, the pre-canonical Synoptic tradition. No one of these four standpoints is altogether adequate for the purpose of acquiring an undistorted view of the pre-canonical Synoptic tradition. The view from each standpoint will doubtless be somewhat distorted. Thus when we claim that the standpoint of Riesenfeld and Gerhardsson is not altogether adequate, we do not mean to say that it is altogether wrong.

It must also be said that our standpoint is not altogether adequate. It should not be thought that a study of the post-canonical tradition can conclusively establish which of the two views on the flexibility of the tradition and the creativity of the community is right. But the evidence derived from this study should be accorded some weight in judging this question. Such as it is, then, it gives no notion of a controlled tradition rigidly memorized and preserved. On this question we stand closer to Bultmann than to the Scandinavians, even while granting that the standpoint of the latter is not altogether invalid. Probably the truth lies between the two poles, and we would put it closer to the pole emphasizing the freedom of the early tradition than to the other.

The tradition moved in the direction of more popular forms of speech.[2] The points which justify this generalization are

[1] Taylor, *Formation*, p. 26.

[2] What we have just said about the inadequacy of any single viewpoint should be kept in mind in reading this section also. We are attempting to describe the pre-canonical tradition from the viewpoint of the post-canonical tradition. Since the viewpoint is not perfectly adequate, the description will not be perfectly accurate.

several. In the first place, we probably should understand the tendency to add detail[1] in this light. Details may well serve the purpose of adding color and thus of increasing popular interest. In the second place, the language of the tradition reveals this tendency. The Apocryphal Gospels, by and large, are more 'folksy' in language than the canonical. The extraordinarily frequent use of *kai* parataxis in the Protev. Jms. and of asyndeton in the Act. Pil., the avoidance of long periods which include subordinating participles, and the simplified vocabulary of the Apocryphal materials are witnesses to this tendency.[2] Even the textual tradition, in which grammatical infelicities are frequently corrected, bears witness to this tendency. Thus the manuscripts, on balance, tend to increase the use of *kai* in Matthew.[3] We may, thirdly, refer to the considerable tendency of later transmitters to change indirect into direct speech.[4] One of the effects of this is to add color and thus popular interest to the narrative. Also to be included here is the tendency to expand conversations,[5] especially by inserting material conveying no new information. Such a device seems to be designed for popular appeal. In the fourth place, many of the new scenes which are added (mostly in the Apocryphal materials)[6] reveal a popular interest. It has been often noted that the Apocryphal Gospels show a marked human interest. They describe character, dwell on secondary figures, give the background of events, and offer sidelights to the main story.[7] The Christian tradition, as Dibelius observed, became reading matter for the early Christians,[8] and so had to acquire a popular flavor. The tendency is sufficiently well marked that we may suppose that many of the popular characteristics in the Synoptic Gospels were added in the course of transmission. An example of such popular characteristics might be the descriptions, mostly in Mark, of Jesus' emotions or of his penetrating glance at someone.[9] These references have been taken as

[1] See above, pp. 144 ff.
[2] See above, pp. 213f., 220.
[3] See above, p. 228.
[4] See above, p. 259.
[5] See above, p. 67.
[6] See above, pp. 67 f.
[7] See the discussion by Oscar Cullmann on the Infancy Gospels, especially pp. 366–7, in Hennecke-Schneemelcher, *op. cit.*
[8] *Die Formgeschichte*, p. 39.
[9] For example, Mk. 1. 41, 43; 3. 5, 34; 8. 12; 10. 21.

indications of an eye-witness account,[1] but it is perhaps better to attribute them to popular interest.

We must reckon, then, with the probability that the Christian tradition was once more formal and less popular than it was when it was first recorded in our Gospels. It is possible, in this case, that the Christian tradition once more nearly approximated the Rabbinic tradition than our Gospels would indicate.[2] It must not be forgotten, however, that the Rabbinic tradition was itself changing, and perhaps in a direction contrary to that of the Christian tradition. That is, it may have once been less formal than the present Mishnah would indicate.[3] We would thus not be justified in arguing that the pre-canonical Christian tradition was formal in the way that Rabbi Judah's Mishnah is. Perhaps it is safest only to conjecture that many of the elements of popular interest which we find in the Synoptics are additions which have been made in the course of transmission.

These two conclusions may seem to be rather meagre results to derive from such a lengthy study. The principal benefits of this study do not lie in the two preceding generalizations, however. We must recall that internal criteria have long been used to determine problems of relative antiquity and authenticity in the Synoptic material. Yet a real test of these criteria, along the lines followed here, has never been made public. The principal point of this study was to conduct such a test and to make available a large body of evidence bearing on each point. Even if one differs from the interpretation of the evidence which has been offered, I hope that the evidence itself will be useful. On the basis of this evidence one should be able to

---

[1] See Vincent Taylor, *The Gospel according to St Mark*, p. 189 (on Mk. 1. 43).

[2] If one accepts the 'tract' theory of W. L. Knox and L. Cerfaux (see p. 5 above), he could argue that the early Synoptic tradition was formally like the Rabbinic.

[3] This is said only to indicate a possibility. Yet we may note that in external form the *Halakah* tradition may have become progressively more formal. According to J. Z. Lauterbach (*Rabbinic essays* [Cincinnati, 1951]), *Halakot* were originally transmitted in Midrash form rather than Mishnah form: that is, in connection with scripture passages rather than independently (pp. 163 f.). Although there were Mishnah-collections before the time of Hillel and Shammai (p. 171), 'there is no doubt that at the time of Hillel and Shammai there were no Mishnah-collections like our Mishnah' (p. 170 n. 12). *Halakot* first began to be separated from their scriptural proofs and taught independently about one hundred years before Hillel and Shammai (p. 171), but 'the topical arrangement of the Mishnah is of later date' (p. 176). Only in the time of Rabbi Akiba (*fl. c.* 110–35) was the principle of topical arrangement introduced (pp. 176, 240).

determine the balance of probability with regard to possible tendencies.

It was, furthermore, as much a purpose of this study to see which categories are not useful for determining relative antiquity of parallel traditions as to see which ones are useful. The negative conclusions of the study are at least as important as the positive ones.

TRANSLATION VARIANTS[1]

It was Torrey's position[2] that Matthew had before him not only the Greek Mark, but also Aramaic material in addition to and paralleling Mark. Luke had both the other two Greek gospels as well as Aramaic in addition to and paralleling them. Matthew and Luke both used Mark's Greek, except where their Aramaic showed a real difference. In this case, the later translator had to show the difference. In this way Torrey accounted for the agreements and the differences of the three Gospels. Later investigation has shown, however, that it is unlikely that the entirety of any one or all of our Gospels is a translation from Aramaic.

Yet both Black and Jeremias give examples which would support Torrey's view, at least in certain passages. It is regrettable that they do not, like Torrey, come to terms with the question of what such passages mean for the Synoptic problem and the history of the tradition.[3] It is our task now to give a brief survey of the major passages which raise the problem of parallel material separately transmitted and to put the question which these passages raise as clearly as possible.

1. Torrey[4] suggests that κτίσις in Mark 10. 6 and ὁ κτίσας in Matthew 19. 4 are different translations of the same Aramaic, *dī b'rā*. There can be no doubt that this hypothesis is credible. Torrey's Aramaic could be translated either 'from the beginning *of creating*' or 'from the beginning *the one creating*'. According to Torrey, Matthew has made the correct translation.

2. In Mark 8. 36//Luke 9. 25, Mark has ψυχή and Luke has ἑαυτός. Torrey[5] and Black[6] agree that these two words translate the same Aramaic, but they do not agree on who has made the correct translation. Black says that ψυχή is used in Mark as a reflexive and is 'a pure Semitism'. 'The difference between Mark 8. 36 and Luke 9. 25 is that between a literal and a more literary version.' Torrey, dealing with Luke 9. 25, thinks that Luke has misinterpreted the word נפש and read it as a reflexive, whereas its proper meaning, 'life', should be pressed. Whether we should have a

---

[1] See p. 4 n. 2 and p. 193 n. 1, above.
[2] *Translated Gospels*, pp. xlvii–liii.
[3] Sparks, 'Some observations on the Semitic background of the New Testament', p. 39, notes that the full implications of arguing for Aramaic sources are not always recognized. He writes that 'it is impossible to maintain at one and the same time both that St Matthew and St Luke were dependent on St Mark in Greek, and also that the differences between them and St Mark are to be explained as different translations of the same Aramaic original'.
[4] *Op. cit.* p. 14.   [5] *Ibid.* pp. 31, 32.
[6] *An Aramaic approach*[2], p. 76 (3rd ed. p. 102).

reflexive here or not is beside the point just now, however. What is important to note is that Torrey and Black agree that Mark and Luke have variant
translations of the same Aramaic word.

3. Jeremias[1] maintains that οἱ ἰσχύοντες in Mark 2. 17 and Matthew
9. 12 and οἱ ὑγιαίνοντες in Luke 5. 31 are variants of *b⁽ᵉ⁾ri'a*, which is
ambiguous. Luke has made the correct translation.

4. According to Jeremias,[2] νηστεύειν (Mark 2. 19a), πενθεῖν (Matthew
9. 15a), and νηστεῦσαι (Luke 5. 34) are 'variant renderings of the ambiguous Aramaic *'ith'anne'*.

5. Black,[3] supported by Jeremias,[4] points out that ἄναλος in Mark 9. 50
and μωρανθῇ in Matthew 5. 13 and Luke 14. 34 are variant translations of תפל.

6. Black[5] conjectures that the inexplicable πρός in Matthew 27. 14 is
a misunderstanding of the adverb עַד 'again' as the preposition עַד 'to,
until'. Mark 15. 5 has the correct translation.

7. Black[6] finds several translation variants in the passage Mark 10. 43 ff.//
Luke 22. 24 ff. They are Mark's μέγας and Luke's μείζων from *rabba*;
πρῶτος and ἡγούμενος from *rish*; δοῦλος and διακονῶν from *'abhda*; and
διάκονος and νεώτερος from *talya*.

8. Black[7] notes that the Q passage Luke 17. 33//Matthew 10. 39 is really
parallel to the triple tradition passage Mark 8. 35. θέλῃ (Mark) and 3ητήσῃ
(Luke) are translation variants, as are σώζειν, περιποιήσασθαι, and
3ωογονήσει.

9. Black[8] and Torrey[9] think that ἵνα (Mk. 4. 12) and ὅτι (Mt. 13. 13)
are variant translations of the Aramaic *d⁽ᵉ⁾*.

Each of the nine cases listed above is credible on the hypothesis that the
Greek variants depend on a common Aramaic word. To take an example
(number 4 above), עֲנִי in the *'ithpael* can mean either 'mourn' or 'fast'.
Neither of these renderings is obviously wrong in the context, so that we
cannot explain the variations among the Gospels as being simply corrections
or alterations for the sake of the meaning. If Matthew had only the Greek
Mark before him, there is no obvious reason why he would have altered
νηστεύειν to πενθεῖν. Some degree of likelihood attaches to the explanation
that the change was influenced by the ambiguity of the Aramaic. To be
sure, this does not wholly explain the passage in Matthew, where 'to fast'
appears three times. Why was the alternative translation chosen only once?
Yet that this particular alternative word to Mark's νηστεύειν was chosen
is unlikely to be pure coincidence, so that Jeremias' view is persuasive.

---

[1] *Parables*[1], p. 100 n.; cf. *Parables*[2], p. 125 n.   [2] *Parables*[1], p. 42 n.
[3] *An Aramaic approach*, pp. 123 ff. (3rd ed. p. 166).
[4] *Parables*[2], p. 168 and *Parables*[1], p. 125.
[5] *An Aramaic approach*, pp. 85–6. (This explanation is deleted in the third edition;
see p. 117.)
[6] *Ibid.* p. 267 (3rd ed. p. 222).   [7] *Ibid.* p. 272 (3rd ed. p. 188).
[8] *Ibid.* p. 155 (3rd ed. p. 213).   [9] Torrey, *Our translated Gospels*, p. 11.

APPENDIX I

By the nature of the evidence, the conjectures for mistranslations which are also made by Aramaists cannot be very persuasive. While some are doubtless credible conjectures, few are of a nature that the hypothesis of mistranslation clearly has the advantage over other hypotheses. The nine passages now under review constitute the strongest evidence for extensive written Aramaic tradition. What was said about example 4 can be said of all: the Greek variants *could* be translation variants, and that *just* these variants appear is probably not coincidental. Just what do these variants indicate?

The scholars whose work is being considered do not deal with the matter in a satisfactory way. Jeremias offers no explanation at all. Black's explanation is not altogether clear. Torrey maintained a consistent position, but it cannot be followed, at least not to the extreme to which he took it. Let us consider what Black says about the matter to see if we can find some light on a vitally important problem.

In the discussion of individual passages,[1] Black clearly has in mind different translations of one Aramaic word, neither translation being seen as necessarily a correction of the other.[2] This seems to be in close agreement with Torrey's view. Yet when summarizing the evidence, he seems to have something else in mind. He actually seems to think that the variant translations of Aramaic came into the canonical Gospels after their composition in Greek, during the early period of textual transmission, from non-canonical sources. Thus he writes that 'Gospel variants which may be traced to an Aramaic source are most probably survivals from the earliest period of the Gospel text...The most probable explanation of the few remaining Greek variants from Aramaic is that, in the earliest period of textual transmission, the writings of the Evangelists have been variously influenced by or assimilated to other well-known extra-canonical Greek versions of the Words of the Lord.'[3]

Using once more as an illustration number 4 in our list, we would, according to this view, explain that Matthew had originally copied Mark's νηστεύειν, but that some scribe, influenced by a Greek version of the story containing a different translation from Aramaic, changed the νηστεύειν to πενθεῖν.

Thus we have before us two ways of accounting for the translation variants in our Gospels. One is that the later Evangelists themselves had independent traditions parallel to their Greek sources. These independent traditions could have been before them in Aramaic or already translated into Greek. The other view is that the translation variants crept into the text during its transmission. With the present uncertainty both as to the extent

---

[1] See pp. 52–4, 76, 86, 100, 155, 267, 272 (3rd ed. pp. 70–2, 102, 137 f., 213, 222, 188).
[2] Cf. Spark's remarks, p. 286 n. 3 above.
[3] *An Aramaic approach*, p. 214 (3rd ed. p. 279).

of non-canonical collections of material parallel to the Gospels and as to the transmission of the text in its earliest years, we cannot make a firm judgement. I find myself somewhat closer to Torrey's view (or a modification of it) than to Black's, however, for the following reasons: (1) All we know of early (and later) textual transmission indicates that the tendency was to harmonize the Gospels to each other, rather than to introduce variants. (2) We already have reason to suspect that even if Matthew and Luke did use Mark, they occasionally had access to a better tradition than Mark. Apart from Q, which is said sometimes to overlap Mark, we may mention primarily Luke's passion narrative, which is widely held to be independent of Mark, at least at some points. But even more to the point, various scholars have from time to time thought that at some particular pericope Matthew or Luke somehow had access to a tradition independent of and better than Mark. A collection of such instances is made in Appendix II.

I do not at all wish to agree with Torrey that the Gospels are *in toto* translations of Aramaic, nor that the Evangelists performed the kind of textual comparison that he suggests. Yet the few apparent translation variants that we have noted are among our best evidence for Aramaic tradition of some extent at some period. They are also strong evidence that the later Evangelists had traditions parallel to and independent of their primary sources. If this is so, it is an important conclusion for the history of the tradition and ultimately for research into the teaching of Jesus.

APPENDIX II

SUGGESTED EXCEPTIONS TO THE PRIORITY OF MARK[1]

From a survey of the work of a few representative scholars—all of whom accept the two-document hypothesis in one form or another—has been culled the following list of instances in which either Matthew or Luke is thought by one or more of these scholars to have a more original form of a certain passage than does Mark. In some instances it is only said that Matthew and/or Luke has a form independent of Mark's. A few passages are also listed in which the relative primitiveness of the passage in Matthew or Luke may be thought to be the result of the influence of Q. Such passages —whether the scholar in question has explicitly mentioned Q or not—are marked with an asterisk (*). A brief explanation is given for each passage, but for fuller details the reader will have to consult the work of the scholar cited.

*1. Mk. 1. 11, cf. Lk. 3. 22 (D). D has the original reading in Luke, and Lk. 3. 22 depends on Q. Mark here also depends on Q, but gives it in a weakened form. J. Weiss, *Das älteste Evangelium*, p. 133.

2. Mk. 1. 29, cf. Mt. 8. 14 and Lk. 4. 38. Mark's 'Andrew with James and John' is secondary. J. Weiss, *op. cit.* p. 148 n.; Bultmann, *Die Geschichte*, pp. 226 f. (E.T. p. 212).

3. Mk. 1. 33, cf. Mt. and Lk. The verse is missing in Matthew and Luke, and was added by a redactor to Mark. J. Weiss, *op. cit.* p. 148. Vincent Taylor states that the verse is in Mark's style, and so must have been known to Matthew and Luke. He does not explain why they agree together in omitting it. *The Gospel according to St Mark*, p. 181.

4. Mk. 1. 35, cf. Lk. 4. 42. Mark's 'and there he prayed' may have been added by a redactor. J. Weiss, *op. cit.* p. 148.

5. Mk. 2. 3, cf. Mt. 9. 2 and Lk. 5. 18. Mark's 'borne by four' is the addition of a redactor. J. Weiss, *op. cit.* p. 155.

6. Mk. 4. 31–2, cf. Mt. 13. 31–2. Matthew retains the original antithetic parallelism. Black, *op. cit.* p. 123 (3rd ed. p. 165).

7. Mk. 4. 41, cf. Mt. 8. 27. Bultmann first raised the possibility that Matthew preserved the earlier text (*op. cit.* p. 230, E.T. p. 216) but later retracted (see the *Ergänzungsheft, ad loc.*).

8. Mk. 6. 8–9, cf. Mt. 10. 9–10 and Lk. 9. 3–4. Mark softens the mission requirements. Karl Kundsin, 'Primitive Christianity in the light of Gospel research', *Form Criticism*, p. 108.

[1] See pp. 7, 279, 289 above.

9. Mk. 7. 24–31, cf. Mt. 15. 21–8. Bultmann thought that Mt. 15. 24 is an old and independent logion, and that part of Mk. 7. 27 is a secondary addition to the text of Mark. Streeter thought that Matthew here had access also to M. See Bultmann, *op. cit.* p. 38 (E.T. p. 38); Streeter, *The Four Gospels*, p. 260. Note also Bultmann, *op. cit.* p. 277 n. 1 (E.T. p. 258 n. 2): in Mt. 15. 21–8, Matthew has 'corrected the text of Mark on the basis of a like tradition'.

10. Mk. 8. 27–33, cf. Mt. 16. 13–23 and Lk. 9. 18–22. Mt. 16. 17–19 is the original ending of the pericope, while Mk. 8. 32–3 (missing in Luke) is a later addition. Bultmann, *op. cit.* p. 277 and n. (E.T. p. 258 and n.).

11. Mk. 8. 32–3, cf. Mt. 16. 22. Matthew's 'far be it from you, Lord', etc., partially supported in Mark by *a b sy*ˢ, represents the 'original Markan text'. Taylor, *St Mark*, p. 379.

12. Mk. 9. 14, cf. Mt. 17. 14 and Lk. 9. 37. The scribes mentioned in Mark are 'a belated addition'. Bultmann, *op. cit.* p. 55 (E.T. p. 52).

13. Mk. 9. 37, cf. Mt. 10. 40. Matthew's form is independent of Mark's and more authentic. Taylor, *St Mark*, p. 406.

14. Mk. 9. 43–7; cf. Mt. 5. 29 (see also Mt. 18. 8–9). Mark's reference to the foot is secondary. Bultmann, *op. cit.* p. 90 (E.T. p. 86). (Mt. 5. 29 is sometimes included in Q, even though there is no Lukan parallel, so perhaps this passage should be marked with an asterisk. We should note what Bultmann failed to mention, however: that Mt. 18. 8–9 also makes no mention of the foot.)

*15. Mk. 10. 11; cf. Lk. 16. 18 and Mt. 5. 32. Mark's forbidding the wife to marry again is secondary. Bultmann, *op. cit.* p. 140 (E.T. p. 132).

16. Mk. 10. 37, cf. Mt. 20. 21. Matthew's 'in your kingdom' may be earlier than Mark's 'in your glory'. Taylor, *St Mark*, p. 440.

17. Mk. 10. 43 ff., cf. Lk. 22. 24 ff. Luke's version is independent of Mark. Black, *op. cit.* p. 267 (3rd ed. p. 222).

18. Mk. 10. 45, cf. Lk. 22. 27. Mark depends upon 'the redemption theories of Hellenistic Christianity'. Luke is more original. Bultmann, *op. cit.* p. 154 (E.T. p. 144).

19. Mk. 11. 25; cf. Mt. 5. 23–4. Matthew's form is earlier and 'presupposes the existence of the sacrificial system in Jerusalem'. Bultmann, *op. cit.* p. 140 (E.T. p. 132).

20. Mk. 12. 25, cf. Lk. 20. 34–6. Luke's version is independent of Mark's. Taylor, *St Mark*, p. 489.

21. Mk. 12. 28–34, cf. Lk. 10. 25 f. In Luke, 'another version of the text is being used than Mark's edition'. Bultmann, *op. cit.* p. 21 (E.T. p. 23).

22. Mk. 12. 28, cf. Mt. 22. 36. Matthew's 'great' may be a more literal translation from the Semitic than Mark's 'first of all'. Taylor, *St Mark*, p. 486.

23. Mk. 12. 36, cf. Mt. 22. 43. Matthew's 'in the Spirit' is earlier than Mark's 'in the Holy Spirit'. Procksch in Kittel, *T.W.B.N.T.* (E.T.), vol. I, p. 103 n. 53.

24. Mk. 13. 1–2, cf. Lk. 21. 6. Luke may be from a different source. Taylor, *St Mark*, p. 501.

25. Mk. 13. 9, cf. Lk. 21. 12 f. Luke is independent of Mark. Taylor, *St Mark*, p. 507.

26. Mk. 13. 13*b*, cf. Lk. 21. 19. Luke is independent of Mark and more original. Taylor, *St Mark*, p. 510.

27. Mk. 13, cf. Lk. 21. 20–36. Luke is independent of Mark 13 and earlier. Taylor, *St Mark*, p. 512.

28. Mk. 13. 11, cf. Mt. 10. 20. Matthew's 'the Spirit of your Father' is earlier than Mark's 'the Holy Spirit'. Procksch, *loc. cit.*; also Taylor, *St Mark*, p. 509.

29. Mk. 14. 17–21, cf. Lk. 22. 21–3. Bultmann originally thought Luke to be earlier (*op. cit.* p. 284, E.T. p. 264), but later changed his mind (see the *Ergänzungsheft, ad loc.*).

30. Mk. 14. 22–5, cf. Lk. 22. 14–18. Luke has here the older tradition. Lk. 22. 19–20 (which parallels Mk. 14. 22–5) is in its entirety an interpolation in the text of Luke. Bultmann, *op. cit.* p. 286 and n. 1 (E.T. pp. 265–6 and n. 1 to p. 266).

31. Mk. 14. 58, cf. Mt. 26. 61. Although Bultmann apparently thinks Matthew used Mark in this passage, he thinks Mark's 'made with hands' and 'not made with hands' to be secondary in comparison with Matthew. See *op. cit.* p. 126 (E.T. p. 120).

32. Mk. 14. 62, cf. Mt. 26. 64 and Lk. 22. 70. Taylor (*St Mark*, p. 568) thinks Mark must originally have written 'you say that I am' (a similar phrase is in Matthew and Luke). J. A. T. Robinson (*Jesus and his coming*, p. 49) comes to a similar conclusion.

33. Mk. 15. 5, cf. Mt. 27. 14. Black writes 'either (*a*) Matthew here preserves the true Marcan reading, or (*b*) (which seems more likely) Matthew has access to a Semitic tradition in addition to his Marcan source'. *Op. cit.* p. 252; see also p. 86.

34. Mk. 15. 44–5, cf. Mt. and Lk. These verses are not in Matthew and Luke. Bultmann regards them as legendary and thinks Matthew and Luke did not have them in their Mark. *Op. cit.* p. 296 (E.T. p. 274).

In addition, we may note that Stanton (*The Gospels as historical documents*, part II, pp. 142–5) gives a list of passages in our Mark which he thinks must have stood otherwise in the Mark used by Matthew and Luke, since one or the other seems to have an earlier form.

1. Those instances in which Mark uses 'the gospel' absolutely (1. 1; 1. 14, 15; 8. 35; 10. 29).

2. 'The Carpenter', Mk. 6. 3, is due to a revising hand. When it is compared with the expression in Matthew and Luke, it is seen that their expressions might easily have been misunderstood.

3. 'The anointing of the sick with oil' may have come from the practice of the church (6. 13).

4. 'The saying "the Sabbath was made for man", etc. at Mk. 2. 27 has the appearance of being an insertion.'

5. Mk. 9. 35–7 'seems to have been rearranged'. The phrase 'and the servant of all' is probably a later insertion.

6. In Mk. 11. 17 the phrase πᾶσιν τοῖς ἔθνεσιν has been inserted later.

7. The phrases in Mk. 4. 35, 36 'on that day when even was come' and 'they take him with them as he was in the boat' are probably later insertions.

8. The linking statements in Mk. 9. 30 f. seem to be secondary to Matthew's blunt statement in the parallel.

9. Mark's dating of the cleansing of the Temple may be due to revision, the original being maintained in Matthew and Luke.

10. The word δίς in Mk. 14. 30, 72 seems later.

11. The same is true of the statement that Jesus was crucified at the third hour (15. 25).

12. Possibly later are the statement in Mk. 2. 26 'while Abiathar was the high priest' and the mention of the scribes in Mk. 9. 14.

APPENDIX III

THE CHRISTIAN METHOD OF
TRANSMISSION OF TRADITION[1]

The question of method of transmission (or pedagogical technique) is the very question with which Gerhardsson has concerned himself. It is his conviction that the method of transmission in early Christianity could not have been altogether dissimilar to the methods used in contemporary Jewish and Hellenistic circles (see *Tradition and transmission*, pp. 7, 47, and frequently). The question of just how closely related Christian pedagogical method was to the methods used in Jewish and Greek circles is both fascinating and important, and Dr Gerhardsson is to be congratulated upon his continuing attempt to illuminate it. Our present point is very simple: that in this area the Christian tradition was probably not handled just like the Rabbinic; it has a claim to some degree of uniqueness. It is unlikely that there could have been enough Christian transmitters trained in the Rabbinic manner to serve the needs of the rapidly spreading Christian movement.

This point is not to be set aside by arguing that Hellenistic pedagogical technique was so close to Rabbinic that the expansion of Christianity into the Greek world would not necessarily have occasioned any change of teaching method. To my knowledge, there is no evidence that purely oral material was transmitted in the Greek world of the first century.[2] Gerhardsson's discussions of memorization in Greek schools (e.g. *Memory and manuscript*, pp. 124 f.) show that *written texts* were memorized, which is quite a different thing from the transmission of purely oral tradition.

Evidence from Christian sources which is sometimes taken to indicate the existence of oral tradition of the Rabbinic type is not so strong as it is

[1] See above, pp. 28 f.
[2] W. D. Davies cites Plato, *Phaedrus*, 274c–275a, as evidence of the esteem in which memorization was held in the ancient world. (See *The Sermon on the Mount*, p. 416.) This esteem, which is similar to Papias's preference for the living voice (see below), need not be questioned. The quotation from Plato itself, which warns of the ill effects of forsaking the exercise of the memory, seems to indicate that memorization was declining in use. In any case, the use of memorization as a learning technique is not in question. We are questioning whether there was any strictly oral tradition in the Rabbinic sense in the Greek world of the first century. Even if some purely oral tradition did exist in the Greek world, the fact that evidence for it is now lacking would seem to indicate that the practice of oral transmission could not have been very widely spread. Thus it would still be doubtful that many trained transmitters could have been available for the oral transmission of Christian material in the Greek world. Purely oral tradition was apparently maintained on the fringes of the Greek world, but in languages other than Greek, among the Jews and Druids.

294

APPENDIX III

sometimes thought to be.[1] The two principal passages which are taken to
establish the existence of a true oral tradition in early Christianity do not
actually do so.[2] The first of these contains Irenaeus's remarks concerning
Polycarp (in Eusebius, *Hist. Eccl.* v. 20). It reads as follows (I use the translation given by Gerhardsson, *Memory and manuscript*, p. 204, omitting, however, many of the Greek phrases he inserts; cf. also the discussion in Davies,
op. cit. pp. 467 ff.):

> 'I can even name the place where the blessed Polycarp sat and taught,
> where he went out and in. I remember his way of life, what he looked like,
> the addresses he delivered to the people, how he told of his intercourse with
> John and with the others who had seen the Lord, how he remembered
> their words and what he had heard from them about the Lord, about his
> miracles, and about his teaching. As one who had received this from
> eyewitnesses of the word of life Polycarp retold everything in accordance
> with the Scriptures. I listened to this then, because of the grace of God
> which was given me, carefully, copying it down, not on paper, but in
> my heart. And I repeat it (ἀναμαρυκῶμαι) constantly in genuine form by
> the grace of God.'

We may remark that Irenaeus does not mention being trained to repeat
what Polycarp taught, but simply says that he remembers what Polycarp
had said in his addresses to the people. Irenaeus explicitly states (*Hist. Eccl.*
v. 20. 5, immediately before the section quoted) that

> 'I remember the events of those days more clearly than those which
> happened recently, for what we learn as children grows up with the soul
> and is united to it, so that I can speak even of the place in which the
> blessed Polycarp sat and disputed...'[3]

It is clear that here we have to do with Irenaeus's personal reminiscence of
impressive events in his childhood, not with the transmission of tradition
in the Rabbinic sense. In the second place, we may note that the translation
of ἀναμαρυκῶμαι as 'repeat' is highly questionable. To have Irenaeus say
that he *repeats* what he heard sounds as if he were passing on tradition, but
actually he did not say so. The verb ἀναμαρυκῶμαι ordinarily means 'chew
the cud'. It doubtless here means 'ruminate' or 'contemplate'. (See
Liddell and Scott, *Greek-English Lexicon, s.v.*) In the third place, we must

---

[1] See R. P. C. Hanson, *Tradition in the early Church* (Philadelphia, 1962), pp. 35 ff.
[2] A third passage discussed by Gerhardsson, *op. cit.* p. 207, and by Davies, *op. cit.*
p. 468, a statement by 'Peter' in the pseudo-Clementine *Recognitiones*, II. 1, is
so questionable as to date that it cannot be regarded as very significant for the
present question.
[3] Translation by Kirsopp Lake in the Loeb Classical Library edition. The word
translated by Gerhardsson 'taught' and by Lake 'disputed' is διελέγετο.
Gerhardsson's translation emphasizes the didactic possibility of the Greek word,
thus fitting it to his hypothesis; but Lake gives the principal meaning of the word.
διαλέγομαι does not really bear the meaning of διδάσκω.

remark that the 'tradition' (which we should better call 'reminiscence') which Irenaeus claims to have from Polycarp is not very trustworthy. If one considers other passages in which Irenaeus mentions knowledge about John gained from Polycarp (*Hist. Eccl.* III. 23. 3 f.; IV. 14. 3–8; V. 8. 4), it becomes clear that the information gained from this source is highly dubious. On this, see C. K. Barrett, *The Gospel according to St John* (London, 1958), pp. 83 ff.

The quotation from Papias (Eusebius, *Hist. Eccl.* III. 3. 9) reads as follows (quoted from Gerhardsson, *op. cit.* p. 206; cf. also Davies, *ad loc.*):

> 'And then whenever someone came who (as a disciple) had accompanied the elders I used to search for the words of the elders: what Andrew or what Peter had said or what Philip or what Thomas or what James or what John or what Matthew or any other disciple of the Lord, or what Aristion or what John the Elder, the disciples of the Lord, say.'

The meaning and significance of this much controverted passage cannot here be discussed in detail. We may only notice two things. In the first place, Papias appears to be searching for personal reminiscence rather than for a body of oral tradition. In the second place, whatever else the passage shows, it certainly indicates that there did not exist a certain body of oral tradition which was learned and taught in the Rabbinic manner: otherwise Papias could have had access to it without waiting for happenstance meetings with people who had personal remembrances of what the elders (whoever they were) said.[1] This passage shows perfectly clearly that the Christian tradition—at least in Papias' generation—was not passed down and spread in the systematic manner which Gerhardsson describes as having taken place in Rabbinic Judaism.[2]

In sum, then, we see that there were probably significant differences between the Christian and Jewish method of transmission, although there may also have been significant similarities.

Just what the method of transmission in Christianity was remains an open question. In a letter of 12 June 1963 Gerhardsson makes several suggestions. He thinks that attention must be concentrated on the use of written notes. In his view, a gradual transition from predominantly oral to predominantly written tradition took place, and written notes served as a vehicle for the transition (see also *Memory and manuscript*, pp. 201 f.). This seems to be a sound suggestion, and the solution may lie along this line.

[1] This also has negative implications for Köster's thesis that oral tradition was a real alternative to the written tradition until about 150 (see p. 52). The evidence from Papias shows that oral tradition was not readily available and could not, then, be an alternative source of information for the widely spread churches.

[2] Geo Widengren ('Tradition and literature in early Judaism and in the early Church', *Numen*, x (1963), 42–83) also discusses Gerhardsson's use of the passages from Irenaeus and Papias. He argues (pp. 72–5) that they prove the use of written sources. Widengren also points out that the traditions which Papias claimed to have received are none too reliable (pp. 74–5, referring to Eusebius' statement to that effect in *Hist. Eccl.* III. 39. 11–12).

SEMITISMS AND THE PROVENANCE OF DOCUMENTS[1]

In chapter IV, we indicated that Semitisms of content might well indicate the environment from which a passage or book comes rather than how early or late it is (see p. 232 above). This is perhaps a rather obvious statement, but we may take an example to indicate just what is meant. Mt. 23. 5 mentions that the scribes and Pharisees 'make their phylacteries broad and their fringes long', while Mk. 12. 38 and Lk. 20. 46 say that the scribes 'like to go about in long robes'. It is clear that Matthew's 'phylacteries' and 'fringes' are more Semitic in content than Mark and Luke's 'long robes'. Phylacteries and fringes were worn only by Jews, while the ostentatious wearing of long robes would be universally understandable. M'Neile comments that Mt. 23. 5 is perhaps the equivalent of Mk. 12. 38 and Lk. 20. 46 'interpreted with more technical Jewish knowledge'.[2] Similarly, where Mk. 5. 27 says that the woman with the issue of blood 'touched his garment', Mt. 9. 20 and Lk. 8. 44 say she 'touched the fringe of his garment'. M'Neile[3] comments that Matthew and Luke mention the sacred part of the garment, the fringe, 'which Mark's Roman readers would not have understood'.

If one were persuaded that Semitisms of content prove relative antiquity, one would have to assign to Matthew (and to Luke in the second example) priority over Mark. But one could argue that Matthew has 're-Judaized' the tradition.[4] In the first example (Mt. 23. 5 parr.), one could also argue that Matthew is drawing on a special source,[5] but this explanation is not available for the second example (Mt. 9. 20 parr.).[6] If one chooses the re-Judaizing hypothesis, judgements about the environment in which each Gospel was written will have to be made. An evangelist presumably did not

---

[1] See pp. 49, 196 n. 4, 232 above.

[2] A. H. M'Neile, *The Gospel according to St Matthew* (London, 1961), p. 331.

[3] M'Neile, *op. cit. ad loc.*

[4] On re-Judaization in Matthew, see G. D. Kilpatrick, *The origins of the Gospel according to St Matthew* (Oxford, 1946), pp. 101 ff. He states (p. 102) that 'if we equate "Jewish" with "original" we are led to conclusions on certain passages which conflict with the main results of synoptic criticism'. See also W. D. Davies, *The setting of the Sermon on the Mount*, pp. 296–315, on Matthew's relation to contemporary Judaism.

[5] So G. D. Kilpatrick, *op. cit.* pp. 30, 31, 35.

[6] On the re-Judaizing hypothesis, the second example offers a small embarrassment for the two-document hypothesis. Why do Luke and Matthew agree together against Mark? Did Luke also re-Judaize?

re-Judaize for himself, but for his readers. This seems to be what M'Neile has in mind when he writes that Mt. 23. 5 displays 'more technical Jewish knowledge'. Presumably such knowledge would have been understood by the readers of Matthew. The re-Judaizing theory must depend upon judgements about environment. Certain environments might invite the re-Judaizing of certain elements in the tradition, thus leading to an appearance of antiquity. Thus we have suggested that such Semitisms of content as those in Mt. 9. 20 and 23. 5 may mean more for assessing the provenance of a passage than for assessing its antiquity.

Is the same thing true for formal Semitisms?[1] We may first observe that formal Semitisms could be introduced into the tradition by someone acquainted with a Semitic language, especially by someone whose native tongue was Semitic. Human mobility, however, would forbid us from making definite judgements about the provenance of a document even if we knew that it had been written by a person whose native speech was Aramaic. A certain probability might attach to an argument for Syrian or Palestinian provenance, but certainty could not be attained. A positive correlation between formal Semitisms and provenance is rendered yet more difficult to prove by another consideration: the ease with which a person far removed from Palestine and Syria and without knowledge of any Semitic tongue could duplicate the style of Semitically influenced Greek by reading the LXX and other Greek literature which depended on Hebrew or Aramaic. We may take a case in point.

The Protev. Jms., as we have frequently noted, contains numerous formal Semitisms.[2] Do these Semitisms indicate Syrian or Palestinian provenance? The date and unity of the Protev. Jms. have been much discussed. Among the earlier discussions, those by Zahn[3] and Harnack[4] are most important. The history of the debate is given by Amann[5] and by de Strycker.[6] Cullmann's view[7]—that the Protev. Jms. must have been written after 150 and that the speech of Joseph in the first person in 18. 2, the prayer of Salome

---

[1] In discussing the sources of the Gospel of Thomas, Quispel argues that one of them must be of Palestinian origin, 'as is shown by the many Aramaisms'. See *N.T.S.* XII (1966), 378.

[2] See pp. 201 f, 213, 228.

[3] Theodor Zahn, *Geschichte des Neutestamentlichen Kanons* II. 2 (Erlangen und Leipzig, 1892), p. 780 and n. 2. Zahn thought that the Protev. Jms. was composed by a Jewish Christian, and commented that 'Jede Seite des Textes bezeugt die Vertrautheit des Verfassers mit der Sprache der Septuaginta z.B. c. 6 p. 13 γένοιτο, γένοιτο, ἀμήν'.

[4] Adolf Harnack, *Die Chronologie der altchristlichen Litteratur bis Eusebius*, I (Leipzig, 1897), p. 599. Harnack notes that if the author of the Protev. Jms. were born a Jew, he never received instruction in his religion and never saw Palestine. All he knew of Judaism is what he found in the Old Testament and the Gospels.

[5] E. Amann, *Le Protévangile de Jacques et ses Remaniements Latins* (Paris, 1910), pp. 77–100.

[6] *Op. cit.* pp. 6–13.   [7] H.-S. pp. 372 f.

in 20. 2, and the narrative about the murder of Zacharias in 22–4 are later additions—is representative of modern scholarship. These issues need not be decided here. Harnack, who divided the Protev. Jms. into three parts, thought that the first part was probably written in Egypt, since Origen shows knowledge of it.[1] But otherwise the provenance of the book has scarcely been discussed.

This was the case, at any rate, until the recent work of de Strycker. For the first time, de Strycker has assembled evidence which points toward a definite country of origin. Palestine and Syria he excludes because of the geographical confusions of the book (pp. 419–21). He thus agrees with Zahn and others,[2] but his evidence is fuller and more convincing. He concludes (p. 421) that 'the terms Jerusalem, Judea, Bethlehem are no more for the author than scarcely differentiated pieces which he moves across the chess-board of the papyrus'.

The Protev. Jms. was originally written in Greek (p. 421). Although the Greek is poor in vocabulary and syntax, it is fairly correct. Further, the precise verbal agreement with the LXX and the New Testament excludes a process of translation. Semitisms are purely literary: they are borrowed from the Greek Bible.[3] The choice seems, then, to rest between Anatolia and Egypt (p. 422), Greece itself being excluded by the lack of variety of the language. Conjunctions are especially limited, and the sequence μέν...δέ appears only once.

De Strycker settles on Egypt by observing that in the Protev. Jms. the concepts of *desert* and *mountain* are precisely the same. To take only one example of those which he brings forward (pp. 422 f.), we may cite 1. 4:

'And Joachim was very sad, and did not show himself to his wife, but betook himself into the wilderness; there he pitched his tent and fasted forty days and forty nights; and he said to himself: "I shall not *go down* either for food or for drink until the Lord my God visits me; prayer shall be my food and drink."'

We see that the verb 'go down' is applied to leaving the desert. The desert is apparently thought of as a mountain. See also 4. 3 and 16. 2 (in the Bodmer papyrus; see de Strycker, *ad loc.*). Desert and mountain, de Strycker argues, are the same in Egypt. Some portions of the alluvial plain are elevated, forming mountains; and these are completely desert. He also notes that in Egypt the desert directly borders fertile areas, with no intermediate

---

[1] *Op. cit.* pp. 598–603, esp. 601 f.
[2] Zahn, *op. cit.* p. 780. Zahn thought that the author was a Jew, but not Palestinian. He cited especially the lack of knowledge of Palestinian geography displayed in chapters 17–21. The assertion (chapter 25) that the book was written in Jerusalem proves that its home 'ziemlich weit von Jerusalem abliegt'. Zahn preferred Egypt or Asia Minor.
[3] See the views of Zahn and Harnack, p. 298 nn. 3 and 4, above, and our discussion, pp. 201 f. above.

region. Significantly, Jerusalem is pictured as having the desert immediately around it in Protev. Jms. 1. 4; 16. 2. The identification of desert and mountain in Egypt is proved by several citations. Mgr. Lefort[1] states that, for a Copt, '"the mountain" designates the desert'. Further, in the Bohairic version of the Old Testament, the 'desert' of Num. 1. 19 is translated as 'mountain'.[2]

In addition to the argument from geography, de Strycker adduces some 'Coptisms' in the Greek of the Protev. Jms. (p. 423). I am not able to judge these, but the geographical evidence seems sufficiently convincing.

We see, then, that the numerous Semitisms in the Protev. Jms. are not a reflection of its provenance. They are derived from knowledge of the Greek Bible. Our conclusion must be that formal Semitisms need not reflect a Palestinian or Syrian provenance.[3]

This discussion shows once again the necessity of distinguishing between Semitisms which could be derived from the LXX and other Jewish–Greek literature and those which could not be. But even if it were established that a document contains Semitisms which could not have been derived from the Greek Bible, Syrian or Palestinian provenance would still not be proved, as we said above, because of human mobility. Thus Zahn thought that the author of the Protev. Jms. was a non-Palestinian Jewish Christian. He took the Semitisms to prove that the author was Jewish, while the geographical confusion of the book proved he was non-Palestinian.[4] Zahn was probably wrong on the first point, but his argument nevertheless shows how difficult it is to pass from formal Semitisms to conclusions about provenance.

[1] 'Les premiers monastères pachômiens', Le Muséon, LII (1939), p. 404.
[2] This is not so striking as it seems at first. The phrase in Num. 1. 19 is 'desert of Sinai'. A change to 'mountain of Sinai' could be explained without appeal to the geographical peculiarity of Egypt, since the mountain of Sinai is frequently mentioned in the Old Testament. The instance may show, however, that the Coptic scribe was insensitive to the difference between the desert and the mountain of Sinai.
[3] Similarly, Moffatt notes the 'Hebraistic colouring' of the periods in Jude, but attributes it to the author's familiarity with apocryphal literature. In a footnote, he argues thus: 'That [Jude] was a Jewish Christian does not necessarily follow, much less that his audience were Jewish Christians...though the former inference is plausible on broader grounds.' See Introduction to the literature of the New Testament[3], p. 347.
[4] See p. 299 n. 2 above.

APPENDIX V

SELECTED PASSAGES[1]

1. Clem. Alex. Strom. II. 9. 45 (de Santos, p. 34; H.-S. p. 164).

As also it stands written in the Gospel of the Hebrews: 'He that marvels shall reign, and he that has reigned shall rest.'

Ibid. v. 14. 96.

To those words this is equivalent: 'He that seeks will not rest until he finds; and he that has found shall marvel; and he that has marvelled shall reign; and he that has reigned shall rest.'

2. Jerome Comm. 1 in Mt. 12. 13 (de Santos, p. 40; H.-S. p. 148).

I was a mason and earned (my) livelihood with (my) hands; I beseech thee, Jesus, to restore to me my health that I may not with ignominy have to beg for my bread.

3. Jerome Contra Pelag. III. 2; cf. Mt. 18. 21 f. (de Santos, p. 42; H.-S. p. 148).

He (*scil.* Jesus) said: 'If thy brother has sinned with a word and has made thee reparation, receive him seven times in a day.' Simon his disciple said to him: 'Seven times in a day?' The Lord answered and said to him: 'Yea, I say unto thee, until seventy times seven times. For in the prophets also after they were anointed with the Holy Spirit, the word of sin was found.'

4. Ps. Origen Lat. Comm. in Mt. 15. 14; cf. Mt. 19. 16 ff. (de Santos, pp. 42 f.; H.-S. pp. 148 f.).

The other of the two rich men said to him: 'Master, what good thing must I do that I may live?' He said to him: 'Man, fulfill the law and the prophets.' He answered him: 'That have I done.' He said to him: 'Go and sell all that thou possessest and distribute it among the poor, and then come and follow me.' But the rich man then began to scratch his head and it pleased him not. And the Lord said to him: 'How canst thou say, "I have fulfilled the law and the prophets?" For it stands written in the law: "Love thy neighbour as thyself"; and behold, many of thy brethren, sons of Abraham, are begrimed with dirt and die of hunger—and thy house is full of many good things and nothing at all comes forth from it to them!' And he turned and said to Simon his disciple, who was sitting by him: 'Simon, son of Jona, it is easier for a camel to go through the eye of a needle than for a rich man to enter the kingdom of heaven.'

[1] See p. 51 above.

301

APPENDIX V

5. Gosp. Heb. Origen, Comm. in Io. II. 6; cf. Hom. in Ier. xv. 4; Jerome, Comm. in Micah 7. 6; Comm. in Is. 40. 9; Comm. in Ezek. 16. 13 (de Santos, p. 35; H.-S. p. 164).

And if any accept the Gospel of the Hebrews—here the Saviour says: 'Even so did my mother, the Holy Spirit, take me by one of my hairs and carry me away on to the great mountain Tabor.'

6. Gosp. Heb. Jerome, Contra Pelag. III. 2 (de Santos, p. 42; H.-S. pp. 146 f.).

Behold the mother of the Lord and his brethren (Mt. 12. 46 parr.) said to him: 'John the Baptist baptizes unto the remission of sins (Mk. 1. 4; Lk. 3. 3), let us go and be baptized by him' (cf. Mt. 3. 13). But he said to them: 'Wherein have I sinned that I should go and be baptized by him? (based on Mt. 3. 14). Unless what I have said is ignorance.'

7. Gosp. Heb. Sedulius Scotus, Comm. on Mt. (II.-S. p. 151).

For thus the Gospel which is entitled 'According to the Hebrews' reports: 'When Joseph looked out with his eyes, he saw a crowd of pilgrims who were coming in company to the cave, and he said: "I will arise and go out to meet them." And when Joseph went out, he said to Simon: "It seems to me as if those coming were soothsayers, for lo, every moment they look up to heaven and confer one with another. But they seem also to be strangers, for their appearance differs from ours; for their dress is very rich and their complexion quite dark; they have caps on their heads and their garments seem to me to be silky, and they have breeches on their legs. And lo, they have halted and are looking at me, and lo, they have again set themselves in motion and are coming here."'

From these words it is clear that not merely three men, but a crowd of pilgrims came to the Lord, even if according to some the foremost leaders of this crowd were named with the definite names Melchus, Caspar, and Phadizarda.

8. Gosp. Ebion. Epiph. Haer. 30. 13. 7 f. (de Santos, pp. 51 f.; H.-S. pp. 157 f.).

When the people were baptized (Lk. 3. 21), Jesus also came and was baptized by John (Mk. 1. 9). And as he came up from the water (apo, Mt. 3. 16), the heavens were opened (closest to Mt. 3. 16) and he saw (Mt. 3. 16) the Holy Spirit in the form of a dove (closest to Lk. 3. 22) coming down and entering into him (closest to Mk. 1. 10). And a voice came (egeneto) out of heaven (closest to Lk. 3. 22) saying (Mt. 3. 16): 'Thou art my beloved Son, in you I am well pleased' (Mk. 1. 11). And again: 'I have begotten you today' (Lk. 3. 22). And immediately a great light shone round about the place. When John saw this, it saith, he saith unto him: 'Who art thou?' And again a voice out of heaven (came) to him: 'This is my beloved son, in whom I am well pleased' (Mt. 3. 17). And then, it says, John falling before him said: 'I beseech thee, Lord, you baptize me.' But he prevented him saying, 'Let it be, because thus it is fitting for all things to be fulfilled' (cf. Mt. 3. 15).

9. Gosp. Ebion. Epiph. Haer. 30. 13. 6 (de Santos, p. 51; H.-S. p. 157).

It happened in the days of Herod the King of Judah (verbatim, Lk. 1. 5 *a*), John came baptizing a baptism of repentance (abbreviated from Mk. 1. 4) in the Jordan river (Mt. 3. 6//Mk. 1. 5); who was said to be of the nation of Aaron the priest, a son of Zacharias and Elisabeth (summary of Lk. 1. 5–18, cf. Lk. 3. 2). And all went out to him (abbreviation of Mt. 3. 5//Mk. 1. 5).

10. Trad. Matt. Clem. Alex. Strom. IV. 6; cf. Lk. 19. 1 ff. (de Santos, p. 59; H.-S. p. 309).

Zacchaeus then (but some say Matthias), a chief tax-gatherer, when he heard that the Lord had seen fit to be with him, (said): 'Behold, the half of my goods I give in alms, O Lord; and if I have extorted anything from any man, I restore it fourfold.' Whereupon the Saviour also said: 'The Son of man is come today, and has found that which was lost.'

11. Oxy. Pap. 840 (de Santos, p. 80; H.-S. pp. 93 f.).

And he took them (the disciples) with him into the place of purification itself and walked about in the Temple court. And a Pharisaic chief priest, Levi by name, fell in with them and said to the Saviour: 'Who gave thee leave to tread this place of purification and to look upon these holy utensils without having bathed thyself and even without thy disciples having washed their feet? On the contrary, being defiled, thou hast trodden the Temple court, this clean place, although no one who has not first bathed himself or changed his clothes may tread it and venture to view these holy utensils!' Forthwith the Saviour stood still with his disciples and answered: 'How stands it then with thee, thou art forsooth (also) here in the Temple court. Art thou then clean?' He said to him: 'I am clean. For I have bathed myself in the pool of David and have gone down by the one stair and come up by the other and have put on white and clean clothes, and (only) then have I come hither and have viewed these holy utensils.' Then said the Saviour to him: 'Woe unto you blind that see not! Thou hast bathed thyself in water that is poured out, in which dogs and swine lie night and day, and thou hast washed thyself and hast chafed thine outer skin, which prostitutes also and flute-girls anoint, bathe, chafe, and rouge, in order to arouse desire in men, but within they are full of scorpions and of badness of every kind. But I and my disciples, of whom thou sayest that we have not immersed ourselves, have been immersed in the living...water which comes down from ...But woe unto them that...'

12. Pap. Oxy. 1. 30–5 (or 31–6) (de Santos, p. 90; H.-S. p. 109).

Jesus says: 'A prophet is not acceptable in his own country, neither does a physician work cures on those who know him.'

13. Pap. Oxy. 1. 36–41 (or 37–42) (de Santos, pp. 90 f.; H.-S. pp. 109 f.).

Jesus says: 'A city which is erected on the top of a high mountain and firmly stablished, can neither fall nor remain hidden.'

303

14. Protev. Jms. 11. 1–2.

11. 1. And she took the pitcher and went forth to draw water, and behold, a voice said: 'Hail, thou that art highly favoured, the Lord is with thee, blessed art thou among women.' And she looked around on the right and on the left to see whence this voice came. And trembling she went to her house and put down the pitcher and took the purple and sat down on her seat and drew out (the thread). 2. And behold, an angel of the Lord (suddenly) stood before her and said: 'Do not fear, Mary; for you have found grace before the Lord of all things and shall conceive of his word.' When she heard this she doubted in herself and said: 'Shall I conceive of the Lord, the living God, and bear as every woman bears?'

15. Ps. Matt. 15. 3, end (de Santos, p. 214).

And coming up she adored the child, saying: 'In him is the redemption of the world.' Cf. Lk. 2. 38: 'And coming up at that very hour, she gave thanks to God, and spoke of him to all who were looking for the redemption of Jerusalem.'

16. Act. Pil. 11. 2.

But the centurion reported to the governor what had happened. And when the governor and his wife heard, they were greatly grieved, and they neither ate nor drank on that day. And Pilate sent for the Jews and said to them: 'Did you see what happened?' But they answered: 'There was an eclipse of the sun in the usual way.'

17. Protev. Jms. 12. 2.	Luke 1. 39–45.
And Mary rejoiced, and went to Elizabeth her kinswoman, and knocked on the door. When Elizabeth heard it, she put down the scarlet, and ran to the door and opened it, and when she saw Mary, she blessed her and said: 'Whence is this to me, that the mother of my Lord should come to me? For behold, that which is in me leaped and blessed thee.' But Mary forgot the mysteries which the archangel Gabriel had told her, and raised a sigh towards heaven and said: 'Who am I, Lord, that all the generations bless me?'	In those days Mary arose and went with haste into the hill country, to a city of Judah, and she entered the house of Zechariah and greeted Elizabeth. And when Elizabeth heard the greeting of Mary, the babe leaped in her womb; and Elizabeth was filled with the Holy Spirit and she exclaimed with a loud cry, 'Blessed are you among women, and blessed is the fruit of your womb! And why is this granted me, that the mother of my Lord should come to me? For behold, when the voice of your greeting came to my ears, the babe in my womb leaped for joy. And blessed is she who believed that there would be a fulfillment of what was spoken to her from the Lord.'

For another example of both addition and omission, see Protev. Jms. 21. 2//Mt. 2. 3–8. Jms. has 99 words, Mt. 101.

18. Just. Apol. 1. 16. 6; cf. Mt. 22. 37 parrs.

The greatest commandment is, 'Thou shalt worship the Lord thy God, and Him only shalt thou serve, with all thy heart and with thy strength, the Lord God that made thee'.

19. Just. Apol. 1. 17. 2; cf. Mt. 22. 17 ff. parrs.

For at that time some came to him and asked him if one ought to pay tribute to Caesar. And he answered: 'Tell me, whose image does the coin bear?' And they said: 'Caesar's.' And again he answered them: 'Render therefore to Caesar the things that are Caesar's, and to God the things that are God's.'

20. Just. Apol. 1. 32. 6; cf. Mt. 21. 1 ff. parr.

For the foal of an ass stood bound to a vine at the entrance of a village, and he ordered his acquaintances to bring it to him then; and when it was brought, he mounted and sat upon it, and entered Jerusalem, where was the vast temple of the Jews which was afterwards destroyed by you. And after this he was crucified, that the rest of the prophecy might be fulfilled.

21. Just. Dial. 49. 4; cf. Mt. 14. 3–12 par.

And this very prophet your king Herod had shut up in prison; and when his birthday was celebrated, and the niece of the same Herod by her dancing had pleased him, he told her to ask whatever she pleased. Then the mother of the maiden instigated her to ask the head of John, who was in prison; and having asked it, (Herod) sent and ordered the head of John to be brought in on a charger.

22. Just. Dial. 53. 2; cf. Mt. 21. 1 ff. parrs.

And truly our Lord Jesus Christ, when he intended to go into Jerusalem, requested his disciples to bring him a certain ass, along with its foal, which was bound in an entrance of a village called Bethphage; and having seated himself on it, he entered into Jerusalem.

23. Just. Dial. 17. 3–4.

It is written: 'My house is a house of prayer, but you have made it a den of robbers' (Mt. 21. 13 parr.). He overthrew also the tables of the money-changers in the temple (Mt. 21. 12). And he cried: 'Woe to you, scribes and Pharisees, hypocrites (Mt. 23. 23), because you tithe mint and rue (Lk. 11. 42; cf. Mt. 23. 23), but do not observe the love of God and justice (close to Lk. 11. 42b). Whited sepulchres! appearing beautiful without, but within full of dead men's bones' (Mt. 23. 27). And to the scribes: 'Woe to you, scribes, because you have the keys, and you yourselves do not enter in, and you hinder (Lk.'s word) those who come in (Mt. 23. 12; Lk. 11. 52). Blind guides!' (Mt. 23. 16).

24. Theoph. III. 13; cf. Lk. 16. 18; Mt. 5. 32.

Theoph. has Lk.'s form for 'and the one marrying (a woman) divorced from her husband commits adultery', but Mt.'s form for 'and whoever divorces a woman except for the reason of fornication makes her commit adultery'.

25. Just. Apol. I. 66. 3.

For the apostles, in the memoirs composed by them, which are called Gospels, have thus delivered unto us what was enjoined upon them; that Jesus took bread, and when He had given thanks, said, 'This do ye in remembrance of Me, this is my body'; and that, after the same manner, having taken the cup and given thanks, He said, 'This is My blood'; and gave it to them alone.

This contains elements from Matthew, Luke, and Corinthians, with considerable abbreviation.

26. Just. Dial. 82. 2.

For He said we would be put to death, and hated for His name's sake; and that many false prophets and false Christs would appear in His name, and deceive many: and so has it come about.

This conflates, apparently from memory, elements from Mt. 24. 5, 9, 11, 24.

27. Fayum Fragment; cf. Mt. 26. 31 par., Mk. 14. 29 f. par. (de Santos, p. 85; H.-S. p. 116; restored after Harnack).

...πάντες ἐν ταύτῃ τῇ νυκτὶ σκανδαλισθήσεσθε κατὰ τὸ γραφέν· Πατάξω τὸν ποιμένα καὶ τὰ πρόβατα διασκορπισθήσεται· εἰπόντος τοῦ Πέτρου, Καὶ εἰ πάντες, οὐκ ἐγώ· πρὶν ἢ ὁ ἀλεκτρυὼν δὶς κοκκύσει σήμερον σὺ τρίς με ἀπαρνήσῃ...

28. Pap. Oxy. I. 6, lines 30–5 (restored) (de Santos, p. 90).

Λέγει ᾽Ιησοῦς· οὐκ ἔστιν (Mt. 13. 57//Mk. 6. 4) δεκτὸς (Lk. 4. 24) προφήτης (all) ἐν τῇ πατρίδι (all) αὐτοῦ (Mk., Lk.).

BIBLIOGRAPHY

I TEXTS AND TRANSLATIONS

Aland, Kurt. *Synopsis Quattuor Evangeliorum.* Stuttgart: Württembergische Bibelanstalt, 1964.

Matthew Black, Bruce M. Metzger, and Allen Wikgren. *The Greek New Testament.* Sponsored by the United Bible Societies. Stuttgart: Württemberg Bible Society, 1966.

Ante-Nicene Fathers, Writings of the, vols. I, II, VIII, X. Grand Rapids: Wm. B. Eerdmans, 1951.

Archambault, Georges. *Justin, Dialogue avec Tryphon.* (Textes et Documents.) Paris: Auguste Picard, 1914.

Bueno, Daniel Ruiz. *Padres Apologistas Griegos* (S. II). (Biblioteca de Autòres Cristianos.) Madrid: La Editorial Catolica, 1954.

Goodspeed, Edgar J. *Die ältesten Apologeten.* Göttingen: Vandenhoeck and Ruprecht, 1914.

Harnack, Adolf. *Bruckstücke des Evangeliums und der Apokalypse des Petrus,* 2nd ed. Leipzig: J. C. Hinrichs'sche Buchhandlung, 1893.

Harris, J. Rendel. *The Apology of Aristides.* (Texts and Studies I. 1.) Cambridge: The University Press, 1891.

Hennecke, Edgar. *New Testament Apocrypha,* vol. I. Edited by W. Schneemelcher. E.T. edited by R. McL. Wilson. Philadelphia: Westminster Press, 1963.

Huck, Albert. *Synopsis of the First Three Gospels.* Revised by Hans Lietzmann and edited by F. L. Cross. New York: American Bible Society, no date.

Justin Martyr. *Apologies.* Edited by Basil L. Gildersleeve. (Douglass Series of Christian Greek and Latin Writers.) New York: Harper and Brothers, 1877.

Legg, S. C. E. *Nouum Testamentum Graece secundum Textum Westcotto-Hortianum.* Oxonii: E Typographeo Clarendoniano. *Euangelium secundum Matthaeum,* 1940. *Euangelium secundum Marcum,* 1935.

Michel, Charles and P. Peeters. *Évangiles Apocryphes,* vol. I. (Textes et Documents.) Paris: Librairie Alphonse Picard et Fils, 1911.

Nestle, Eberhard and Kurt Aland. *Novum Testamentum Graece,* 25th ed. Stuttgart: Württembergische Bibelanstalt, 1963.

Peeters, Paul. *Évangiles Apocryphes,* vol. II. (Textes et Documents.) Paris: Auguste Picard, 1914.

Robinson, J. A. and M. R. James. *The Gospel according to Peter, and the Revelation of Peter,* 2nd ed. London: C. J. Clay and Sons, 1892.

Rushbrooke, W. G. *Synopticon. An exposition of the common matter of the Synoptic Gospels.* London: Macmillan and Co., 1880.

de Santos Otero, Aurelio. *Los Evangelios Apocrifos*, 2nd ed. (Biblioteca de Autores Cristianos.) Madrid: La Editorial Catolica, 1963.

Scrivener, F. H. *Bezae Codex Cantabrigiensis*. Cambridge: Deighton, Bell and Co., 1864.

Swete, H. B. *The Akhmîn Fragment of the Apocryphal Gospel of Peter*. London: Macmillan and Co., 1893.

Tischendorf, Constantinus. *Evangelia Apocrypha*. Lipsiae: Avenarius et Mendelssohn, 1853.

Walker, Alexander. *Apocryphal Gospels, Acts, and Revelations*. (Ante-Nicene Christian Library, vol. XVI.) Edinburgh: T. and T. Clark, 1870.

Westcott, B. F. and F. J. A. Hort. *The New Testament in the Original Greek*. London: Macmillan and Co., 1956.

II GENERAL

Abbott, Edwin A. and W. G. Rushbrooke. *The common tradition of the Synoptic Gospels*. London: Macmillan and Co., 1888.

Aland, Kurt. 'Neue Neutestamentliche Papyri II', *N.T.S.* XII (1966), 193–210.

Allen, W. C. 'The Aramaic element in St Mark', *Exp. Times*, XIII (1901), 328–30.

The Gospel according to St Matthew, 3rd ed. (The International Critical Commentary.) Edinburgh: T. and T. Clark, 1912.

'The original language of the Gospel according to St Mark', *The Expositor*, 6th series, I (1900), 436–43.

Amann, E. *Le Protévangile de Jacques et ses Remaniements Latins*. Paris: Letouzey et Ané, 1910.

Argyle, A. W. 'Did Jesus speak Greek?' *Exp. Times*, LXVII (1955/6), 92 f., 383.

'An alleged Semitism', *Exp. Times*, LXVII (1955/6), 247.

Audet, Jean-Paul. *La Didachè: Instructions des Apôtres*. Paris: Librairie Lecoffre, 1958.

Bacon, B. W. *Is Mark a Roman Gospel?* (Harvard Theological Studies, VII.) Cambridge, Mass.: Harvard University Press, 1919.

Studies in Matthew. New York: Henry Holt and Co., 1930.

Bellinzoni, A. J. *The sayings of Jesus in the writings of Justin Martyr*. Leiden: E. J. Brill, 1967.

Bertram, Georg. *Neues Testament und historische Methode*. Tübingen: J. C. B. Mohr, 1928.

Beyer, Klaus. *Semitische Syntax im Neuen Testament*, vol. I (Satzlehre, Teil I). (Studien zur Umwelt des Neuen Testaments.) Göttingen, Vandenhoeck and Ruprecht, 1962.

Black, Matthew. *An Aramaic approach to the Gospels and Acts*, 2nd ed. Oxford: The Clarendon Press, 1957. 3rd ed. 1967. Cited as *An Aramaic approach*.

Page references are to the second edition with references to the third edition added in parentheses.

'The problem of the Aramaic element in the Gospels', *Exp. Times*, LIX (1947/8), 171 ff.

'The recovery of the language of Jesus', *N.T.S.* III (1956/7), 305 ff.

'Second Thoughts: IX. The Semitic element in the New Testament', *Exp. Times*, LXXVII (1965), 20–3.

Blass, F. and A. Debrunner. *A Greek grammar of the New Testament and other early Christian literature.* Translated and edited by R. W. Funk. Cambridge: The University Press, 1961.

Bonnard, Pierre. 'La Tradition dans le Nouveau Testament', *R.H.Ph.R.* XL (1960), 20–30.

Bornkamm, G., G. Barth, and H. J. Held. *Tradition and interpretation in Matthew.* E.T. by Percy Scott. (New Testament Library.) London: S.C.M., 1963.

Bornkamm, Günther. *Jesus of Nazareth.* E.T. by Irene and Fraser McLuskey with J. M. Robinson. New York: Harper and Brothers, 1960.

Bousset, Wilhelm. *Die Evangeliencitate Justins des Märtyrers.* Göttingen: Vandenhoeck and Ruprecht, 1891.

Bowman, John. *The Gospel of Mark: The New Christian Jewish Passover Haggadah.* (Studia Post-Biblica, VIII.) Leiden: Brill, 1965.

Brown, Raymond E., S. S. *The Gospel according to John (i–xii).* (The Anchor Bible.) Garden City, N.Y.: Doubleday and Co., 1966.

Bultmann, Rudolf. *Die Erforschung der synoptischen Evangelien*, 4th ed. Berlin: Alfred Töpelmann, 1961. Cited as *Die Erforschung.*

'The Study of the Synoptic Gospels', *Form Criticism*. Edited by F. C. Grant. New York: Harper Torchbooks, 1962. Cited as *Die Erforschung* (E.T.).

Die Geschichte der synoptischen Tradition, 5th ed. Göttingen: Vandenhoeck and Ruprecht, 1961. Cited as *Die Geschichte.*

The history of the Synoptic tradition. E.T. by John Marsh. New York: Harper and Row, 1963. Cited as *Die Geschichte* (E.T.).

'The new approach to the Synoptic problem', *Journal of Religion*, VI (1926), 337–62. Cited as 'The New Approach'.

Burkitt, F. C. *The earliest sources for the life of Jesus*, 2nd ed. London: Houghton Mifflin Co., 1922.

The Gospel history and its transmission, 3rd ed. Edinburgh: T. and T. Clark, 1911.

Burney, C. F. *The Aramaic origin of the Fourth Gospel.* Oxford: The Clarendon Press, 1922.

The poetry of Our Lord. Oxford: The Clarendon Press, 1925.

Burton, Ernest De Witt. *Principles of literary criticism and the Synoptic problem.* (From vol. 5 of the Decennial Publications of the University of Chicago.) Chicago: The University of Chicago Press, 1904.

Bussmann, Wilhelm. *Synoptische Studien*, 3 vols. Halle: Buchhandlung des Waisenhauses, 1925, 1929, 1931.

Butler, B. C. 'The literary relations of Didache, Ch. xvi', *J.T.S.* XI (1960), 265–83.

The originality of St Matthew. Cambridge: The University Press, 1951.

Cadbury, H. J. 'Between Jesus and the Gospels', *H.T.R.* XVI (1923), 81–92.

The making of Luke-Acts. London: S.P.C.K., 1958.

The style and literary method of Luke. (Harvard Theological Studies, VI.) Cambridge, Mass.: Harvard University Press, 1920.

Cambier, J. and others. *La Formation des Évangiles: Problème synoptique et Formgeschichte*. Bruges: Desclée De Brouwer, 1957. The following articles: J. Heuschen, 'La Formation des évangiles', pp. 11–23; L. Cerfaux, 'En marge de la question synoptique. Les Unités littéraires antérieures aux trois premiers évangiles', pp. 24–33; J. W. Doeve, 'Le rôle de la tradition orale dans la composition des Évangiles synoptiques', pp. 70–84.

Cerfaux, L. See under Cambier, J.

Chadwick, H. M. and N. K. Chadwick. *The growth of literature*, 3 vols. Cambridge: The University Press, 1932, 1936, 1940.

Clark, A. C. *The Acts of the Apostles*. Oxford: The Clarendon Press, 1933.

The descent of manuscripts. Oxford: The Clarendon Press, 1918.

The primitive text of the Gospels and Acts. Oxford: The Clarendon Press, 1914.

Clark, Kenneth W. 'The theological relevance of textual variation in current criticism of the Greek New Testament', *J.B.L.* LXXXV (1966), 1–16.

Colwell, E. C. 'The complex character of the Late Byzantine text of the Gospels', *J.B.L.* LIV (1935), 211–21.

Couchoud, P. L. 'L'Évangile de Marc a-t-il été écrit en Latin?' *R.H.R.* XCIV (1926), 161–92.

Dahl, Nils A. 'Anamnesis', *Studia Theologica*, I (1948), 69–95.

Dalman, Gustaf. *Jesus-Jeschua*. Leipzig: J. C. Hinrichs'sche Buchhandlung, 1922.

Jesus-Jeshua. E.T. by Paul Levertoff. London: S.P.C.K., 1929.

Die Worte Jesu. Darmstadt: Wissenschaftliche Buchgesellschaft, 1965. Reprint of the second edition of 1930.

The words of Jesus. E.T. by D. M. Kay. Edinburgh: T. and T. Clark, 1902.

Daube, David. *The New Testament and Rabbinic Judaism*. London: Athlone Press, 1956.

'Rabbinic methods of interpretation and Hellenistic rhetoric', *H.U.C.A.* XXII (1949), 239–64.

Davies, W. D. *Christian origins and Judaism*. Philadelphia: The Westminster Press, 1962.

Invitation to the New Testament. Garden City, New York: Doubleday and Co., Inc., 1966.

'Paul and Judaism', *The Bible in modern scholarship* (ed. by J. Philip Hyatt). Nashville/New York: Abingdon Press, 1965.

Paul and Rabbinic Judaism: some Rabbinic elements in Pauline Theology, 2nd ed. London: S.P.C.K., 1958.

The setting of the Sermon on the Mount. Cambridge: The University Press, 1964.

Deissmann, Adolf. *Bible Studies*, 2nd ed. E.T. by Alexander Grieve. Edinburgh: T. and T. Clark, 1909.

Dibelius, Martin. *Die Formgeschichte des Evangeliums*, 4th ed. Tübingen: J. C. B. Mohr (Paul Siebeck), 1961. Cited as *Die Formgeschichte*.

A fresh approach to the New Testament and early Christian literature. London: Ivor Nicholson and Watson, 1937. Cited as *A Fresh Approach*.

'The structure and literary character of the Gospels', *H.T.R.* xx (1927), 151–70.

'Zur Formgeschichte der Evangelien', *Theologische Rundschau*, n.F. 1 (1929), 185–216. Cited as 'Zur Formgeschichte'.

Dodd, C. H. 'Present tendencies in the criticism of the Gospels', *Exp. Times*, XLIII (1931–2), 246–51.

Doeve, J. W. See under Cambier, J.

Draper, H. Mudie. 'Did Jesus speak Greek?' *Exp. Times*, LXVII (1955–6), 317.

Easton, B. S. 'The first Evangelic tradition', *J.B.L.* L (1931), 148 ff.

The Gospel before the Gospels. New York: Charles Scribner's Sons, 1928.

Enslin, M. S. *The literature of the Christian movement.* (Christian Beginnings, part III.) New York: Harper Torchbooks, 1956.

Farmer, W. R. *The Synoptic problem.* New York: The Macmillan Co., 1964.

Fascher, Erich. *Die formgeschichtliche Methode.* Giessen: Alfred Töpelmann, 1924.

Textgeschichte als hermeneutisches Problem. Halle: M. Niemeyer, 1953.

Fortna, R. T. *The Gospel of signs: a reconstruction of the chief narrative source used by the Fourth Evangelist.* Unpublished dissertation, Union Theological Seminary. New York, 1965.

Gärtner, Bertil. *The theology of the Gospel according to Thomas.* E.T. by Eric J. Sharpe. New York: Harper and Brothers, 1961.

Gerhardsson, Birgir. *Memory and Manuscript: Oral Tradition and Written Transmission in Rabbinic Judaism and Early Christianity.* (Acta Seminarii Neotestamentici Upsaliensis xxii.) Lund: C. W. K. Gleerup, 1961.

Tradition and transmission in Early Christianity. (Coniectanea Neotestamentica xx.) Lund: C. W. K. Gleerup, 1964.

Glasson, T. F. 'Did Matthew and Luke use a "Western" Text of Mark?' *Exp. Times*, LV (1943/4), 180–4.

Glover, Richard. 'The Didache's quotations and the Synoptic Gospels', *N.T.S.* v (1958), 12–29.

Goguel, M. 'Une nouvelle école de critique évangélique', *R.H.R.* XCIV (1926), 114–60.

Goodenough, Erwin R. *Jewish symbols in the Greco-Roman Period,* 12 vols. New York: Pantheon Books, 1953–65.

Grant, F. C. *The Earliest Gospel.* Nashville: Abingdon Cokesbury, 1943.

The Gospels: their origin and their growth. London: Faber and Faber, 1957.

'Where form criticism and textual criticism overlap', *J.B.L.* LIX (1940), 11–21.

Grant, Robert M. *The Apostolic Fathers,* vol. I. New York: Thomas Nelson and Sons, 1964.

with D. N. Freedman. *The secret sayings of Jesus.* London: Collins (Fontana Books), 1960.

Grintz, Jehoshua M. 'Hebrew as the spoken and written language in the last days of the Second Temple', *J.B.L.* LXXIX (1960), 32–47.

Guillaumont, Antoine. 'Sémitismes dans les Logia de Jésus retrouvés à Nag-Hamâdi', *Journal Asiatique,* CCXLVI (1958), 113–23.

and others. *The Gospel according to Thomas.* Leiden: E. J. Brill, 1959.

Gundry, Robert H. 'The language milieu of first-century Palestine: its bearing on the authenticity of the Gospel tradition', *J.B.L.* LXXXIII (1964), 404–8.

Hadorn, Wilhelm. *Die Entstehung des Markus-Evangeliums.* (B.F.C.T. II, 4.) Gütersloh: C. Bertelsmann, 1898.

Hanson, R. P. C. *Tradition in the early Church.* (The Library of History and Doctrine.) Philadelphia: The Westminster Press, 1962.

Harnack, Adolf. *Die Chronologie der Litteratur bis Irenäus. (Geschichte der altchristlichen Litteratur bis Eusebius,* Theil II, Bnd. I.) Leipzig: J. C. Hinrichs'sche Buchhandlung, 1897.

Harris, J. Rendel. *Four lectures on the Western text of the New Testament.* London: C. J. Clay and Sons, 1894.

Hatch, W. H. P. *The 'Western' Text of the Gospels.* Evanston, Illinois: Seabury-Western Theological Seminary, 1937.

Hawkins, Sir John C. *Horae Synopticae,* 2nd ed. Oxford: The Clarendon Press, 1909.

Heuschen, J. See under Cambier, J.

Hoffmann, R. A. *Das Marcusevangelium und seine Quellen.* Königsberg: Thomas und Oppermann, 1904.

Howard, W. F. See under Moulton, J. H.

Hunkin, J. W. '"Pleonastic" ἄρχομαι in the New Testament', *J.T.S.* XXV (1924), 390–402.

Hunzinger, Claus-Hunno. 'Aussersynoptisches Traditionsgut im Thomas-Evangelium', *Th. Lit. Zeit.* LXXXV (1960), 843–6.

Iber, Gerhard. 'Zur Formgeschichte der Evangelien', *Theologische Rundschau,* n.F. XXIV (1957–8), 283–338.

Jeremias, Joachim. *The Eucharistic words of Jesus.* E.T. by Arnold Ehrhardt. Oxford: Basil Blackwell, 1955. Revised ed. trans. by Norman Perrin. London: S.C.M., 1966.

The parables of Jesus. Second English edition, translated by S. H. Hooke. New York: Charles Scribner's Sons, 1963.

Unknown Sayings of Jesus. Translated by Reginald H. Fuller. London: S.P.C.K., 1958.

Johannessohn, Martin. 'Das biblische καὶ ἐγένετο und seine Geschichte', *Zeitschrift für vergleichende Sprachforschung,* LIII (1925), 161–212.

de Jonge, M. 'Christian Influence in the Testaments of the Twelve Patriarchs', *Nov. Test.* IV (1960), 181–235.

Testamenta XII Patriarcharum. Leiden: E. J. Brill, 1964.

Jülicher, Adolf. *An introduction to the New Testament.* E.T. by Janet Penrose Ward. London: Smith, Elder and Co., 1904.

Katz, Peter. 'Zur Übersetzungstechnik der Septuaginta', *Welt des Orients,* II (1954–9), 267–73.

Kenyon, F. G. *Handbook to the textual criticism of the New Testament.* London: Macmillan and Co., 1901.

The Western Text in the Gospels and Acts. (From the Proceedings of the British Academy, vol. XXIV.) London: Humphrey Milford, 1939.

Kilpatrick, G. D. 'Atticism and the Text of the Greek New Testament', *Neutestamentliche Aufsätze* (Festschrift für Prof. Josef Schmid zum 70. Geburtstag, edited by J. Blinzler and others).

'The Greek New Testament Text of Today and the *Textus Receptus*', *The New Testament in historical and contemporary perspective* (Essays in Memory of G. H. C. Macgregor, edited by Hugh Anderson and William Barclay). Oxford: Basil Blackwell, 1965, pp. 189–208.

The origins of the Gospel according to St Matthew. Oxford: The Clarendon Press, 1946.

'Western Text and Original Text in the Gospels and Acts', *J.T.S.* XLIV (1943), 24–36.

Klijn, A. F. J. 'Scribes, Pharisees, Highpriests, and Elders in the New Testament', *Nov. Test.* III (1959), 259–67.

'A survey of the researches into the Western Text of the Gospels and Acts', *Nov. Test.* III (1959), 1–27, 161–73.

Knox, W. L. *The sources of the Synoptic Gospels,* 2 vols. Edited by H. Chadwick. Cambridge: The University Press, 1953, 1957.

Köhler, L. *Das formgeschichtliche Problem des neuen Testaments,* Tübingen: J. C. B. Mohr, 1927.

Köster, Helmut. *Synoptische Überlieferung bei den apostolischen Vätern.* (T.U. 65.) Berlin: Akademie-Verlag, 1957.

Kümmel, W. G. *Einleitung in das neue Testament.* Begründet von P. Feine und J. Behm. Thirteenth edition. Heidelberg: Quelle and Meyer, 1964.

Das neue Testament: Geschichte der Erforschung seiner Probleme. Freiburg/ München: Verlag Karl Alber, 1958.

Kundsin, K. 'Autopsie oder Gemeindeüberlieferung?' *Studia Theologica,* I (1935), 101–17.

'Primitive Christianity in the Light of Gospel Research', *Form Criticism.* Edited by F. C. Grant. New York: Harper Torchbooks, 1962.

Lacocque, André. 'La Tradition dans le Bas-Judaïsme', *R.H.Ph.R.* XL (1960), 2–18.

Lauterbach, Jacob Z. *Rabbinic essays.* Cincinnati: Hebrew Union College Press, 1951.

Lieberman, Saul. *Greek in Jewish Palestine.* New York: The Jewish Theological Seminary of America, 1942.

Hellenism in Jewish Palestine, 2nd ed. New York: The Jewish Theological Seminary of America, 1962.

'How much Greek in Jewish Palestine', *Biblical and Other Studies.* (Studies and Texts, vol. I, edited by Alexander Altmann.) Cambridge, Mass.: Harvard University Press, 1963.

Lightfoot, J. B. *The Apostolic Fathers,* vol. I, pt. ii, 2nd ed. London: Macmillan and Co., 1889.

Lindsay, R. L. 'A modified two-document theory of the Synoptic Dependence and Interdependence', *Nov. Test.* VI (1963), 239–63.

Lohr, C. H. 'Oral techniques in the Gospel of Matthew', *Catholic Biblical Quaterly,* XXIII (1960), 403–35.

McGinley, L. J. *Form-criticism of the Synoptic healing narratives.* Woodstock, Maryland: Woodstock College Press, 1944.

MacKinnon, Ian F. '"Formgeschichte" and the Synoptic problem: present position', *The Canadian Journal of Religious Thought,* IX (1932), 190–6.

M'Neile, A. H. *The Gospel according to St Matthew.* London: Macmillan and Co., 1961.

Manson, T. W. *The teaching of Jesus: studies in its form and content.* Second edition, first published in 1935. Cambridge: The University Press, 1963.

Marxsen, Willi. *Einleitung in das Neue Testament.* Gütersloh: Gerd Mohr, 1963.

'Bemerkungen zur "Form" der sogenannten synoptischen Evangelien', *Th. Lit. Zeit.* LXXXI (1956), 345–8.

Metzger, Bruce M. *Chapters in the history of New Testament textual criticism.* (New Testament Tools and Studies, IV.) Grand Rapids: W. B. Eerdmanns, 1963.

The Text of the New Testament: its transmission, corruption, and restoration. New York: Oxford University Press, 1964.

Moffatt, James. *Introduction to the literature of the New Testament,* 3rd ed. Edinburgh: T. and T. Clark, 1961.

Montefiore, Hugh and H. E. W. Turner. *Thomas and the Evangelists*. London: S.C.M., 1962.

Moulton, J. H. *A grammar of New Testament Greek*. Vol. I (3rd ed.), 1908; vol. II, edited by W. F. Howard, 1956; vol. III, by Nigel Turner, 1963. Edinburgh: T. and T. Clark.

'The language of the New Testament', *A commentary on the Bible* (ed. by A. S. Peake). New York: Thomas Nelson and Sons, 1920, pp. 591–3.

The New Testament in the Apostolic Fathers. By a committee of the Oxford Society of Historical Theology. Oxford: The Clarendon Press, 1905.

Nineham, D. E. 'Eye-witness testimony and the Gospel tradition', *J.T.S.* IX (1958), 13–25, 243–52 and XI (1960), 253–64.

Palmer, N. H. 'Lachmann's Argument', *N.T.S.* XIII (1967), 368–78.

Pautrel, R. 'Des Abréviations subies par quelques sentences de Jésus dans la rédaction synoptique', *Recherches de Science Religieuse*, XXIV (1934), 344–65.

Porúbčan, Štefan. 'Form criticism and the Synoptic problem', *Nov. Test.* VII (1964), 81–118.

Preuschen, Erwin. *Antilegomena: Die Reste der ausserkanonischen Evangelien und urchristlichen Überlieferungen*, 2nd ed. Giessen: Alfred Töpelmann, 1905.

Purves, George T. *The testimony of Justin Martyr to early Christianity*. New York: Anson D. F. Randolph and Co., 1889.

Quispel, G. 'L' Évangile selon Thomas et les Clémentines', *Vig. Chr.* XII (1958), 181–96.

'L' Évangile selon Thomas et le Diatessaron', *Vig. Chr.* XIII (1959), 87–117.

'L' Évangile selon Thomas et le "Texte Occidental" du Nouveau Testament', *Vig. Chr.* XIV (1960), 204–15.

'"The Gospel of Thomas" and the "Gospel of the Hebrews"', *N.T.S.* XII (1966), 371–82.

'The Gospel of Thomas and the New Testament', *Vig. Chr.* XI (1957), 189–207.

'Some remarks on the Gospel of Thomas', *N.T.S.* V (1958), 276–90.

Rabinowitz, I. '"Be Opened" = Ἐφφαθά (Mark 7. 34): Did Jesus speak Hebrew?' *Z.N.T.W.* LIII (1962), 229–38.

Riesenfeld, Harald. *The Gospel tradition and its beginnings*. London: A. R. Mowbray and Co., 1957.

Robinson, J. A. T. *Jesus and his coming*. London: S.C.M., 1957.

Robinson, J. M. 'ΛΟΓΟΙ ΣΟΦΩΝ. Zur Gattung der Spruchquelle Q', *Zeit und Geschichte* (Dankesgabe an Rudolf Bultmann, edited by E. Dinkler). Tübingen: J. C. B. Mohr, 1964, pp. 77–96.

Rohde, Joachim. *Formgeschichte und Redaktionsgeschichte in der neutestamentlichen Forschung der Gegenwart*. Diss. Berlin, 1962. Summary in *Th. Lit. Zeit.* XC (1965), 226–8.

BIBLIOGRAPHY

Sanday, William. *The Gospels in the second century*. London: Macmillan and Co., 1876.

editor. *Studies in the Synoptic problem*. Oxford: The Clarendon Press, 1911.

Schmid, Josef. *Matthäus und Lukas: eine Untersuchung des Verhältnisses ihrer Evangelien*. (Biblische Studien, 23.) Freiburg im Breisgau: Herder and Co., 1930.

Schmidt, K. L. *Der Rahmen der Geschichte Jesu*. Berlin: Trowitzsch und Sohn, 1919.

'Die Stellung der Evangelien in der allgemeinen Literaturgeschichte', EYXAPIΣTHPION (Festschrift Hermann Gunkel, edited by Hans Schmidt [F.R.L.A.N.T., n.F., 19]). Göttingen: Vandenhoeck and Ruprecht, 1923, 2. Teil, pp. 50–134.

Schniewind, J. 'Zur Synoptiker-Exegese', *Theologische Rundschau*, n.F. II (1930), 129–89.

Scholten, J. H. *Das älteste Evangelium*. Translated by E. R. Redepenning. Elberfeld: R. L. Friderichs, 1869.

Das paulinische Evangelium. Translated by E. R. Redepenning. Elberfeld: R. L. Friderichs, 1881.

Schrage, Wolfgang. *Das Verhältnis des Thomas-Evangeliums zur synoptischen Tradition und zu den koptischen Evangelienübersetzungen*. Berlin: Verlag Alfred Töpelmann, 1964.

Segal, M. H. *A grammar of Mishnaic Hebrew*. Oxford: The Clarendon Press, 1958.

Slotki, I. W. 'Long and shorter versions of Ancient Hebrew poems', *The American Journal of Semitic Languages and Literatures*, L (1933), 15–31.

Smith, D. M., Jr. *The composition and order of the Fourth Gospel: Bultmann's Literary Theory*. New Haven: Yale University Press, 1965.

Smith, Morton. 'The Jewish elements in the Gospels', *J.B.R.* xxiv (1956), 90–6.

'Palestinian Judaism in the first century', *Israel: Its Role in Civilization* (edited by Moshe Davis). New York: Harper and Brothers, 1956, pp. 67–81.

Sparks, H. F. D. 'The Semitisms of St Luke's Gospel', *J.T.S.* xliv (1943), 129–38.

'Some observations on the Semitic background of the New Testament', *Bulletin of Studiorum Novi Testamenti Societas*, II (1951), 33–43.

Spitta, F. *Die synoptische Grundschrift in ihrer Überlieferung durch das Lukasevangelium*. Leipzig: J. C. Hinrichs'sche Buchhandlung, 1912.

Stanton, V. H. *The Gospels as historical documents*. Part II: *The Synoptic Gospels*. Cambridge: The University Press, 1909.

Stauffer, Ethelbert. *Jesus and his story*. E.T. by Dorothea M. Barton. London: S.C.M., 1960.

Streeter, B. H. *The Four Gospels*. London: Macmillan and Co., 1961.

316

de Strycker, Émile. *La Forme la plus ancienne du Protévangile de Jacques.* (Subsidia Hagiographica 33.) Bruxelles: Société des Bollandistes, 1961.

Styler, G. M. 'The Priority of Mark', Excursus IV in *The birth of the New Testament* by C. F. D. Moule. New York: Harper and Row, 1962, pp. 223–232.

Taylor, R. O. P. 'Did Jesus speak Aramaic?' *Exp. Times*, LVI (1944/45), 95–7.

Taylor, Vincent. *The Formation of the Gospel Tradition.* London: Macmillan and Co., 1957. Cited as *The Formation.*

The Gospel according to St Mark. London: Macmillan and Co., 1959.

Taylor, W. S. 'Memory and the Gospel tradition', *Theology Today*, XV (1958), 470–9.

Thackeray, H. St John. *A grammar of the Old Testament in Greek.* Cambridge: The University Press, 1909.

Thompson, B. H. 'To what extent did Jesus use Greek?' *Religion in Life*, XXXII (1962/3), 103–15.

Titus, E. L. *The motivation of changes made in the New Testament text by Justin Martyr and Clement of Alexandria.* Chicago: The University of Chicago Press, 1945.

Torrey, C. C. *Our translated Gospels.* New York: Harper and Brothers, 1936.

Turner, C. H. 'Marcan usage: notes, critical and exegetical, on the second Gospel', *J.T.S.* XXVIII (1926/7), 9–30, 349–62.

Turner, H. E. W. *Historicity and the Gospels.* London: A. R. Mowbray and Co., 1963.

See under Montefiore, H.

Turner, N. 'The language of the New Testament', *Peake's commentary on the Bible* (ed. by Matthew Black and H. H. Rowley). London: Thomas Nelson and Sons, 1962, pp. 659–62.

'Second Thoughts—VII. Papyrus Finds', *Exp. Times*, LXXVI (1964), 44–8.

See under Moulton, J. H.

Vaganay, L. *Le Problème Synoptique: une Hypothèse de Travail.* Tournai: Desclée and Co., 1954.

Vogels, H. J. *Die Harmonistik im Evangelientext des Codex Cantabrigiensis.* (T.U. 36, 1a.) Leipzig: J. C. Hinrichs'sche Buchhandlung, 1910.

Votaw, C. W. 'The Gospels and contemporary biographies', *American Journal of Theology*, XIX (1915), 45–73, 217–49.

Weiss, Bernhard. *Das Marcusevangelium und seine synoptischen Parallelen.* Berlin: Wilhelm Hertz, 1872.

Die Quellen der synoptischen Überlieferung. (T.U. 32, 3.) Leipzig: J. G. Cotta, 1908.

Weiss, Johannes. *Das älteste Evangelium.* Göttingen: Vandenhoeck und Ruprecht, 1903.

Earliest Christianity, 2 vols. E.T. edited by F. C. Grant. New York: Harper and Brothers (Harper Torchbooks), 1959.

Weisse, C. H. *Die evangelische Geschichte*, 2 vols. Leipzig: Breitkopf und Härtel, 1838.

Wernle, Paul. *Die synoptische Frage*. Tübingen: J. C. B. Mohr (Paul Siebeck), 1899.

Westcott, B. F. and F. J. A. Hort. *The New Testament in the original Greek*, vol. II (Introduction and Appendix). New York: Harper and Brothers, 1882.

Widengren, Geo. 'Tradition and literature in early Judaism and in the early Church', *Numen*, x (1963), 42–83.

Wilcox, Max. *The Semitisms of Acts*. Oxford: The Clarendon Press, 1965.

Wilder, Amos. 'Form-history and the oldest tradition', *Neotestamentica et Patristica* (Freundesgabe Oscar Cullmann, edited by W. C. van Unnik [Supplements to *Nov. Test.* VI]). Leiden: E. J. Brill, 1962, pp. 3–13.

Williams, C. S. C. *Alterations to the Text of the Synoptic Gospels and Acts*. Oxford: Basil Blackwell, 1951.

Woods, F. H. 'The origin and mutual relation of the Synoptic Gospels', *Studia Biblica et Ecclesiastica: Essays Chiefly in Biblical and Patristic Criticism*, vol. II (edited by S. R. Driver, T. K. Cheyne, and W. Sanday). Oxford: The Clarendon Press, 1890, pp. 59–104.

Wright, L. E. *Alterations of the words of Jesus as quoted in the literature of the second century*. Cambridge, Mass.: Harvard University Press, 1952.

Yoder, James D. 'Semitisms in Codex Bezae', *J.B.L.* LXXVIII (1959), 317–21.

Zahn, Theodore. *Geschichte des Neutestamentlichen Kanons*, II, 2. Erlangen und Leipzig: Andreas Deichert, 1892.

INDEX

I. INDEX OF PASSAGES QUOTED*

A. OLD TESTAMENT

B. NEW TESTAMENT

* The index includes only passages which are referred to outside of the lists.

C. OTHER EARLY CHRISTIAN LITERATURE

II. INDEX OF AUTHORS

Wernle, Paul 6 n., 207
Westcott, B. F. 35, 48 n., 209
Widengren, Geo 296 n.
Wilcox, Max 190 n., 200 n.
Wilder, Amos 28 n.

Williams, C. S. C. 251 n.
Woods, F. H. 93 n., 278

Yoder, James D. 33 f.

Zahn, Theodore 298–300

III. INDEX OF SUBJECTS

abbreviation 50, 64–6, 274
actions 61–3, 67, 80–3
Acts of Pilate 67, 202, 229 f., 283
adjectives and adjectival phrases 116–
    19, 144, 163–5, 184, 275
Alexandrian text-type 31
Apocryphal Gospels 17, 20, 25, 40–5,
    51, 66 f., 92 f., 145, 147, 148 n.,
    185 f., 194, 209, 228–31, 259, 283
Apologists 37–40. See also Justin
    Martyr.
apophthegmata 16, 19 n., 88, 90, 146 n.
Apostolic Fathers 3, 35–7, 205, 280
Aramaism, see Semitism
Aristides 37
Armenian Infancy Gospel 48
asyndeton 214–20, 228 f., 240–2, 251–3
Athenagoras 37, 40

Bodmer papyrus 43, 49
Byzantine text-type, see Koine text-
    type

casus pendens 207
Christian tradition about Jesus
    change in 1 f., 17, 27, 29
    characteristics of the forms of 9,
        14–17, 19, 22
    compared to other traditions 9 f.,
        17–22, 27 f., 294, 296. See also
        Rabbinic literature, Hellenistic
        literature
    continuity of 1, 27, 281
    creation of by Christian communities
        1 f., 281
    criteria for determining the relative
        antiquity of 2–26, (esp. 2–4, 7 f.,
        10 f., 14–17, 22 f.), 45, 147, 190,
        192 f., 252, 274 f., 276
    extra-canonical Christian tradition
        2 f., 38. See also Gospel of Thomas
    laws of transmission or development
        of, tendencies of change in 2–26
        (esp. 2, 7–10, 12–14, 16–22, 24–6),

    29, 43, 45, 50, 68, 69 n., 146,
        256 f., 272, 274 f.
    method of transmission of 28, 294–6
    nature of 1, 11 f.
    pre-canonical Christian tradition 7 f.
        29, 45, 279–85
    post-canonical Christian tradition 7,
        45, 53–68, 96–146, 209–32, 258 f.,
        265–8, 281 f. See also Apocryphal
        Gospels, textual tradition, Apolo-
        gists, Church Fathers
Church Fathers 35–40, 67
    See also Apostolic Fathers and indi-
        vidual Fathers
Circumstances 139 f., 145 f., 176–8,
    186, 275
Clement of Alexandria 36
I Clement 37
II Clement 37
Codex Bezae (D) 31–4, 46–8, 185, 192,
    290
    See also 'Western' text-type
Codex Sinaiticus (ℵ, Al) 33 f., 43,
    46–8, 51
Codex Vaticanus (B) 33 f., 43, 46–8
Conclusions and results 141 f., 145,
    180 f., 186
Conflation 32, 42, 262–71

Details 19 n., 23 f., 45, 88–189, 274,
    283
Dialogues 59 f., 67, 76–8, 83, 274 f.
Diatessaron 33, 41
Didache 3, 36
direct discourse 256–62, 274 f., 283
direct objects 104–7, 144, 155–7,
    184

Egerton papyrus 43
emotion 143, 145, 181 f., 186
ethical dative 34
expansion 19, 19 n., 63
explanations 140 f., 145, 179 f., 186
Fayum fragment, 43

326

scenes and events 60, 67, 78–80, 83, 274 f.
Semitic wording 225–9, 246–9, 254 f.
Semitism 10, 33 f., 42, 45, 94, 190–255, 274, 297–300
Septuagintalisms 199–202, 298, 300
speeches 54–8, 66 f., 71–6, 82 f., 274 f.
Streitgespräche 15, 19 n.
subjects 96–103, 144, 152–5, 183, 275
Synoptic Gospels
  order of pericopes in 7, 277 f.
  overlap of sources of 4 f.
  relations of to each other 69–87 (length) 146–89 (detail), 232–55 (Semitism) 259–62 (direct discourse), 268–71 (conflation)
  sources of 5, 38. *See also* Q, M
Synoptic problem 5–7, 10, 183 ff., 276–9
Syriac Infancy Gospel 49

Syrian text-type, *see* Koine text-type

tales (*Novellen*) 24
Tatian 37
temporal references 90, 94
Testaments of the Twelve Patriarchs 30, 202 n.
textual criticism 17, 29–35, 46–8
textual tradition 17, 20, 25, 29–35, 44–8, 66 f., 145, 185, 209, 228, 230, 250, 289
Theophilus of Antioch 37, 40
translation variants 4, 286–9

Ur-Markus 6, 17, 152 n.

'Western' text-type 31–5, 39, 41, 46, 48
  See also Codex Bezae (D)